MW00714080

PACKERS
"VERSES"
VIKINGS

A Poetic Perspective

Carl "Gator" Nelson (signature)

Carl Nelson

PACKERS "VERSES" VIKINGS
A Poetic Perspective
By Carl Nelson

First Edition

Copyright 2006, Carl Nelson

First Printing
05 06 07 08 10 9 8 7 6 5 4 3 2 1

All rights reserved, including the right to reproduce this book or portions thereof, in any form, except for brief quotations embodied in articles and reviews, without written permission from the publisher.

ISBN Number 1-886028-78-8

Library of Congress Catalog Card Number: 2006922951

Published by:

Savage Press
P.O. Box 115
Superior, WI 54880

Phone: 715-394-9513

E-mail: mail@savpress.com

Web Site: www.savpress.com

Printed in the U.S.A.

Box 115, Superior, WI 54880 (715) 394-9513

DEDICATION

This book is dedicated to the person who has done the most to make it a reality, my lovely bride, Debbie.

She is the one who spent many, many hours scouring my computer and scattered papers, bringing as many of the fifteen years worth of poetry together, having to retype and format many of them because they were written long before I was computer-enabled or my word processing program and hers wouldn't interact, and all to provide a surprise Christmas gift for me.

She then continued with the surprises, contacting publishers all over North America until Mike Savage of Savage Press in Superior, Wisconsin, responded favorably to the idea that a decade's worth of poetry might just be marketable.

Debbie has since then been my sounding board, my marketing guru, motivator, cheerleader and occasionally, my cold-hearted taskmaster.

She is also the only reason that this book is in your hands right now, rather than scattered throughout various desk drawers and cardboard boxes, computer hard drives and note books.

For all you have done, Debbie—this book's for you!

ACKNOWLEDGEMENTS

I'd like to thank all of those wonderful people from around the world who helped me assemble this collection of poetry. From Mike, Nan, and Debbie at Savage Press, to my family, especially my grandchildren who are featured so prominently, to the many fans of the Green Bay Packers and the Minnesota Vikings who lent both their photographic images and their enthusiasm for the project, thank you so much.

Many of the images contained in this book were collected by me over the course of years of attending both Packers and Vikings games and events. Many of the others were submitted by fans of both teams. Here is a list of those who submitted photographs for my book.

First, the commercial establishments that let me reproduce their imagery: Prevea Health, Saint Mary's and Saint Vincent Hospitals, Bellin Health, Bellin Health Partners and the Green Bay Packers, Stadium Sports and Antiques, WestmorelandFlint and Krenzen Auto, and the Nummi Jewelers' otter.

Next, there is a group of very colorful and easily recognized characters who are so frequently seen at Packers' functions that they seem to be part of the organization. Some of these people are: The Packalope, Saint Vincent, Cheese Louise, the 'G' man, the Packers' Santa Claus who works the parking lots at Lambeau, the Big Dawg, Mike the Lambeau Guy, and many others, who all make the experience of being at Lambeau Field an enjoyable one.

There are also photographs of family members: Kate, Eric and Scott Nelson, Lin Stoningpot, as well as Helen Nelson and Shirley Williams, Ali and AJ, Pete and Diane Isabell, Lydia Surface, Mike Roberts and Marcus Nelson, Chelsea, Robert, Briana and Andrew Nelson and the newest members of the family, Karou Nelson and Olivia Isabell.

And of course, the photographs of friends and acquaintances and most of all, fans of both football and fun: Ben Boucher, Anna Warren & father, Alex & George Garnett, Bridger, Carson and their dad, Simon Zadina, Jake Edwards, Doug Hinderks, Heidi & Elsa Marty, Cori Carlson, Victoria Kucera, Ian M, Dieu Phuong, Mai Kim, Huaong, Thom, Hong, Tai, Phuoc, Phi Phi, Phi Yen, Jeff & Nancy, Marshall, Carl & Elizabeth Ohvall, Mark Traun, Mike & Joyce Olson, Kerry Hilleren, Peggy Dahl, Chris Mahoney, Loren, Zac, Ben & Diane Erickson, Dale and Sharon, Katie and Jozie Nummi, Adrian Bowser, Karen Nelson, Mike & Devin Pillar, Jordan Pearson, Victoria and Eric Pascutti, Tony and Marilyn Mears, Maria Clark, Janie Doran, Becky and Danny Thomas, Ryan & Maggie Kelnhofer, Melissa Nazal, Teresa and Gary Eskuri, Bob & Kathy Marincel, Todd &Nina Bucher, Kathy & Kristin Marincel, Kylen Grand, Kim & Audrey Kostuch, Lynne & Kris Jones, Earl Jamieson from Maine, Paul Brown, Mike Robers, Seth & Derek Pykkonen, the DeNucci family, Kyla Williams, Shawn Butler and his Dad, Matt & Nolan Baker, Sebastian Holte, Chuck Fredrick& Greg Culver, the Fraiser family, the Dickman family, Alex Larson, McKinley Herda, Kevin Cothell & Noah Jameson, Jenna Ebbers & Abbey Arnold, Norm & Brenda Mayer, Corey & Debra Mayer, Jeff & Nancy Radimecky, Shaun Murphy from England, Chris & Abby Benser, Sue Johnson & Ida Anderson, Patty & Denny Peterson, Susan St. Marie, Lorne Brusletter and his family, Elliott, Courtney, Madison and Huston, Lauren & Jacob Sekelsky, Olivia Sekelsky, Peter Larson, Peter Salnick Jr., Thomas Woldmoe, Rachel, Katy & Amanda Woldmoe, Samantha Salnick, Nancy Carlson, Amy Tridgell, Diane Haworth, Deb Stone, Nadine Robison, Fern Burdick, the Sislo family, and last but not least, Jim Sterzinger. And the four-legged fans: Trolley the guinea pig, along with Windsor and Mister the wonder dogs.

If you find your photograph in this book and can't find your name, please contact me at CoachCarl@PackersversesVikings.com.

PACKERS
" VERSES "

VIKINGS

TABLE OF CONTENTS

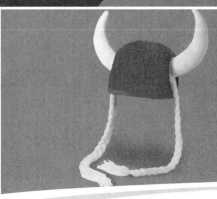

For whatever road you're on.  Krenzen

PACKERS

" VERSES "

VIKINGS

Green Bay Packers
Regular Season 13-3
Postseason 2-0
Super Bowl XXXI Champion

Minnesota Vikings
Regular Season 9-7
Postseason 0-1

1996

Carl "Gator" Nelson

PACKERS "VERSES" VIKINGS
~ Carl Nelson

OPENING WEEK 96

GB: 0-0
MN: 0-0

SUMMER IS COMING TO A CLOSE
MORNINGS ARE GROWING CHILLY
IT'S TIME AGAIN FOR FOOTBALL SEASON
A TIME SOME FOLKS FIND DOWNRIGHT SILLY

BUT THIS IS A TIME FOR CELEBRATION
FOR THOSE OF US WHO LOVE THE GAME
WE'LL WATCH MULTIPLE FORMATIONS
AND TRY TO LEARN THE ROOKIES' NAMES

WE'LL SEE THE POWER OF THE RUNNING GAME
THE BEAUTY OF THE LONG TOUCHDOWN PASS
WE'LL COMPLAIN ABOUT BAD ASTROTURF
AND WISH ALL FOOTBALL FIELDS HAD GRASS

THE TWO TEAMS THAT MATTER MOST
MINNESOTA AND GREEN BAY
SEEM TO BE ENTERING THIS SEASON
TRAVELING IN TWO SEPARATE WAYS

THE PACKERS' TEAM IS ON THE RISE
THEIR DESTINY WILL BE FULFILLED
WITH ANOTHER NFL CHAMPIONSHIP
AND WE FANS WILL BE QUITE THRILLED

~ ~ ~ ~ ~ ~ ~ ~ ~ ~ ~ ~ ~ ~ ~ ~ ~ ~

THE VIKINGS ON THE OTHER HAND
SEEM TO HAVE BEGUN TO SLUMP
DENNIS GREEN WILL HAVE TO WORRY
ABOUT HIS BIG BUTT GETTING DUMPED!

MINNESOTA PLAYS DETROIT AT HOME
IN A GAME THEY CAN'T SELL OUT
BARRY SANDERS AND THE LIONS
MAY WELL PRODUCE A ROUT!

THE PACKERS GO TO TAMPA BAY
TO TAKE ON TONY DUNGY AND THE BUCS
GREEN BAY'S TEAM WON'T BE STOPPED
AND WILL CRUSH THEM LIKE ENORMOUS TRUCKS

GOD BLESS CARL

DRAFT PARTY
HERE

IMMEDIATE SEATING AVAILABLE

RESULTS:
Green Bay beat the
Tampa Bay Buccaneers 34-3

Minnesota beat the
Detroit Lions 17-13

GB: 1-0
MN: 1-0

PACKERS "VERSES" VIKINGS ~ Carl Nelson

AFTER ONE WEEK OF FOOTBALL SEASON
THE YEAR IS OFF TO A GOOD START
SOME TEAMS HAVE SHOWN THAT MARGINAL TALENT
CAN BE OVERCOME WITH LOTS OF HEART

THE MINNESOTA VIKINGS' TEAM
SHOWED THAT SOME THINGS NEVER CHANGE
THE DEFENSE WAS LOOKING SHABBY
'TIL LINEBACKER JEFF BRADY SHOWED HIS RANGE

THE OFFENSE ALSO STRUGGLED
UNTIL WARREN MOON WENT DOWN
THEN BRAD JOHNSON AND ROBERT SMITH
TOOK THE BALL AND REALLY WENT TO TOWN

THIS WEEK THE VIKINGS HIT THE ROAD
GOING DOWN TO THE GEORGIADOME
WHERE THEY'LL GET TO SEE A SELLOUT CROWD
SOMETHING THEY'LL RARELY SEE AT HOME

THE FALCONS ARE TRUE MASTERS
OF THE STYLE CALLED "RUN AND SHOOT"
WHERE THE BALL GETS TOSSED TO A RECEIVER
AND DOWN THE FIELD HE SCOOTS

~ ~ ~ ~ ~ ~ ~ ~ ~ ~ ~ ~ ~ ~ ~ ~ ~ ~

GREEN BAY MADE A TRIP DOWN SOUTH
AND HAMMERED TAMPA BAY
THE DEFENSE CRUSHED THE HAPLESS BUCS
AND BRETT FAVRE HAD QUITE A DAY

NOW IT'S BACK TO LAMBEAU FIELD
PRO FOOTBALL'S PUREST SHRINE
TO PLAY AGAINST THE EAGLES
ON MONDAY NIGHT IN PRIME TIME

THE GAME SHOULD BE A CHALLENGE
PHILLY IS A TEAM WHICH HAS IMPROVED
THE COACH EVEN USED TO WORK FOR HOLMGREN
BEFORE HE PICKED UP AND MOVED

BUT RICKY WATTERS AND RODNEY PEETE
JUST MAY NOT BE ENOUGH
TO KEEP UP WITH THE PACKERS
WHO ARE LOOKING PRETTY TOUGH

AND ONCE THE DUST HAS SETTLED
AND THE LAST PASS PLAY HAS BEEN RUN
GREEN BAY WILL BE TWO-AND-0
WHILE MINNESOTA'S ONE-AND-ONE

RESULTS:
Green Bay beat the
Philadelphia Eagles 39-13

Minnesota beat the
Atlanta Falcons 23-17

GB: 2-0
MN: 2-0

PACKERS "VERSES" VIKINGS ~ Carl Nelson

WHEN YOU PLAY TEAMS FROM THE CENTRAL
AS THE FALCONS AND EAGLES LEARNED
YOU'D BEST HANG ON TO THE BALL
OR YOU'RE GOING TO GET BURNED

THE VIKINGS BEAT ATLANTA
WHILE OUT AND ON THE ROAD
OF COURSE, THE WAY THE FUMBLES BOUNCED
HELPED TO LIGHTEN MINNESOTA'S LOAD

THIS WEEK IT'S OFF TO SOLDIER FIELD
TO DO BATTLE WITH CHICAGO'S BEARS
WARREN MOON WILL GET THE START
AND WILL ACQUIRE MORE GRAY HAIR

THE BEARS' DEFENSE KNOWS WARREN MOON
AND HOW TO GET HIM OFF HIS GAME
ONCE THE VIKING RUNNING BACKS ARE STOPPED
WARREN WILL COME TO KNOW REAL PAIN

THE BEARS' OFFENSE HAS MANY FACES
THE VIKES WON'T KNOW WHAT TO EXPECT
CHICAGO CAN RUN RIGHT UP THE MIDDLE
OR LEAVE THE VIKING SECONDARY WRECKED

~ ~ ~ ~ ~ ~ ~ ~ ~ ~ ~ ~ ~ ~ ~ ~ ~ ~

BRETT FAVRE AND THE PACKERS
HAVE CERTAINLY COME OUT SMOKIN'
TO SAY THEY ARE CONTENDERS
TRULY IS NOT JOKIN'

WHEN THE CHARGERS COME TO TOWN THIS WEEK
WITH AN OFFENSE THAT'S RATED SECOND BEST
GREEN BAY'S GREAT DEFENSIVE TEAM
WON'T GET MUCH OF A REST

BUT REGGIE SEAN AND ALL THE BOYS
KNOW WHAT THEY HAVE TO DO
AND WILL CAUSE SAN DIEGO'S TEAM
TO TURN BLACK AND "CHARGER BLUE"

AS FOR THE PACKERS' OFFENSE
THERE'S TOO MANY STARS TO NAME
FOR TWO WEEKS THEY'VE BEEN ASTOUNDING
SUNDAY SHOULD BE THE SAME

BUT IF BOTH THE PACK AND VIKINGS WIN
IT WOULDN'T BE THE WORST
WHAT A SETUP FOR THE NEXT WEEK'S GAME
WITH BOTH TEAMS TIED FOR FIRST!

9

RESULTS:
Green Bay beat the
San Diego Chargers 42-10

Minnesota beat the
Chicago Bears 20-14

GB: 3-0
MN: 3-0

HOW COULD THERE BE A BETTER STAGE
FOR SUNDAY'S FOOTBALL GAME?
THE PACK VISITS THE VIKINGS
BOTH TEAMS' RECORDS ARE THE SAME

NEITHER TEAM HAS LOST A GAME
BOTH ARE PLACED AT THREE-AND-O
THE VIKES HAVE SQUEAKED OUT ALL THEIR WINS
WHILE THE PACK PUTS ON QUITE A SHOW

THE PACKERS' OFFENSE IS NUMBER ONE
GREEN BAY WILL FEEL THEY'VE GONE TO HEAVEN
WHEN THEY FACE MINNESOTA'S DEFENSE
WHICH IS RATED NUMBER TWENTY-SEVEN

THE PACKERS HAVE BEEN WINNING
BY TWENTY-NINE POINTS A GAME
THE VIKES' AVERAGE SCORE IS TWENTY
NO DOUBT THIS WEEK WILL BE THE SAME

BUT GREEN BAY HASN'T FARED TOO WELL
THE LAST FOUR TRIPS TO THE 'DOME
LUCK SEEMS TO BE ON THE VIKINGS' SIDE
WHEN THEY PLAY THE PACK AT HOME

THE DOME SEEMS LIKE A BLACK HOLE
WHERE GOOD TEAMS DISAPPEAR
BUT GREEN BAY HAS TOO MUCH FIREPOWER
TO HAVE THAT OCCUR THIS YEAR

THE PACKERS JUST HAVE TO PLAY THEIR GAME
AND LET THE TALENT SHINE ON THROUGH
EDGAR WILL SCORE ONE TOUCHDOWN
KEITH JACKSON WILL ADD TWO

OH, THE VIKINGS WON'T JUST LIE DOWN
AND LET THE PACKERS HAVE THEIR WAY
THEY'LL FIGHT AND BLOCK AND TACKLE
TRYING TO PRODUCE THAT ONE BIG PLAY

MOON'S LONG PASSES WILL FILL THE AIR
(WHEN HE'S NOT LYING ON HIS BACK)
TOO BAD FOR OLD WARREN
SOME WILL GO TO GREEN BAY'S DEFENSIVE BACKS!

ROBERT SMITH WILL RUN THE BALL
AND TRY TO MOVE IT ON THE GROUND
BUT IN A SEA OF YELLOW HELMETS
HE'LL BE LUCKY NOT TO DROWN

BUT THAT'S ENOUGH RHETORIC
TIME FOR THE GAME AT HAND
THE OUTCOME OF SUNDAY'S CONTEST
WILL CAUSE UPSET IN VIKING-LAND

PACKERS "VERSES" VIKINGS   ~ Carl Nelson

RESULTS:
Green Bay lost to
Minnesota 21-30

10

PACKERS "VERSES" VIKINGS

~ Carl Nelson

LAST SUNDAY AT THE METRODOME
THE VIKINGS' DEFENSE STOLE THE GAME
AND JUST LIKE THE LAST FOUR TRIES
THE OUTCOME WAS THE SAME

SO ENJOY YOUR TIME YOU VIKING FANS
YOUR TEAM IS FOUR-AND-O
BUT WHAT THE REMAINING SEASON HOLDS
THERE IS NO WAY TO KNOW

THIS WEEK THE VIKINGS TRAVEL EAST
TO JIMMY HOFFA'S FINAL RESTING PLACE
IT WILL BE OF GREAT INTEREST
TO SEE IF MINNESOTA FALLS FLAT ON THEIR FACE

THE GIANTS AREN'T A STRONG TEAM
IN FACT THEY SEEM QUITE WEAK
BUT THAT'S A DANGEROUS OPPONENT
AFTER ONE'S TEAM HAS HIT ITS PEAK

BECAUSE THE VIKES PLAY TO THE LEVEL
OF THE NEXT UPCOMING FOE
THEY'LL HAVE TO BE QUITE CAREFUL
NOT TO TAKE ONE ON THE NOSE

~ ~ ~ ~ ~ ~ ~ ~ ~ ~ ~ ~ ~ ~ ~ ~ ~

THE VIKINGS' DEFENSE HAD THEIR WAY
WITH A SHAKY PACKERS' LINE
THE BACKS AND TIGHT ENDS TRIED TO BLOCK
BUT STILL BRETT FAVRE HAD NO TIME

THREE WEEK'S WORTH OF ERRORS
SEEMED TO CATCH UP WITH THE PACK
FUMBLES AND AN INTERCEPTION
AND OF COURSE THOSE SEVEN SACKS

BUT NO TEAM GOES UNDEFEATED
AND THE PACKERS WERE NOT SHATTERED
FOR BY THE TIME THE SEASON ENDS
THIS LOSS JUST WON'T MATTER!

THIS WEEK IT'S ON THE ROAD AGAIN
TO VISIT ANOTHER DOME
THIS ONE'S OUT IN SEATTLE
AND IS THE SEAHAWKS' HOME

RESULTS:
Green Bay beat the
Seattle Seahawks 31-10

Minnesota lost to the
New York Giants 10-15

THOSE SEAHAWKS SHOULD BE NERVOUS
AS GREEN BAY CORRECTS ITS ERRORS
THE PACKERS' TEAM SEATTLE PLAYS
SHOULD FILL THOSE BOYS WITH TERROR!

11

PACKERS "VERSES" VIKINGS

~ Carl Nelson

WELL GOD'S BACK IN HIS HEAVEN
ALL IS RIGHT WITHIN THIS WORLD
THE PACKERS PLAYED AS THEY SHOULD
THE VIKINGS PLAYED LIKE GIRLS

MINNESOTA TRAVELED TO NEW JERSEY
THE PLACE WHERE JIMMY HOFFA CROAKED
AND MADE THE GAME PLAYED AGAINST THE PACKERS
SEEM LIKE JUST A CRUEL JOKE

AGAINST THE "MIGHTY" GIANTS
THE VIKINGS COULDN'T PASS OR RUN
THIS WEEK'S GAME AGAINST THE PANTHERS
WILL PROVE THE SLIDE HAS NOW BEGUN

ALTHOUGH FOLKS LIVING IN THE TWIN CITIES
WON'T BE ABLE TO WATCH THE GAME AT HOME
THE PANTHERS WHO HAVE ALSO ONLY LOST ONE TIME
SHOULD LIGHT UP THE METRODOME

SEVERAL OF WARREN'S OLD FRIENDS
NOW CALL CAROLINA HOME
THEY'LL PROVIDE SEVERAL FORCEFUL REUNIONS
AND LEAVE THE VIKES LAID OUT IN THE 'DOME

~ ~ ~ ~ ~ ~ ~ ~ ~ ~ ~ ~ ~ ~ ~ ~ ~ ~

"CAN'T WIN ON TURF OR IN A DOME"
THAT'S WHAT WAS SAID ABOUT THE PACKERS
BUT IN THE GAME AGAINST SEATTLE
THEY SURELY DIDN'T LOOK LIKE SLACKERS

GREEN BAY'S DEFENSE TOOK THE BALL
A TOTAL OF FIVE TIMES
WHILE SEATTLE'S COACHING STAFF
WAS GOING OUT OF THEIR MINDS

THIS WEEK IT'S OFF TO CHICAGO
TO FACE THOSE HATED BEARS
GIVEN THE PAST FEW YEARS' RECORD
GREEN BAY WILL BE ON A TEAR

FOR IF THERE'S A TEAM THE PACKERS OWN
THEY PLAY AT SOLDIER FIELD
GREEN BAY ALWAYS PLAYS THEM TOUGH
AND THE BEARS NEARLY ALWAYS YIELD

FAVRE WILL CONTINUE HIS RECORD PACE
DOWNFIELD EDGAR BENNETT WILL RUN
BLOOD WILL FLOW AND GRASS WILL FLY
AND GREEN BAY WILL BE AT FIVE-AND-ONE

RESULTS:
Green Bay beat the
Chicago Bears 37-6

Minnesota beat the
Carolina Panthers 14-12

12

GB: 5-1
MN: 5-1

PACKERS "VERSES" VIKINGS ~ Carl Nelson

HOW DO THE VIKINGS DO IT?
PULLING THOSE WINS OUT OF THEIR BUTTS
TO WATCH THEM STRUGGLE AGAINST "SO-SO" TEAMS
MUST MAKE VIKINGS FANS GO COMPLETELY NUTS

YET IN SOME WAY THEY HAVE DONE IT
AND HAVE SOMEHOW WON FIVE GAMES
THEY HAVEN'T LOOKED VERY PRETTY
BUT THE WINS COUNT JUST THE SAME

NOW IT'S OFF ON A TRIP TO TAMPA
TO PLAY THOSE HAPLESS BUCS
THE VIKES SHOULD BE ABLE TO BEAT THEM
AND NOT EVEN NEED TO USE THEIR LUCK

TAMPA HOWEVER MAY FEEL DIFFERENTLY
AND NOT LET THE VIKINGS CRUISE
ABOUT HALF THE TIME THE LAST FEW YEARS
THIS IS A GAME THE VIKINGS MANAGE TO LOSE

TAMPA BAY HASN'T TASTED VICTORY
WILL THE BUCCANEERS STAND TALL?
THE VIKES ARE PRETTY CONFIDENT
MEANING IT'S THE PERFECT SETUP FOR A FALL

~ ~

LAST WEEK THE BEARS SEEMED UPSET
AT THE WAY THE PACKERS WHIPPED 'EM
THIS WEEK SAN FRANCISCO
WILL BE GREEN BAY'S NEXT VICTIM

THIS WEEK COMING TO WISCONSIN
IS THE "FORTY-NINERS' SHOW"
THAT 'FRISCO WANTS SOME REVENGE
EVERY GREEN BAY PACKER KNOWS

LATE LAST YEAR THE PACKERS
STOPPED THE 'NINERS PLAYOFF RUN
THEY JUST OUTPLAYED OLD 'FRISCO
AND SEEMED TO HAVE LOTS OF FUN

THIS MONDAY NIGHT AT LAMBEAU
THEY'LL GO AT IT ONCE MORE
SAN FRANCISCO HAS BEEN STRUGGLING
WILL THE PACK RUN UP THE SCORE?

WITHOUT YOUNG SAN FRANCISCO
JUST ISN'T THE SAME TEAM
ALL OF WHICH FEEDS INTO THE PACKERS' PLAN
AND THIS YEAR'S PLAYOFF DREAM

RESULTS:
Green Bay beat the
San Francisco 49ers 23-20

Minnesota lost to the
Tampa Bay Buccaneers 13-24

GB: 5-1
MN: 5-1

Week Eight was the Bye week for both teams
Which means there were no poems written

~ ~ ~ ~ ~ ~ ~ ~ ~ ~ ~ ~ sorry ~ ~ ~ ~ ~ ~ ~ ~ ~ ~ ~

PACKERS "VERSES" VIKINGS ~ ~ Carl Nelson

14

GB: 6-1
MN: 5-2

PACKERS "VERSES" VIKINGS

~ Carl Nelson

THE LAST TIME WE SAW THE VIKINGS
THEY WERE A WHIPPED AND SORRY GROUP
LIMPING INTO THE BYE WEEK
HOPING THAT THEY COULD REGROUP

THE LOSS TO THE BUCCANEERS
HAD BROUGHT THE VIKES CRASHING DOWN TO EARTH
LOSING TO A TEAM LIKE THAT
MAKES PLAYERS QUESTION THEIR OWN WORTH

MINNESOTA'S OFFENSE HAS BEEN STRUGGLING
WITH JUST THREE TOUCHDOWNS IN THE LAST THREE GAMES
THE DEFENSE NOW HAS ALSO FALTERED
WILL THEY EVER PLAY THE SAME?

THE BEARS NOW COME TO THE METRODOME
LOOKING TO PAY THE VIKINGS BACK
MINNESOTA HURT FOUR BEARS WHILE IN CHCAGO
LOOK FOR AN EVEN MORE VICIOUS BEAR ATTACK

THE BEARS ALWAYS PLAY THE VIKINGS TOUGH
AND THEY FEEL THIS TIME THEY HAVE A REASON
TAKE A GOOD LONG LOOK AT WARREN MOON
HE MAY NOT BE SEEN AGAIN THIS SEASON

~ ~ ~ ~ ~ ~ ~ ~ ~ ~ ~ ~ ~ ~ ~ ~ ~ ~

TWO WEEKS AGO ON A MONDAY NIGHT
WAS PLAYED A GAME 'TWAS SIMPLY AWESOME
THE PACKERS WON IT IN OVERTIME
BUT AN INJURED ROBERT BROOKS IT COST 'EM

BUT ANTONIO FREEMAN AND DON BEEBE
SHOWED THEY CAN TAKE UP THE SLACK
THE LOSS OF ONE WIDE RECEIVER
WON'T DERAIL THE PACK

PACKER FANS WILL HAVE TO ADMIT
WE GOT SOME BREAKS DURING THAT GAME
BUT WHEN ALL IS SAID AND DONE
THEY BEAT THE 'NINERS JUST THE SAME

THE BYE WEEK GAVE THE PACKERS
A CHANCE TO REVISE SOME OF THEIR PLANS
THIS WEEK TAMPA'S BUCCANEERS
PLAY BEFORE LAMBEAU'S RABID FANS

NOW THAT THE GREEN BAY PACKERS
ARE SETTLED FIRMLY IN FIRST PLACE
THEY MUST NOT BE LIKE MINNESOTA'S TEAM
AND FALL FLAT ON THEIR FACE

RESULTS:
Green Bay beat the
Tampa Bay Buccaneers 13-7

Minnesota lost to the
Chicago Bears 13-15

GB: 7-1
MN: 5-3

THE VIKINGS PLAYED TRUE TO FORM
MONDAY NIGHT AGAINST THE BEARS
TWELVE PENALTIES TWO BLOCKED KICKS
AND ROBERT SMITH IN A SURGEON'S CARE

MANY VIKING FANS ARE ASKING THEMSELVES
"WHO ARE THOSE GUYS IN THE PURPLE HATS?"
"THEY SHOULD HAVE OVERWHELMED THE BEARS
HOW COULD THEY PLAY LIKE THAT?"

THAT'S A REAL GOOD QUESTION
THE ANSWER IS NOT EASILY FOUND
THE VIKE DEFENSE ISN'T GETTING IT DONE
THEY CAN'T PASS OR MOVE IT ON THE GROUND

IT WON'T BE GETTING ANY EASIER
STARTING THIS WEEK WITH THE CHIEFS
THE NEXT EIGHT GAMES ARE TOUGH ONES
AND IN SIGHT THERE'S NO RELIEF

THOSE VIKINGS' BOYS MUST SUCK IT UP
AND PLAY JUST AS HARD AS THEY CAN
OR THE NEXT ENDANGERED SPECIES
WILL BE THE ELUSIVE "VIKINGS' FAN"

~ ~ ~ ~ ~ ~ ~ ~ ~ ~ ~ ~ ~ ~ ~ ~ ~ ~

WHILE NOT A THING OF BEAUTY
THE PACKERS DEFEATED TAMPA BAY
GREEN BAY HAD TO WORK MUCH HARDER
THAN THEY SHOULD HAVE LAST SUNDAY

BUT IN THE GREATER SCHEME OF THINGS
IT'S WINS NOT FORM THAT REALLY MATTERS
HOWEVER IT WAS ANOTHER EXPENSIVE GAME
NOW ANTONIO'S ARM IS SHATTERED

GREEN BAY HAD TO TURN TO A PLAYER
ONCE WAIVED NOW GETTING A SECOND CHANCE
ANTHONY MORGAN'S BACK TO CATCH THE BALL
AND TO DO THE TOUCHDOWN DANCE

NOW IN THE LAST HOME GAME UNTIL DECEMBER
THE DETROIT LIONS COME TO TOWN
THEY CAN MOVE THE BALL THROUGH THE AIR
AND HAVE BARRY SANDERS ON THE GROUND

WHILE THE LIONS CAN BE PRODUCTIVE
THEY'VE BEEN UP AND DOWN THIS YEAR
LOOK FOR GREEN BAY'S OFFENSE TO OPEN UP
AND THE DEFENSE WILL KNOCK BARRY ON HIS REAR

PACKERS "VERSES" VIKINGS ~ Carl Nelson

RESULTS:
Green Bay beat the Detroit Lions 28-18

Minnesota lost to the Kansas City Chiefs 6-21

16

GB: 8-1
MN: 5-4

PACKERS "VERSES" VIKINGS

~ Carl Nelson

"WE HAVE THE SAME RECORD AS THE COWBOYS"
SAYS THE VIKINGS' DENNY GREEN
AS HE STANDS UPON THE SIDELINE
GAZING AT HIS "WELL-OILED MACHINE"

WE'VE SEEN THE WAY THE VIKES HAVE PLAYED
DURING THE LAST FEW WEEKS
UNLIKE HIGH-SPEED SCORING MACHINES
THEY'RE MORE LIKE THIN-NECKED GEEKS

AGAINST THE CHIEFS OF KANSAS CITY
THE VIKINGS DEFENSE HELD ITS OWN
BUT BECAUSE THE OFFENSE IS BROKEN
MINNESOTA COULDN'T GET TO THE END ZONE

THE WAY FOR THE MINNESOTA VIKINGS
TO BREAK THEMSELVES OUT OF THIS SLUMP
IS TO RE-EVALUATE THE COACHING STAFF
AND TOSS DENNY IN THE DUMP

THAT'S WHAT SHOULD REALLY HAPPEN
BUT THE VIKINGS "WON'T" OR "CAN'T"
A NEW HEAD COACH IS NEEDED
EVEN A STUMP LIKE OLD BUD GRANT

~ ~ ~ ~ ~ ~ ~ ~ ~ ~ ~ ~ ~ ~ ~ ~ ~ ~ ~

THE LIONS LEARNED A LESSON
BEING TAUGHT TO THE NFC
"IF YOU'RE NOT PLAYING FOR THE PACKERS
LAMBEAU IS NOT THE PLACE TO BE"

THE LIONS BROUGHT ALL THEY HAD
INCLUDING FOOTBALL'S BEST RUNNING BACK
BUT NONE OF THAT WAS ENOUGH
TO DEFEAT AN AROUSED PACK

THE PACK IS PLAYING THROUGH SOME INJURIES
THAT WOULD CRIPPLE MANY TEAMS
BUT PLAYERS LIKE BEEBE AND MICKENS
ARE SUPPORTING GREEN BAY'S DREAM

THIS WEEK ON THE ROAD IN KANSAS CITY
THEY'LL PLAY THE TEAM WHO JUST KILLED THE VIKES
GREEN BAY'S OFFENSIVE LINE IS NICKED UP
WHICH THE CHIEFS' DEFENSE WILL LIKE

RESULTS:
Green Bay lost to the
Kansas City Chiefs 20-27

Minnesota lost to the
Seattle Seahawks 23-42

DESPITE THAT FACT THE PACKERS
SHOULD CONTINUE THEIR WINNING WAYS
REMINDING US THAT THESE ARE INDEED
GREEN BAY'S "GLORY DAYS"

PACKERS "VERSES" VIKINGS

~ Carl Nelson

WHO WOULD HAVE EVER THOUGHT IT?
WE'RE FEELING SORRY FOR THE VIKES
AND WATCHING THEM GET POUNDED
HAS SLIPPED FROM THE LIST OF "LIKES"

SEEING SEATTLE MAUL THEM
MADE MANY STOMACHS QUEASY
NEVER IN OUR WILDEST DREAMS
HAS MINNESOTA EVER LOOKED SO EASY

THE RAIDERS WILL BE THE NEXT TEAM
TO FEAST UPON THE "QUEENS"
HOW MUCH LONGER WILL THE VIKES PUT UP
WITH HEAD COACH DENNY GREEN?

~ ~ ~ ~ ~ ~ ~ ~ ~ ~ ~ ~ ~ ~ ~ ~ ~ ~

THIS WEEK THERE'LL BE SOME EXTRA LINES
TALKING ABOUT THE PACK
IN THREE YEARS THEY'VE PLAYED SIX GAMES IN DALLAS
AND AGAIN THIS YEAR THEY'RE GOING BACK

YES, WE ALL WATCHED KANSAS CITY
GIVE THE PACKERS A GOOD SPANKING
BUT IF YOU THINK GREEN BAY'S GOING DOWN THE TUBE
IT'S YOUR OWN CHAIN YOU'RE YANKING

THE PACKERS HAVE TO FACE THE 'POKES
LOOKING LIKE THEY'VE BEEN THROUGH A BLENDER
NOW EDGAR BENNETT'S PULLED A GROIN
WHILE FAVRE HAS A HIP THAT'S TENDER

AIKMAN IRVIN AND THE REST
ARE PRIMARILY A DISTRACTION
FOR THERE'S A BACK IN DALLAS
WHO PROVIDES MOST OF THE COWBOYS' ACTION

GREEN BAY PLAYS THE COWBOYS TOUGH
BUT EMMITT USUALLY TURNS THE TIDE
AGAIN THIS WEEK THE 'POKES WILL SADDLE UP
AND UPON HIS BACK THEY'LL RIDE

MICKENS, REGGIE, AND ALL THE GUYS
WILL SHOW THE PACKERS HAVE A LOT OF HEART
THIS WILL BE THE WEEK THAT SHOWS
THEY'RE MORE THAN THE SUM OF THE PARTS

SO DON'T LOOK FOR GREEN BAY
TO ROLL OVER IN THAT JOINT
DO YOURSELF A FAVOR...
TAKE THE PACKERS AND THE POINTS

18

RESULTS:
Green Bay lost to the
Dallas Cowboys 6-21

Minnesota beat the
Oakland Raiders 16-13

GB: 8-3
MN: 6-5

PACKERS "VERSES" VIKINGS

~ Carl Nelson

EVEN THOUGH THE VIKINGS WON
IN OAKLAND SUNDAY NIGHT
IT MAY BE TOO SOON TO THINK THAT TEAM
IS MOVING BACK TOWARD THE LIGHT

BRAD JOHNSON'S PLAY WAS ADEQUATE
LEROY HOARD LOOKED PRETTY GOOD
JUGGLING THE OFFENSIVE LINE
HELPED THEM PLAY THE WAY THEY SHOULD

HOWEVER KEEPING THINGS IN PERSPECTIVE
WINNING JUST ONE GAME OUT OF FIVE
DOESN'T MAKE THE VIKINGS DOMINANT
BUT KEEPS DENNY'S JOB ALIVE

THIS WEEK IT'S THE DENVER BRONCOS
ROLLING INTO THE METRODOME
MINNESOTA'S BEST HOPE OF A VICTORY
IS THE CALLS THEY GET AT HOME

DENVER'S TEAM HAS WON TEN TIMES
WHILE LOSING ONLY ONCE
TO NOT PICK THE WINNER OF THIS GAME
YOU WOULD HAVE TO BE A DUNCE

~ ~ ~ ~ ~ ~ ~ ~ ~ ~ ~ ~ ~ ~ ~ ~ ~ ~ ~

IN SUCCESSIVE WEEKS IT'S HAPPENED
GREEN BAY HAS TAKEN IT ON THE CHIN
BUT DON'T DESPAIR YOU PACKERS' FANS
GREEN BAY SHALL RISE AGAIN

DALLAS STRETCHED THEIR WINNING STREAK
TO SEVEN GAMES ON MONDAY NIGHT
THOUGH THE 'POKES COULD ONLY SCORE FIELD GOALS
WHEN THEY SCORED THEM STARTED QUITE A FIGHT

WELL IT DOESN'T MATTER AT THIS TIME
AND PLAYOFF REVENGE WILL BE SWEET
FOR IF THE COWBOYS GET THERE
IT WILL BE AT LAMBEAU WHERE THEY MEET

THE PACKERS NEED TO TURN AROUND
AND REGAIN THEIR WINNING WAYS
THIS WEEK'S GAME OUT IN ST LOUIS
STARTS THE RETURN TO THE GLORY DAYS

RESULTS:
Green Bay beat the
St Louis Rams 24-9

Minnesota lost to the
Denver Broncos 17-21

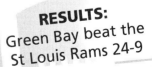

THIS GAME COMES AT THE RIGHT TIME
TO GIVE THE PACK A BREAK...
WITH RETIREMENTS AND INJURIES
HOW MUCH MORE CAN THEY TAKE?

GB: 9-3
MN: 6-6

THE BRONCOS PULLED OFF A MIRACLE
IN THE CLOSING SECONDS LAST SUNDAY
IT DIDN'T HAVE MUCH TO DO WITH THE VIKINGS
BUT SHOWED THE MAGIC OF JOHN ELWAY

THE VIKINGS HIT THE PLAYING FIELD
LOOKING LIKE THE TEAMS OF YORE
BUT THE ORANGE CRUSH'S DEFENSIVE PLAY
LEFT LEROY (AND HIS SHOES) UPON THE FLOOR

THE VIKES PLAYED QUITE A GOOD GAME
BETTER THAN THEY HAVE IN SEVERAL WEEKS
THEY SHOULD HAVE PROBABLY BEATEN DENVER
IF NOT FOR SOME DEFENSIVE LEAKS

NOW FROM THE ARIZONA DESERT
TO THE LAND OF FROZEN LAKES
COMES BOOMER AND THE CARDINALS
TO PROVE THEIR RECORD'S NOT A FAKE

BOTH TEAMS SIT AT SIX-AND-SIX
AND BOTH HAVE FADING PLAYOFF HOPES
MINNESOTA MUST PLAY A PERFECT GAME
AND NOT LIKE A BUNCH OF DOPES

~ ~ ~ ~ ~ ~ ~ ~ ~ ~ ~ ~ ~ ~ ~ ~ ~ ~

THE PACKERS SEEMED TO GET HEALTHY
ALTHOUGH IT WAS AT THE RAMS' EXPENSE
A TENACIOUS FIRST HALF DEFENSE
SET UP THE SECOND HALF'S OFFENSE

WHILE GREEN BAY IN THE FIRST HALF
GAVE PACKERS' FANS SOME FITS
THE HEART AND TALENT OF THE PACKERS
JUST WOULDN'T LET THEM QUIT

FINALLY THE PACKERS HEAD HOME
AFTER A ROAD TRIP FROM HELL
THEY HAVE ACQUIRED A NEW WEAPON
AND ANTONIO IS FINALLY WELL

SINCE THINGS ARE GETTING BETTER
AND THE PACK'S SHEDDING ITS CARES
WHAT BETTER TEAM FOR THEM TO PLAY
THAN THE LOWLY CHICAGO BEARS

THE BEARS KNOW THE PACKERS OWN THEM
BUT WILL STILL DO THEIR BEST TO WIN
BETWEEN EDGAR'S RUNNING AND THE "RISON" STAR
THE PACK WILL BEAT THEM ONCE AGAIN

PACKERS "VERSES" VIKINGS

~ Carl Nelson

RESULTS:
Green Bay beat the
Chicago Bears 28-17

Minnesota beat the
Arizona Cardinals 41-17

PACKERS "VERSES" VIKINGS ~ Carl Nelson

GB: 10-3
MN: 7-6

ALL THE VIKINGS' FANS ARE REJOICING
AS MINNESOTA REARS ITS PURPLE HEAD
WHO WOULD HAVE EVER THOUGHT IT?
A FEW WEEKS AGO THEY JUST SEEMED DEAD

EVEN THE "REAL FANS" WERE SORT OF GROUSING
BUT NOW THEY SING A DIFFERENT TUNE
THE MAJOR REASON FOR THE TURNAROUND
IS BRAD JOHNSON'S "ECLIPSE" OF WARREN MOON

OF COURSE THE ARIZONA CARDINALS
ARE NOT AN ELITE TEAM
SO LAST SUNDAY'S VIKINGS' WIN
MAY BE WORTH LESS THAN IT SEEMED

THIS WEEK MINNESOTA'S ON THE ROAD
HEADED INTO THE LION'S DEN
DETROIT'S HAD ITS WAY WITH THE VIKES THERE
WILL THAT HAPPEN ONCE AGAIN?

PLAYING THE LIONS IN THE SILVERDOME
IS NEVER AN EASY TASK
ON MONDAY THE VIKES' HOPES WILL BE CRUSHED
OR ONCE AGAIN IN GLORY THEY WILL BASK

~ ~ ~ ~ ~ ~ ~ ~ ~ ~ ~ ~ ~ ~ ~ ~ ~ ~

THE PACK IS GETTING HEALTHIER
AS WAS SHOWN SUNDAY AGAINST THE BEARS
THIS WEEK CHMURA REJOINS THE FOLD
AND WILL BE WARMLY WELCOMED THERE

ANTONIO'S RETURN WAS SPECTACULAR
PLAYING WITH ONE ARM IN A CAST
HE CAUGHT TEN BALLS AND HAD A BIG DAY
AND IT WON'T BE HIS LAST

NOW THE BRONCOS COME TO TOWN
WITH JOHN ELWAY AND HIS MAGIC ARM
DENVER'S RUNNING GAME AND DEFENSE
WILL ALSO TRY TO DO THE PACKERS HARM

REGGIE AND THE DEFENSE
MUST RISE UP FROM THE STARTING BELL
IF THEY CAN SLOW DOWN TERRELL DAVIS
GREEN BAY SHOULD DO QUITE WELL

RESULTS:
Green Bay beat the
Denver Broncos 41-6

Minnesota beat the
Detroit Lions 24-22

NOW AS THE SEASON TAPERS DOWNWARD
TOWARD THE FINAL FEW SUNDAYS
THE PACKERS MUST LOOK TOWARD THE PLAYOFFS
AND MAKE SURE "THE ROAD" GOES THROUGH GREEN BAY

GB: 11-3
MN: 8-6

PACKERS "VERSES" VIKINGS ~ Carl Nelson

THE VIKINGS HAVE WON TWO GAMES IN A ROW
AND COULD BE SAID TO BE GATHERING SOME SPEED
WINS AGAINST THE CARDINALS AND THE LIONS
ARE GIVING THEM THE CONFIDENCE THEY NEED

THOUGH PERHAPS THE WIN OVER IN DETROIT
SHOULDN'T HAVE VIKINGS' FANS TOO EXCITED
IT TOOK THE LIONS MISSING A TWO-POINT CONVERSION
BEFORE THIS GAME WAS FINALLY DECIDED

ON PAPER THE LIONS REALLY WON THIS GAME
BUT IT GOES TO SHOW HOW MISLEADING STATS CAN BE
BECAUSE THEY REALLY WERE NEVER IN IT
AND THAT WAS VERY PLAIN TO SEE

THIS WEEK THEY'LL WELCOME THE BUCCANEERS
WHO'VE BEEN HAVING A RESURGENCE OF THEIR OWN
TONY DUNGY'S MESSAGE MAY BE GETTING THROUGH
AS THE RECENT VICTORIES HAVE SHOWN

THE VIKES CAN'T AFFORD TO SLIP UP
AND TAKE A LOSS THIS LATE IN THE SEASON
A PLAYOFF BERTH IS STILL WITHIN REACH
THAT SHOULD BE ENOUGH OF A REASON

~ ~ ~ ~ ~ ~ ~ ~ ~ ~ ~ ~ ~ ~ ~ ~ ~ ~

WHILE IT CAN BE SAID THAT THE DENVER BRONCOS
WEREN'T TOO INTERESTED IN LAST SUNDAY'S GAME
THE FACT THAT GREEN BAY SIMPLY CRUSHED THEM
HAS GOT TO STING SOMEWHAT JUST THE SAME

BRETT FAVRE MADE A COUPLE OF THOSE PLAYS
THAT SHOWS WHY HE'S A MULTI-TIME MVP
AND THE WAY THE PACKERS' DEFENSE PLAYED
WAS A BEAUTIFUL THING TO SEE

WHILE THIS WIN MEANS THAT THE PACKERS
CAN MOVE ON WITH THE CENTRAL CROWN IN HAND
THEY WILL STILL NEED TO WIN OUT
TO BRING PLAYOFF GAMES BACK TO PACKERLAND

THE DETROIT LIONS ARE THE NEXT OPPONENT
SITTING SQUARELY IN THE PACKERS' SIGHTS
BUT WAYNE FONTES' SHIP IS SINKING
AND THERE'S NOT TIME TO SET IT RIGHT

THE LIONS ARE WATCHING THIS SEASON
SPIRAL SLOWLY DOWN THE DRAIN
THE BEATING THEY'LL GET FROM THE PACKERS
WILL ONLY INCREASE THEIR PAIN

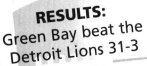

RESULTS:
Green Bay beat the
Detroit Lions 31-3

Minnesota beat the
Tampa Bay Buccaneers 21-10

GB: 12-3
MN: 9-6

MERRY CHRISTMAS TO ALL!

PACKERS "VERSES" VIKINGS ~ Carl Nelson

MINNESOTA HAS LOOKED MUCH IMPROVED
DURING THE PAST FEW WEEKS
BUT EXCEPT FOR THE DENVER BRONCOS
THE COMPETITION HAS BEEN PRETTY WEAK

SOMEHOW THE VIKES HAVE PUT TOGETHER
A THREE-GAME STRING OF WINS
UNFORTUNATELY FOR MINNESOTA
THIS SUNDAY THEY'LL PROBABLY LOSE AGAIN

THE LIONS' CARDS AND BUCCANEERS
AREN'T IN THE SAME CLASS AS THE PACK
GREEN BAY HAS WON THEIR LAST FOUR GAMES
AND THEY WON'T BE LOOKING BACK

THIS WEEK IT'S OFF TO GREEN BAY
AND THE GRASS OF LAMBEAU FIELD
WHERE THE TURF WILL SLOW THE VIKES
AND THE COLD WILL MAKE THEM YIELD

THE VIKINGS FOUND OUT EARLIER THIS SEASON
THE PACKERS DIDN'T LIKE BEING "MOONED"
NOW WATCH THEIR "JOHNSON" GET SLAPPED AROUND
THIS COMING SUNDAY AFTERNOON

THE PACKERS WON THEIR FOURTH STRAIGHT GAME
ALTHOUGH IT WAS TO BE EXPECTED
THE WAY THE DEFENSE CRUSHED BARRY SANDERS
SHOWED WHY THEY'RE SO WELL- RESPECTED

FAVRE AND THE REST OF HIS TEAMMATES
HAVE REGAINED THE BALANCE AND THE DRIVE
THAT HELPED OVERCOME THE INJURIES
AND KEPT POSTSEASON HOPES ALIVE

BOTH THE OFFENSE AND THE DEFENSE
HAVE MADE QUITE A TURNABOUT
DOMINATING BOTH SIDES OF THE LINE OF SCRIMMAGE
AND GIVING FANS MANY REASONS TO SHOUT

WHILE PLAYING OUTSIDE IN DECEMBER
THE VIKES CAN SAY IS "NO CONCERN"
WE'LL SEE WHAT'S SAID WHEN FEET ARE NUMB
AND THE COLD MAKES THEIR SKIN BURN

THIS WEEK'S GAME AT LAMBEAU
BEGINS A LONG HOME FIELD PLAYOFF RUN
THE OUTSTANDING WAY THE PACK HAS PLAYED
HAS BROUGHT PACKERS' FANS THIS FUN!

RESULTS:
Green Bay beat the
Minnesota Vikings 38-10

23

PACKERS "VERSES" VIKINGS ~ Carl Nelson

THE SEASON IS FINALLY OVER
THE PLAYOFFS ARE SET TO BEGIN
THE PACKERS EASILY WON THE CENTRAL
WHILE THE VIKINGS WEASELED THEIR WAY IN

LAST SUNDAY UP AT LAMBEAU
THE PACKERS THUMPED THE VIKES
GREEN BAY'S DEFENSE CONTAINED 'EM
'TIL THE OFFENSE CHOSE TO STRIKE

NOW THE PACKERS HAVE A WEEK OFF
TO HEAL ANY INJURIES THAT MAY LINGER
BUT THE ONLY REAL DAMAGE DONE SUNDAY
CAME FROM COREY FULLER'S FINGER

IT WAS A GAME PLAYED WITH ANGER
WITH HITS BOTH CLEAN AND LATE
BUT IN THE END, GREEN BAY'S RUNNING GAME
SEALED THE MINNESOTA VIKINGS' FATE

SO WHILE THE PACKERS TAKE THE WEEKEND OFF
THE VIKINGS HEAD OUT ON THE ROAD
TO FACE TROY AIKMAN AND THE COWBOYS
WHICH IS A VERY HEAVY LOAD

WHILE EMMITT'S BEEN A BIT OFF
HIS PERFORMANCE OF SOME YEARS PAST
HE STILL HAS HIS TERRIFIC MOVES
AND HE'S PRETTY DOGGONE FAST

AS FOR THE COWBOYS' AIR GAME
THEY SAY AIKMAN IS ONE OF THE BEST
SOME FOLKS MAY NOT AGREE WITH THAT
BUT HE'LL BE UP TO THE TEST

THE COWBOYS' DEFENSE IT MUST BE SAID
IS ONE OF THE TOUGHEST AROUND
ALTHOUGH SINCE LEON WAS SUSPENDED
THEY MAY FEEL A LARGE "LETT" DOWN

MINNESOTA'S GOT A TOUGH GAME AHEAD
PROBABLY MORE THAN THEY CAN HANDLE
THE DEFENSE WILL HAVE A REAL LONG DAY
IF DALLAS CAN CONTROL "BIG" JOHN RANDLE

THE LIMITS OF THE VIKINGS' OFFENSE
WERE LAST WEEK SHOWN TO THE WHOLE WORLD
THE BACKS AND RECEIVERS WERE ROUGHED UP
AND BRAD JOHNSON TO THE GROUND WAS HURLED

SO FOR ALL YOU VIKINGS' FANS
LOOKING FOR A PACKERS' REMATCH NEXT WEEKEND
THE COWBOYS' TEAM WILL BE JUST TOO TOUGH
AND BACK TO THE CITIES THE VIKES THEY WILL SEND

GB: 13-3
Central
Champs!

MN: 9-7
Wildcard

RESULTS:
Green Bay had a
"Bye Week"

Minnesota lost to the
Dallas Cowboys 15-40

24

PACKERS "VERSES" VIKINGS ~ Carl Nelson

WELL SOMEONE HAS TO SAY IT
REGARDING LAST SUNDAY'S GAME
THOUGH THE VIKES WERE IN THE PLAYOFFS
THE RESULT WAS JUST THE SAME

THE TEAM IN WHITE AND SILVER
ATE MINNESOTA'S BOYS ALIVE
IF YOU BELIEVED THE VIKES COULD WIN
YOU MUST HAVE LISTENED TO DENNY'S JIVE

DENNY'S RECORD IN THE PLAYOFFS
DOESN'T SHOW THE THINGS IT SHOULD
IT'S NOT JUST BAD COACHING THAT COSTS THEM GAMES
THE VIKES JUST AREN'T VERY GOOD

PHYSICALLY THE VIKINGS' TEAM
DOESN'T MATCH UP WITH THE ELITE
IT'S NOT RANDLE OR JOHNSON'S ARM
OR THE LACK OF ROB SMITH'S FEET

HERE'S SOME ADVICE FOR THE VIKES
ALTHOUGH THE TEAM'S IN LOVE WITH SPEED
IN BOTH OFFENSIVE AND DEFENSIVE LINES
IT'S MORE TALENT AND "BEEF" YOU NEED

~ ~ ~ ~ ~ ~ ~ ~ ~ ~ ~ ~ ~ ~ ~ ~ ~ ~

WHILE THE VIKES WERE TAKING LUMPS
THE PACKERS WERE RESTING IN THEIR HOMES
SECURE IN KNOWING THE NEXT TEAM PLAYED
WOULDN'T DRAG THEM INTO A DOME

THIS WEEK IT IS THE 'NINERS
WHO STRIDE INTO THE PACKERS' DEN
BUT EVEN WITH STEVE YOUNG PLAYING
SAN FRANCISCO WILL LOSE AGAIN

FAR EARLIER THIS SEASON
ON AN EVENTFUL MONDAY NIGHT
THESE TWO TEAMS MET AT LAMBEAU
AND THE GAME LOOKED LIKE A STREET FIGHT

THE SAN FRANCISCO FORTY-NINERS
LOST IN OVERTIME THAT NIGHT
CHRIS JACKE'S GAME-WINNING FIELD GOAL
WAS A TRULY BEAUTIFUL SIGHT

GREEN BAY CAN'T LOOK PAST THESE GUYS
ALTHOUGH THEY'VE BEATEN THEM IN THE PAST
DESPITE THE BEST EFFORTS OF THE 'NINERS
THE PACK WILL KNOCK THEM TO THE GRASS

GB: 0-0
(1st Game)

MN: 0-1
(back in MPLS)

RESULTS:
Green Bay beat the
San Francisco 49ers 35-14

25

PACKERS "VERSES" VIKINGS ~ Carl Nelson

Playoff Records
GB: 1-0
Carolina: 1-0

LAST WEEK AT LAMBEAU IT WAS RAINING
TURNING THE FIELD INTO FREEZING SLOPPY GOO
CAUSING THE FORTY-NINERS TEAM TO WONDER
"WHATEVER IS THERE TO DO?"

DESMOND HOWARD RETURNED ONE FOR A SCORE
SOON AFTER THE GAME BEGAN
AND THOUGH FAVRE TOSSED A SCORE TO RISON
THE GAME DEPENDED ON HOW EDGAR BENNETT RAN

AND EDGAR DIDN'T DISAPPOINT
ALTHOUGH HIS STYLE MAY NOT BE FLASHY
HE "GROUND" IT OUT AND SCORED TWO TIMES
DESPITE CONDITIONS BEST DESCRIBED AS "TRASHY"

THE DEFENSE SHONE ONCE AGAIN
AS SHURMUR'S TROOPS ARE TRULY ON A ROLL
THEY JUST PLAYED TOUGH HARD-NOSED FOOTBALL
AND NEVER LET THE 'NINERS GET OUT OF CONTROL

ALL IN ALL IT WAS ALMOST A PERFECT DAY
AS THE SAN FRANCISCO TEAM WENT DOWN TO DEFEAT
THE CITY OF GREEN BAY WAS REALLY ROCKIN'
AS ALL BUT THREE FANS FILLED LAMBEAU'S SEATS

~ ~ ~ ~ ~ ~ ~ ~ ~ ~ ~ ~ ~ ~ ~ ~ ~ ~ ~

THE PANTHERS ARE ONLY IN THEIR SECOND SEASON
AND ALREADY THE CONFERENCE CROWN THEY SEEK
AMAZINGLY THEY'LL PLAY ONE OF THE OLDEST TEAMS
FACING THE PACKERS AT LAMBEAU FIELD THIS WEEK

WHILE COUGHLIN AND HIS COACHING STAFF
HAVE BROUGHT CAROLINA'S TEAM A LONG WAY
IT WILL BE UP TO COLLINS' ARM AND JOHNSON'S LEGS
TO TAKE THEM THE REST OF THE WAY

SAM MILLS LEADS A DEFENSE THAT'S AGGRESSIVE
AND READY TO EXPLOIT ANY WEAKNESS SEEN
TACKLING ANYBODY WITH THE BALL
WHO CAN GET PAST LINEMAN KEVIN GREENE

BOTH CAROLINA AND THE PACKERS ARE READY
PREPARED TO TAKE EACH OTHERS' MEASURE
AND TO CLAIM THE HALAS TROPHY
SHOWING THE CHAMPIONSHIP THEY WILL TREASURE

ONCE THE GAME HAS ENDED SUNDAY
AND ONE TEAM'S DOMINANCE HAS BEEN SEEN
IT'S OFF TO THE SUPER BOWL IN NEW ORLEANS
FOR THE TEAM WEARING GOLD AND GREEN

RESULTS:
Green Bay beat the
Carolina Panthers 30-13

SUPER BOWL EDITION
THIS IS THE YEAR WE'VE WAITED FOR
HOPING WITH ALL OUR HEARTS AND SOULS
THIS YEAR THE GREEN BAY PACKERS
ARE RETURNING TO THE SUPER BOWL

THE LAST TIME THIS HAPPENED
I WAS NOT YET THIRTEEN
AND THE YEARS BETWEEN FOR PACKERS' FANS
HAVE BEEN MORE THAN A LITTLE LEAN

FOR ALL OF US WHO'VE WAITED
THROUGH ALL OF THOSE LONG YEARS
WATCHING THE PACKERS BEAT THE PANTHERS
NEARLY MOVED US ALL TO TEARS

SO THIS COMING SUNDAY AFTERNOON
DOWN IN SWINGING NEW ORLEANS
WILL BE THE SUPER BOWL RETURN
OF WHO IS REALLY "AMERICA'S TEAM"

SO WHAT WILL HAPPEN SUNDAY
AS THE PACKERS FACE THE PATS
BEFORE A SOLD-OUT SUPERDOME CROWD
MOSTLY WEARING BIG CHEESE HATS

RECENT YEARS WOULD SEEM TO SAY
THE EDGE MUST GO TO THE NFC
WILL HISTORY REPEAT ITSELF?
TUNE IN SUNDAY NIGHT TO SEE

WHILE BILL PARCELLS AND THE PATRIOTS
ARE THE AFC AT ITS BEST
THEY MUST NOW FACE THE PACKERS
CAN THEY SURVIVE THE TEST?

NEW ENGLAND'S OFFENSE CAN BE POTENT
ON THE GROUND AND THROUGH THE AIR
AND THE SHIFTY PATRIOT DEFENSE
HAS GIVEN MANY QUARTERBACKS GRAY HAIR

BUT THAT JUST WON'T MATTER
AS YOU WILL COME TO SEE
GREEN BAY WILL TAKE HOME THE TROPHY
AND BRETT FAVRE THE MVP

FOR THOSE OF US WHO KEPT THE FAITH
WHEN IT SEEMED THEY NEVER WOULD GET BACK
WHAT A SWEET REWARD THIS IS
FOR THOSE OF US WHO LOVE THE PACK!

GO PACK!!

PACKERS "VERSES" VIKINGS   ~ Carl Nelson

27

RESULTS:
Green Bay beat the
New England Patriots 35-21

PACKERS

" VERSES "

VIKINGS

<u>Green Bay Packers</u>
Regular Season 13-3
Postseason 2-0
Lost Super Bowl XXXII

<u>Minnesota Vikings</u>
Regular Season 9-7
Postseason 1-1

1 9 9 7

Carl "Gator" Nelson

Season Opener!
Sept. 1
1 9 9 7

World Champion
GB: 0-0
MN: 0-0

PACKERS "VERSES" VIKINGS ~ Carl Nelson

SUMMERTIME IS ENDING
FALL'S CRISPNESS FILLS THE AIR
IT'S THE TIME FOR FOOTBALL
PACKERS VIKINGS LIONS BUCS AND BEARS

THE TIME FOR TALK HAS ENDED
IT'S TIME FOR THEM TO SHOW THEIR STUFF
WILL THE CHANGES MADE BY THESE TEAMS
TO GET BETTER BE ENOUGH?

THIS WEEK IN THE OPENER
THE VIKES GO TO VISIT THE BILLS
MOST TIMES BACK IN HISTORY
THIS GAME WOULD HAVE PROVIDED THRILLS

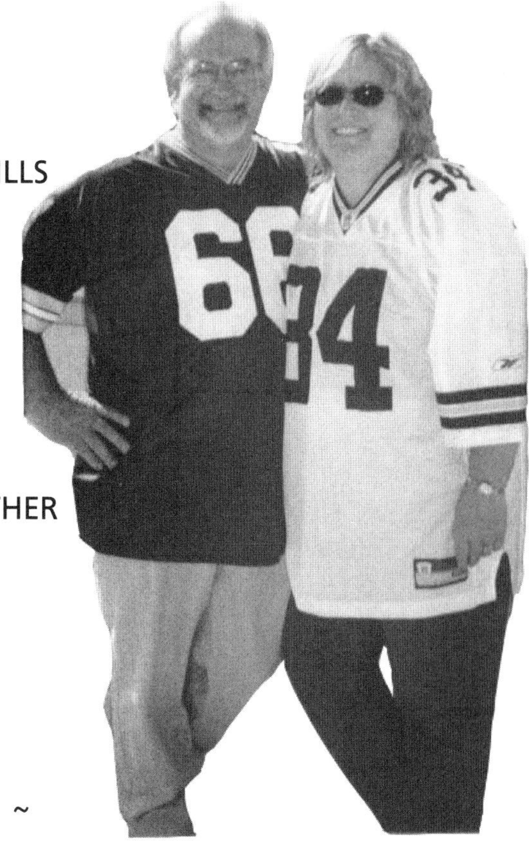

BUT THE WAY THINGS LOOK NOW
THIS GAME JUST WON'T BE SO GREAT
BETWEEN THESE TWO COMBATANTS
THE LOST SUPERBOWL'S NUMBER EIGHT

WHILE THIS NUMBER IS SIGNIFICANT
ALL IT REALLY GOES TO SHOW
IS THAT WHEN TWO LOSERS COME TOGETHER
THEY'LL PUT ON A PALTRY SHOW

THE BILLS ARE GOING TO WIN THIS GAME
AND NOT WORK UP A SWEAT
THE VIKINGS MAY HAVE HIGH HOPES
BUT THEY DON'T HAVE THE TALENT YET

~ ~ ~ ~ ~ ~ ~ ~ ~ ~ ~ ~ ~ ~ ~ ~

THE SUPER BOWL IS OVER
GREEN BAY SHOWED THEY ARE THE BEST
NOW THIS UPCOMING SEASON
WILL PROVIDE AN ONGOING TEST

OPENING THIS YEAR WITH CHICAGO
ON THE FIRST MONDAY NIGHT
THE PACKERS WILL BE PROVIDED
WITH THEIR FIRST DIVISION FIGHT

BENNETT USED TO OWN THE BEARS
RUNNING FOR YARDS AT WILL
BUT NOW IT'S FAVRE AND LEVENS
THAT WILL GIVE PACKERS FANS THEIR THRILLS

AS THE FIRST WEEK COMES TO A CLOSE
BRINGING AN END TO ALL OUR FUN
THE PACKERS WILL BE ONE-AND-O
THE VIKINGS O-AND-ONE

RESULTS:
Green Bay beat the Chicago Bears 38-24

Minnesota beat the Buffalo Bills 34-13

PACKERS "VERSES" VIKINGS ~ Carl Nelson

THE VIKINGS GAVE US A BIG SURPRISE
THE WAY THEY TROUNCED THE BILLS
DEFENSIVELY THEY JUST ABUSED THEM
WHILE SMITH RAN THE BALL AT WILL

THE QUESTION IS AND MUST REMAIN
'TIL THIS SUNDAY'S GAME IS SEEN
"ARE THE BILLS REALLY ALL THAT BAD
OR IS IT AN ASCENDANT VIKINGS' TEAM?"

ON THE ROAD AGAIN THIS SUNDAY
THE VIKES WILL VISIT CHICAGO'S TROOPS
WHILE THE BEARS MAY NOT BE CONTENDERS
THEY'RE ALWAYS A ROWDY GROUP

BRYAN COX AND THAT "BAD BEAR D"
ARE HUNGRY AND WANT TO DINE
CARTER SMITH AND JOHNSON
WILL FILL THE MENU OUT JUST FINE

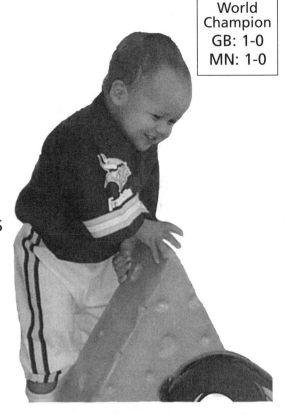

~ ~ ~ ~ ~ ~ ~ ~ ~ ~ ~ ~ ~ ~ ~ ~

MONDAY NIGHT THE PACKERS
SHOWED THEY'RE NOT SUPERMEN
BUT GREEN BAY'S TENACITY
PULLED OUT THE WIN AGAIN

GREEN BAY NEEDS SOME INSECTICIDE
TO KILL THAT "INJURY BUG "
THAT'S ALREADY SCORING PACKERS' KNEES
EVEN BEFORE THEY PLAY ON A RUG

THE LOSS OF NEWSOME AND CHMURA
PUTS SOME HILLS IN THE PACKERS' ROAD
BUT AGAINST PHILADELPHIA'S EAGLES
THE BACKUPS CAN SHOULDER THE LOAD

WILL IT BE RODNEY PEETE OR TY DETMER
AT THE HELM AGAINST THE PACK?
IT REALLY JUST WON'T MATTER
THEY'LL SPEND THE DAY FLAT ON THEIR BACKS

AS FOR RICKY"RUNNING" WATERS
DESPITE HOW HARD HE TRIES
HE'LL FIND THE GREEN BAY DEFENSE
WILL LEAVE HIM HIGH AND DRY

AS THIS COMING SUNDAY
FADES WITH THE SETTING SUN
THE PACKERS WILL BE TWO-AND-O
THE VIKINGS ONE AND ONE

RESULTS:
Green Bay lost to the
Philadelphia Eagles 9-10

Minnesota beat the
Chicago Bears 27-24

WHAT A STRANGE POSITION
TO SEE THE VIKES IN FIRST
TIED WITH A TEAM FROM TAMPA BAY
USUALLY THOUGHT TO BE THE WORST

THE VIKINGS NEEDED A LITTLE LUCK
TO GET BY CHICAGO'S BEARS
FOR WITHOUT THAT DEFENSIVE TOUCHDOWN
THE CHANCE TO WIN WOULDN'T HAVE BEEN THERE

THIS WEEK BEFORE THE HOME "CROWD"
THEY'LL FACE TAMPA'S BUCCANEERS
A TEAM WHOSE DEFENSIVE STARS
HAVE BROUGHT OPPONENTS' FANS TO TEARS

THROUGHOUT THE PAST COUPLE OF YEARS
MINNESOTA'S HAD PROBLEMS WITH THE BUCS
AND THE FEW TIMES THAT THEY'VE BEAT THEM
HAS REFLECTED THE VIKINGS' GOOD LUCK

WHO KNOWS HOW IT WILL END THIS WEEK?
WILL THE VIKINGS STAY ON TOP?
OR WILL TAMPA'S GOOD BASIC FOOTBALL
BRING THE VIKES' RUN TO A STOP?

~ ~ ~ ~ ~ ~ ~ ~ ~ ~ ~ ~ ~ ~ ~ ~ ~ ~

THERE IS NOTHING TO BE SAID
ABOUT THE LOSS SUFFERED BY THE PACK
A MISSED KICK ATTEMPTED BY A ROOKIE...
BUT GREEN BAY'S PACKERS WILL BE BACK

THE INJURIES HAD TO PLAY A PART
BUT THEY CAN'T TAKE THE BLAME ALONE
BRETT WAS ALWAYS HURRIED
AND FREEMAN'S HANDS WERE HARD AS STONE

BUT PACKERS' FANS AREN'T WORRIED
'CUZ THE BEST HAS NOT BEEN SEEN AS YET
THE PACK SHOULD COLLECT THE DOLPHINS
JUST LIKE A LETHAL TUNA NET

WHILE MARINO'S BEEN A GREAT ONE
HIS SKILLS ARE ON THE DECLINE
THIS SUNDAY IT'S ON THE LAMBEAU TURF
WHERE HE OFTEN WILL RECLINE

THE PACKERS' OFFENSE WILL BREAK OUT
FROM THE CLOUDS INTO THE SUN
AND WHEN THE PACKERS PLAY THE 'QUEENS
BOTH WILL BE AT TWO-AND-ONE

PACKERS "VERSES" VIKINGS ~ Carl Nelson

World
Champion
GB: 1-1
MN: 2-0

RESULTS:
Green Bay beat the
Miami Dolphins 23-18

Minnesota lost to the
Tampa Bay Buccaneers 14-28

31

World
Champion
GB: 2-1
MN: 2-1

PACKERS "VERSES" VIKINGS ~ Carl Nelson

THIS IS THE FOURTH WEEK OF THE SEASON
THE ONE WE'VE ALL BEEN WAITING FOR
THE WEEK THE PACKERS AND THE VIKINGS
STRAP ON THEIR HATS AND GO TO WAR

THE PLAYOFFS AND THE SUPERBOWL
ARE QUITE DISTANT GOALS FROM HERE
BUT THIS WEEKEND'S FOOTBALL CONTEST
WILL GIVE ONE TEAM'S FANS THE RIGHT TO CHEER

THE VIKES TOOK ONE ON THE CHIN LAST WEEK
FROM THE TAMPA "PEWTER AND RED"
EVERYONE THOUGHT THE VIKES WOULD ROLL
BUT 'TWAS THE BUCCANEERS INSTEAD

ON SUNDAY THE VIKINGS HEAD TO LAMBEAU
A FIELD AS LOVELY AS IT CAN BE
WHERE THEY WILL TRY TO NOT BECOME
PACKERS' VICTIM NUMBER THREE

~ ~ ~ ~ ~ ~ ~ ~ ~ ~ ~ ~ ~ ~ ~ ~

IN GETTING BY THE DOLPHINS
THE PACKERS AGAIN DID PAY THE PRICE
AS WHOMEVER DOLES OUT INJURIES
COME NOT JUST ONCE BUT TWICE

THE VIKES WILL ROLL IN ON SUNDAY
AGAINST A PACKER TEAM SO "NICKED"
THAT FIELDING TWENTY-TWO GOOD PLAYERS
IS BECOMING QUITE A TRICK

WHILE THE PACKERS HAVE BEEN STRUGGLING
TO GET THEIR GAME ON TRACK
MINNESOTA WILL WORK QUITE HARD
TO REGAIN THEIR POTENT ATTACK

BRAD JOHNSON SMITH AND RANDLE
WILL PROVIDE THE VIKINGS' KEYS
IT WILL BE UP TO THE GREEN BAY PACKERS
TO KNOCK THEM TO THEIR KNEES

BRETT FAVRE AND THE PACKERS
FACE A GAME THAT SEEMS QUITE TOUGH
BUT A TEAM WITH FREEMAN WHITE AND LEVENS
SHOULD PROVE TO BE ENOUGH

IF THE PACK'S OFFENSIVE LINE
CAN KEEP BRETT FAVRE UP ON HIS FEET
GREEN BAY AND LAMBEAU'S MAGIC
WILL SEND THE VIKES DOWN TO DEFEAT

32

RESULTS: Green Bay beat the Minnesota Vikings 38-32

PACKERS "VERSES" VIKINGS

~ Carl Nelson

ALTHOUGH THE VIKINGS GOT BACK IN IT
LAST WEEK IN THE SECOND HALF
THE PACKERS CRUSHED THE VIKINGS' HOPES
AND HAD A GOOD LAST LAUGH

WHILE THE VIKES' RECEIVERS WERE PRETTY GOOD
AND JOHNSON WAS SOLID AS A ROCK
THE DEFENSE TOOK SOME VACATION
AND SMITH NEEDED AN OFFICIAL'S BLOCK

NOW SUNDAY NIGHT PHILLY'S EAGLES
WILL INVADE THE VIKINGS' HOME
RANDALL'S EX-TEAM SHOULD HAVE SOME FUN
IN THE HALF-EMPTY METRODOME

THE EAGLES' RICKY "RUNNING" WATERS
HAS BEEN WAITING FOR THIS CHANCE
TO STREAK THROUGH THE VIKINGS' DEFENSE
AND TO DO HIS TOUCHDOWN DANCE

THE VIKES HOWEVER SIGNED JERRY BALL
TO GIVE THE "D" LINE SOME MUCH NEEDED WEIGHT
BUT EVEN IF HE ESCAPES A HEART ATTACK
THE MOVE IS TOO LITTLE, AND HAS COME MUCH TOO LATE

~ ~ ~ ~ ~ ~ ~ ~ ~ ~ ~ ~ ~ ~ ~ ~ ~ ~ ~

THE PACKERS ON THE OTHER HAND
DID WHAT THEY SET OUT TO DO
BEATING UP THE VIKINGS IN THE FIRST HALF
THEN HOLDING ON IN NUMBER TWO

THE PACK IT SHOULD BE MENTIONED
IN THE FIRST HALF LOOKED SIMPLY GREAT
DESPITE TWO TURNOVERS IN THE THIRD QUARTER
THEIR DEFENSE STIFFENED LATE

GREEN BAY'S VICTORIES AREN'T PRETTY
COMPARED TO LAST YEAR THEY SEEM HARD
BUT AS THE WORLD CHAMPIONS
EVERYBODY TRIES TO BE THE BULLY IN THEIR YARD

BARRY SANDERS AND THE LIONS
ARE THIS WEEK'S PACKERS' TEST
ALTHOUGH THE GAME IS IN THE SILVERDOME
THE PACK SHOULD BE EQUAL TO THE TEST

THAT GREEN BAY CAN STOP THE LIONS
EVERYONE WILL PLAINLY SEE
ON MONDAY THE PACK IS FOUR AND ONE
THE VIKINGS TWO AND THREE

RESULTS:
Green Bay lost to the
Detroit Lions 15-26

Minnesota beat the
Philadelphia Eagles 28-19

World Champion
GB: 3-2
MN: 3-2

PACKERS "VERSES" VIKINGS

~ Carl Nelson

THE VIKES PULLED OUT ANOTHER ONE
ON THIS LAST SUNDAY PAST
THE EAGLES WERE THE LAST TEAM
ON WHOM THE VIKINGS' SPELL WAS CAST

YET ANOTHER GOOD TEAM WENT INTO
THAT "ACCURSED METRODOME"
WHERE THE TEAM THAT SHOWS UP
IS OFTEN NOT THE ONE THAT LEFT THEIR HOME

THIS WEEK HOWEVER IT'S THE VIKES
THAT GO INTO A FOREIGN LAND
WHERE THE TEMPERATURE WILL BE NINETY-PLUS
AND HADES' GATES SEEM NEAR AT HAND

DENNY'S BOYS DON'T SEEM TO DO WELL
IN THE WESTERN DESERT HEAT
WHERE THE LACK OF OUTDOOR CONDITIONING
WILL LEAD TO THEIR THIRD DEFEAT

~ ~ ~ ~ ~ ~ ~ ~ ~ ~ ~ ~ ~ ~ ~ ~ ~ ~ ~

GREEN BAY LOOKED PRETTY SHABBY
WHEN IN THE SILVERDOME THEY FELL
THE PACKER'S TEAM'S NOT HAVING FUN
AND TO PLAY LIKE THAT IS HELL

FAVRE AND THE BOYS MUST JUST RELAX
TO LET THEIR TRUE TALENT SHOW
STUPID PLAYS CAN BE EXPENSIVE
AS THE SCORE LAST WEEK WILL SHOW

THANK GOODNESS IT'S THE BUCS THIS WEEK
AND NOT A TEAM THAT POSES A REAL THREAT
WHILE TAMPA BAY MAY BE UNDEFEATED
THEY'VE NOT PLAYED A REAL TEAM AS YET

THE NINERS MINUS RICE AND YOUNG
THE VIKES, LIONS, CARDS AND FISH
NONE OF THOSE CAN GIVE THE KIND OF GAME
A HOME FIELD PACKERS' TEAM CAN DISH

TAMPA'S WEAKNESSES WILL BE EXPOSED
FOR ALL THE WORLD TO SEE
ESPECIALLY IN THE TWIN CITIES
WHERE THIS GAME'S THE ONLY ONE ON TV

THE VIKINGS' FANS WILL BE UPSET
AND WE'LL HEAR THEIR CRY AND ROAR
AS THEY MISS THE 'QUEENS GOING THREE-AND-THREE
WHILE THE PACK WINS NUMBER FOUR

RESULTS:
Green Bay beat the
Tamp Bay Buccaneers 21-16

Minnesota beat the
Arizona Cardinals 20-19

PACKERS "VERSES" VIKINGS ~ Carl Nelson

World
Champion
GB: 4-2
MN: 4-2

THE VIKES MANAGED ANOTHER MIRACLE
IN THE SCORCHING DESERT HEAT
THE CARDS SEEMED TO HAVE THE GAME LOCKED UP
'TIL TWO KICKERS SENT THEM TO DEFEAT

WHAT A STUNNING GAME PLAN
COOKED UP BY DENNY AND HIS STAFF
LETTING ARIZONA PUSH THEM AROUND
FOR ALL BUT TWO MINUTES OF THE SECOND HALF

IT WASN'T PRETTY, BUT IT WORKED OUT
AS DO MANY OF THE VIKINGS' TRICKS
AND IN THE END THE GAME WAS WON BY
A KICKER BORN IN NINETEEN FIFTY-SIX

THE PANTHERS ARE THE NEXT TEAM
WITH WHOM THE VIKES WILL STRUGGLE
THOUGH IN LAST YEAR'S CHAMPIONSHIP GAME
THIS YEAR REALITY HAS BURST THAT BUBBLE

CAROLINA IS JUST NOT VERY GOOD
WHICH IS WHY VIKINGS' FANS SHOULD WORRY
MINNESOTA WILL PLAY DOWN TO THAT LEVEL
AND COULD GET BEATEN IN A HURRY

~ ~ ~ ~ ~ ~ ~ ~ ~ ~ ~ ~ ~ ~ ~ ~ ~ ~ ~

TAMPA BAY HAS BEEN SHOWN AS MORTAL
THE PERFECT SEASON HAS FALLEN TO THE SIDE
THEY PLAYED LIKE THE BUCCANEERS OF OLD
AND COULDN'T WIN NO MATTER WHAT THEY TRIED

THE PACKERS DIDN'T MAKE IT EASY FOR THEMSELVES
MAKING MISTAKES IN THE WISCONSIN SUN
THOUGH BRETT FAVRE THREW TWO TOUCHDOWNS
THE GAME WAS STOLEN BY GABE WILKENS' TOUCHDOWN RUN

AT THE SOUTH END OF LAKE MICHIGAN
IS A PLACE CALLED "SOLDIER FIELD"
WHERE CHICAGO'S BEARS PLAY FOOTBALL
AND TRULY HATE TO YIELD

GREEN BAY CAN'T TAKE THE BEARS TOO LIGHTLY
THOUGH CHICAGO'S PLAY HAS SIMPLY BEEN ABYSMAL
TO BE OVERCONFIDENT AND TAKE A LOSS
COULD MAKE THE FUTURE LOOK A LITTLE DISMAL

BUT DON'T WORRY FAITHFUL ONES
OUR PACKERS WON'T MAKE US FEEL BLUE
GOING INTO THE COMING BYE WEEK
GREEN BAY'S RECORD WILL BE FIVE-AND-TWO

RESULTS:
Green Bay beat the
Chicago Bears 24-23

Minnesota beat the
Carolina Panthers 21-14

35

PACKERS "VERSES" VIKINGS ~ Carl Nelson

THIS IS THE WEEK THAT COMES ALONG
IN THE MIDDLE OF EVERY YEAR
MINNESOTA AND GREEN BAY HAVE THE WEEK OFF
WHICH CAUSES OUR WOMEN TO CHEER

THIS IS A GOOD TIME PERHAPS
TO TAKE A MOMENT TO REFLECT
ON THE HAPPENINGS OF THIS SEASON
THOUGH IT'S NOT HALF OVER YET

~ ~ ~ ~ ~ ~ ~ ~ ~ ~ ~ ~ ~ ~ ~ ~

MINNESOTA HAS SURPRISED A LOT OF FOLK
BY BEING TIED FOR FIRST
THE OFFENSE WAS EXPECTED TO DO WELL
BUT WHO THOUGHT THE DEFENSE WOULD BE WORST

BRAD JOHNSON IS DEVELOPING
INTO A GOOD QUARTERBACK
AND HE HAS A GREAT RUNNING GAME
TO KEEP DEFENSES OFF HIS BACK

THAT RUNNING GAME DEPENDS OF COURSE
ON KEEPING ROBERT SMITH UP ON HIS FEET
IF HE CAN CONTINUE THE YEAR UNINJURED
THAT VIKINGS' OFFENSE COULD BE SWEET

REED AND CARTER ARE LOOKING FINE
WHICH DEFENSES MUST FIND A DRAG
IT'S JUST TOO BAD THAT THEY CAN'T REALIZE
EVERY NON-CATCH DOES NOT DESERVE A FLAG

THE DEFENSE HOWEVER IS NOT SO GOOD
THOUGH JOHN RANDLE HAS BEEN PRETTY GREAT
THE REST OF THAT BUNCH IS PRETTY BAD
AND SHOULD STOP HITTING PEOPLE LATE

~ ~ ~ ~ ~ ~ ~ ~ ~ ~ ~ ~ ~ ~ ~ ~ ~

THE PACKERS TOO ARE SURPRISING US
AS CLOSE AS ALL THE GAMES HAVE BEEN
BUT AS THEY SAY "IT DON'T HAVE TO BE PRETTY—
A WIN'S A WIN'S A WIN"

THE INJURY TOLL HAS BEEN TREMENDOUS
AS EACH WEEK'S INJURY REPORT WILL SHOW
EACH OF THOSE WOUNDS CREATES PROBLEMS
THAT ONLY THE COACHING STAFF CAN KNOW

CONTINIUED...

FAVRE HAS BEEN PRESSING FAR TOO HARD
AS IS REFLECTED IN SOME DUMB THROWS
HOW MUCH BENNETT'S MISSED IN THE RUNNING GAME
IS THE ONE FACT THAT SURELY SHOWS

WHILE THE RECEIVERS SEEM TO BE STRUGGLING
THAT PROBABLY REFLECTS THE QB'S STRESS
THEY HAVEN'T PLAYED THE SAME "O" LINE TWO WEEKS IN A ROW
WHICH THROWS THE GAME'S TIMING INTO DURESS

THE DEFENSE TOO HAS HAD ITS PROBLEMS
EVEN WITH THE PRESENCE OF REGGIE WHITE
THEY JUST CAN'T SEEM TO GET OFF THE FIELD
WHICH CAN MAKE FOR A LONG NIGHT

BUT AS THE CHAMPIONS OF THE LEAGUE
THE PACK GETS EVERYONE'S BEST GAME
THEY WON'T BE A SURPRISE TO ANYONE
BUT WE WANT THEM TO BE WINNERS JUST THE SAME

BUT IT'S NOT TIME TO PANIC
SEASON'S END IS NOT VERY NEAR
THERE IS TIME FOR MANY REVERSALS
IN THE FORTUNES OF THIS YEAR

Both Green Bay and Minnesota were on their "Bye Week"

BUT BOTH THE PACKERS AND THE VIKINGS
SHOULD BE AWARE THE CENTRAL'S POWER MAY BE MOVING
TAMPA BAY IS ALSO TIED FOR FIRST
AND THE DETROIT LIONS ARE IMPROVING

THIS YEAR HOWEVER THOSE TEAMS
SHOULDN'T BE MUCH MORE THAN DISTRACTION
THE MINNESOTA AND WISCONSIN TEAMS
WILL PROVIDE THE SIGNIFICANT ACTION

SO LET'S ALL HOPE THAT OUR FAVORITE TEAMS
CAN USE THE WEEK TO REST AND HEAL
THE REST OF THIS FOOTBALL SEASON
SHOULD HOLD REAL EXCITEMENT AND APPEAL

World
Champion
GB: 5-2
MN: 5-2

PACKERS "VERSES" VIKINGS

~ Carl Nelson

THE MIDSEASON VACATION'S OVER
THE SEASON'S SECOND HALF NOW WILL START
THIS IS THE TIME OF THE FOOTBALL YEAR
WHERE TEAMS MUST SHOW THEIR HEART

THE VIKES HAVE BEEN SURPRISING
KEEPING THEIR SHARE OF FIRST PLACE
BUT IT IS ABOUT THIS TIME OF YEAR
WHEN THEY FALL FLAT ON THEIR FACE

FAST STARTS SEEM TO BE THE RULE
OF THE LAST FEW VIKINGS' SEASONS
BUT THE SECOND HALF HASN'T BEEN SO GOOD
ONE MUST WONDER ABOUT THE REASONS

THIS WEEK IT'S A TRIP TO TAMPA BAY
TO PLAY IN THE WARM SUNSHINE
IF THE VIKES DON'T WIN THIS GAME
BE PREPARED TO HEAR THEM WHINE

THE BUCS SIMPLY WHIPPED THE VIKINGS
IN THE GAME UP AT THE METRODOME
THERE'S NO REASON TO THINK THINGS WILL BE DIFFERENT
WHEN TAMPA PLAYS THE 'QUEENS AT HOME

~ ~ ~ ~ ~ ~ ~ ~ ~ ~ ~ ~ ~ ~ ~ ~ ~ ~ ~

THE PACKERS GET AN EXTRA DAY OFF
SINCE THEY PLAY ON MONDAY NIGHT
IT'S A REMATCH OF THE SUPERBOWL
AND SHOULD BE QUITE A FIGHT

"TIME" IT'S SAID "CAN HEAL ALL WOUNDS"
GREEN BAY MUST HOPE THAT'S TRUE
BECAUSE IF THEY ARE NOT HEALTHY
PACKERS' FANS MAY FEEL QUITE BLUE

BUT THERE'S TRUE HOPE FOR THE FAITHFUL
THE PACKERS' TEAM HAS HEALED AND GOTTEN STRONGER
THE TIME FOR CLOSE AND HARD-FOUGHT GAMES
WILL BE WITH THE TEAM NO LONGER

THE PATRIOTS ARE PRETTY GOOD
BUT STILL CAN'T MATCH UP WITH THE PACK
THIS WEEK LOOK FOR THE BLOWOUT SCORE
AND THE START OF THE LONG-AWAITED COMBACK

THE STRETCH RUN TO THE PLAYOFFS
IS NOW SET TO BEGIN
WHAT BETTER WAY THAN WITH A VIKINGS' LOSS
AND A MASSIVE PACKERS' WIN

RESULTS:
Green Bay beat the
New England Patriots 28-10

Minnesota beat the
Tampa Bay Buccaneers 10-6

PACKERS "VERSES" VIKINGS

~ Carl Nelson

THE VIKINGS CONTINUE TO AMAZE
WINNING GAMES IN WAYS UNKNOWN
THEY EVEN USE THE "PHANTOM TOUCHDOWN" PLAY
AS THE REPLAYS HAVE CLEARLY SHOWN

BUT MINNESOTA IS NOW IN TURMOIL
DUE TO THE THREATS IN DENNY'S BOOK
AND NOW FINDING THAT THE TEAM'S FOR SALE
HAS SHAKEN THE FANS' OUTLOOK

CAN THE VIKINGS KEEP ON WINNING
WITH ALL THIS DISTRACTION GOING ON?
OR WILL THE MIDSEASON SLIDE START NOW
UNTIL THE PLAYOFF HOPES ARE GONE?

ROBERT SMITH'S TAKING THE WEEK OFF
WHICH SHOULD FILL VIKINGS' FANS WITH FEAR
WITH HIS HISTORY OF NAGGING INJURIES
HE MAY NOT RETURN THIS YEAR

THIS WEEK IT'S THE PATS WHO CHALLENGE
ANGRY FROM TAKING A LOSS AT HOME
THE VIKES WILL HAVE THEIR HANDS FULL
EVEN AT THE METRODOME

~ ~ ~ ~ ~ ~ ~ ~ ~ ~ ~ ~ ~ ~ ~ ~ ~ ~

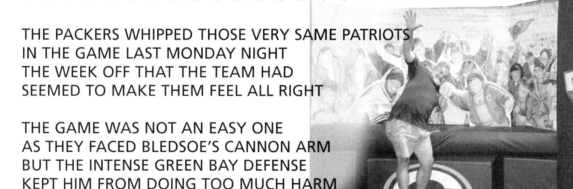

THE PACKERS WHIPPED THOSE VERY SAME PATRIOTS
IN THE GAME LAST MONDAY NIGHT
THE WEEK OFF THAT THE TEAM HAD
SEEMED TO MAKE THEM FEEL ALL RIGHT

THE GAME WAS NOT AN EASY ONE
AS THEY FACED BLEDSOE'S CANNON ARM
BUT THE INTENSE GREEN BAY DEFENSE
KEPT HIM FROM DOING TOO MUCH HARM

THE DIFFERENCE IN THE PACK WAS SURPRISING
FAVRE AND THE TEAM JUST SEEMED TO CLICK
THE RECEIVERS CAUGHT THE BALL WHEN NEEDED
AND LEVENS' LEGS REALLY TURNED THE TRICK

SUNDAY NIGHT THE LIONS COME TO LAMBEAU
TRYING TO BEAT THE PACK AGAIN
DETROIT IS NOT SO GOOD ON GRASS
WHERE BARRY SANDERS CANNOT SPIN

SO ONCE THE VIKINGS HAVE BEEN TROUNCED
WATCH GREEN BAY WIN ON SUNDAY NIGHT
THE TIE FOR THE LEAD WILL BE BROKEN
AND THE UNIVERSE WILL BE JUST RIGHT

RESULTS:
Green Bay beat the
Detroit Lions 20-10

Minnesota beat the
New England Patriots 23-18

WHOEVER HELPS THE VIKES EACH WEEK
APPEARED IN LAST SUNDAY'S GAME AGAIN
ALLOWING THEM TO RECOVER CARTER'S FUMBLE
WHICH GAVE THEM THE POINTS NEEDED TO WIN

NEW ENGLAND PUT UP A LITTLE STRUGGLE
BEFORE ROLLING OVER ON THEIR BACKS
THE PATRIOTS' DEFENSE PLAYED PRETTY WELL
BUT BLEDSOE AND THE OFFENSE NEVER GOT ON TRACK

THE "MONSTERS OF THE MIDWAY"
INVADE THE METRODOME THIS WEEK
THEY'RE CALLED "MONSTERS" BECAUSE THEIR GAME
IS SO BAD IT MAKES ONE WANT TO SHRIEK

WILL THE VIKINGS HAVE THE STUFF
THAT IT WILL TAKE TO WIN THIS GAME?
WITH BOTH SMITH AND LEROY OUT
THE OFFENSE IS JUST NOT THE SAME

MINNESOTA WILL NEED ALL THE BREAKS
FOR THE BEARS ALWAYS PLAY THEM TOUGH
THIS WEEK JOHNSON'S ARM AND CARTER'S HANDS
MAY PROVE TO NOT BE QUITE ENOUGH

~ ~ ~ ~ ~ ~ ~ ~ ~ ~ ~ ~ ~ ~ ~ ~ ~ ~

THE PACKERS SPLIT THIS SEASON'S GAMES
WITH THE LIONS OF DETROIT
THE DEFENSE HANDLED BARRY SANDERS
AND MADE MITCHELL LOOK LIKE A MALADROIT

THE PACKERS SEEM TO BE A BETTER TEAM
SINCE THE MIDSEASON BREAK
BOTH THE OFFENSE AND THE DEFENSE
HAVE CUT DOWN ON THEIR MISTAKES

THIS WEEK THE RAMS COME TO LAMBEAU
TO PLAY IN THAT HALLOWED PLACE
A FORTUNATE OCCURANCE
THAT WILL KEEP THE PACKERS IN FIRST PLACE

BUT THE PACK CAN'T BE RELAXED
THEY MUST KEEP THE GOAL FIRMLY IN THEIR SIGHTS
BECAUSE SOMETIMES A TWO-AND-SEVEN TEAM
WILL PUT UP QUITE A FIGHT

BOTH THE PACKERS AND THE VIKINGS
HAVE THEIR WORK CUT OUT THIS WEEK
THE VIKINGS CAN'T AFFORD TO STUMBLE
AND GREEN BAY MUST START BUILDING TOWARD THE PEAK

PACKERS "VERSES" VIKINGS ~ Carl Nelson

World
Champion
GB: 7-2
MN: 7-2

RESULTS:
Green Bay beat the
St Louis Rams 17-7

Minnesota beat the
Chicago Bears 29-22

40

PACKERS "VERSES" VIKINGS ~ Carl Nelson

IN THE METRODOME LAST SUNDAY
THERE WAS A LESSON LEARNED
FOR THE VIKES NO TEAM IS EASY
AND THEY WERE NEARLY BURNED

CHICAGO GAVE THE VIKINGS
THE BEST GAME THAT THEY COULD
AND CAME VERY CLOSE TO WINNING
IF THEY WERE ONLY ANY GOOD

THIS WEEK THE VIKES ARE ON THE ROAD
TO FACE DETROIT ONCE AGAIN
FOR VISITING TEAMS THE SILVERDOME
CAN TRULY BE THE "LIONS' DEN"

THE VIKINGS ARE STILL NICKED-UP
ROBERT SMITH'S ANKLE IS STILL NOT RIGHT
AND THE LIONS WILL DO THEIR LEVEL BEST
TO MAKE SURE JOHNSON'S SORE ON SUNDAY NIGHT

BARRY SANDERS' BIGGEST GAMES
USUALLY COME ON HIS HOME FIELD
IF THE VIKES CAN'T STOP HIM
MINNESOTA WILL SURELY YIELD

~ ~ ~ ~ ~ ~ ~ ~ ~ ~ ~ ~ ~ ~ ~ ~ ~ ~

MEANWHILE OVER AT LAMBEAU
THE PACKERS ALSO WENT TO SCHOOL
TO FINALLY BEAT THOSE PESKY RAMS
GREEN BAY HAD TO USE ALL THEIR TOOLS

THE RAMS DEFENSE PLAYED VERY WELL
AND GAVE THE PACKER OFFENSE FITS
THEY EVEN BROKE SOME OF BROOKS' RIBS
WITH ONE OF THE VICIOUS HITS

THE LOSS OF BROOKS IS ANOTHER PROBLEM
THAT THE PACKERS WILL HAVE TO FACE
IT'S NOT BEEN AN EASY SEASON
BUT THE PACKERS ARE STILL IN FIRST PLACE

THIS WEEK IT'S ON THE ROAD AGAIN
TO PLAY AGAINST THE WINLESS COLTS
WHOSE RECORD WON'T IMPROVE THIS WEEK
AS THEY FALL TO BRETT FAVRE'S LIGHTNING BOLTS

THE PACKERS CAN'T OVERLOOK THESE GUYS
WHO AREN'T QUITE AS BAD AS THEY MAY SEEM
BUT AS THE DUST SETTLES DOWN ON SUNDAY
GREEN BAY WILL BE THE ONLY FIRST PLACE TEAM

World
Champion
GB: 8-2
MN: 8-2

RESULTS:
Green Bay lost to the
Indianapolis Colts 38-41

Minnesota lost to the
Detroit Lions 15-38

41

PACKERS "VERSES" VIKINGS ~ Carl Nelson

World
Champion
GB: 8-3
MN: 8-3

THE VIKINGS REALLY BLEW A CHANCE
TO GAIN SOLE POSESSION OF FIRST PLACE
WHEN THEY TRAVELED TO THE SILVERDOME
AND FELL FLAT ON THEIR COLLECTIVE FACE

SCOTT MITCHELL PASSED AND BARRY RAN
THROUGH MINNESOTA'S DEFENSE AT WILL
IF THERE WERE NO TIME LIMIT
THEY'D BE ZOOMING THROUGH THEM STILL

THE LOSS TO THE DETROIT LIONS
WAS LIKE A SLAP TO THE VIKINGS' FACE
NOW THE VIKES GO TO THE MEADOWLANDS
WHICH WILL BE A VERY HOSTILE PLACE

THE JETS JUST LIKE THE VIKINGS
HOLD ONTO A SHARE OF FIRST
QUITE A CHANGE FROM LAST YEAR
WHEN THEY WERE ONE OF FOOTBALL'S WORST

WITH MURRELL TO RUN THE BALL
AND NEIL O'DONNELL THERE TO THROW
AGAINST MINNESOTA'S WIMPY DEFENSE
THE JETS SHOULD PUT UP QUITE A SHOW

~ ~ ~ ~ ~ ~ ~ ~ ~ ~ ~ ~ ~ ~ ~ ~ ~ ~ ~

THERE ARE NO EXCUSES TO BE MADE
ABOUT GREEN BAY'S LOSS AGAINST THE COLTS
WHILE THE OFFENSE WAS TREMENDOUS
THE DEFENSE PLAYED LIKE DOLTS

THE LAST THING THE PACKERS NEEDED
WAS TO END (L)INDY'S LOSING STREAK
A BIG GAME WAS IN ORDER
WITH THE 'POKES IN TOWN THIS WEEK

FOR YEARS THE PACK HAS STATED
THAT UP IN LAMBEAU THEY'D PREVAIL
THIS IS THE PACKERS' BIG CHANCE
TO KICK THOSE ROTTEN COWBOYS' TAILS

AIKMAN SMITH AND IRVIN
ALWAYS GIVE THE PACKERS FITS
LET'S HOPE THEIR INSURANCE IS PAID UP
BECAUSE THEY'LL TAKE SOME FEARFUL HITS

THE PLAY OF BROOKS AND LEVENS
AND BRETT FAVRE'S PASSING SPEED
COMBINED WITH THE VIKINGS' LOSS
WILL FILL THE FIRST PLACE SEED

RESULTS:
Green Bay beat the
Dallas Cowboys 45-17

Minnesota lost to the
New York Jets 21-23

42

MONDAY NIGHT IT HAPPENS
THE REMATCH FROM WEEK FOUR
AS YOU MAY RECALL FROM THAT GAME
THE VIKES COUND NOT MATCH THE PACKERS' SCORE

World
Champion
GB: 9-3
MN: 8-4

THE VIKINGS HAVE NOT BEEN PLAYING WELL
FOR THE LAST COUPLE OF WEEKS
TAKING LOSSES FROM TWO FOOTBALL TEAMS
THAT SOME FOLKS MIGHT CALL "GEEKS"

COULD IT BE THAT MINNESOTA
IS FINALLY STARTING THEIR LATE SEASON STUMBLE?
OR HAS THE OVERALL LACK OF TALENT
FORCED THEM TO BECOME QUITE HUMBLE

BUT THIS WEEK THE PACKERS
COME ROLLING INTO THE 'DOME
WE ALL KNOW GREEN BAY DOESN'T DO TOO WELL
IN THE BALLOON THE VIKINGS CALL THEIR HOME

THIS TIME IT WILL BE DIFFERENT
FOR THE PACK IS TRULY PLAYING WELL
WHETHER THAT CAN OVERCOME THE VIKINGS' LUCK
ONLY MONDAY NIGHT WILL TELL

~ ~ ~ ~ ~ ~ ~ ~ ~ ~ ~ ~ ~ ~ ~ ~ ~ ~ ~

IT'S TIME TO EXORCISE THE DEMONS
THAT HAVE TORMENTED GREEN BAY'S PACK
LAST WEEK THEY FINALLY BEAT THE COWBOYS
NOW THERE'S ONLY ONE MORE MONKEY ON THEIR BACK

MINNESOTA IS ABOUT TO LEARN
THAT LUCK CAN CARRY ONE JUST SO FAR
ENTER BRETT FAVRE AND DORSEY LEVENS
THE PACKERS' OFFENSIVE STARS

THE VIKINGS HAVE STARS OF THEIR OWN
BUT RIGHT NOW THEY'RE NOT SHINING BRIGHTLY
JOHNSON WILL SPEND TIME ON HIS BACK
WHILE CARTER'S COVERED TIGHTLY

THE MINNESOTA'S "FAMOUS" DEFENSE
SHOWN TO BE SUSPECT AT BEST
WILL THROW RANDLE AT THE OFFENSIVE LINE
WHICH FOR ONCE WILL BE UP TO THE TEST

THE DEFENSE OF THE PACKERS
WHILE NOT AS PROFICIENT AS LAST YEAR
HAS WREAKED ENOUGH HAVOC THE LAST FEW WEEKS
TO CAUSE THE VIKES TO FEAR

SO IN THE LAST HOURS OF MONDAY NIGHT
AS THE PACKERS COMPLETE A SEASON SWEEP
GREEN BAY'S LEAD WILL GROW TO TWO
WHILE VIKINGS' FANS BEGIN TO WEEP

RESULTS:
Green Bay beat the
Minnesota Vikings 27-11

PACKERS "VERSES" VIKINGS ~ Carl Nelson

43

PACKERS "VERSES" VIKINGS ~ Carl Nelson

MINNESOTA TOOK ONE ON THE NOSE
IN THE 'DOME LAST MONDAY NIGHT
WHILE THE PACKERS LOOKED SIMPLY SUPER
THE VIKINGS HARDLY PUT UP A FIGHT

BRAD JOHNSON AND THE PURPLE BOYS
WENT OUT AND PLAYED THEIR BEST
BUT THE LIMITED VIKINGS' TALENT POOL
COULDN'T MATCH UP TO THE TEST

THE PLAYOFF HOPES ARE WANING
BECOMING WISPY AS A GHOST
AND WHAT A "TREAT" FOR MINNESOTA
TO PLAY THE 'NINERS ON THE COAST

RANDALL CUNNINGHAM IS NOW THE MAN
ON WHOM THE VIKINGS' HOPES ARE PINNED
WHEN THE 'FRISCO "D" LINE HEARD OF THIS
TO A MAN, THEY ONLY GRINNED

WHILE IT WOULD BE NICE TO SEE AN UPSET
AND SEE THE 'QUEENS PULL OUT THE WIN
SAN FRANCISCO'S TEAM IS JUST TOO GOOD
AND THE VIKINGS WILL LOSE AGAIN

~ ~ ~ ~ ~ ~ ~ ~ ~ ~ ~ ~ ~ ~ ~ ~ ~ ~

HOLMGREN'S BOYS WERE ECSTATIC
WHEN THEY CRUSHED THE "METROGNOMES"
AND JUDGING BY THE CROWD NOISE
THEY MUST HAVE ALMOST FELT AT HOME

THERE WAS NOT AN ASPECT OF THE GAME
IN WHICH THE VIKES EXCELLED
GREEN BAY QUITE SIMPLY WHIPPED 'EM
FROM THE GAME'S STARTING BELL

NOW FOR A DECEMBER VACATION
DOWN IN FLORIDA'S STEAMY HEAT
THE PACKERS CAN'T LET THAT BE A FACTOR
AND MUST SEND THE BUCS DOWN TO DEFEAT

TAMPA IS A BETTER TEAM
THAN THEY'VE ALMOST EVER BEEN
ONE TIME THEY NEARLY REACHED THE SUPER BOWL
AND ARE TRYING HARD AGAIN

RESULTS:
Green bay beat the
Tampa Bay Buccaneers 17-6

Minnesota lost to the
San Francisco 49ers 17-28

WITH THE WIN THE GREEN BAY PACKERS
WRAP UP FIRST PLACE AND THE FIRST ROUND BYE
AND WHILE THE VIKES SHOULD LOSE TO THE 'NINERS
FOR THE WIN I HOPE THEY'LL TRY

World & 1997
Central Division
Champion!
GB: 11-3
MN: 8-6

PACKERS "VERSES" VIKINGS ~ Carl Nelson

BOTH THE PACKERS AND THE VIKINGS
THIS WEEK HAD A LOT AT STAKE
GREEN BAY WAS LOOKING FOR THE DIVISION CROWN
THE VIKES HAD A PLAYOFF SPOT TO MAKE

MINNESOTA TOOK THEIR "BAD OL' SELVES"
OUT TO THREE COM PARK
BUT AGAINST THE FORTY-NINERS
THEY COULDN'T PRODUCE A SPARK

WHILE CUNNINGHAM WAS FUN TO WATCH
HE COULDN'T PRODUCE ENOUGH SCORES
WHILE STEVE YOUNG AND THE 'NINERS
MADE THE "D" LOOK LIKE A REVOLVING DOOR

ONCE AGAIN JOHN RANDLE
WAS TAKEN OUT OF HIS GAME
THIS WEEK AGAINST THE LIONS
THE OUTCOME WILL BE THE SAME

THIS WEEK TO THE METRODOME
COMES BARRY SANDERS' FLASHING FEET
AND WITH THE VIKINGS' LACK OF DEFENSE
THAT SURELY SPELLS DEFEAT

~ ~ ~ ~ ~ ~ ~ ~ ~ ~ ~ ~ ~ ~ ~ ~

DOWN IN TAMPA SUNDAY
THE BUCS TRIED THEIR BEST
BUT NOT ONLY DID THE PACKERS WIN
THEY ALLOWED GILBERT BROWN TO REST

THE RUNNING GAME THAT DUNGY LOVES
FAILED THE BUCS WHEN NEEDED MOST
AND THE DEFENSE MADE TAMPA SEEM
LIKE A VERY GRACIOUS HOST

FAVRE CONTINUES TO LEAD THE LEAGUE
IN TOUCHDOWN PASSES THROWN
AND IF THERE'S A BETTER QUARTERBACK
THIS YEAR IT'S NOT BEEN SHOWN

NOW IT'S A TRIP TO CAROLINA
TO PLAY A TEAM THAT JUST LAST YEAR
CONTENDED FOR THE SUPER BOWL
WHEN THE PANTHERS CAME UP HERE

GREEN BAY IS TRYING FOR THE HOME FIELD
WHICH WOULD WARM THE HOME FANS' HEARTS
THE WIN AGAINST THE PANTHERS
WILL BE A REAL NICE PLACE TO START

RESULTS:
Green Bay beat the
Carolina Panthers 31-10

Minnesota lost to the
Detroit Lions 13-14

45

~ Carl Nelson

PACKERS "VERSES" VIKINGS

THE END OF THE YEAR IS UPON US
AS THIS SEASON DRAWS TO A CLOSE
IT'S TIME TO REVIEW OUR FAVORITES
AND TO TRY NOT TO STEP ON TOES

THE VIKES ARE ALIVE IN THE PLAYOFF RACE
ALTHOUGH ON INTENSE LIFE SUPPORT
THE FIVE-GAME DIVE HERE AT THE END
MAY LEAVE THE 'QUEENS JUST A LITTLE SHORT

THE LOSS TO THE LIONS MAY TYPIFY
THE FRUSTRATION OF THE VIKINGS' YEAR
THOUGH THEY LED FOR ALMOST THE WHOLE GAME
THEY LOST WHEN THE END WAS NEAR

THIS LAST WEEK IT'S THE LOWLY COLTS
WHO COME TO THE METRODOME
BUT WHERE THE GAME'S PLAYED WON'T MAKE MUCH DIFFERENCE
THE VIKINGS LOSE EQUALLY WELL AT HOME

THE ONLY WAY THE PLAYOFF TRAIN
WILL VISIT THE LAND OF LAKES
IS IF THE VIKES CAN WIN THIS GAME
AND IF THEY HAVE WHAT IT TAKES

~ ~ ~ ~ ~ ~ ~ ~ ~ ~ ~ ~ ~ ~ ~ ~ ~ ~ ~

THE PACKERS ON THE OTHER HAND
HAVE PICKED UP AFTER A SHAKY START
FOR A WHILE IT SEEMED THEY WOULD FALTER
AND THAT THEY MAY FALL APART

THE LOSS OF BENNETT AND NEWSOME
SEEMED TO PREVIEW THE PACKERS' DOOM
HOWEVER GREEN BAY PICKED UP THE SLACK
AND AGAIN THE "BIG SHOW" LOOMS

THEY'VE LIVED ON THE LEGS OF LEVENS
AND ON THE ARM OF A TWO-TIME MVP
AND THE WAY THE DEFENSE HAS PLAYED
HAS SIMPLY BEEN A JOY TO SEE

WHEN THE PACKERS CRUSHED THE PANTHERS
OUT ON THE ROAD THIS WEEK
BUFFALO HAD TO TAKE NOTICE
THAT THE PACKERS ARE REACHING THEIR PEAK

THE BILLS THIS WEEK COME TO LAMBEAU
WHERE THEY WILL TAKE THEIR LUMPS
THE DIVISION CHAMPS WILL WIN AGAIN
WHILE VIKES' FANS WIND UP IN THE DUMPS

World & 1997
Central Division
Champion!
GB: 12-3
MN: 8-7

RESULTS:
Green Bay beat the
Buffalo Bills 31-21

Minnesota beat the
Indianapolis Colts 39-28

Wildcard Week Dec. 27 1997

PACKERS "VERSES" VIKINGS ~ Carl Nelson

CHRISTMAS CAME A LITTLE EARLY
FOR THE VIKINGS' TEAM THIS YEAR
THEIR LAST GAME WAS AGAINST THE COLTS
A TEAM THAT CAUSES NO ONE FEAR

MINNESOTA RAN UP A FIRST HALF LEAD
BUT THE COLTS CAME GALLOPING BACK
THEY COULD HAVE PERHAPS WON THAT GAME
BUT FOR A CRIPPLING JOHN RANDLE SACK

A HIT THAT SOME THOUGHT A LITTLE ROUGH
KNOCKED HARBAUGH FROM THE GAME
AND WHEN HOLCOMB TOOK THE HELM
INDIANAPOLIS WAS NOT THE SAME

SOMEHOW MINNESOTA RALLIED AT YEAR'S END
BREAKING A FIVE-GAME LOSING STREAK
SNEAKING PAST THOSE PITIFUL COLTS
AND INTO THE PLAYOFF GAME THIS WEEK

SO IT'S OFF TO NEW JERSEY
AND JIMMY HOFFA'S LAST RESTING PLACE
TO DO BATTLE WITH THE GIANTS
WHO FINISHED FIRST OUT IN THE EAST

THE GIANTS ARE A TEAM UNKNOWN
TO THOSE OF US IN THE MIDWEST
BUT THEY ARE NOT NOBODIES
AND HAVE BEATEN SOME OF THE BEST

BUT AS THE VIKES MAKE THEIR PLAYOFF RUN
ONE MUST RECALL THE LAST FEW YEARS
WILL IT BE THE USUAL LOSS
OR SAVING DENNY'S JOB THAT BRINGS THE TEARS?

THE PACK ALSO GOT A CHRISTMAS TREAT
AFTER WALLOPING THE BILLS
THEY RECEIVED SOME EXTRA DAYS OFF
TO REST AND HEAL THEIR ILLS

THE PACKERS NOW ONLY HAVE TO WAIT
TO SEE WHO COMES UP TO LAMBEAU
WHETHER IT'S THE BUCS OR THE LIONS
IT SHOULD BE QUITE A SHOW

THE PACK CAN'T AFFORD TO LOOK AHEAD
AND MUST KEEP THEIR FOCUS CLEAR
BUT THE WAY GREEN BAY IS PEAKING
IT SEEMS THAT THEY'LL REPEAT THIS YEAR

World & 1997 Central Division Champion!
GB: 13-3
MN: 9-7

RESULTS:
Green Bay was on a "bye"
Minnesota beat the New York Giants 23-22

47

PACKERS "VERSES" VIKINGS ~ Carl Nelson

THE OUTCOME OF SATURDAY'S GAME
LEFT DENNY LOOKING SOMEWHAT SURPRISED
FOR IT MUST HAVE SEEMED A MIRACLE
HAD OCCURRED BEFORE HIS EYES

WHEN THE GIANTS TOOK THE FIELD
THEY HAD THE 'QUEENS SQUARE IN THEIR SIGHTS
AND FOR FIFTY MINUTES PUSHED THE VIKES AROUND
IT SEEMED THEY HAD MINNESOTA DEAD TO RIGHTS

BUT IT HAPPENED AS IT HAS BEFORE
THE VIKINGS FOUND A WAY BACK INTO THE GAME
GETTING A COUPLE OF CALLS AND A TOUCHDOWN CATCH
LET THE VIKINGS WIN ALTHOUGH THEY LOOKED A LITTLE LAME

THIS WEEK THEY'RE ON THE ROAD AGAIN
GOING TO PLAY IN THE CALIFORNIA SUN
BUT THIS GAME AGAINST THE 'NINERS
WON'T SEEM LIKE A LOT OF FUN

THE VIKINGS LOST TO THIS TEAM
IN A GAME JUST A FEW WEEKS PAST
THE FORTY-NINERS SHOULD ROLL AGAIN
AND MAKE THIS GAME DENNY'S LAST

~ ~ ~ ~ ~ ~ ~ ~ ~ ~ ~ ~ ~ ~ ~ ~ ~

TAMPA WAS IMPRESSIVE SUNDAY
STOPPING BARRY SANDERS IN HIS TRACKS
HOWEVER THIS WEEK IT'S OFF TO LAMBEAU
AND THE LIONS ARE NOT THE PACK

WHILE FOCUSING ON THE RUNNING BACK
WILL GET YOU PAST MANY FOOTBALL TEAMS
THE PACKERS HAVE SO MANY WEAPONS
THE BUC DEFENDERS MUST HAVE BAD DREAMS

FREEMAN BROOKS AND CHMURA
WILL BE REELING IN BRETT FAVRE'S DARTS
AT THE SAME TIME HENDERSON AND LEVENS
WILL TEST THE TAMPA DEFENSE'S HEART

THE PACKERS' DEFENSE IS RESTED
EVEN GILBERT IS AT "FULL SPEED"
DILFER AND THE RUNNING BACKS SHOULD WORRY
FOR THE ODDS ARE THAT THEY WILL BLEED

RESULTS:
Green Bay beat the
Tampa Bay Buccaneers 21-7

Minnesota lost to the
San Francisco 49ers 22-38

OH THIS WON'T BE AN EASY GAME
TAMPA BAY IS AN EXCELLENT TEAM
BUT THEY HAVE THE MISFORTUNE OF COMING TO LAMBEAU
AND STANDING IN THE WAY OF GREEN BAY'S DREAM

~ Carl Nelson

PACKERS "VERSES" VIKINGS

WATCHING THOSE MINNESOTA VIKINGS' THIS WEEK
HAD TO BE HARD FOR TRUE VIKINGS' FANS
WHILE THEY CAME OUT AND LOOKED RESPECTABLE
THEY LET THE GAME SLIP THROUGH THEIR HANDS

DENNY AND HIS FOOTBALL TEAM
SEEMED TO BE WAITING TO MAKE THAT ONE BIG PLAY
HOWEVER THE FORTY-NINERS
WERE MAKING THAT BIG PLAY ALL DAY

THOUGH WASHINGTON WAS BENCHED EARLY ON
AND RANDLE WAS HITTING THE QB LATE
THINGS LIKE THREE STRAIGHT ILLEGAL MOTION FLAGS
REALLY SEALED THE VIKINGS' FATE

ONE MUST PLAY GOOD FUNDAMENTAL FOOTBALL
WHEN UP AGAINST THE ELITE TEAMS
AT LEAST THIS SHOULD END THE REIGN
OF "THE SHERIFF" DENNY GREEN

~ ~ ~ ~ ~ ~ ~ ~ ~ ~ ~ ~ ~ ~ ~ ~ ~ ~ ~

THE PACKERS HAD THEIR HANDS FULL
DISPATCHING TAMPA'S BUCS
GREEN BAY COULDN'T SEEM TO CATCH THE BALL
AND EARLY ON SEEMED TO HAVE NO LUCK

BUT THE PACKERS NEVER FALTERED
AND KEPT ON PLUGGING AWAY
IN THE END IT WAS DORSEY LEVENS' LEGS
THAT SAVED THE GREEN BAY TEAM SUNDAY

OH THE PACKERS' DEFENSE PLAYED QUITE WELL
WITH GILBERT BROWN ON CENTER STAGE
BUT THE SECONDARY COULDN'T CATCH A PICK
UNTIL WELL INTO THE GAME'S LAST PAGE

NOW IT'S A TRIP TO THE 'NINERS' HOME
WHERE THE "WEST COAST" OFFENSE STARTED
WHILE GREEN BAY WOULD RATHER BE AT LAMBEAU
THEY WON'T ENTER THIS GAME DOWN-HEARTED

FOR TWO YEARS NOW THE PACKERS
HAVE KEPT THE 'NINERS FROM THE BIG SHOW
THE RESULT SHOULD BE THE SAME THIS YEAR
EVEN LACKING COLD AND SNOW

STEVE YOUNG AND THE REST OF HIS TEAM
WILL PROVIDE QUITE A FOOTBALL TEST
BUT THE PACKERS ARE THE DEFENDING CHAMPIONS
AND WILL RISE TO PROVE THAT THEY'RE THE BEST

World & Defending NFC Champions!
GB: 1-0
MN: 1-1
(Eliminated from the postseason)

RESULTS:
Green Bay beat the San Francisco 49ers 23-10

PACKERS "VERSES" VIKINGS

~ Carl Nelson

THE BRONCOS ALMOST MADE IT LOOK EASY
WHEN THEY GOT BY THE "MEN OF STEEL"
ALTHOUGH THERE WAS SOME TURNOVER HELP
DENVER PROVED TO BE THE REAL DEAL

OH ELWAY LOOKED PRETTY GOOD
(ESPECIALLY FOR A MAN HIS AGE)
BUT FOR ONCE THE BRONCO'S DEFENSE
ALLOWED THEM TO APPEAR UPON THIS PAGE

WHILE "THE BUS" RAN THE BALL QUITE WELL
IT WAS KORDELL STEWART WHO LOST THIS GAME
NEXT YEAR IN THE SAME POSITION
HIS JUDGEMENT WON'T BE THE SAME

EXPERIENCE MAKES A BOLD MAN WISE
AS MANY A QUARTERBACK HAS LEARNED
AND TO PLAY IN THE SUPER BOWL
IS A PRIVILEGE THAT MUST BE EARNED

DON'T DESPAIR YOU STEELERS FANS
FOR THIS WAS NOT A ONE-TIME TRIP
NEXT YEAR WHEN THE STEELERS PLAY HERE
KORDELL WILL THROW THE BALL WITH ZIP

NOW AS FOR THE DENVER BRONCOS
THEIR VICTORY WAS HARD-EARNED
EVEN THOUGH THEIR OFFENSE WAS EFFECTIVE
IT WAS ON MISCUES THE GAME WAS TURNED

TERRELL DAVIS WAS IMPRESSIVE
AS HE HAS BEEN FOR MOST OF THE YEAR
BUT EXCUSE THE GREEN BAY PACKERS
IF HE DOESN'T FILL THEM WITH FEAR

FOR NOW THE BRONCOS GO TO PLAY
WITH THE BIG BOYS OF THE LEAGUE
AND HANDLING DENVER'S SMALL "O" LINE
WON'T CAUSE THE PACKER DEFENSE TO FATIGUE

PEOPLE SAY THAT JOHN ELWAY
"DESERVES" TO WIN THIS GAME
WELL, HE'S BEEN TO IT THREE TIMES BEFORE
AND THIS YEAR'S OUTCOME WILL BE THE SAME

FOR IT'S TALENT NOT EMOTION
THAT BRINGS THE LOMBARDI TROPHY HOME
AND WHEN ONE COMPARES THE BRONCOS TO THE PACKERS
ONLY ONE TEAM STANDS ALONE

THE TIME HAS COME FOR TRUTH TO BE TOLD
AS THE SUPER BOWL MATCH-UP NEARS
THE FANS OF THE PACKERS WILL BE ECSTATIC
WHILE BRONCO FANS WILL BE IN TEARS

WHILE SOME MAY FEEL FOR JOHN ELWAY
WITH THREE SUPER BOWL LOSSES IN HIS PAST
IN THIS WHICH MAY BE HIS LAST TRY
THE DIE ALREADY HAS BEEN CAST

THERE IS NO WAY THE BRONCOS
COULD MATCH UP TO GREEN BAY'S PACK
THE ONLY TEAM IN RECENT YEARS
WHICH SHOULD WIN THE TROPHY BACK TO BACK

THE BRONCOS JUST DON'T MATCH UP
WITH GREEN BAY IN ANY WAY OR FORM
AND CONSIDERING THE LAST THIRTEEN YEARS
THAT SEEMS TO BE THE NORM

DENVER'S ELWAY IS AN EXAMPLE
THAT "TIME PASSES BY NO MAN"
THE THINGS THAT HE CAN NO LONGER DO
THE PACKERS' BRETT FAVRE CAN

IT USED TO BE THAT ELWAY'S LEGS
COMBINED WITH HIS ARM'S POWER
CAUSED OPPONENTS TO BE AFRAID
BUT NOW BRETT FAVRE CAUSES THEM TO COWER

AS FAR AS RECEIVERS AND THE OTHER THINGS
THAT PEOPLE LIKE TO TALK ABOUT
GREEN BAY HAS THE ADVANTAGE
AND ABOUT THAT THERE IS NO DOUBT

RUNNING BACK IS THE ONLY PLACE
WHERE THESE TEAMS ARE EVEN CLOSE
BUT I'M AFRAID THE PACKERS WILL MAKE
DAVIS SEEM LIKE UN"LEVENS"ED TOAST

GREEN BAY SHOULD DOMINATE
FROM THE KICKOFF TO THE GUN
AND FOR THOSE OF US WHO LOVE THEM
THIS GAME WILL BE FILLED WITH FUN

RESULTS:
Unfortunately Green Bay
lost to the
Denver Broncos 24-31

TRUE PACKERS' FANS WILL CELEBRATE
AS WE'VE LATELY HAD THE CHANCE TO DO
AS HOLMGREN WINS CONSECUTIVE CHAMPIONSHIPS
LIKE LOMBARDI WON ONE AND TWO

PACKERS

" **VERSES** "

VIKINGS

Green Bay Packers
Regular Season 11-5
Postseason 0-1

Minnesota Vikings
Regular Season 15-1
Postseason 1-1

1998

Carl "Gator" Nelson

~ Carl Nelson

PACKERS "VERSES" VIKINGS

GB: 0-0
MN: 0-0

A WONDEROUS SUMMER IS WINDING DOWN
AUTUMN WILL SOON BE UPON US
IT'S TIME TO WATCH PRO FOOTBALL
IN A SEASON FILLED WITH PROMISE

THE VIKINGS THINK THEY'VE FOUND THE KEY
TO UNLOCK THE CHAMPIONSHIP DOOR
STARTING SUNDAY THEY'LL HAVE TO PROVE
THAT IT'S NOT ALL BIG TALK ONCE MORE

THE DEFENSE IT'S SAID IS MUCH IMPROVED
AND WILL BE IMPOSSIBLE FOR TEAMS TO HANDLE
BUT IT'S NOT OBVIOUS JUST WHAT HAS CHANGED
EXCEPT THE BIG BUCKS TO OL' JOHN RANDLE

THE OFFENSE HOWEVER WILL GIVE PAUSE
TO ANY TEAM WHO HAS TO FACE 'EM
IF THE INJURY BUGS STAY FAR AWAY
MOST TEAMS WILL HAVE TO CHASE THEM

BUT HISTORY SAYS THE BUCCANEERS
ALWAYS PLAY THE VIKINGS TOUGH
WITH MINNESOTA'S POROUS DEFENSE
THAT OFFENSE JUST WON'T BE ENOUGH

~ ~ ~ ~ ~ ~ ~ ~ ~ ~ ~ ~ ~ ~ ~ ~ ~ ~ ~

THIS TOO IS A TIME OF QUESTIONS
FOR GREEN BAY'S BELOVED PACK
THERE ARE ANSWERS FOR THE RUNNING GAME
NOW THAT DORSEY LEVENS IS BACK

BRETT FAVRE THE THREE-TIME MVP
WILL TAKE THE SNAPS AGAIN
AND ANY GAME IN WHICH HE PLAYS
IS ONE THE PACKERS HAVE A CHANCE TO WIN

THE DEFENSE PROVIDES THE MOST CONCERN
BUT THEY WON'T CAUSE US TO LOSE MUCH SLEEP
THE STARTING BUNCH WILL DO JUST FINE
ALTHOUGH THEY ARE NOT VERY DEEP

THIS WEEK AGAINST DETROIT'S LIONS
BARRY SANDERS WILL TRY TO RUN ON GRASS
AND JUST LIKE THE LAST FEW TIMES
THE PACK WILL KNOCK HIM ON HIS ASS

WHEN THE WEEKEND'S GAMES WIND DOWN
AND TAMPA HAS WON THEIR GAME
THEY'LL FIND THEY'RE TIED WITH THE PACKERS
WHOSE RECORD WILL BE THE SAME

RESULTS:
Green Bay beat the Detroit Lions 38-19

Minnesota beat the Tampa Bay Buccaneers 31-7

GB: 1-0
MN: 1-0

PACKERS "VERSES" VIKINGS

~ Carl Nelson

"JUST CALL OFF THE SEASON—"
ALL THE MINNESOTA SPORTSWRITERS SAY
"NO ONE CAN TOUCH THE VIKINGS
AFTER ALL, THEY BEAT TAMPA BAY"

SORRY ALL YOU VIKINGS FANS
I'M AFRAID THAT'S NOT TO BE
WHILE THE TAMPA TEAM MAY BE PRETTY GOOD
THEY'RE NOT THE CLASS OF THE NFC

WHILE THE VIKINGS DID LOOK IMPRESSIVE
AND EXCEPT FOR JIMMY HITCHCOCK DIDN'T STRUGGLE
THE MOST NOTABLE THING THAT I SAW
WAS THE WAY THAT RANDY MOSS CAN JUGGLE

YES BRAD JOHNSON THREW PRETTY WELL
AND SMITH RAN THE BALL JUST FINE
THE QUESTION IS, WILL THEY BE STANDING UPRIGHT
WHEN IT COMES DOWN TO PLAYOFF TIME?

THIS WEEK IT'S OFF TO SAINT LOUIS
TO PLAY THE WORST TEAM IN THE LAND
IF LIKE THEY DO THE VIKES PLAY TO THAT LEVEL
THEY'LL COME HOME WITH THEIR HELMETS IN HAND

~ ~ ~ ~ ~ ~ ~ ~ ~ ~ ~ ~ ~ ~ ~ ~ ~ ~

THE GREEN BAY PACKERS SCORED ALMOST EVERY WAY
THAT A FOOTBALL TEAM POSSIBLY CAN
AND WHILE THE DEFENSE GAVE UP SOME CATCHES
THEY KEPT BARRY SANDERS WELL IN HAND

DORSEY LEVENS SHOWED NO ILL EFFECTS
FROM HIS EXTENDED OFF-SEASON REST
AND THE PACK'S RECEIVING CORPS
SHOWED WHY THEY ARE AMONG THE BEST

THE PASSES THROWN BY BRETT FAVRE
WERE BEAUTIFUL TO SEE
IT WAS A GOOD REMINDER
OF WHY HE'S A THREE-TIME MVP

THIS WEEK IT'S TAMPA'S BUCCANEERS
TRAVELING TO LOVELY LAMBEAU FIELD
THEY'LL HAVE A CHIP UPON THEIR SHOULDERS
SINCE THE 'QUEENIES MADE THEM YIELD

DUNGY'S TEAM WON'T MATCH UP WELL
WITH THE GAME THE PACK WILL SHOW
LEVENS AND FAVRE WILL CARVE THEM UP
AS THE PACK MOVES TO TWO-AND-O

RESULTS:
Green Bay beat
Tampa Bay Buccaneers 23-15

Minnesota beat the
St Louis Rams 38-31

GB: 2-0
MN: 2-0

PACKERS "VERSES" VIKINGS ~ Carl Nelson

THE VIKINGS SHOW THAT THE MORE THINGS CHANGE
THE MORE THEY STAY THE SAME
THEY PLAYED DOWN TO THE LEVEL OF THE RAMS
AND NEARLY LOST THAT GAME

OR MAYBE THAT WASN'T THE REASON
MAYBE THE VIKINGS JUST AREN'T ALL THAT GOOD
THE DEFENSE HAS NOT BEEN IMPRESSIVE
THOUGH THE OFFENSE PLAYS LIKE IT SHOULD

NOW JOHNSON IS THE FIRST VIKE
TO GRAB SOME INJURY TIME
HOWEVER RANDALL IS A GREAT BACKUP
(WHEN HE THROWS FROM BEHIND THE LINE)

THIS WEEK IT'S THE DETROIT LIONS
PROVIDING THE VIKINGS' TEST
THAT MEANS BARRY SANDERS
AT RUNNING BACK HE'S THE BEST

IF THE 'QUEENS DON'T FIND SOMEONE TO HELP
THE AGING JOHNNY RANDLE
THE DEFENSE WILL CONTINUE TO FAIL
AND THE LIONS WILL BE MORE THAN THEY CAN HANDLE

~ ~ ~ ~ ~ ~ ~ ~ ~ ~ ~ ~ ~ ~ ~ ~ ~

ONE MUST WONDER WHAT MIKE HOLMGREN'S DONE
TO DRAW DOWN THE WRATH OF THE HEAVENS
AS YET AGAIN A BRIGHT STAR IS LOST
THIS YEAR IT'S DORSEY LEVENS

FOR THE LAST THREE YEARS IN GREEN BAY
ANOTHER PLAYER HAS PICKED UP THE SLACK
NOW HARRIS AND JERVEY MUST DO IT
UNTIL DORSEY MAKES IT BACK

BUT THERE'S NO DESPAIR IN GREEN BAY
DUE TO THE PRESENCE OF "NUMBER FOUR"
AS LONG AS BRETT IS ON HIS FEET
THE PACK HAS A CHANCE TO SCORE

LAST WEEK UP AT LAMBEAU FIELD
WITH THE HELP OF A STUNNING REGGIE WHITE
THE PACKERS PUT DOWN THE BUCCANEERS
WHO MAY AS WELL JUST SAY "GOOD NIGHT"

THIS WEEK IN CINNCINATI
THE BENGALS MUST FACE THE PACK
THEY'LL LEARN HOW BAD IT FEELS TO LOSE
TO A TEAM WITH A BACK-UP RUNNING BACK

RESULTS:
Green Bay beat the
Cincinnati Bengals 13-6

Minnesota beat the
Detroit Lions 29-6

GB: 3-0
MN: 3-0

PACKERS "VERSES" VIKINGS ~ Carl Nelson

THE VIKES DID AWAY WITH THE LIONS
WITH THEIR USUAL DISPATCH
THE DEFENSE STEPPED UP AND DID THEIR PART
IN HARASSING DETROIT'S ROOKIE CHARLIE BATCH

THE LIONS PLAYED THE VIKINGS TOUGH
THROUGHOUT THE GAME'S FIRST HALF
BUT WHEN DETROIT TURNED AWAY FROM BARRY SANDERS
THEY GAVE MINNESOTA THE LAST LAUGH

MINNESOTA'S OFFENSE HOWEVER DIDN'T SEEM
TO HAVE ITS NORMAL FLAIR
THE VIKES COULDN'T MOVE ON THE GROUND
AND WEREN'T IMPRESSIVE THROUGH THE AIR

CHICAGO'S BEARS THIS WEEK'S OPPONENT
DOESN'T LIKE THE MINNESOTA'S TEAM
AND SINCE THEIR RECORD IS O-AND-THREE
TO BEAT THE VIKINGS WOULD BE A DREAM

ON THE SURFACE IT SEEMS THE BEARS ARE EASY
BUT IT'S NOT CLEAR IF THAT IS TRUE
WHILE THE 'QUEENS WILL PROBABLY WIN
THEY'LL WIND UP BEATEN BLACK-AND-BLUE

~ ~ ~ ~ ~ ~ ~ ~ ~ ~ ~ ~ ~ ~ ~ ~ ~ ~

LAST SUNDAY THE PACKERS' OFFENSE
JUST COULDN'T SEEM TO FIND THE "ZONE"
THE TIMING AND EASE JUST WASN'T THERE
THE CAUSE REMAINS UNKNOWN

RAYMONT HARRIS FUMBLED ONE TIME
AND ONCE WAS KNOCKED FROM THE GAME
HE'S CLEARLY NOT DORSEY LEVENS
BUT HE'LL BE EFFECTIVE JUST THE SAME

IT'S A GOOD THING THAT GREEN BAY'S DEFENSE
TOOK CONTROL OF THE ENTIRE FIELD
AND EXCEPT FOR ONE HAIL-MARY PASS
A BIG PLAY JUST DIDN'T YIELD

NOW IT'S OFF TO TAKE ON CAROLINA
UNDER A SHINING SOUTHERN SUN
THAT PACKER DEFENSE IS SMILING
SINCE THE PANTHERS CAN'T PASS OR RUN

TWO TIMES THE PACK HAS FACED THESE GUYS
AND THE OUTCOME WILL BE REPEATED
AS THE PACKERS CLOSE OUT WEEK FOUR
THEY WILL REMAIN UNDEFEATED

RESULTS:
Green Bay beat the
Carolina Panthers 37-30

Minnesota beat the
Chicago Bears 31-28

GB: 4-0
MN: 4-0

PACKERS "VERSES" VIKINGS ~ Carl Nelson

A QUICK NOTE TO ALL THE VIKINGS' FANS
WHO THINK THEIR TEAM RULES THE STACK
MINNESOTA'S NOT YET FACED AN OPPONENT
WITH THE TALENT OF THE PACK

YES THEY "WEASELED" BY THE BEARS
BUT WE ALL KNOW HOW GOOD THEY ARE
FOR MUCH OF THE DAY MINNESOTA LOOKED
LIKE THEY'D BEEN RUN OVER BY A CAR

ERIK KRAMER HAD HIS WAY
WITH THE VAUNTED VIKES' DEFENSE
WHO MUCH OF THE DAY SLOWED THE "MIGHTY" BEARS
LIKE A RUN-DOWN PICKET FENCE

THEN THE VIKINGS' RECEIVERS
WHO CAN WIN MANY A FOOT RACE
FOUND IT'S HARD TO CATCH THE BALL
WHEN CUNNINGHAM'S BEING CHASED

~ ~ ~ ~ ~ ~ ~ ~ ~ ~ ~ ~ ~ ~ ~ ~ ~ ~ ~ ~

REGGIE WHITE WATCHED THAT GAME
WITH A SMILE UPON HIS LIPS
KNOWING THAT INTO THAT BACKFIELD
HE'LL BE MAKING MANY TRIPS

FREEMAN, BROOKS AND DERRICK MAYES
ARE PREPARING TO CATCH BRETT FAVRE'S DARTS
AND TIGHT ENDS CHMURAS AND DAVIS
WILL DRIVE THE STAKE THROUGH MINNESOTA'S HEART

TWICE LAST YEAR WE HEARD THE RHETORIC
AND ALL THE REASONS THE VIKINGS WOULD COME THROUGH
BUT AT SEASON'S END IT WAS PLAIN TO SEE
'TWAS THE PACKERS WHO'D WON TWO

LAMBEAU FIELD HAS BEEN THE PLACE
WHERE MANY TEAMS HAVE STUMBLED
I'M AFRAID THE MINNESOTA VIKINGS
ARE THE NEXT GROUP TO BE HUMBLED

DENNY, RED AND THE "PURPLE PRIDE"
JUST WON'T BE UP TO THE TEST
AND WILL BE GLAD TO HAVE A WEEK OFF
TO LICK THEIR WOUNDS AND REST

AS HOLMGREN'S BOYS LEAVE THE FIELD
AND HEAD OFF TO THEIR HOMES
THEY'LL BE SECURE IN THE KNOWLEDGE
THAT ATOP THE CENTRAL THEY'RE ALONE

RESULTS:
Green Bay lost to
Minnesota 24-37

GB: 4-1
MN: 5-0

PACKERS "VERSES" VIKINGS

~ Carl Nelson

AFTER THE GAME ON MONDAY NIGHT FOOTBALL
THE PACKERS WERE MORE THAN A LITTLE SHAKEN
IT WAS WIDELY THOUGHT THEY'D CRUSH THE VIKES
BUT IT TURNED OUT THEY WERE BADLY MISTAKEN

GREEN BAY WAS RIDING A FOUR-GAME WIN STREAK
AS THEY WERE GETTING READY FOR THIS GAME
THEY HADN'T FACED A SERIOUS CHALLENGE YET
WHY WOULDN'T THIS WEEK BE THE SAME?

BRETT FAVRE WAS LOOKING PRETTY GOOD
AND THE RUNNING GAME WAS COMING AROUND
THE DEFENSE HAS BEEN PRETTY DOMINANT
HATING TO GIVE UP ANY GROUND

FOR TWENTY-FIVE GAMES LAMBEAU FIELD
HADN'T SEEN THE GREEN BAY PACKERS LOSE
BUT THAT STREAK WAS EASILY BROKEN
BEFORE IT WAS TIME FOR LATE LOCAL NEWS

THE PACKERS' OFFENSE WAS JUST HORRIBLE
WITH THE DEFENSE PLAYING NO BETTER
TO THEIR CREDIT THEY ADMITTED TO BEING OUTCLASSED
WITHOUT TRYING TO BLAME IT ALL ON THE WEATHER

~ ~ ~ ~ ~ ~ ~ ~ ~ ~ ~ ~ ~ ~ ~ ~ ~ ~

THE VIKINGS WERE UNDEFEATED AS WELL
BUT SEEMED PRIMED TO TAKE A FALL
THEIR STARTING QUARTERBACK HAD BEEN INJURED
AND THE DEFENSE WASN'T PLAYING WELL AT ALL

RANDALL CUNNIGHAM CAME OFF THE BENCH
AND STARTED THROWING THE FOOTBALL LONG
EVERY TIME GREEN BAY TRIED TO DEFEND
IT WAS APPARENT THE DEFENDER GUESSED WRONG

RANDY MOSS FINALLY SHOWED US IN THIS GAME
WHY HE HAD BEEN DRAFTED IN THE FIRST ROUND
AS HE OUTRAN AND OUTWRESTLED DEFENDERS
THAT WERE TRYING TO PUSH HIM AROUND

THE TEAM IN PURPLE MADE LAMBEAU FIELD
LOOK LIKE THEIR OWN PRACTICE SITE
THEIR DEFENSE SMOTHERED THE PACKERS
WHO LOOKED LIKE THEY COULDN'T PUT UP A FIGHT

RESULTS:
Both Green Bay
and Minnesota
were on their
"Bye Week"

THE PACKERS' TEAM HAS BEEN LOOKING STRONG
AT LEAST UNTIL THIS POINT OF THE SEASON
BUT THE VIKINGS PUMMELED AND EMBARRASSED THEM
AND GREEN BAY HAS TO SEARCH OUT THE REASON

GB: 4-1
MN: 5-0

PACKERS "VERSES" VIKINGS ~ Carl Nelson

INTO THE METRODOME ON SUNDAY
COMES THE WASHINGTON REDSKINS
A TEAM THAT IS SO PATHETIC
THERE SHOULD BE NO DOUBT THE VIKES CAN WIN

BUT MINNESOTA DIALS ITS GAME UP AND DOWN
DEPENDING ON THE TEAM THEY'RE FACING
IF THE 'QUEENS SET IT DOWN TOO FAR
ON THE SIDELINES DENNY WILL BE PACING

FOR THE REDSKINS WON'T ROLL OVER
THEY'RE GOING TO GIVE IT THEIR BEST SHOT
LOSING EX-VIKING TERRY ALLEN
AND MAKING THE SWITCH TO GUS FERROTTE

TEAMS WITH RECORDS LIKE THE REDSKINS
ARE WHAT GIVE COACHES GRAY HAIR
FOR EACH GAME BECOMES THEIR SUPER BOWL
AND THEY WILL PLAY WITHOUT A CARE

THE VIKINGS CAN BE CONFIDENT
BUT MUST PLAY THEIR GAME WITH CARE
FOR IT'S EASIER TO REACH FIRST PLACE
THAN IT IS TO REMAIN UP THERE

~ ~ ~ ~ ~ ~ ~ ~ ~ ~ ~ ~ ~ ~ ~ ~ ~ ~ ~

IN THIS SEASON'S OPENING GAME
THE LIONS WERE MANHANDLED BY THE PACK
TONIGHT GREEN BAY GOES TO THE SILVERDOME
WHERE DETROIT WILL TRY TO GIVE SOME BACK

THE DETROIT TEAM WILL TAKE THE FIELD
BEHIND ROOKIE CHARLIE BATCH
AND OF COURSE THERE'S BARRY SANDERS
ON THAT TURF HE'S HARD TO CATCH

BUT GREEN BAY SEEMS TO HAVE HIS NUMBER
AND THE DEFENSE HAS SOMETHING TO PROVE
TONIGHT THE LIONS' RUNNING BACK
WILL FIND IT HARD TO MAKE A MOVE

BRETT FAVRE AND THE RECEIVERS
ALSO HAVE SOME THINGS TO MAKE UP FOR
ADD JERVEY STARTING AT RUNNING BACK
AND THE PACKERS WILL SLAM THE DOOR

THE LIONS ALWAYS PRESENT SOME PROBLEMS
THEY'RE HARD TO BEAT IN THEIR HOME
BUT THE PACKERS WILL BE READY
FOR THE RECENT LOSS THEY WILL ATONE

RESULTS:
Green Bay lost to the
Detroit Lions 20-27

Minnesota beat the
Washington Redskins 41-7

BOTH THE PACK AND VIKES SHOULD WIN THESE GAMES
AS THEY HEAD INTO A STRETCH OF TEN MORE WEEKS
HOW THE STANDINGS LOOK AT SEASON'S END
WILL DEPEND ON WHEN THEY REACH THEIR PEAKS

GB: 4-2
MN: 6-0

PACKERS "VERSES" VIKINGS ~ Carl Nelson

THE VIKINGS DID TO WASHINGTON
PRETTY MUCH WHAT WAS EXPECTED
WHILE THE POINT TOTAL WAS IMPRESSIVE
THE 'SKINS SHOWED WHY THEY'RE NOT MUCH RESPECTED

THIS WEEK IT'S OFF TO PONTIAC
FOR DETROIT PROVIDES THE NEXT TEST
WALKING INTO THAT LIONS' DEN
CAN BE LIKE STEPPING INTO A HORNETS' NEST

BARRY SANDERS IS FINDING THE WAY
TO MOVE HIS BOTTOM DOWN THE FIELD
AND CHARLIE BATCH HAS THE COMPOSURE
TO NOT BE FRIGHTENED FOLD AND YIELD

THE LIONS SEEM TO BE POISED
TO PUT TOGETHER THEIR MIDSEASON STREAK
AND VIKINGS FANS JUST HAVE TO WONDER
HOW LONG THE 'QUEENS CAN REMAIN AT THEIR PEAK

THIS SUNDAY'S GAME FEELS UP IN THE AIR
WITHOUT THE WINNER SEEMING CLEAR
THE ODDS MAY BE AGAINST THE VIKINGS
WINNING AT THE SILVERDOME THIS YEAR

~ ~ ~ ~ ~ ~ ~ ~ ~ ~ ~ ~ ~ ~ ~ ~ ~ ~

THE GREEN BAY TEAM MAY HAVE FOUND ITSELF
LICKING ITS WOUNDS ONCE AGAIN
BUT LET'S RECALL THIS IS THE PACKERS
AND NOT THE WASHINGTON REDSKINS

THE OFFENSE HAS FOUND ITSELF OFF TRACK
PERHAPS DUE TO THE PLAY OF THE OFFENSIVE LINE
ONCE THE PROBLEMS CAN BE FOUND AND FIXED
IT WILL BE BACK TO WINNING TIME

THE DEFENSE HAS TAKEN A LITTLE HEAT
FOR THE PLAYS OF THE LAST TWO WEEKS
BUT UNTIL THE OFFENSE CAN RETAIN THE BALL
THEY'RE BOUND TO SPRING SOME LEAKS

THE THING THAT IS MISSING IS CONFIDENCE
THE BELIEF THAT THEY'LL FIND A WAY TO WIN
THE PACK MUST JUST PLAY THROUGH THIS
AND PICK UP THE MOMENTUM ONCE AGAIN

THE RAVENS MAY BE COMING ALONG
AT WHAT IS JUST THE PERFECT TIME
TRUTH BE TOLD THEY'RE NOT VERY GOOD
AND THE PACKERS SHOULD DO JUST FINE

60

RESULTS:
Green Bay beat the
Baltimore Ravens 28-10

Minnesota beat the
Detroit Lions 34-13

GB: 5-2
MN: 7-0

THE LIONS LOOKED LIKE THEY HAD A CHANCE
WHEN THEY WENT TO THE HALF TIME LOCKER ROOM
BUT WHEN THE VIKINGS RETOOK THE FIELD
THEIR POOR PLAY SPELLED THE LIONS' DOOM

ROBERT SMITH WITH HIS TOUCHDOWN RUN
AND HITCHCOCK'S PICK-OFF RETURN
LEFT THE DETROIT TEAM IN RUINS
LOOKING LIKE THEY HAD CRASHED AND BURNED

NOW JUST RELAX YOU VIKINGS FANS
THIS WEEK YOUR TEAM PLAYS THE BUCCANEERS
WHO WERE SUPPOSED TO BE CONTENDERS
BUT WHO LOOK WORSE THAN THEY HAVE IN YEARS

BUT THE VIKINGS STILL HAVE ONE TEAM TO FACE
WHO HAVE ALWAYS BEEN THAT TEAM'S GREATEST FOE
IT'S NOT ONE OF THE UPCOMING OPPONENTS
AS LONG-TERM VIKINGS FANS ALL KNOW

IT WON'T TAKE MAGIC TO DERAIL THE TRAIN
NOT A GROUP OF WITCHES, TROLLS OR ELVES
THE HURDLE MINNESOTA MUST OVERCOME
IS THE VIKINGS TEAM THEMSELVES

~ ~ ~ ~ ~ ~ ~ ~ ~ ~ ~ ~ ~ ~ ~ ~ ~ ~ ~

THE PACKERS PLUCKED THE RAVENS
ON LAMBEAU'S HALLOWED GRASS
THEY STEPPED UP WHEN THEY HAD TO
AND KNOCKED THOSE RAVENS ON THEIR ASS

THE WEEK THE FORTY-NINERS COME TO TOWN
BRINGING WITH THEM A LONG-TERM GRUDGE
FOR FROM THE FAST TRACK TO THE CHAMPIONSHIP
FOR THREE YEARS THE PACK HAS GIVEN THEM A NUDGE

THAT THE PACKERS WILL HAVE THEIR HANDS FULL
SHOULD BE QUITE OBVIOUS TO ALL
THE OFFENSIVE LINE IS SHAKY
AND THE BACKS CAN'T MOVE THE BALL

BUT THE PASSING GAME IS IMPROVING
FAVRE'S AIM AND ARM ARE MUCH MORE TRUE
AND ONCE JERVEY LEARNS TO SEE THE HOLES
THE 'NINERS DEFENSE WILL BE FEELING BLUE

GREEN BAY'S TEAM CAN WIN THIS GAME
DESPITE THEIR SHAKY START
THE KEY WILL BE FOR THE PACKERS
TO PLAY WITH ALL THEIR PRIDE AND HEART

RESULTS:
Green Bay beat the
San Francisco 49ers 36-22

Minnesota lost to the
Tampa Bay Buccaneers 24-27

GB: 6-2
MN: 7-1

PACKERS "VERSES" VIKINGS ~ Carl Nelson

REALITY REARED ITS UGLY HEAD
IN FLORIDA LAST SUNDAY
THE VIKINGS KIND OF COASTED IN
WHILE THE BUCS CAME PREPARED TO PLAY

DUNN AND ALSTOTT "GROUND" IT OUT
RUNNING THROUGH THE VIKES AT WILL
MINNESOTA'S DEFENSIVE TEAM
DIDN'T PROVIDE TOO MANY THRILLS

STARTING SUNDAY THE VIKINGS PLAY
THREE HOME GAMES IN A ROW
NEW ORLEANS IS THE FIRST OPPONENT
AGAINST WHOM THEIR CHARACTER MUST SHOW

THE SAINTS ARE A TEAM FILLED WITH TURMOIL
WITHOUT A SUPERSTAR IN THE BUNCH
ON PAPER THE VIKES SHOULD CRUSH THEM
AND EAT THESE GUYS FOR LUNCH

BUT HISTORICALLY THE VIKES HAVE FAILED
IN THE PAST WHEN IN THIS PLACE
WILL THEY PUT THE LOSS BEHIND THEM
OR FALL FLAT ON THEIR COLLECTIVE FACE?

~ ~ ~ ~ ~ ~ ~ ~ ~ ~ ~ ~ ~ ~ ~ ~ ~ ~ ~

THE PACKERS STARTED OFF QUICKLY
AGAINST SAN FRANCISCO'S TEAM
BUT WHEN THEY LET THE MOMENTUM GO
IT SEEMED LIKE A BAD DREAM

WHAT FUN WHEN THE GREEN BAY DEFENSE
THEN RETOOK THAT FOOTBALL FIELD
SACKING STEVE YOUNG AN AMAZING NINE TIMES
AND FORCING THE 'NINERS TO YIELD

NOW THE PACKERS MUST UNDERTAKE
A LONG THREE-GAME ROAD TRIP
WITH THE COMPETITION IN THE CENTRAL
IT COULD BE DISASTEROUS TO SLIP

THIS WEEK JEROME BETTIS AND KORDELL STEWART
ARE THE MAIN THREAT THE PACK WILL FACE
AND PITTSBURGH'S THREE RIVERS STADIUM
CAN BE A VERY HOSTILE PLACE

BUT THE PACK IS COMING 'ROUND
THE BOYS IN YELLOW HATS WILL COME THROUGH
THE STEELERS WILL BE QUITE DISMAYED
TO FIND THEY'VE BEEN BEATEN BLACK-AND-BLUE

RESULTS:
Green Bay lost to the
Pittsburgh Steelers 20-27

Minnesota beat the
New Orleans Saints 31-24

PACKERS "VERSES" VIKINGS ~ Carl Nelson

GB: 6-3
MN: 8-1

LAST WEEK THE "PURPLE-HELMETED WARRIORS"
HAD THEIR JOHNSON STANDING TALL AND ERECT
AFTER AN INJURY TO RANDALL CUNNINGHAM
THAT MANY FEEL MAY BE SOMEWHAT SUSPECT

BRAD TOOK THE REINS FROM RANDALL
AND HAD THE VIKINGS ON THE MOVE
HE SEEMED TO HAVE REGAINED HIS RHYTHM
AND SETTLED DOWN INTO THE GROOVE

BUT AS OFTEN HAPPENS AT TIMES LIKE THIS
(AND NOT JUST TO THE VIKES ALONE)
FATE PLAYS OUT HER TRUMP CARD
IN THIS CASE 'TWAS A BROKEN THUMB BONE

ADDING TO THE CONFUSION OF THE WEEK
ON MONDAY RANDALL'S KNEE WAS 'SCOPED
DESPITE DENNY'S ASSURANCES HE WILL PLAY
ON FIEDLER THE VIKES WILL HANG THEIR HOPES

"IT'S A GOOD THING IT'S JUST CINCINNATI"
IS HOW THE VIKINGS' TALK HAS RUN
BUT DON'T FORGET TWO WEEKS AGO THEY LED THE BUCS
UNTIL JUST BEFORE THE FINAL GUN

~ ~ ~ ~ ~ ~ ~ ~ ~ ~ ~ ~ ~ ~ ~ ~ ~ ~

THE PACKERS CONTINUED WITH THEIR TREND
OF LOSING NIGHT-TIME FOOTBALL GAMES
THEY ARE SIX-AND-0 ON SUNDAYS
IF ONLY THE OFF-DAY RECORD COULD BE THE SAME

THEN TRAGEDY STRUCK THE PACKERS
ONCE AGAIN WITH JERVEY'S LOSS
IT SEEMS THE PACKERS' BACKS HAVE BEEN UNLUCKY
FROM THE SEASON'S OPENING COIN TOSS

BUT THE GREEN BAY TEAM WON'T GIVE UP
HOLMES AND HARRIS WILL SHOULDER THE LOAD
AND ALTHOUGH THE PATH WON'T BE EASY
THE PACK IS STILL ON THE PLAYOFF ROAD

THE GREEN BAY TEAM IS SMARTING
FROM THE LOSS TO THE PITTSBURGH TEAM
BOTH THE PLAYERS AND COACHES ARE FRUSTRATED
AND LOOKING TO BLOW OFF SOME STEAM

RESULTS:
Green Bay beat the
New York Giants 37-3

Minnesota beat the
Cincinnati Bengals 24-3

THE NEW YORK GIANTS ARE THE TEAM
WHO WILL FEEL THE PACKER'S WRATH
DON'T LET THE KIDS WATCH ON SUNDAY
FOR IT WILL BE A "GIANT" BLOODBATH

63

GB: 7-3
MN: 9-1

PACKERS "VERSES" VIKINGS

~ Carl Nelson

ON A MONDAY NIGHT BACK IN OCTOBER
THE PACK WAS EMBARRASSED BY THE 'QUEENS
COULD THAT SCENARIO BE REPLAYED?
THE ANSWER ON SUNDAY WILL BE SEEN

SINCE THAT GAME THE PACKERS
AT TIMES HAVE PLAYED LIKE THEY'RE STILL SHAKEN
BUT IF ONE ASSUMES THEY'VE LOST THEIR EDGE
I'M AFRAID THAT YOU'RE SADLY MISTAKEN

THE VIKES HAVE BEEN A JUGGERNAUT
LOSING ONLY ONE GAME UP 'TIL NOW
THE RUNNING GAME HAS BEEN WORKING
AND THE LONG BOMBS PROVIDE THE "WOW"

BUT THE WINS HAVEN'T COME AS EASILY
FOR THE VIKES THE LAST FEW WEEKS
WHILE THAT TEAM REMAINS PRODUCTIVE
I WONDER IF THEY'VE REACHED THEIR PEAK

CUNNINGHAM HAS A SORE KNEE
RANDY MOSS IS NO LONGER A SURPRISE
CARTER REED AND ROBERT SMITH WILL BE THE FOCUS
OF THE PACKERS' DEFENSE'S EYES

BUT HOW CAN THAT GROUP BE DEFENDED
WHEN THEY ATTEMPT TO RUN OR PASS?
KEEP ROBERT SMITH GOING LEFT AND RIGHT
AND KNOCK CUNNINGHAM ON HIS ASS

THE VIKINGS' LINE IS A LITTLE NICKED
AND IS LETTING SOME DEFENDERS THROUGH
AND WHEN IT'S HOLLIDAY BUTLER AND REGGIE WHITE
RANDALL WILL BE SINGING THE BLUES

THE PACK'S DEFENSE WHO TOOK THE GAME OFF
ON THAT RAINY OCTOBER MONDAY NIGHT
HAS SINCE REGAINED ITS FOOTING
AND WON'T GIVE UP YARDS WITHOUT A FIGHT

~ ~ ~ ~ ~ ~ ~ ~ ~ ~ ~ ~ ~ ~ ~ ~ ~ ~ ~ ~

NOW BRETT FAVRE MAY HAVE TOSSED A FEW PICKS
BUT HE'S THROWN THE TOUCHDOWNS TOO
THE DEFENSIVE BACK WHO BITES ON THE FAKE
WILL QUICKLY FIND HE'S SCREWED

THAT THE RUNNING GAME HAS STUMBLED
SINCE LEVENS' LOSS IS SADLY TRUE
BUT DARICK HOLMES MAY JUST HAVE THE TALENT
TO HELP THE PACKERS' TEAM COME THROUGH

FREEMAN BROOKS AND MARK CHMURA
ALONG WITH TYRONE DAVIS AN EMERGING STAR
ALL HAVE GOOD SPEED AND SURE HANDS
A COMBO THAT WILL HELP THE PACK GO FAR

BACK IN OCTOBER THE VIKINGS' DEFENSE
GAVE THE GREEN BAY PACKERS FITS
THE LINE GOT GOOD PENETRATION
AND THE SECONDARY GOT SOME LATE HITS

AS ALWAYS THAT GROUP IS ANCHORED
BY THE HYPERACTIVE JOHNNY RANDLE
WHO DUE TO HIS SPEED AND INTENSITY
CAN BE PRETTY TOUGH TO HANDLE

BUT GREEN BAY'S "O" LINE IS PLAYING BETTER
THAN IT WAS ON THAT FATEFUL NIGHT
NO ONE WILL GET TO THE PACKERS' QUARTERBACK
WITHOUT FACING QUITE A FIGHT

TOSS IN THE REVENGE FACTOR
FOR DOUG PEDERSON'S BROKEN JAW
AND WE WILL SEE A PACKERS' TEAM
WHO TRULY INSPIRES AWE

WHILE THE VIKES HAVE BEEN THIS GOOD ALL YEAR
THE PACKERS CONTINUE TO IMPROVE
THEY'LL HAVE SOME STARS REJOINING THEM SOON
WHEN IT'S TIME TO MAKE THEIR MOVE

THE PACK HAS PLAYED THROUGH INJURIES
THAT WOULD HAVE CRIPPLED MANY TEAMS
AND REMAIN ALIVE IN THE PLAYOFF HUNT
RETAINING THEIR "SUPER" DREAM

THERE'S TALK FROM AND ABOUT THE VIKINGS
HOSTING SOME PLAYOFF GAMES AT THEIR HOME
THE OUTCOME OF THE NEXT FEW GAMES
WILL SHOW IF THERE'LL BE ANY IN THE 'DOME

TO SAY SUNDAY'S GAME HAS SOME IMPORTANCE
MAY BE THE UNDERSTATEMENT OF THE YEAR
A VIKINGS' WIN WILL PUT THEM NEARLY OUT OF REACH
A LOSS BRINGS GREEN BAY UNCOMFORTABLY NEAR

THE PACK WILL FINISH SUNDAY
FAR CLOSER THAN MINNESOTA LIKES
WHILE GETTING EVEN FOR THE OTHER GAME
AS THEY DEFEAT THE VIKES

RESULTS:
Green Bay lost to the
Minnesota Vikings 28-14

GB: 7-4
MN: 10-1

~ Carl Nelson

PACKERS "VERSES" VIKINGS

THE VIKINGS SHOWED WHY THEY'RE IN FIRST
WITH THEIR HANDLING OF THE PACK
THEY SCORED ON TWO EARLY TURNOVERS
TAKING THE LEAD AND NEVER LOOKING BACK

WHILE THEY WEREN'T TOTALLY DOMINANT
THEY KEPT THE GAME IN HAND ALL DAY
THEY MADE THE BIG PLAY WHEN THEY HAD TO
AND THAT WAS ENOUGH TO WIN SUNDAY

BUT "THERE'S NO REST FOR THE WICKED"
AS THE OLD-TIME SAYING GOES
THAT THE VIKES PLAY IN DALLAS ON THURSDAY
IS THE EXAMPLE THIS YEAR'S SCHEDULE SHOWS

THE 'POKES AFTER A SLOW START
ARE BEGINNING TO PICK UP SOME SPEED
THEY ARE ALWAYS TOUGH ON THANKSGIVING DAY
AND NOW THE VIKES HAVE LOST JAKE REED

THE COWBOYS LIVE AND DIE WITH POWER RUNNING
THERE'S SOME PASSING BUT IT MOSTLY FALLS TO EMMITT
LOOK FOR MINNESOTA'S "D" LINE TO BE MANHANDLED
AND FOR THE 'POKES TO GIVE THE VIKINGS FITS

~ ~ ~ ~ ~ ~ ~ ~ ~ ~ ~ ~ ~ ~ ~ ~ ~ ~ ~

THE "BLACK HOLE OF PRO FOOTBALL"
IS WHERE THE MINNESOTA VIKINGS PLAY
STRANGE THINGS HAPPEN ON THAT FIELD
AS WAS EVIDENCED LAST SUNDAY

BRETT FAVRE FUMBLED NOT ONCE BUT TWICE
AND THEN THREW THE TOUCHDOWN PICK
ALTHOUGH HE PLAYED WELL AFTER THAT
THE EARLY MISCUES DID THE TRICK

RANDY MOSS COULD MAKE A CAREER
OUT OF PLAYING AGAINST THE PACK
HOW DOES HE MANAGE TO CATCH THOSE BALLS
WHILE SURROUNDED BY DEFENSIVE BACKS?

THE PACK MUST NOW READJUST THEIR SIGHTS
THEY'LL NOT WIN THE CENTRAL DIVISION CROWN
A WILD CARD WILL BE THE PLAYOFF TICKET
AND PROVIDE A CHANCE TO BRING THE VIKINGS DOWN

THE PHILADELPHIA EAGLES WILL PROVIDE THE START
TO A SEASON-ENDING WINNING STREAK
THAT WILL ALLOW THE PACK TO ROLL INTO THE PLAYOFFS
JUST AS THEY'RE REACHING THEIR PEAK

RESULTS:
Green Bay beat the
Philadelphia Eagles 24-16

Minnesota beat the
Dallas Cowboys 46-36

GB: 8-4
MN: 11-1

PACKERS "VERSES" VIKINGS

~ Carl Nelson

SINCE THE VIKES CRUSHED THE 'POKES ON TURKEY DAY
THERE HAS BEEN A LINGERING DOUBT
SINCE THE VIKINGS APPEAR ABLE TO SCORE AT WILL
WHY WASN'T THAT GAME MORE OF A BLOWOUT?

THE VIKINGS ARE TRULY AN AMAZING TEAM
CLEARLY THE CLASS OF THE NFC
SO WHAT IS IT ABOUT THESE GUYS
THAT SOMEHOW DOESN'T FEEL QUITE REAL TO ME?

MY PERCEPTION IS NEITHER HERE NOR THERE
AND DOESN'T MATTER MORE THAN A WHIT
BUT HAVEN'T ALL THOSE FANS IN THEIR NEW PURPLE
FELT IT JUST A LITTLE TINY BIT?

REED IS GONE FOR THE SEASON
THOUGH HE'LL BE BACK FOR THE PLAYOFFS NEVER FEAR
AND THE KNEE OF SMITH IS INJURED
AS IT IS ALMOST EVERY YEAR

SUNDAY NIGHT IT WILL BE THE BEARS
WHO TRY TO SLOW THE VIKE'S MACHINE
WILL THE OFFENSIVE ONSLAUGHT CONTINUE?
THE ANSWER TO THAT MUST STILL BE SEEN

~ ~ ~ ~ ~ ~ ~ ~ ~ ~ ~ ~ ~ ~ ~ ~ ~ ~

THE PACKERS HAD TO WORK HARD
TO LEAVE PHILLY IN THE DUST
EVEN THOUGH PLAYING AT HOME
THEY SEEMED COVERED WITH LAMBEAU RUST

THIS GAME SHOWED THE HAZARDS
OF THIS TIME OF THE SEASON
AND WHY NO OPPONENT CAN BE OVERLOOKED
THE POTENTIAL FOR UPSET IS THE REASON

WHILE THE PACK IS GETTING HEALTHIER
WITH LEVENS' RETURN AND THAT OF MAYES
THE INJURY BUG GOT FREEMAN AND CHMURA
ON THE FOOTBALL FIELD SUNDAY

WHILE THAT WILL MAKE THE TASK MORE DIFFICULT
AND CERTAINALY NOT TO THE PACKERS' LIKING
GREEN BAY MUST STILL WIN OUT
TO EARN A THIRD SHOT AT MINNESOTA'S VIKINGS

RESULTS:
Green Bay lost to the
Tampa Bay Buccaneers 22-24

Minnesota beat the
Chicago Bears 48-22

THE BUCCANEERS OF TAMPA BAY
ARE THE NEXT TEAM IN THE PACKERS' SIGHTS
AND THE MYTH WILL FINALLY BE LAID TO REST
THAT GREEN BAY CAN'T WIN GAMES PLAYED AT NIGHT

Week 15
Dec. 13
1998

GB: 8-5
MN: 12-1
Central
Division
Champs

PACKERS "VERSES" VIKINGS ~ Carl Nelson

SOMETIMES IT SEEMS THE VIKINGS
JUST CAN'T DO ANYTHING WRONG
IF THE RUNNING GAME'S NOT WORKING
THEY JUST TOSS THE FOOTBALL LONG

THIS IS NOT THE VIKINGS' TEAM
NORMALLY SEEN AT THIS TIME OF YEAR
FIGURING OUT THE SLIM WILD-CARD CHANCES
THAT IN THE POST SEASON THEY'LL APPEAR

THE VIKE FANS AREN'T QUITE USED TO THIS
THEY'RE STILL TRACING OUT THE PLAYOFF PATH
A TASK THAT'S NEVER AN EASY ONE
EVEN WHEN PROFICENT WITH THE "NEW" MATH

BUT THE MESSAGE HERE IS A SIMPLE ONE:
"YOUR TEAM'S WINNING YOU DAMNED FOOLS!"
JUST RELAX AND ENJOY THE RIDE
AND LEAVE THE MATH TO THOSE IN SCHOOL

THE VIKES WILL HAVE THE HOME FIELD
FROM THE PLAYOFFS' START UNTIL THEIR END
UNLESS THINGS LIKE TAUNTING OPPONENTS
COMES BACK TO BITE THEM IN THE END!

~ ~ ~ ~ ~ ~ ~ ~ ~ ~ ~ ~ ~ ~ ~ ~ ~

MONDAY NIGHT THE PACKERS LOOKED
QUITE A LOT LIKE THE TEAM THEY ARE
ONE WITH AN OVERWHELMING INJURY LOAD
AND A STRUGGLING SUPERSTAR

THE PACKERS HAVE THE MARKET CORNERED
ON PLAYERS WITH BROKEN BONES
BILLY SCHROEDER JUST GOT HIS CLAVICLE
AND THERE HAVE BEEN FOUR BROKEN LEGS ALONE

THROW IN SOME ANKLES, KNEES AND HAMSTRINGS
AND THE USUAL LIGAMENT AND CARTILAGE TEARS
AND IT WILL BE SURPRISING IF THE PACKERS
CAN FIELD A TEAM AGAINST THE BEARS

RESULTS:
Green bay beat the
Chicago Bears 26-20

Minnesota beat
Baltimore Ravens 38-28

BUT HOLD YOUR HEADS HIGH PACKERS FANS
THERE'S REALLY NO REASON TO WORRY
FOR THIS WEEK CHICAGO COMES TO LAMBEAU
AND THAT WILL MAKE THE PACK FEEL BETTER IN A HURRY

IT'S REALLY TOO BAD OUR FAVORITE EX-PACKER
EDGAR BENNETT IS THE RUNNING BACK'S NAME
STANDS IN GREEN BAY'S ROAD INTO THE PLAYOFFS
AND MUST BE CRUSHED DURING THIS GAME

PACKERS "VERSES" VIKINGS ~ Carl Nelson

MINNESOTA'S WIN IN BALTIMORE
LEFT A LITTLE SOMETHING TO BE DESIRED
THE OFFENSE PRODUCED ONLY TWO TOUCHDOWNS
BUT THE KICKER'S LEG GOT TIRED

YES FANS THE RAVENS' DEFENSE
GAVE DENNY AND HIS STAFF FITS
THEY COMPLETELY SNUFFED THE RUNNING GAME
AND GOT TO CUNNINGHAM WITH SOME HITS

BUT WHEN THINGS ARE GOING WELL
THE BREAKS SEEM TO FALL YOUR WAY
SIX TIMES THE RAVENS TURNED IT OVER
AND NO GAME IS WON THAT WAY

SPEAKING OF LUCK HOW ABOUT THIS WEEK'S GAME
WITH THE JAGS FORCED TO START A THIRD-STRING QB?
WHAT SHOULD HAVE BEEN QUITE A FOOTBALL GAME
HAS BEEN DECIDED BY INJURIES TO TWO KNEES

SO THE VIKES SHOULD END THE SEASON
WITHOUT LOSING A GAME AT HOME
THE BRUNELL-LESS JAGUARS DON'T HAVE A CHANCE
IN THE HOT AIR-FILLED METRODOME

~ ~ ~ ~ ~ ~ ~ ~ ~ ~ ~ ~ ~ ~ ~ ~ ~ ~

THE BEARS ROLLED INTO LAMBEAU
AND STARTED THE GAME OFF WITH A ROAR
EDGAR BENNETT HAD HIMSELF A LONG RUN
AND THE BEARS MOVED DOWN THE FIELD TO SCORE

THE PACKERS STARTED SLOWLY
AS THEY SEEM TO DO THESE DAYS
BUT BEHIND THE ARM OF FAVRE
THEY RETURNED TO THEIR WINNING WAYS

DORSEY LEVENS LOOKED QUITE GOOD
RUNNING THROUGH THE BEARS AT WILL
TO SEE HIM BREAKING TACKLES ONCE AGAIN
PROVIDED PACKER FANS WITH THRILLS

TENNESEE'S SOON-TO-BE "TITANS"
PROVIDE THE CHALLENGE FOR THIS WEEK
THEY'LL BRING A GOOD BACK IN WITH THEM
AND A QB WHO'S QUICK ON HIS FEET

BUT THE PACKERS DON'T LOSE IN DECEMBER
ESPECIALLY AT LAMBEAU FIELD
TENNESEE STANDS IN THE PLAYOFF PATH
AND THEY WILL QUICKLY BE FORCED TO YIELD

GB: 9-5
MN: 13-1
Central
Division
Champs

RESULTS:
Green Bay beat the
Tennessee Oilers 30-22

Minnesota beat the
Jacksonville Jaguars 50-10

GB: 10-5
MN: 14-1
Central
Division
Champs

PACKERS "VERSES" VIKINGS ~ Carl Nelson

HOLY SMOKES! IT'S CHRISTMAS
FOOTBALL SEASON IS NEARLY DONE
FOR ALL MINNESOTA VIKINGS FANS
IT'S BEEN A SEASON FULL OF FUN

SANTA CAME EARLY TO MINNESOTA
WAY BACK THERE IN THE SPRING
GIVING RANDY MOSS TO THE VIKINGS
AND WASN'T THAT A WONDEROUS THING?

RANDALL CUNNINGHAM'S PLAY IS A GIFT TOO
COMPLETING PASSES SHORT AND LONG
HOARD AND SMITH HAVE BEEN RUNNING WELL
SPARKING THE VIKINGS' TOUCHDOWN SONG

YES THIS SEASON HAS BEEN A GIFT
TO VIKING FANS WHO WERE SOMEWHAT NEEDY
NOW THEY MUST JUST TRY TO NOT ANGER SANTA
BY BEING MORE THAN A LITTLE GREEDY

THE OILERS ARE THIS WEEK'S FOE
A TEAM PLAYING FOR ONLY PRIDE
THEY'LL DO THEIR BEST TO BEAT THE VIKES
BUT WON'T SLOW THE VICTORY RIDE

~ ~ ~ ~ ~ ~ ~ ~ ~ ~ ~ ~ ~ ~ ~ ~ ~ ~

THE PACKERS TOO WERE VISITED
BUT IT WAS SANTA'S EVIL TWIN
WHO HAS THROWN A MULTITUDE OF INJURIES
IN THE PATH OF PACKERS' WINS

YES THE ORTHOPAEDISTS HAVE EARNED THEIR FEES
WITH 'SCOPES AND SCREWS AND PLASTER
ONLY GREAT HEART AND BRETT FAVRE'S ARM
KEPT THIS YEAR FROM BEING A DISASTER

THE BRIGHT SPOTS HAVE BEEN FEW AND FAR BETWEEN
BUT STILL THE PACK HAS WON TEN GAMES
JUST IMAGINE, FANS, HOW GOOD THEY'D HAVE LOOKED
COULD THE LINEUP HAVE JUST REMAINED THE SAME

YET THE PACKERS HAVE REACHED THE PLAYOFFS
FOR THE SIXTH YEAR IN A ROW
IT'S UP TO THEM AND THEIR HEALTH
JUST HOW FAR THE PACK CAN GO

THE BEARS THIS WEEK HOST THE BOYS
IN GOLD AND HUNTER GREEN
WHETHER THEY WILL LIE DOWN OR RISE UP STRONG
ON SUNDAY WILL BE SEEN

SO MERRY CHRISTMAS TO ONE AND ALL
WHETHER YOU TEAM WEARS PURPLE OR GREEN
MAY YOUR FAMILY AND FRIENDS ENRICH YOU
BEYOND YOUR WILDEST DREAMS

70

RESULTS:
Green Bay beat the
Chicago Bears 16-13

Minnesota beat the
Tennessee Oilers 26-16

~ Carl Nelson

PACKERS "VERSES" VIKINGS

WHAT A SEASON FOR THE VIKINGS
SETTING RECORDS BY THE SCORE
AND NOW TO PLAY IN THE BIG GAME
THEY HAVE TO WIN ONLY TWO MORE

AS IS BEFITTING OF THEIR POSITION
THEY HAVE THE FIRST WEEK AS A "BYE"
NOW THEY'LL WATCH THE OTHER TEAMS
TO BE THEIR NEXT OPPONENT VIE

THERE'LL BE MORE TO SAY ABOUT THE VIKINGS
BUT SINCE THEY WON'T PLAY A GAME THIS WEEK
IT IS THE GREEN BAY PACKERS
ABOUT WHOM THIS TOME WILL SPEAK

~ ~ ~ ~ ~ ~ ~ ~ ~ ~ ~ ~ ~ ~ ~ ~ ~ ~ ~

FOUR STRAIGHT YEARS WITH AT LEAST ELEVEN WINS
AND SIX STRAIGHT TIMES IN THE POST-SEASON
PACKERS FANS HAVE BECOME QUITE SPOILED
AND THE TEAM'S EXCELLENCE HAS BEEN THE REASON

GREEN BAY HAS BATTLED BRAVELY
AGAINST ODDS SO VERY LONG
AND NOW BEGINS THE PLAYOFFS
WHICH IS WHERE THE PACK BELONGS

THIS YEAR'S TRIP INTO THE PLAYOFFS COMES
THROUGH THE ENTRANCE LABELED "WILD CARD"
THAT MEANS NO GAME AT LAMBEAU
AND THAT THE JOURNEY WILL BE HARD

THE PACK WILL TRAVEL TO CALIFORNIA
TAKING ON THE 'NINERS SUNDAY AFTERNOON
WHILE GREEN BAY HAS BEATEN THEM SIX TIMES RUNNING
I'M SURE TO THEM THIS REMATCH COMES FAR TOO SOON

THE PACKERS' WOUNDED SHOULD HAVE RETURNED
BY THE TIME OF SUNDAY'S STARTING GUN
BUT SAN FRANCISO WILL BE READY TO PLAY
BENEATH A SHINING CALIFORNIA SUN

THE PACKERS NEED TO PLAY A PERFECT GAME
WITH THE PASS AND GROUND GAMES MESHING
SHURMER'S DEFENSE MUST PLAY SMART
AND BLITZ ENOUGH TO KEEP THE 'NINERS GUESSING

WHEN THOSE PARTS COME ALL TOGETHER
UNDER HOLMGREN'S GUIDING HAND
THE PACK WILL MOVE ON THROUGH THE PLAYOFF MAP
AND HEAD OFF TO VIKINGLAND!

GB: 0-0
Defending NFC Champs

MN: 0-0
Central Division Champs

RESULTS:
Green Bay lost to the San Francisco 49ers 27-30

Minnesota was on their "Bye Week"

GB: 0-1
(Eliminated from
the post season)
MN: 0-0

PACKERS "VERSES" VIKINGS ~ Carl Nelson

THE PACKERS CHECKED OUT OF THE PLAYOFFS
IN ABOUT THE BEST WAY A TEAM COULD
LOSING A CLOSE GAME TO AN EXCELLENT TEAM
AFTER PLAYING JUST AS HARD AS THEY COULD

BUT THE PACKERS CAN GO INTO THE OFF-SEASON
HOLDING THEIR HEADS UP PROUD AND HIGH
THEY HAD TO OVERCOME A LOT THIS YEAR
AND STILL GAVE IT A HELL OF A TRY

~ ~ ~ ~ ~ ~ ~ ~ ~ ~ ~ ~ ~ ~ ~ ~ ~ ~ ~

THE VIKES SHOULD BE HAPPY AND HEALTHY
AFTER A COUPLE OF WEEKS TO WATCH AND WAIT
THEY'LL ROLL INTO THIS WEEK'S GAME AT THE METRODOME
BELIEVING THAT THEIR CHANCES WILL BE GREAT

AFTER ALL IT'S THE ARIZONA CARDINALS
TRAVELING TO THE LAND OF FROZEN LAKES AND SNOW
IN THE PLAYOFFS FOR THE FIRST TIME SINCE EIGHTY-TWO
HOW FAR DO THEY THINK THEY'LL GO?

THE VIKING TEAM BRINGS TO THE FIELD
A TEAM WITH INCREDIBLE OFFENSIVE FIREPOWER
HAVING A STRONG-ARMED AND CRAFTY OLD QUARTERBACK
AND RECEIVERS SO TALL OVER DEFENSES THEY ALL TOWER

MINNESOTA'S DEFENSE IS ALSO FORMIDABLE
AS LONG AS THAT OFFENSE GIVES THEM THE LEAD
THOUGH NOT KNOWN FOR BEING VERY LARGE
THEY COMPENSATE WITH GREAT SPEED

SO WHAT CHANCE DO THE CARDINALS HAVE?
WHY WOULD THEY RISK RAISING THE VIKING IRE?
THEY'RE A YOUNG TEAM, THAT IS PRETTY GOOD
AND THEY PLAY WITH HEART AND FIRE

BEHIND THE ARM OF A MAN KNOWN AS "THE SNAKE"
AND THE LEGS OF ADRIAN MURRELL
THE CARDS COULD MAKE THIS GAME INTERESTING
IF THEY CAN TRANSLATE THAT FIRE INTO PLAYING WELL

THE CARDS' DEFENSE IS A STINGY ONE
NOT YIELDING YARDS WITHOUT A FIGHT
THEY POSSESS TWO TALENTED CORNERBACKS
WHO CAN PLAY A COVERAGE TIGHT

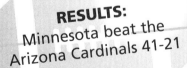

RESULTS:
Minnesota beat the
Arizona Cardinals 41-21

BUT THE VIKES WILL SURELY WIN THIS GAME
AS LONG AS THEY KEEP ONE THOUGHT IN THEIR HEAD
IF THEY SHOW UP THE LEAST BIT COMPLACENT
THEIR SUPER BOWL HOPES COULD WIND UP DEAD

PACKERS "VERSES" VIKINGS ~ Carl Nelson

THE VIKINGS HAD THE CARDS FOR LUNCH
IN THE METRODOME ON SUNDAY LAST
THE CARDS' RUNNING GAME GOT STUFFED EARLY ON
AND THE SNAKE NEVER GOT SET TO PASS

YES ANOTHER VICTIM FELL
IN THE VIKINGS' PLAYOFF ONSLAUGHT
MINNESOTA HAS A LOT OF TALENT
AND THEY ARE QUITE SIMPLY HOT

RANDALL CUNNINGHAM HAS BEEN REBORN
DISCOVERING AN ARM EVEN HE DIDN'T KNOW EXISTED
WHICH MADE THE SWITCHOVER FROM BRAD JOHNSON
ONE THAT JUST COULDN'T BE RESISTED

THE RECEIVERS HAVE BEEN REMARKABLE
THOSE TARGETS OF EVERY RANDALL TOSS
CHRIS CARTER DOESN'T SEEM TO HAVE LOST ANY SPEED
AND THERE'S NOTHING MORE TO SAY 'BOUT RANDY MOSS

MINNESOTA'S DEFENSE IS THE ONE AREA
WHICH MAY GIVE VIKINGS FANS A LITTLE WORRY
IF THEY CAN'T CONTAIN MR. ANDERSON
ATLANTA COULD TAKE THE LEAD IN A HURRY

~ ~ ~ ~ ~ ~ ~ ~ ~ ~ ~ ~ ~ ~ ~ ~ ~ ~ ~

THE FALCONS FLY INTO THE METRODOME
CARRYING A RECORD OF FOURTEEN AND TWO
WHICH SHOWS THAT FOR THE CHAMPIONSHIP
THEY'RE LEGITIMATE CONTENDERS TOO

THEY BRING WITH THEM JAMAL ANDERSON
KIND OF A BARRY SANDERS BUT WITH SIZE
HE'S A YOUNG MAN GIFTED WITH FLASHING FEET
AND CARRIES REAL POWER IN HIS THIGHS

THE FALCONS' RECEIVERS ARE ALWAYS READY
TO GIVE OPPONENT'S DEFENSES A SCARE
AND SINCE CHRIS CHANDLER HAS STAYED HEALTHY
THE BALL IS OFTEN IN THE AIR

THE FALCONS' DEFENSE, LIKE MINNESOTA'S
IS BUILT TO PLAY ON TURF AND HAS GOOD SPEED
THEY'VE CAUSED MORE TURNOVERS THAN THE VIKES
AND THAT MAY PROVIDE THE EDGE THEY'LL NEED

THE MINNESOTA VIKINGS SHOULD WIN THIS GAME
THOUGH IT WON'T BE A WALKOVER LIKE LAST WEEK
THE FALCONS WILL GIVE THEM A PRETTY GOOD GAME
AND INTO THE SUPER BOWL MAY EVEN SNEAK

MN: 1-1
Atlanta: 1-0

Hell
It's that cold...

RESULTS:
Minnesota lost to the
Atlanta Falcons 27-30

73

PACKERS "VERSES" VIKINGS

HOW TO PUT INTO RHYMING WORDS
THE EMOTIONS OF THIS WEEK
HOW TRAGIC TO SEE THE VIKINGS FALL
JUST AS THE FRENZY REACHED ITS PEAK

WHEN THE VIKINGS' TEAM TOOK THE FIELD
IN THAT RAUCOUS METRODOME
NO ONE PRESENT (EXCEPT THE FALCONS)
BELIEVED THEY COULD LOSE A GAME AT HOME

THE VIKINGS MAY HAVE FIGURED
THAT THE NOISE WOULD SHAKE UP THE "BIRDS"
BUT AS THE GAME GROUND ON THE CROWD QUIETED
AND BY THE END A PIN'S DROP COULD HAVE BEEN HEARD

THE FALCONS SCORED AND THEN THE VIKES
THEN MINNESOTA THRICE AGAIN
THE GAME WAS READY TO BE PUT AWAY
THE ONLY QUESTION REMAINING WAS "WHEN"

TRYING TO PUT THIS GAME OUT OF REACH
DENNY CALLED FOR A PASSING PLAY
CUNNINGHAM WAS SACKED AND LOST THE BALL
AND THE DREAM BEGAN SLIP-SLIDING AWAY

IN THE SECOND HALF THE VIKINGS LOOKED
AS THOUGH THEY WERE A LITTLE SHAKEN
AND THOSE WHO HAD ASSUMED THE VIKES WOULD WIN
SOON WERE TO BE SHOWN THEY WERE MISTAKEN

THE HIGH-SPEED OFFENSE OF THE VIKINGS
PLAYED THAT SECOND HALF WITH SOMETHING LACKING
WHILE THEY APPEARED DAZED AND CONFUSED
ATLANTA'S TEAM JUST KEPT ATTACKING

THE FALCONS WERE WITHIN A TOUCHDOWN
WHEN GARY ANDERSON MISSED A KICK
STILL, WITH ONLY TWO MINUTES LEFT
THE VIKES WOULD SURELY TURN THE TRICK

BUT ALAS THAT DIDN'T HAPPEN
SEVENTY-ONE YARDS THE FALCONS FLEW
THEY SCORED THE TYING TOUCHDOWN
AND THEN SCORED IN THE OT, TOO

TO GIVE CREDIT TO THE FALCONS
THEY DID JUST WHAT THEY HAD TO DO
PLAYING WELL ENOUGH TO SHUT UP THE FANS
AND TO BEAT THE VIKINGS TOO

FROM DEFEAT THE FALCONS SEIZED A VICTORY
THAT STOPPED MINNESOTA'S MIAMI RUN
WHEN YOU WONDER HOW IT HAPPENED—
"THE VIKES JUST DIDN'T GET IT DONE."

Atlanta
NFC Champions

Viking's New Goal Posts

Super Bowl XXXIII
Jan. 31
1999

~ Carl Nelson

PACKERS "VERSES" VIKINGS

Denver: 1-4
Atlanta: 0-0

THE SUPER BOWL IS UPON US
THIS SEASON IS VERY NEARLY THROUGH
LAST FALL THIRTY TEAMS BEGAN A JOURNEY
THAT NUMBER HAS DWINDLED TO ONLY TWO

SOME WOULD SAY THESE AREN'T THE BEST TEAMS
IN THE CONFERENCES THEY REPRESENT
THOUGH BY WINNING ALL BUT TWO GAMES EACH
THE MESSAGE CLEARLY HAS BEEN SENT

THE BRONCOS COME INTO THIS GAME
AS THE DEFENDERS OF THE CROWN
THE FALCONS' TEAM IS THE UPSTART
WHO WILL TRY TO BRING THE BIG BOYS DOWN

THE FALCONS CAME FROM OUT OF NOWHERE
SCRATCHING AND CLAWING THEIR WAY TO THE TOP
EVERYONE THOUGHT THAT IN THE METRODOME
THE MAGICAL SEASON WOULD COME TO A STOP

BUT THE 'BIRDS GOT BY THE VIKINGS
PLAYING WITH A LOT OF GRIT AND POISE
CUNNINGHAM TO MOSS COULDN'T BEAT 'EM
NOR EVEN THE MINNESOTA FIELD'S CROWD NOISE

THE DENVER BRONCOS ON THE OTHER HAND
ALL SEASON WERE FAVORED TO REPEAT
OVERCOMING THE PRESSURE FOR FOURTEEN WEEKS
BEFORE GOING DOWN TO DEFEAT

THE PAPERS THIS WEEK ARE OVERFLOWING
WITH CONFIDENT WORDS THAT MAY NOT BE WISE
A FALCON HAS GUARANTEED A WIN
WHILE DENVER'S SHARPE IS SLAMMING ALL THOSE GUYS

BUT ON SUNDAY THE TIME FOR TALK IS THROUGH
AND IT WILL BE TIME FOR BOTH TO SHOW THEIR STUFF
JOHN ELWAY WILL BE ENDING HIS CAREER
WILL HE AND DAVIS BE ENOUGH?

CHRIS CHANDLER WHILE NOT A YOUNG MAN
IS PLAYING IN HIS VERY FIRST BIG SHOW
WITH JAMAL ANDERSON AND THAT GREAT ARM
THERE'S NO TELLING JUST HOW FAR THEY'LL GO

WATCH FOR A GAME THAT'S QUITE INTENSE
WITH HITS AND TACKLES THAT WILL MORE THAN STING
IF THE FALCONS DON'T TURN THE FOOTBALL OVER
THEY'LL LEAVE MIAMI WITH THE CHAMPION'S RING

I MAY BE REACTING TO THE FACT
THAT DENVER IS THE "CHAMP-ANNOINTED"
BUT TAKE THE FALCONS AND THE POINTS
AND YOU WON'T BE DISAPPOINTED!

RESULTS:
The Denver Broncos beat the
Atlanta Falcons 34-19

75

PACKERS

" VERSES "

VIKINGS

Green Bay Packers
Regular Season 8-8
No Postseason

Minnesota Vikings
Regular Season 10-6
Postseason 1-1

1999

Carl "Gator" Nelson

LABOR DAY HAS COME AND GONE
THE KIDS ARE ALL BACK IN SCHOOL
AFTERNOONS ARE OFTEN WARM AND SUNNY
THOUGH THE MORNINGS ARE GETTING COOL

GB: 0-0
MN: 0-0

TIME FOR OUR THOUGHTS TO TURN TO FOOTBALL
UP HERE IT'S THE VIKINGS AND THE PACK
LAST YEAR BOTH TEAMS WERE IN THE PLAYOFFS
WILL THEY BE ABLE TO MAKE IT BACK?

THE VIKINGS HAD THE KIND OF YEAR
OF WHICH DREAMS ARE MADE
BUT THEIR TRIP TO THE SUPER BOWL
HAS BEEN SOMEWHAT DELAYED

LAST YEAR THE MINNESOTA VIKINGS PLAYED
THROUGH A SEASON TOUCHED BY MAGIC
THAT THEY FELL SHORT IN THE CHAMPION'S GAME
WAS NOTHING SHORT OF TRAGIC

THE ATLANTA FALCONS CAME TO PLAY
ON A WINTER'S DAY SO COLD
THE VIKINGS TOOK AN EARLY LEAD
WHICH, ALAS, THEY COULDN'T HOLD

AND THERE IN THE MIGHTY METRODOME
WHERE MOMENTS BEFORE THE CHEERS HAD RANG
THE VIKINGS' SEASON CAME TO AN END
WITH A WHIMPER—NOT WITH A BANG

THIS SEASON OPENS WITH A TRIP
TO PLAY THOSE FALCONS ONCE AGAIN
DOWN SOUTH IN THE GEORGIADOME
WHERE THE VIKES EXPECT THIS YEAR TO END

THE VIKINGS' OFFENSE STILL LOOKS QUITE STRONG
LIKE THEY HAVEN'T REALLY CHANGED AT ALL
BUT THE LACK OF DOMINANT DEFENSE
WILL BE THIS TEAM'S DOWNFALL

THEY FOUND OUT THE OLD SAYING
"DEFENSE WINS CHAMPIONSHIPS" IS TRUE
AND UNTIL THE VIKES EMBRACE THAT CONCEPT
MINNESOTA FANS WILL WIND UP BLUE

PACKERS "VERSES" VIKINGS

~ Carl Nelson

77

PACKERS "VERSES" VIKINGS ~ Carl Nelson

THE PACKERS' SEASON CLOSED WITH A CRUSHING CATCH
OUT IN 'FRISCO'S THREE-COM PARK
THE GREEN BAY TEAM SEEMED TO HAVE IT WON
'TIL A YOUNG PASS TO OWENS FOUND ITS MARK

BUT THE PACKERS' TEAM HAD SHOWN TRUE GUTS
AT THE END OF A SEASON FILLED WITH PAIN
FOR AFTER LEVENS BROKEN LEG IN WEEK TWO
THE OFFENSE WAS NEVER QUITE THE SAME

THE LOSSES IN THE OFF-SEASON
OF HOLMGREN BROOKS AND REGGIE WHITE
HAVE CAUSED MANY FANS TO WONDER
IF THE PACK CAN BE UP FOR THE FIGHT

THE HEART OF THE PACKERS IS STILL INTACT
AS LONG AS THEY STILL HAVE BRETT FAVRE'S ARM
AND WITH A HEALTHY LEVENS AND FREEMAN'S HANDS
THE SCOREBOARD NUMBERS WILL STAY QUITE WARM

RAY RHODES ENTERS AS THE HEAD COACH
IN A TIME OF NEW BEGINNINGS
AS THE RAIDERS WILL FIND ON SUNDAY
THIS WILL BE A TIME OF WINNING

THE DEFENSE HAS A LOT TO PROVE
AND WITH REGGIE'S SHOES TO FILL
THE YOUNG PLAYERS ON THAT SIDE OF THE BALL
MUST SHOW THEY FIT THE BILL

BUT OVERALL THE PACKERS' TEAM
IS LOOKING PRETTY GOOD
AND WHEN THE POSTSEASON BERTHS ARE HANDED OUT
THE PACK WILL BE THERE LIKE THEY SHOULD

RESULTS:
Green Bay beat the
Oakland Raiders 28-24

Minnesota beat the
Atlanta Falcons 17-14

GB: 1-0
MN: 1-0

PACKERS "VERSES" VIKINGS ~ Carl Nelson

"IT'S THE REMATCH OF THE CHAMPIONSHIP"
WAS HOW LAST WEEK'S VIKINGS' GAME WAS BILLED
BUT THOSE WHO LOOKED FOR AN OFFENSIVE SHOOTOUT
AT GAME'S END WERE SOMEWHAT LESS THAN THRILLED

THE VIKINGS SHUT DOWN JAMAL AGAIN
WHILE THE 'BIRDS DID LIKEWISE TO RANDY MOSS
WHOSE BIGGEST CONTRIBUTION
CAME WHEN THE YELLOW FLAGS WERE TOSSED

MINNESOTA OWNED THE FIRST HALF
WHILE IT WAS THE FALCONS IN PART TWO
AND WASN'T IT IRONIC THAT THE WINNING POINTS
CAME FROM GARY ANDERSON'S SHOE?

NOW THE RAIDERS COME TO TOWN THIS WEEK
AFTER LOSING A CLOSE ONE TO THE PACK
WITH EX-VIKE RICH GANNON AT THE HELM
THEIR OFFENSE FINALLY SEEMS ON TRACK

NOW WILL THE VIKINGS' OFFENSE GET A WAKE-UP CALL?
OR WILL THEY CONTINUE TO LOOK AS IF THEY'RE SNOOZING?
UNLESS THEY FIND A WAY TO TURN UP THE HEAT
MINNESOTA COULD END THIS GAME BY LOSING

~ ~ ~ ~ ~ ~ ~ ~ ~ ~ ~ ~ ~ ~ ~ ~ ~ ~ ~ ~

THE PACKERS FANS WERE SCREAMING SUNDAY
CELEBRATING ANOTHER SEASON'S START
BUT BY THE END OF LAST WEEK'S GAME
THEY WERE CHEERING BRETT'S NERVE AND HEART

WITH A BRUISED AND SWOLLEN PASSING HAND
HE LED THE PACKERS DOWN THE FIELD
FOR A LAST-SECOND GAME-WINNING TOUCHDOWN
SIMPLY BECAUSE HE REFUSED TO YIELD

THIS WEEK GREEN BAY IS ON THE ROAD
TO THE PONTIAC SILVERDOME
THE PACKERS HAVE OFTEN HAD THEIR PROBLEMS
IN WHAT WAS 'TIL THIS YEAR BARRY SANDERS' HOME

BUT THIS YEAR THERE IS NO BARRY
AND THE QB IS STILL CHARLIE BATCH
WHO BY NO STRETCH OF THE IMAGINATION
COMES CLOSE TO BEING BRETT FAVRE'S MATCH

RESULTS:
Green Bay lost to the
Detroit Lions 15-23

Minnesota lost to the
Oakland Raiders 17-22

WHILE THE PACKER DEFENSE MUST BE ALERT
AND PLAY A MORE CONSISTENT GAME
IT'S THE GREEN BAY OFFENSE THAT WILL TAKE CONTROL
AND PUT THE DETROIT LIONS' TEAM TO SHAME

GB: 1-1
MN: 1-1

PACKERS "VERSES" VIKINGS ~ Carl Nelson

THERE'S AN EERIE KIND OF SILENCE
SURROUNDING THIS WEEK'S FOOTBALL GAME
NORMALLY PACKER/VIKING "SMACK" IS FLOWING
THIS YEAR IT'S JUST NOT THE SAME

COULD IT BE THAT CONFIDENCE IS LACKING
AMONG FANS OF MINNESOTA AND THE PACK?
I'M SURE THAT A BIG WIN ON SUNDAY
WILL HELP TO BRING IT BACK

~ ~ ~ ~ ~ ~ ~ ~ ~ ~ ~ ~ ~ ~ ~ ~ ~

THE RAIDERS CAME AND SAW AND CONQUERED
LAST WEEK DOWN IN THE METRODOME
MINNESOTA'S NOT USED TO BEING PUSHED AROUND
ESPECIALLY WHEN THEY ARE AT HOME

BUT THAT IS EXACTLY WHAT OCCURRED THERE
THE VIKES WERE HARDLY IN THAT GAME
LAST YEAR MINNESOTA WAS A POWERHOUSE
THIS YEAR THEY LOOK A LITTLE PLAIN

~ ~ ~ ~ ~ ~ ~ ~ ~ ~ ~ ~ ~ ~ ~ ~ ~

THE PACKERS TOO HAVE QUESTIONS
THOUGH LAST WEEK THEY PLAYED A DECENT GAME
BUT FOR TWO LIONS' DEFENSIVE LAPSES
THAT OUTCOME WOULD NOT HAVE BEEN THE SAME

THE THUMB OF BRETT FAVRE IS A PROBLEM
AS IS THE INJURY KEEPING CHEWY OFF THE FIELD
BUT LEVENS KEEPS PILING UP THE YARDS
AND THE OFFENSIVE LINE JUST DOESN'T YIELD

LAST YEAR AT LAMBEAU ON A MONDAY
MINNESOTA JUST LIT UP THE PACK
SHOWING THE TALENT OF RANDY MOSS
AGAINST MUCH SHORTER DEFENSIVE BACKS

BUT THIS YEAR RANDY HAS BEEN MORE QUIET
THOUGH THERE'S NO PROBLEM WITH RANDALL'S ARM
IT'S JUST THE VIKINGS' OFFENSIVE LINE
CAN'T KEEP HIM FROM RECURRENT HARM

THAT THE DEFENSE OF THE PACKERS
WILL HAVE ITS HANDS FULL IS SURELY TRUE
BUT WITH JUST A LITTLE PASS RUSH
THE VIKES WILL BE TRULY SCREWED

RESULTS:
Green Bay beat
Minnesota 23-20

SO WHEN THE GAME IS OVER SUNDAY
AND THE TEAMS ARE SHOWERING OFF THE BLOOD AND GRASS
ONE LOOK UP AT THE SCOREBOARD WILL SHOW
THAT THE PACKERS KICKED THE VIKINGS' ASS!

GB: 2-1
MN: 1-2

MINNESOTA FANS ARE BEGINNING TO WONDER
"WHAT IN THE WORLD IS GOING ON?"
AND MAYBE THE VIKES ARE STARTING TO REALIZE
LAST YEAR'S MAGIC MAY WELL BE GONE

WHILE THE WAY THE PACKERS PLAYED
WAS AT TIMES FAR FROM PRETTY
WHEN THE TIME CAME TO STEP UP AND WIN
GREEN BAY'S GAME WAS DOWNRIGHT GRITTY

WHILE FAVRE TO BRADFORD WAS THE PLAY
THAT SENT THE VIKINGS TO DEFEAT
THE VERY CHANCE TO MAKE THAT PLAY
CAME FROM DORSEY LEVENS' FEET

MORE THAN THAT IT WAS THE TEAM
PUTTING ALL THE PIECES TOGETHER
AFTER GIVING UP AN EARLY SCORE
THE DEFENSE SEEMED TO SAY "WHATEVER"

WHILE THE VIKINGS MOVED THE BALL
IT WAS OUT IN THE MIDDLE OF THE FIELD
BUT WHEN THE ENDZONE BEGAN TO LOOM
THE PACKERS' "D" REFUSED TO YIELD

THE PACKERS' OFFENSE TOOK WHAT MINNESOTA GAVE
AND CHIPPED AWAY AT THE LEAD THE VIKINGS HAD
BUT WHEN MOSS SCORED WITH TWO MINUTES LEFT
THINGS WERE LOOKING PRETTY BAD

BRETT FAVRE THEN TOOK THE FIELD
KEEPING THE FAITHFUL'S HOPES ALIVE
AFTER ALL IT TAKES LESS THAN TWO MINUTES
TO MOUNT A TOUCHDOWN DRIVE

DOWN THE FIELD THE PACKERS DROVE
USING RUNS AND PASSES SHORT AND LONG
BUT WHEN SCHROEDER LEFT THEM WITH FOURTH AND THREE
IT ALL SEEMED TO BE GOING WRONG

BUT THE REST AS THEY SAY IS HISTORY
WHAT ARE THE LESSONS TO BE LEARNED?
UNLESS MINNESOTA FINDS A WAY TO PLAY TOGETHER
THE SUPER BOWL DREAMS MAY SOON BE BURNED

~ ~ ~ ~ ~ ~ ~ ~ ~ ~ ~ ~ ~ ~ ~ ~ ~ ~ ~

THE BUCCANEERS ARE THE NEXT FOE
THAT THE MINNESOTA TEAM MUST FACE
LAST YEAR THE VIKINGS ONLY LOSS
CAME IN TAMPA BAY'S HOME PLACE

THE VIKINGS HAVE TO WIN THIS GAME
TO AVOID DISINTEGRATION FROM WITHIN
WHILE THE PACKERS HAVE THIS WEEK OFF
TO WEAR THE WINNER'S GRIN

PACKERS "VERSES" VIKINGS   ~ Carl Nelson

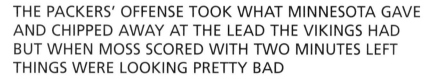

RESULTS:
Green Bay was on their
"Bye Week"

Minnesota beat
Tampa Bay 21-14

GB: 2-1
MN: 2-2

PACKERS "VERSES" VIKINGS ~ Carl Nelson

FOR JUST A LITTLE WHILE SUNDAY
IT SEEMED THE "OLD" VIKINGS HAD RETURNED
DEMONSTRATING THE DOMINATING OFFENSE
FOR WHICH THEIR FANS HAVE YEARNED

TWENTY-ONE POINTS THEY ROLLED UP
IN THE FIRST QUARTER OF THAT GAME
BUT THEN THE VIKINGS' SCORING STOPPED
AND THE OFFENSE SEEMED TO PULL UP LAME

AGAIN THE VIKINGS FOUND THEMSELVES
READY TO LOSE WITH JUST SECONDS LEFT
IT'S A GOOD THING FOR MINNESOTA
TRENT DILFER JUST ISN'T VERY DEFT

THE CHIGAGO BEARS THIS WEEK COME TO PLAY
FRESH FROM A WIN WITH SPIRITS UNDAUNTED
PERHAPS LOOKING FOR A LITTLE REVENGE
FOR THE GAME IN WHICH THEY WERE TAUNTED

DWAYNE RUDD MAY HAVE BOUGHT THE VIKES
MORE THAN THEY ARE BARGAINING FOR
IF THE BEARS CAN MOVE THE BALL
LOOK FOR THEM TO RUN UP THE FINAL SCORE

~ ~ ~ ~ ~ ~ ~ ~ ~ ~ ~ ~ ~ ~ ~ ~ ~

THE PACKERS RETURN FROM THE BYE WEEK
STILL FEELING THE GLOW FROM THEIR LAST WIN
A LAST SECOND VICTORY OVER THE VIKINGS
WHICH LEFT GREEN BAY IN FIRST AGAIN

THIS WEEK TAMPA COMES TO LAMBEAU
BRINGING A DEFENSE THAT'S PRETTY TOUGH
WARREN SAPP WILL BE BACK THIS WEEK
WILL HIS PRESENCE BE ENOUGH?

FOR THE PACK IS TOUGH TO STOP
WHEN PLAYING 'NEATH THE 'SCONNIE SKY
BRETT'S THUMB IS HEALING NICELY
SO LOOK FOR THE PIGSKIN TO REALLY FLY

TAMPA BRINGS TWO GOOD RUNNING BACKS
BUT AT QB IS OL' TRENT DILFER
WHO'S PASSING SKILLS ARE SO LIMITED
LOOK FOR GREEN BAY TWO PASSES TO PILFER

RESULTS:
Green Bay beat the
Tampa Bay Buccaneers 26-23

Minnesota lost to the
Chicago Bears 22-24

THIS GAME WON'T BE PLAYED 'TIL SUNDAY NIGHT
SO THE VIKES WILL BE ABLE TO SEE
THAT AS A BIRTHDAY GIFT TO BRETT FAVRE
THE PACK WILL PICK UP WIN NUMBER THREE

GB: 3-1
MN: 2-3

PACKERS "VERSES" VIKINGS ~ Carl Nelson

THE SEASON JUST GOT LONGER
FOR THE MINNESOTA VIKES
THERE WASN'T MUCH ABOUT LAST WEEK'S GAME
THAT ANYONE COULD LIKE

THE BEARS HAVE BEEN THE KIND OF TEAM
THAT THE VIKINGS SIMPLY KILL
BUT SUNDAY IT WAS THE BEAR FANS
WHO WERE FILLED WITH WINNING THRILLS

THIS YEAR THE THRILLS HAVE BEEN FEW
AND PRETTY FAR BETWEEN
FOR THE FANS OF THE MINNESOTA VIKINGS
"HISTORY'S MOST POTENT SCORING MACHINE"

NOW IT'S ON THE MARCH THE VIKINGS GO
TO THE PONTIAC SILVERDOME
WHERE AS THE GREEN BAY PACKERS CAN ATTEST
THE LIONS ARE HARD TO BEAT AT HOME

THE VIKINGS HAVE TO HAVE A BREAKOUT WEEK
TO GET THEMSELVES ON TRACK
OR THEY WILL PROVE THEMSELVES AS HELPLESS
AS DENNY GREEN WOULD BE UPON HIS BACK

~ ~ ~ ~ ~ ~ ~ ~ ~ ~ ~ ~ ~ ~ ~ ~ ~

LAST WEEK THE BUCS CAME TO GREEN BAY
WITH THE FEELING IN THEIR HEARTS
THAT TO BE SEEN AS TRUE CONTENDERS
A WIN AT LAMBEAU WOULD BE THE START

THEY BROUGHT THE GAME THEY PLAY BEST
AND FELT IT WOULD BE ENOUGH
NEVER ONCE GIVING CONSIDERATION
THAT IT'S AT HOME THE PACK IS MOST TOUGH

WHILE THEY GAVE IT ALL THEY HAD
AND TOOK THE LEAD QUITE NEAR THE END
AGAINST THE PACKERS' HOME MAGIC
THEY WEREN'T ABLE TO DEFEND

THIS WEEK THE PACK FLIES OFF TO DENVER
TO PLAY A BRONCOS TEAM
THAT A MERE TWO YEARS AGO
SHATTERED GREEN BAY'S REPEAT DREAM

RESULTS:
Green Bay lost to the
Denver Broncos 10-31

Minnesota lost to the
Detroit Lions 23-25

WHILE REVENGE SHOULD BE THE MOTIVE
THAT CHAMPIONSHIP TEAM IS A MERE SHELL
THE PACK SHOULD BE ABLE TO POUND THE BRONCS
AND MAKE THIS GAME A LIVING HELL

83

GB: 3-2
MN: 2-4

PACKERS "VERSES" VIKINGS ~ Carl Nelson

MINNESOTA'S STRUGGLES CONTINUED
LAST WEEK IN THE SILVERDOME
THEY'RE NOT PLAYING WELL ON THE ROAD
AND NOT MUCH BETTER WHEN AT HOME

THE VIKINGS' TEAM PLAYED A GAME
THAT WAS LARGELY UNINSPIRED
THEY SEEMED TO JUST GO THROUGH THE MOTIONS
AND LOOKED AS IF THEY WERE TIRED

GIVING CREDIT TO THE LIONS
THEY GAVE THE VIKINGS ALL THEY HAD
THE QUESTION IS "ARE THEY THAT GOOD?
OR IS MINNESOTA JUST THAT BAD?"

CUNNINGHAM FINALLY FOUND THE BENCH
THIS WEEK IT'S GEORGE WHO'LL GET THE START
HE BRINGS A REAL TALENT TO QUARTERBACK
THE ONLY QUESTION IS HIS HEART

THE 'NINERS ARE A TEAM IN FLUX
SURELY NOT THE TEAM THEY WERE LAST YEAR
BUT THEY STILL SHOULD HAVE ENOUGH
TO BRING VIKINGS FANS TO TEARS

~ ~ ~ ~ ~ ~ ~ ~ ~ ~ ~ ~ ~ ~ ~ ~ ~ ~

THE BRONCOS GAVE THE PACKERS
WHAT COULD BE CALLED A WHIPPIN'
DENVER'S GAME PLAN HAD GREEN BAY
A-STUMBLIN' AND A-TRIPPIN'

THE TACKLING DIDN'T LOOK SO GOOD
THE OFFENSE FAILED AS WELL
GREEN BAY WASN'T IN THIS GAME
FROM THE VERY STARTING BELL

CHANGES TO THE OFFENSIVE LINE
ALLOWED DENVER TO BRING THE HEAT
AND LETTING DORSEY LEVENS GET SHUT DOWN
SENT THE PACKERS TO DEFEAT

THIS WEEK IT IS THE CHARGERS
WHO WILL TEST THE COURAGE OF THE PACK
CAN RAY RHODES CORRECT THE PROBLEMS
AND BRING THE PACKERS ROARING BACK?

RESULTS:
Green Bay beat the
San Diego Chargers 31-3

Minnesota beat the
San Francisco 49ers 40-16

SAN DIEGO HAS NATRONE MEANS
A DOUBLE HANDFUL AT RUNNING BACK
BUT THIS WEEK HE WON'T BE ENOUGH
TO DERAIL A RESURGENT PACK

GB: 4-2
MN: 3-4

PACKERS "VERSES" VIKINGS   ~ Carl Nelson

THE VIKINGS OF MINNESOTA
HAVE BEEN A DISAPPOINTMENT TO THEIR FANS
BUT NOW THE RESOUNDING CHEER GOES UP
"JEFF GEORGE IS THE MAN"

IT SURELY SEEMED ON SUNDAY
HE HAD THE KEY TO THE FIREPOWER
HIS QUICK RELEASE AND CANNON ARM
LED THE VIKINGS TO THEIR FINEST HOUR

BUT THIS IS NOT UNEXPECTED
IT'S FOR THIS THAT HE IS KNOWN
THE QUESTION IS" HAS HE GROWN UP?"
THAT'S WHAT MUST STILL BE SHOWN

FLYING OUT TO DENVER
TO FACE THE BRONCS THIS WEEK
WILL PROVIDE SOME OF THE ANSWERS
THAT THE VIKINGS AND THEIR FANS SEEK

THE DENVER TEAM HAS STRUGGLED
BUT LOOK AS THOUGH THEY MAY BE REBOUNDING
GEORGE FOR THEM HOLDS NO SURPRISES
LOOK FOR THE VIKES TO TAKE A POUNDING

~ ~ ~ ~ ~ ~ ~ ~ ~ ~ ~ ~ ~ ~ ~ ~ ~ ~

THE CHARGERS ENTERED LAST SUNDAY'S GAME
WITH A DEFENSE HIGHLY REGARDED
BUT WHEN THE FINAL GUN WAS FIRED
THOSE RATINGS HAD BEEN DISCARDED

DORSEY SCORED THE FIRST RUSHING TOUCHDOWN
THE 'BOLTS HAD ALLOWED IN SIX LONG WEEKS
AND BRETT AND THE RECEIVERS
EXPLOITED THE SECONDARY'S LEAKS

THE PACKERS' DEFENSE CRUISED THE FIELD
LIKE A SCHOOL OF HUNGRY SHARKS
PICKING OFF SIX CHARGER PASSES
AND EXTINGUISHING ALL OFFENSIVE SPARKS

MONDAY NIGHT MIKE HOLMGREN
BRINGS HIS SEAHAWKS TO LAMBEAU FIELD
THE SITE OF THE FINEST YEARS
HIS FOOTBALL CAREER MAY YIELD

SEATTLE IS A GOOD YOUNG TEAM
HOLMGREN HOPES TO TAKE THEM TO THE TOP
BUT THIS WEEK ON THE GRASS AT GREEN BAY
THAT TRIP WILL MAKE AN UNEXPECTED STOP

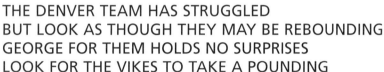

RESULTS:
Green Bay lost to the
Seattle Seahawks 7-27

Minnesota beat the
Denver Broncos 23-20

85

GB: 4-3
MN: 4-4

PACKERS "VERSES" VIKINGS ~ Carl Nelson

DENVER SEEMED TO HAVE THE NUMBER
OF JEFF GEORGE AND THE VIKES
RUNNING THE BALL NEARLY AT WILL
AND PASSING WHEN THEY LIKED

THEN THE DENVER OFFENSE FALTERED
GRIESE FUMBLED AT THE FIVE
A COUPLE OF DEFENSIVE ERRORS
LET THE VIKINGS REMAIN ALIVE

WHILE NOT EXACTLY OVERPOWERING
THE VIKINGS LAST WEEK GOT THE WIN
HELPED IN SOME SMALL WAY BY THE IMPACT
OF DWAYNE RUDD'S HELMET WITH MCCAFFERY'S CHIN

MONDAY NIGHT DALLAS BRINGS "NEON DEION"
TO TAKE ON JEFF GEORGE AND MOSS "THE FREAK"
THE 'POKES ARE MORE THAN A LITTLE BATTERED
WHILE MINNESOTA APPEARS READY TO PEAK

THE VIKES BELIEVE THEY CAN WIN OUT
THIS WEEK THEY'LL FIND THAT JUST ISN'T TRUE
AIKMAN DEION AND EMMITT SMITH
WILL LEAVE THE VIKINGS "COWBOY BLUE"

~ ~ ~ ~ ~ ~ ~ ~ ~ ~ ~ ~ ~ ~ ~ ~ ~ ~

MIKE HOLMGREN CAME BACK TO GREEN BAY
WANDERING LAMBEAU'S SIDELINES YET AGAIN
AND AS HAPPENED SO OFTEN IN THE PAST
HIS TEAM CAME AWAY WITH THE WIN

THE OFFENSE WAS NOT OUTSTANDING
HIS DEFENSE WAS LESS THAN GREAT
IT WAS INSTEAD THE MELTDOWN OF BRETT FAVRE
THAT SEALED THE PACKERS' FATE

HE THREW FOUR PICKS AND FUMBLED TWICE
HE DID MORE DAMAGE THAN THE SEAHAWKS' TEAM
BRETT MUST REALIZE HE'S NOT SUPERMAN
BEFORE HE SINKS GREEN BAY'S POSTSEASON DREAM

IT HAS BEEN FIVE LONG YEARS
SINCE CHICAGO MANAGED TO BEAT THE PACK
THIS WEEK'S GAME IS AN IMPORTANT CHANCE
FOR GREEN BAY TO GET THEMSELVES ON TRACK

THE MEN IN GREEN MUST CONCENTRATE
AND KEEP THAT WINNING STREAK ALIVE
A MORE BALANCED OFFENSE IS THE KEY
TO MAKING THE PACKERS' OFFENSE THRIVE

RESULTS:
Green Bay lost to the
Chicago Bears 13-14

Minnesota beat the
Dallas Cowboys 27-17

86

GB: 4-4
MN: 5-4

PACKERS "VERSES" VIKINGS ~ Carl Nelson

DALLAS CAME OUT LOOKING STRONG
AGAINST MINNESOTA MONDAY NIGHT
THE VIKINGS LOOKED AS IF THEY'D ROLL OVER
AND GIVE UP WITHOUT A FIGHT

BUT BEFORE THE HALF IT HAPPENED
TWO BREAKS WENT MINNESOTA'S WAY
THE FIRST BREAK WAS EMMITT'S FINGER
THE SECOND A SNAP THAT GOT AWAY

SOMEHOW GEORGE MANAGED TO THROW A BALL
INTO THE ENDZONE FOR THE SCORE
IN THE SECOND HALF THE VIKES TOOK OVER
AND THE 'POKES WERE A THREAT NO MORE

THIS WEEK THE CHICAGO BEARS ARE WONDERING
JUST WHICH VIKING TEAM THEY'LL FACE
THE ONE THAT CAN DOMINATE LATE IN A GAME
OR THE ONE THAT STINKS UP THE PLACE

A FEW WEEKS AGO BY PLAYING HARD
THE BEARS SENT THE VIKINGS TO DEFEAT
AS LONG AS THE LINEMEN WEAR THEIR CUPS
THEY HAVE A GOOD CHANCE TO REPEAT

~ ~ ~ ~ ~ ~ ~ ~ ~ ~ ~ ~ ~ ~ ~ ~ ~ ~

SUNDAY THE PACKERS TOOK TO LAMBEAU FIELD
TO FACE THE CHIGAGO BEARS
A TEAM THEY'D BEATEN TEN STRAIGHT TIMES
AND SHOULDN'T LOSE TO ON A DARE

BUT THE BEARS HAD A GAME PLAN SO CLEVER
IT MUST HAVE BEEN DEVISED BY ELVES
"SIMPLY PLAY THE PACKERS CLOSE AND TOUGH—
AND THEY'LL PROBABLY BEAT THEMSELVES"

SO THEY CAME OUT AND PLAYED BASIC BALL
RUNNING FOR MORE YARDS THAN THEY PASSED
AND AFTER BLOCKING A KICK AT GAME'S END
IT WAS THE PACKERS WHO'D BEEN OUTCLASSED

NOW IT'S ON THE ROAD TO DALLAS
TO PLAY A LONG-TIME BITTER FOE
BUT THE 'POKES ARE RIDDLED BY INJURIES
FROM AIKMAN'S HEAD TO DEION'S TOE

THIS IS NOT A GAME TO TAKE LIGHTLY
GARRETT HAS BEATEN THE PACK BEFORE
GREEN BAY'S OFFENSE HAS TO FIND ITSELF
AND PROVE THAT IT CAN RUN UP A SCORE

RESULTS:
Green Bay lost to the
Dallas Cowboys 13-27

Minnesota beat the
Chicago Bears 27-24

PACKERS "VERSES" VIKINGS ~ Carl Nelson

GB: 4-5
MN: 6-4

THE CHIGAGO BEARS GAVE MINNESOTA
ALMOST AS MUCH AS THE VIKES COULD HANDLE
BEHIND A THIRD-STRING QUARTERBACK
THEY LIT THE VIKES' DEFENSE UP LIKE CANDLES

BUT THE VIKINGS MANAGED TO HOLD ON
AND FINALLY TURNED THE TRICK
THOUGH THE GAME DID GO TO OVERTIME
THANKS TO ANDERSON'S ERRANT KICK

AS THE VIKES GO TO THE BYE WEEK
THE COACHING STAFF MUST BE PUZZLED
WHILE AT TIMES THE VIKES LOOK TERRIFIC
AT OTHER TIMES IT SEEMS THEY'RE MUZZLED

IF IT WEREN'T FOR CHRIS CARTER'S HANDS
MINNESOTA WOULDN'T HAVE A FOUR-GAME STREAK
HOW LONG CAN HE CARRY THIS TEAM
WHO WITHOUT HIM WOULD LOOK PRETTY WEAK?

CONSISTENCY IS WHAT THE GOAL MUST BE
AND WHAT THE VIKINGS TRULY NEED
FOR IF THEY ONLY PLAY WELL HALF THE TIME
THE PLAYOFF PLANS JUST WON'T SUCCEED

~ ~ ~ ~ ~ ~ ~ ~ ~ ~ ~ ~ ~ ~ ~ ~ ~ ~ ~

AS IT HAS HAPPENED SO MANY TIMES
DALLAS KICKED GREEN BAY'S BUTT AGAIN
THE PACKERS LOOKED SIMPLY AWFUL
AND THE EXCUSES ARE WEARING THIN

THE TALENT LEVEL HASN'T CHANGED THAT MUCH
SO WHY IS IT SO HARD TO PASS AND RUN?
THE TEAM SEEMS TO HAVE NO RHYTHM
AND NO ONE SEEMS TO BE HAVING FUN

IS FAVRE'S RIGHT HAND THAT DAMAGED?
OR IS IT MOTIVATION THIS TEAM LACKS?
RAY RHODES HAS TO FIND THE ANSWERS
BEFORE THE FANS DEMAND HE GETS THE AX

THIS WEEK THE DETOIT LIONS
WILL PLAY AT THE HALLOWED LAMBEAU SITE
AND IF THE PACKERS CAN'T WIN THIS GAME
THEY MAY AS WELL JUST SAY "GOOD NIGHT"

RESULTS:
Green Bay beat the
Detroit Lions 26-17

Minnesota was on their
"Bye Week"

IN THE PAST WHEN THE PACKERS PLAYED AT HOME
IT ALMOST ALWAYS GUARANTEED A WIN
THIS WEEK'S GAME WILL BE A CHANCE
TO RE-ESTABLISH THAT TRADITION ONCE AGAIN

88

GB: 5-5
MN: 6-4

PACKERS "VERSES" VIKINGS ~ Carl Nelson

COMING OUT OF THE BYE WEEK
NEW QUESTIONS FACE DENNY AND HIS STAFF
DO THE VIKINGS HAVE THE TALENT
TO SEPARATE FROM THE CENTRAL'S CHAFF?

HOW MUCH MONEY IS JEFF GEORGE WORTH?
WHAT'S THE REAL STORY ON LEROY HOARD?
IF THE VIKINGS DON'T GO ON WINNING
WILL THEIR FANS GET BORED?

WILL THE VIKINGS' LACK OF DEFENSE HURT THEM
AS THE OFFENSE REACHES ITS PEAK?
THESE THINGS ALL REMAIN TO BE SEEN
THROUGHOUT THE NEXT SIX WEEKS

THIS WEEK THE CHARGERS OF SAN DIEGO
INVADE THE TWIN CITIES' METRODOME
THIS GAME SHOULDN'T PRESENT A CHALLENGE
ESPECIALLY WITH THE VIKES AT HOME

BUT THESE GAMES ARE OFTEN TOUGHER
THAN THE OPPONENT'S RECORD SHOWS
BECAUSE THE VIKINGS TEND TO PLAY DOWN
TO THE LEVEL OF THEIR FOE

~ ~ ~ ~ ~ ~ ~ ~ ~ ~ ~ ~ ~ ~ ~ ~ ~

GREEN BAY STANDS AT A CROSSROADS
WITH PLAYOFF HOPES STILL STRANGELY ALIVE
AFTER A WIN AGAINST THE LIONS
EVENED THEIR RECORD AT FIVE AND FIVE

THE PACKERS STARTED SLOWLY
GIVING UP TWO EARLY LIONS' SCORES
GREEN BAY'S OFFENSE CONTINUED TO STRUGGLE
WORRYING PACKERS' FANS ONCE MORE

THEN GREEN BAY PICKED UP THE PACE
BRADFORD CAUGHT A TD THAT WAS ASTOUNDING
BRETT FAVRE BEGAN TO SMILE AGAIN
AND THE PACKERS STARTED REBOUNDING

FAVRE'S THUMB IS FINALLY HEALING
AND HE'S FULL OF HIS OLD TRICKS
IF THE PACKERS CAN GET BACK TO NORMAL
THEY'LL BE A FACTOR IN THE PLAYOFF MIX

MONDAY NIGHT IT'S THE FORTY-NINERS
WHO WON THE PLAYOFF GAME LAST YEAR
BUT THIS TIME IT'S THE TEAM FROM 'FRISCO
WHO WILL SHED THE LOSER'S TEARS

RESULTS:
Green Bay beat the
San Francisco 49ers 20-3

Minnesota beat the
San Diego Chargers 35-27

GB: 6-5
MN: 7-4

PACKERS "VERSES" VIKINGS ~ Carl Nelson

WHEN THE CHARGERS CAME TO MINNESOTA
NO ONE GAVE THEM A CHANCE IN HELL
BUT AFTER GIVING UP A BIG LEAD EARLY
THEY TOOK THE VIKES TO THE CLOSING BELL

WHILE THE VIKINGS' OFFENSE LOOKED IMPRESSIVE
IN THE FIRST HALF OF THE GAME
THEY TOOK A SNOOZE IN THE THIRD QUARTER
AND NEVER AGAIN REALLY LOOKED THE SAME

MINNESOTA'S DEFENSE ONCE AGAIN
PROVED TO BE THAT TEAM'S ACHILLES' HEEL
THEY COULDN'T MOUNT A PASS RUSH
AND HITCHCOCK GOT BURNED MORE THAN WILLIE TEAL

THIS WEEK THE VIKINGS GO TO TAMPA BAY
TO FACE ANOTHER TEAM TIED FOR FIRST PLACE
WILL MINNESOTA'S LINE BE UP TO THE CHALLENGE
OF KEEPING JEFF GEORGE OFF HIS FACE?

WARREN SAPP AND THE TAMPA "D"
CAN HARDLY WAIT TO GET AT THE VIKINGS
UNLESS MINNESOTA PLAYS FOUR FULL QUARTERS
THIS GAME WON'T END UP TO THEIR LIKING

~ ~ ~ ~ ~ ~ ~ ~ ~ ~ ~ ~ ~ ~ ~ ~ ~ ~ ~

WHILE THEY DON'T LOOK LIKE THE PACK OF OLD
GREEN BAY'S TEAM IS PLAYING BETTER
AS THEY SHOWED IN SAN FRANCISO
ON A NIGHT THAT COULDN'T GET ANY WETTER

WHILE THE FIRST QUARTER WASN'T IMPRESSIVE
CONTROL WAS SOON SEIZED BY THE PACK
WHO STARTED MOVING THE BALL AT WILL
AND JUST NEVER ONCE LOOKED BACK

WHILE THE PACKERS MAY HAVE WON THE GAME
ONE HAS TO WORRY ABOUT THE COST
DORSEY NOW HAS A BROKEN RIB
AND WITH ONE HIT COULD EASILY BE LOST

CHICAGO'S BEARS HAVE FACED NO OTHER TEAM
AS MANY TIMES AS THEY HAVE THE PACK
BUT THIS TIME DUE TO STEROID USE
THEY WILL HAVE LOST THEIR QUARTERBACK

RESULTS:
Green Bay beat the
Chicago Bears 35-19

Minnesota lost to the
Tampa Bay Buccaneers 17-24

DESPITE THIS THE GAME WILL BE TOUGH ANYWAY
AS THESE WARRIORS STRIVE TO PROVE WHO'S BEST
AND WHEN THE SUN GOES DOWN ON SUNDAY
CHICAGO'S PLAYOFF HOPES WILL HAVE BEEN PUT TO REST

GB: 7-5
MN: 7-5

PACKERS "VERSES" VIKINGS

~ Carl Nelson

ONE OF THE ETERNAL FOOTBALL TRUTHS
WAS AGAIN PROVEN MONDAY NIGHT
"IF YOU KEEP YOUR HEAD AND PLAY DEFENSE
IN THE END YOU'LL BE ALL RIGHT"

MONDAY NIGHT THE VIKINGS TOOK THE FIELD
RIDING A FIVE-GAME WINNING STREAK
THEIR WALK WAS SMOOTH AND CONFIDENT
SURELY THIS TEAM WAS AT ITS PEAK

TAMPA HAD A ROOKIE AT THE HELM
AND WERE MISSING A RUNNING BACK
IT WAS UP TO ALSTOTT AND THE DEFENSE
TO STEP UP AND REEL IN THE SLACK

AND THAT THEY DID WITH JARRING HITS
SHORT PASSES AND POWER RUNNING
THE BUCS CONTROLLED THE TEMPO OF THE GAME
WHICH MINNESOTA FOUND QUITE STUNNING

THE VIKES HAVE FOUND THEY'RE VULNERABLE
AND AT A TIME WHEN THEY COULD USE RELIEF
WILL HAVE TO BE LUCKY TO NOT TAKE A LOSS
FROM THE KANSAS CITY CHIEFS

~ ~ ~ ~ ~ ~ ~ ~ ~ ~ ~ ~ ~ ~ ~ ~ ~ ~

WHILE THE PACKERS STARTED SLOWLY
AND WITH A MISTAKE OR TWO
THEY TOOK CONTROL OF LAST WEEK'S GAME
HELPED BY A ROOKIE WITH "SMOKING SHOES"

THE WEATHER DOWN IN CHIGAGO
WAS REMINISCENT OF GAMES OF OLD
SOLDIER FIELD'S WINDS WERE SWIRLING
AND IT WAS RAINY WET AND COLD

MAYBE THAT WAS THE REASON THE PACKERS
REDISCOVERED THEIR RUNNING GAME
EVERYONE THOUGHT THAT WITH LEVENS OUT
IT JUST COULDN'T BE THE SAME

HOW NICE TO SEE YOUNG MR. PARKER
ADMIRABLY FILLING IN WHILE DORSEY HEALS
THIS WEEK AGAINST THE PANTHERS
WE'LL GET TO SEE IF HE'S FOR REAL

THE CAROLINA PANTHERS COME TO LAMBEAU
BRINGING A RECORD OF SEVEN AND FIVE
WITH THE RE-EMERGENCE OF THE PACKERS
THEY'LL BE LUCKY TO ESCAPE ALIVE

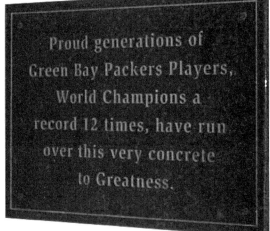

Proud generations of
Green Bay Packers Players,
World Champions a
record 12 times, have run
over this very concrete
to Greatness.

RESULTS:
Green Bay lost to the
Carolina Panthers 31-33

Minnesota lost to the
Kansas City Chiefs 28-31

BOTH THE PACKERS AND THE VIKINGS
LAST WEEKEND MANAGED TO STUMBLE
AND THE LOSSES TAKEN BY THESE TEAMS
MAY CAUSE THEIR POSTSEASON HOPES TO CRUMBLE

GB: 7-6
MN: 7-6

THE CHIEFS OF KANSAS CITY
WELCOMED THE VIKINGS TO ARROWHEAD
AN ENVIRONMENT QUITE HOSTILE
TO THOSE WHOSE UNIFORMS WEREN'T RED

THE CHIEFS MANHANDLED THE VIKE'S DEFENSE
AND TOOK AN EARLY THREE-SCORE LEAD
BUT A BIG KICK RETURN FOR A TD
WAS THE BREAK THE VIKINGS SEEMED TO NEED

MINNESOTA TRIED TO MAKE A COMEBACK
WITH THE HELP OF JEFF GEORGE AND RANDY MOSS
WHO DESPITE PUTTING TWO TD'S ON THE BOARD
WILL BE MORE REMEMBERED FOR THE FUMBLES HE LOST

~ ~ ~ ~ ~ ~ ~ ~ ~ ~ ~ ~ ~ ~ ~ ~ ~

THE PACKERS ON THE OTHER HAND
SEEMED ABLE TO MOVE THE BALL AT WILL
BUT THE INEFFECTIVENESS OF THE DEFENSE
WOULD ALLOW THE PANTHERS THE FINAL THRILL

FAVRE WAS HOT AND HIS THROWS WERE ON
AND DESPITE THE LACK OF A RUNNING GAME
IT APPEARED THAT GREEN BAY WOULD PULL IT OFF
AND COME OUT WINNERS JUST THE SAME

ALAS HOWEVER THAT WAS NOT TO BE
AS BEUERLEIN SLOWLY PICKED THE PACK APART
WAS THE PACKERS' GAME PLAN ILL-CONCEIVED?
OR WERE THE COACHES JUST NOT VERY SMART?

~ ~ ~ ~ ~ ~ ~ ~ ~ ~ ~ ~ ~ ~ ~ ~ ~ ~ ~

SO ON MONDAY OUR TEAMS MEET AGAIN
NOT IN A BATTLE FOR FIRST PLACE
BUT FOR A CHANCE TO STAY ALIVE
IN THE WILD CARD PLAYOFF RACE

THE VIKES WILL BE WITHOUT CARTER
WHILE DORSEY LEVENS WILL MAKE HIS RETURN
AS ALWAYS IT WILL BE ON ONE BIG PLAY
THAT THIS GAME'S OUTCOME WILL TURN

WHILE THE PACKERS DON'T SEEM TO PLAY WELL
IN THE HUBERT H HUMPHREY METRODOME
IT WILL TYPIFY THE VIKINGS' YEAR
TO BE SWEPT BY THE PACK AT HOME

PACKERS "VERSES" VIKINGS ~ Carl Nelson

92

RESULTS:
Green Bay lost to the
Minnesota Vikings 20-24

GB: 7-7
MN: 8-6

PACKERS "VERSES" VIKINGS ~ Carl Nelson

'TWAS THE WEEK BEFORE CHRISTMAS
AND ALL THROUGH THE 'DOME
VIKES FANS WERE ROCKING
FOR A BIG GAME AT HOME

RAY RHODES PACED THE SIDELINES
CHOMPING ON HIS GUM
WHILE DENNY HOPED HIS VIKINGS
WOULDN'T MAKE HIM LOOK DUMB

THE GAME STARTED BADLY
FOR THE FANS OF THE PACK
WITH TWO BRETT FAVRE FUMBLES
AS THE RESULT OF TWO VIKINGS' SACKS

BUT THE PACKERS REBOUNDED
WITH THE HELP OF DORSEY LEVENS
WHOSE RUNS THROUGH THE VIKINGS
LOOKED LIKE GIFTS FROM THE HEAVENS

THE PACKERS' PASSES HOWEVER
DIDN'T WORK OUT SO NEAT
WITH GREEN BAY'S RECEIVERS
HAVING THE BALLS HIT THEIR FEET

EARLY IN THE GAME MINNESOTA
WASN'T EXACTLY WHAT YOU'D CALL "NIFTY"
ONE TIME JEFF GEORGE FUMBLED
LEAVING THEM WITH THIRD-AND-FIFTY

WHILE THE PACKERS' DEFENSE
PLAYED WELL IN PATCHES
THEY STILL COULDN'T DEFEND
RANDY MOSS AND HIS CATCHES

NOW BOTH TEAMS' PLAYOFF HOPES
ARE IN THE HANDS OF OTHERS
WITH THE VIKES SENDING GOOD WISHES
TO THEIR WISCONSIN BROTHERS

THE PACKERS LIKEWISE
NEED THE VIKINGS TO WIN
A LOSS BY THE GIANTS
MAY HELP GREEN BAY SNEAK IN

SO WITH TWO WEEKS REMAINING
WE'LL SEE WHAT FATE DISHES
ALL THAT REMAINS TO BE SAID IS
"BEST HOLIDAY WISHES!!"

RESULTS:
Green Bay lost to the
Tampa Bay Buccaneers 10-29

Minnesota beat the
New York Giants 34-17

PACKERS "VERSES" VIKINGS ~ Carl Nelson

THE VIKES WENT OUT TO THE MEADOWLANDS
WHERE JIMMY HOFFA RESTS
TO FACE THE NEW YORK GIANTS' TEAM
BOTH WERE ON A PLAYOFF QUEST

THE VIKES AS USUAL STARTED SLOWLY
ALLOWING THE "G-MEN" LONG SCORING DRIVES
BUT THAT SCORING WAS ONLY FIELD GOALS
LETTING MINNESOTA STAY ALIVE

THEN AS OFTEN SEEMS TO HAPPEN
BIG VIKINGS' PLAYS APPEARED
RANDY MOSS THREW FOR A TOUCHDOWN
AND SMITH SCORED HIS FIRST OF THE YEAR

THE VIKINGS LOCKED UP A PLAYOFF SPOT
BY BEATING UP THE LOWLY "ANTS"
A TEAM THAT WAS LESS THAN STELLAR
AND NEVER REALLY HAD A CHANCE

THIS WEEK'S FOE THE DETROIT LIONS
GOT OVER ON THE VIKINGS ONCE THIS YEAR
IF THE VIKES LOOK PAST THIS TEAM
THEY'LL BE KICKING THEMSELVES IN THE REAR

~ ~ ~ ~ ~ ~ ~ ~ ~ ~ ~ ~ ~ ~ ~ ~ ~ ~

HOW MUCH MORE MOTIVATION
COULD HAVE BEEN NEEDED BY THE PACKERS?
THEIR DESTINY WAS IN THEIR HANDS
WHY DID OUR TEAM APPEAR SUCH SLACKERS?

BRETT FAVRE NEVER GOT IN THE GROOVE
LEVENS NEVER GOT ON TRACK
THE DEFENSE PLAYED WELL FOR A HALF
BUT WOUND UP ON THEIR BACK

THE BUCCANEERS JUST GROUND IT OUT
AND SHOWED A DEFENSE THAT IS TOUGH
WHILE THEY WEREN'T QUITE SPECTACULAR
THEY MADE PLAYS THAT WERE BIG ENOUGH

THIS WEEK THE ARIZONA CARDINALS
ARE THE SEASON'S CLOSING FOE
WILL THE JANUARY TRIP TO LAMBEAU
MAKE THEM PLAY IN THE COLD AND SNOW?

THE BALMY WEATHER TYPIFIES
THE PACKERS' CRAZY SEASON
WHO'D HAVE THOUGHT THEY'D HAVE TO WIN
TO SIMPLY MAKE THEIR RECORD EVEN?

(Hanging on
by a thread)
GB: 7-8
MN: 9-6
(Cinched
playoff spot)

RESULTS:
Green Bay beat the
Arizona Cardinals 49-24

Minnesota beat the
Detroit Lions 24-17

PACKERS "VERSES" VIKINGS ~ Carl Nelson

CONGRATS ARE DUE TO THE VIKINGS
FOR AFTER A START THAT WAS PRETTY WEAK
THEY MADE IT INTO THE PLAYOFFS
AND APPEAR TO HAVE REACHED THEIR PEAK

THE VIKINGS WON LAST SUNDAY
AND SO GET A PLAYOFF GAME AT HOME
THE DALLAS COWBOYS IS THE REWARD
IN THIS WEEK'S GAME AT THE METRODOME

WHEN THESE TWO TEAMS PLAYED EARLIER
DALLAS STARTED OUT PRETTY STRONG
BUT INJURIES TO EMMITT AND AIKMAN
MEANT THEIR LEAD WOULDN'T LAST TOO LONG

THIS TIME BOTH TEAMS ARE AT FULL STRENGTH
EVEN DEION'S BIG TOE IS HEALED
RANDY MOSS HAS SAID "CLIMB ON MY BACK"
SURELY HE CAN MAKE THE COWBOYS YIELD

SORRY FANS BUT THAT WON'T HAPPEN
MINNESOTA'S LACK OF DEFENSE IS THE REASON
LOOK FOR EMMITT TO HAVE A HUGE DAY
AND THE VIKES TO EXIT EARLY THIS POSTSEASON

~ ~ ~ ~ ~ ~ ~ ~ ~ ~ ~ ~ ~ ~ ~ ~ ~

ON SUNDAY THE PACKERS LOOKED LIKE
THE TEAM THAT SHOULD HAVE BEEN
AS THEY RAN UP THE SCORE WITH EASE
AND SMACKED THE CARDINALS ON THE CHIN

LEVENS RAN LIKE THE HORSE HE IS
SCHROEDER PULLED IN TWO SCORING PASSES
THE DEFENSE PLAYED LIKE ANIMALS
KNOCKING THE CARDS TO LAMBEAU'S GRASSES

THEY DID EVERYTHING THEY HAD TO
TO REMAIN EVEN FAINTLY IN THE RACE
BUT TO BE PUT OUT OF IT BY THE COWBOYS
WAS THE FINAL SLAP TO THE PACKERS' FACE

SO RONNIE WOLF IN ONE BOLD MOVE
FIRED RAY AND THE COACHING STAFF
IN A GESTURE THAT IS SO ASININE
THAT IF NOT SO TRAGIC WOULD MAKE ME LAUGH

WITH INJURIES, FREE AGENCY AND A FEW MISTAKES
THE PACKERS WENT AS FAR AS THEY DESERVED
BY GIVING RHODES ANOTHER YEAR
THE PACKERS WOULD HAVE BEEN FAR BETTER SERVED

Playoff
Spectator
GB: 8-8
MN: 10-6
Qualified
Wild Card

RESULTS:
Green Bay was edged from the playoffs

Minnesota beat the Dallas Cowboys 27-10

THE VIKINGS TOOK ONE STEP CLOSER
TO WHAT SEEMS THEIR ETERNAL GOAL
ANOTHER CHANCE FOR REDEMPTION
IN YET ANOTHER SUPER BOWL

MN: 1-0
(Wild Card
Winner)

THE COWBOYS ROLLED INTO THE METRODOME
AND SEEMED TO TAKE THE GAME IN HAND
BUT WHEN THEY GOT NEAR THE GOAL LINE
DALLAS ENTERED "NEVERLAND"

THEY NEVER CROSSED THE LINE THAT DRIVE
THEY NEVER REALLY GOT GOING AGAIN
EMMITT SMITH NEVER AGAIN WAS A FACTOR
AND THE COWPOKES NEVER GOT THE WIN

MINNESOTA MANAGED TO LOOK PRETTY GOOD
IN PICKING UP THIS WILD-CARD WIN
NOW THEY MUST TAKE THEIR SHOW TO ST LOUIS
AND TRY TO PLAY THAT WELL AGAIN

THE RAMS ARE THE SORT OF TEAM
THAT THE VIKINGS WERE LAST YEAR
SORT OF COMING OUT OF NOWHERE
WITH AN OFFENSE THAT KNOWS NO FEAR

THAT OFFENSE SHOULD BE GIVING ULCERS
TO THE PASS DEFENDERS OF THE VIKES
WHETHER MARSHALL FAULK OR ISSAC BRUCE
THERE'S NOT MUCH FOR THEM TO LIKE

THIS IS AN OFFENSE THAT WILL TEST YOU
AND LOVES TO GO DEEP WITH THE BALL
ANY MISTAKES BY THE VIKE'S SECONDARY
AND "TOUCHDOWN!" WILL BE THE CALL

THE VIKES HAVE WEAPONS OF THEIR OWN
BUT THEY OFTEN PUT THE BALL ON THE GROUND
AND ST LOUIS HAS A NASTY HABIT
OF TAKING THOSE TURNOVERS DOWNTOWN

WHILE VIKES ARE USED TO PLAYING INSIDE
THIS WILL BE A VERY HOSTILE CROWD
UNLESS THE VIKES TAKE THE LEAD EARLY
THE NOISE WILL BE UNBEARABLY LOUD

THE ONLY WAY THE VIKES CAN WIN
WILL BE TO PLAY A PERFECT GAME
THEY HAVEN'T DONE IT YET THIS YEAR
THIS WEEK SHOULD TURN OUT THE SAME

PACKERS "VERSES" VIKINGS ~ Carl Nelson

PACKERS "VERSES" VIKINGS ~ Carl Nelson

THE END HAS COME THE FAT LADY'S SUNG
THE VIKINGS' SEASON HAS ENDED
FOR THE SECOND STRAIGHT TIME MINNESOTA
FOUND THEIR SUPER BOWL HOPES UPENDED

THE RAMS STRUCK FIRST ON SUNDAY
LOOKING LIKE THEY HAD THE FASTER TRACK
BUT TO THE CREDIT OF THE VIKINGS
BY HALFTIME THEY'D FOUND THEIR WAY BACK

A COUPLE BIG PLAYS GAVE MINNESOTA
THE EMOTION FROM WHICH THEY FEED
MINNESOTA'S DEFENSE THEN STEPPED UP
AND THE HALF ENDED WITH A SLIM VIKINGS' LEAD

THEN THE DISASTER HAPPENED
THE RAMS TOOK THE KICKOFF BACK
FROM THAT MOMENT FORWARD
THE VIKINGS NEVER AGAIN GOT ON TRACK

THE THIRD QUARTER WAS ALL ST LOUIS
THE VIKES WERE EMBARRASSING TO SEE
PICKS AND FUMBLES AND BOTCHED SNAPS
AND DEFENSE THAT LET THE RAMS RUN FREE

THE FOURTH QUARTER STARTED OUT THE SAME
AS THE RAMS CONTINUED TO RUN UP THE SCORE
THE VIKES PUT UP SOME POINTS IN GARBAGE TIME
BUT WERE A REAL THREAT NO MORE

WHAT HAPPENED TO THIS VIKINGS' TEAM?
HOW DID THEY GET BLOWN OUT OF THIS GAME?
LAST YEAR IT WAS A LACK OF DEFENSE
THIS YEAR IT'S NOT SO PLAIN

UNLIKE LAST YEAR THE WHOLE TEAM
CAN TAKE THE CREDIT FOR THIS GAME
OFFENSE DEFENSE AND SPECIAL TEAMS
ALL SHOULD FEEL THE SHAME

SPEAKING OF WHICH, MR RANDY MOSS
SQUIRTED A REF AFTER AN UNCAUGHT PASS
SHOWING THAT WHILE HE HAS ALL-PRO HANDS
HE POSSESSES "POP WARNER" CLASS

SO WHERE DO THE VIKES GO AFTER THIS?
ALL IN ALL THE FUTURE'S UNCLEAR
THEY MUST RETIRE AND LICK THE WOUNDS
AND TRY IT AGAIN NEXT YEAR

VIKINGS

Super Bowl Trophy Case

RESULTS:
Minnesota lost to the
St Louis Rams 37-49

Super Bowl
XXXIV
Jan. 30
2000

PACKERS "VERSES" VIKINGS ~ Carl Nelson

WHEN THE SEASON STARTED IN SEPTEMBER
THE CONTENDERS NUMBERED THIRTY-ONE
THE SEASON PARED THAT DOWN TO TWO
FACING THEIR MOMENT IN THE SUN

THE TITANS FINALLY FOUND A HOME
AFTER BOUNCING AROUND A BIT
THEY GRABBED THE CONCEPT OF "HOME FIELD"
AND MADE THE MOST OF IT

THEY'VE GOT ONE OF THOSE QUARTERBACKS
WHO'S A THREAT WHEN HE RUNS THE BALL
ALTHOUGH HE CAN COMPLETE THE LONG PASS
WHEN THE HEAD GUY MAKES THAT CALL

IN ASSESSING THE TITAN RUNNING BACKS
EDDIE GEORGE IS FAST AND TOUGH
AND THEY POSSESS AN OVERWHELMING DEFENSE
THAT JUST LOVES TO SHOW THEIR STUFF

LOOKING AT THIS FOOTBALL TEAM
THERE AREN'T TOO MANY TOUGHER
BUT THE TITANS HAVE TWO STARTERS OUT
THAT WILL MAKE THIS GAME MUCH ROUGHER

~ ~ ~ ~ ~ ~ ~ ~ ~ ~ ~ ~ ~ ~ ~ ~ ~

THE RAMS ALSO WERE A REAL SURPRISE
INJURIES GAVE KURT WARNER THE CALL
THIS MAN CAME IN AND LIT UP THE LEAGUE
WITH THE WAY HE CAN THROW THE BALL

MARSHALL FAULK CAME THROUGH A TRADE
THE HAMSTRINGS HELD UP ON ISSAC BRUCE
THE GAME PLANS WORKED LIKE MAGIC
AND OTHER TEAMS FELT "WHAT'S THE USE?"

THE ST LOUIS DEFENSE DID THEIR PART
CRUSHING OPPONENTS INTO THE GROUND
FINDING THE BEST WAY TO DEFEND THE PASS
WAS TO PUT THE QUARTERBACK QUICKLY DOWN

THIS IS A TEAM BUILT ON SPEED
THE BIG PLAY AND FINESSE
THOUGH TAMPA SHOWED A STINGY DEFENSE
CAN PUT THIS OFFENSE TO THE TEST

SO WHICH TEAM WILL LEAVE WEARING THE RING?
THIS GAME IS A TOUGH ONE TO CALL
TENNESSEE WILL KEEP IT CLOSE
BUT LOOK FOR ST LOUIS TO WIN IT ALL

Super Bowl
Records
St. Louis: 0-1
Tennessee: 0-0

RESULTS:
St Louis Rams beat the
Tennessee Titans 23-16

PACKERS

" VERSES "

VIKINGS

Green Bay Packers
Regular Season 9-7
No Postseason

Minnesota Vikings
Regular Season 11-5
Postseason 1-1

Y2K bugs tackled my computer, thus devouring
several verses for the 2000 season. I'm handing off
what was recovered after this unfortunate infestation.

2 0 0 0

Carl "Gator" Nelson

PACKERS "VERSES" VIKINGS ~ Carl Nelson

IT IS PERHAPS QUITE FITTING
FOOTBALL STARTS THIS TIME OF THE YEAR
AS SUMMER IS COMING TO A CLOSE
AND THE START OF SCHOOL IS NEAR

AT EVERY LEVEL THIS HALLOWED GAME
LETS YOUNG MEN TRY TO PROVE WHO'S BEST
THEORY AND PRACTICE AND INTUITION
WILL SOON BE PUT TO THE TEST

MOST OF US WHO LIVE IN WISCONSIN
FIND THE GREEN BAY PACKERS TO OUR LIKING
WHILE THOSE FROM ACROSS THE RIVER
USUALLY FOLLOW THE MINNESOTA VIKINGS

BOTH OF THESE TEAMS HAVE THRILLED US
BOTH WITH THEIR STARS AND SUPPORTING CASTS
UNFORTUNATELY AS POTENTIAL CHAMPIONS
FOR NOW THEIR TIME MAY HAVE PASSED

THERE ARE YOUNGER TEAMS OUT IN THE CENTRAL
WHOSE ASCENDANCY HAS JUST BEGUN
THAT NEEDN'T MEAN HOWEVER
THAT WATCHING OUR BOYS WON'T STILL BE FUN

THE VIKINGS HAVE SOME QUESTIONS
AS TO HOW THEIR SEASON WILL GO
BUT OFFENSIVELY THEY'LL BE ALRIGHT
WITH MOSS PULLING IN CULPEPPER THROWS

THE VIKINGS' "D" HOWEVER WILL BE THE PLACE
THAT DECIDES THE POSITION AT THE END
UNLESS THEY FIND SOME MAGIC
THE VIKES WILL BE HOME FOR CHRISTMAS ONCE AGAIN

THE PACKERS DEFENSE SEEMS SHAKY, TOO
WITH TEAMS RUNNING EASILY UP THE MIDDLE
THE LOSS OF GILBERT BROWN AT THE NOSE
MEANS ALL THOSE GUYS ARE JUST TOO LITTLE

OFFENSIVELY THEY SHOULD BE ALRIGHT
AS LONG AS BRETT FAVRE'S ELBOW HEALS
THE RUNNING GAME MAY BE A LITTLE NICKED
BUT LEVENS WILL SOON REGAIN HIS WHEELS

BOTH OF THESE TEAMS WILL NEED TO FIND
THE WAY TO MAKE ALL THE PIECES MESH
AS FOR HOW THOSE TEAMS WILL FINISH
IT COULD BE ANYBODY'S GUESS —

GB: 0-0
MN: 0-0

PACKERS "VERSES" VIKINGS   ~ Carl Nelson

GOING INTO THE FIRST WEEK OF THE SEASON
THE VIKINGS WILL FACE THE CHICAGO BEARS
WHO COME INTO THE METRODOME
TRYING TO GAIN THE WINNER'S SHARE

THE BEARS' DEFENSE HAS BEEN SOMWHAT WIMPY
IN THE GAMES DURING THIS PRESEASON
THEY HAVE LAST YEAR'S TALENT LEVEL
SO THE COACHES ARE SEARCHING FOR THE REASON

AT QUARTERBACK IT'S CADE MCNOWN
WHO ALTHOUGH ERRATIC IS STRONG-ARMED
THE TEST WILL BE FOR HIS "O" LINE
TO KEEP HIM FROM VIKINGS' HARM

DAUNTE CULPEPPER ON THE OTHER SIDE
WILL HAVE THE CHANCE TO BECOME THIS YEAR'S HERO
IF HE CAN PLAY LIKE IN THE PRESEASON
ALTHOUGH HIS "REAL" STARTS NUMBER ZERO

CARTER, MOSS AND ROBERT SMITH
SHOULD KEEP THE SCOREBOARD NUMBERS SPINNING
IT COULD ONLY BE THE VIKINGS "D"
THAT WILL KEEP THIS TEAM FROM WINNING

~ ~ ~ ~ ~ ~ ~ ~ ~ ~ ~ ~ ~ ~ ~ ~ ~ ~

AS SUNDAY'S SUN SHINES DOWN ON LAMBEAU
THE NEW YORK JETS WILL COME TO PLAY
AGAINST AN UNSETTLED PACKERS' TEAM
ON THIS MILLENNIUM'S OPENING DAY

INJURIES HAVE ALREADY STRUCK THE PACK
FROM FAVRE'S ARM TO DORSEY'S KNEE
THROWING WHAT SHOULD BE A WELL-PLANNED OFFENSE
DEEP INTO TURMOIL AND UNCERTAINTY

THESE AILMENTS SHOULD ALL PASS WITH TIME
ALLOWING THE OFFENSE TO GREATLY IMPROVE
UNFORTUNATELY IT'S THE PACKERS' DEFENSIVE TEAM
THAT'S LEFT WITH LOTS TO PROVE

THE PLAYERS ON THAT SIDE OF THE BALL
HAVEN'T SHOWN THAT THEY CAN GET IT DONE
OPPOSING TEAMS HAVE HAD THEIR WAY
USING EITHER PASS OR RUN

THE DEFENSE HAS GOT TO SUCK IT UP
FOR GREEN BAY TO HAVE A CHANCE TO WIN
LET'S HOPE THEY GIVE NEW COACH SHERMAN
THE CHANCE TO WEAR A WINNER'S GRIN

RESULTS:
Green Bay lost to the New York Jets 16-20

Minnesota beat the Chicago Bears 30-27

GB: 3-4
MN: 6-0

PACKERS "VERSES" VIKINGS ~ Carl Nelson

THE BEARS DID EVERYTHING THEY COULD
TO DERAIL THE VIKINGS' VICTORY TRAIN
THE FIELD WAS SOFT, THE GRASS WAS LONG
AND THE GAME STARTED IN POURING RAIN

THE VIKINGS' DEFENSE DID THEIR PART, TOO
ALLOWING THE BEARS THE FIRST TD
BUT WHEN CHICAGO MISSED THE EXTRA POINT
IT WAS A SIGN OF THINGS TO BE

WHILE THE VIKINGS FOLLOWED THE PATTERN
OF LOOKING A LITTLE SHABBY EARLY ON
ONCE AGAIN THEY RESPONDED LATE IN THE (
AND THE BEARS' HOPE WAS COMPLETELY GO(

THIS WEEK THE BILLS FROM BUFFALO
INVADE THE HUMPHREY METRODOME
THE VIKINGS SHOULD BE HAPPY AND RELAXE
AS THEY ALWAYS ARE AT HOME

THIS IS TIME OF THE SEASON
WHEN THE VIKINGS MUST BE MOST ALERT
BEING CONFIDENT IS OK FOR THEM
BUT COMPLACENCY WILL REALLY HURT

~ ~ ~ ~ ~ ~ ~ ~ ~ ~ ~ ~ ~ ~ ~ ~ ~ ~

LAST SUNDAY'S GAME AT LAMBEAU
WAS REMINISCENT OF GREAT GAMES PAST
WHEN BOTH THE PACKERS AND THE 'NINERS
SIMPLY CAME TO KICK THE OTHER'S ASS

THE PACKERS WON LAST SUNDAY
IN A GAME WHERE THEY NEVER TRAILED
SAN FRANCISO MADE A LATE GAME RALLY
WHICH HOWEVER, ULTIMATELY FAILED

FOR ONCE THIS GREEN BAY PACKERS' TEAM
PULLED A WIN FROM THE JAWS OF DEFEAT
BRETT FAVRE TWICE ESCAPED THE 'NINERS' PASS RUSH
AND THAT SIGHT WAS MIGHTY SWEET

COULD IT BE THAT IT'S COMING TOGETHER
AND THAT THE PACK'S GAME'S ON THE UPSWING?
THE PLAYERS ONCE HURT ARE RETURNING
AND WE ALL HAVE SEEN MUCH STRANGER THINGS

~ ~ ~ ~ ~ ~ ~ ~ ~ ~ ~ ~ ~ ~ ~ ~ ~ ~

FOR NOW, THE PACKERS HEAD INTO THE BYE WEEK
LOOKING FORWARD TO HEALING AND MUCH-NEEDED REST
BECAUSE THE NEXT FOUR GAMES THE PACKERS PLAY
WILL SURELY PUT THEM TO THE TEST

RESULTS:
Green Bay was on their
"Bye Week"

Minnesota beat the
Buffalo Bills 31-27

GB: 3-4
MN: 7-0

PACKERS "VERSES" VIKINGS ~ Carl Nelson

THE BUFFALO BILLS GAVE THE VIKES A SCARE
BY PLAYING TOUGH AND KEEPING THEIR HEADS
IT WASN'T 'TIL A FOURTH-QUARTER FUMBLE
THAT THE BILLS WERE OFFICIALLY CONSIDERED DEAD

WITH THE CHIEFS STOMPING THE ST LOUIS RAMS
MINNESOTA MOVED INTO THE LEAGUE'S TOP SPOT
SEVEN-AND-O AND LOOKING STRONG
THOSE VIKINGS FEEL THEY'RE PRETTY HOT

DOWN TO TAMPA THOSE VIKES NOW GO
TO FACE THOSE "SCARY" BUCCANEERS
WHO'S ABSOLUTELY AWFUL RECENT PLAY
SHOULD BE EMBARRASSING THEM TO TEARS

THE BUCS WOULD LOVE TO WIN THIS GAME
TO PROVE THEY'RE STILL ONE OF THE ELITE
BUT THE VIKINGS WOULD REALLY HAVE TO CHOKE
TO DEPART FROM TAMPA AFTER A DEFEAT

BUT HEAVY IS THE HEAD THAT WEARS THE CROWN
AND HAPPINESS OFT TURNS INTO DESPAIR
FOR IT'S FAR EASIER TO REACH THE TOP
THAN IT IS TO REMAIN WAY UP THERE

~ ~ ~ ~ ~ ~ ~ ~ ~ ~ ~ ~ ~ ~ ~ ~ ~ ~ ~

IN MIAMI THIS COMING SUNDAY
FOR THE VERY FIRST TIME THIS FALL
THE COMPLETE GREEN BAY PACKERS' TEAM
WILL BE ABLE TO TAKE THE STARTING CALL

THE PACKERS' PLAY HAS BEEN UP AND DOWN
AND THEIR THREE AND FOUR RECORD REFLECTS JUST THAT
FOR THE PACK TO HAVE A CHANCE AT RESPECTABILITY
THEY MUST DEFINITELY CLEAN UP THEIR ACT

RESULTS:
Green Bay lost to the
Miami Dolphins 20-28

Minnesota lost to the
Tampa Bay Buccaneers 13-41

THE 'FINS HAVE A DEFENSE THAT IS WELL-KNOWN
FOR FEROCITY AND FOR HEAVY HITS
THEY ARE TOUGH AND HARD AND TENACIOUS
AND IT IS SAID THEY NEVER EVER QUIT

BUT MONDAY NIGHT THE NEW YORK JETS
SIMPLY TOOK THAT GROUP APART
WHAT EFFECT WILL THAT LOSS HAVE
ON THAT DOLPHINS' DEFENSES' HEARTS?

HOPEFULLY IT WILL BE ENOUGH TO GIVE
THE PACKERS' OFFENSE A CHANCE TO GET ON TRACK
A WEEK OFF TO REST AND REVISE THE PLAN
MAY HELP GREEN BAY START ON THE LONG ROAD BACK

GB: 6-7
MN: 11-2

PACKERS "VERSES" VIKINGS ~ Carl Nelson

EVER SINCE THIS SEASON STARTED
THE VIKES HAVE WORRIED ABOUT THE RAMS
THEN AMAZINGLY AS THE GAME APPROACHES
THE CHAMPS LOOK MORE LIKE A FLOCK OF LAMBS

MINNESOTA'S VIKINGS ON THE OTHER HAND
ARE LOOKING TO TURN THE HOME FIELD LOCK
THIS WILL PRESENT THEM WITH NO PROBLEMS
IF ONE CAN ACCEPT THE VIKINGS' TALK

BUT THE RAMS ARE RECOVERING FROM SOME INJURIES
THIS WEEK MORE TIMING AND POLISH WILL RETURN
THE QB IS STILL KURT WARNER
AND HIS OFFENSE STILL HAS SPEED TO BURN

CULPEPPER AND THE VIKING "O"
ARE NO SLOUCHES IN THEIR OWN RIGHT
AND SINCE NEITHER DEFENSE IS EXACTLY STELLAR
LOOK FOR THE SCORE TO REACH AMAZING HEIGHTS

AT GAME'S END THE DECIDING FACTOR WILL BE
THE RAMS NEED A WIN WHILE THE VIKINGS DON'T
DESPERATION IS SUCH A GREAT MOTIVATOR
ST LOUIS WILL—AND MINNESOTA WON'T

~ ~ ~ ~ ~ ~ ~ ~ ~ ~ ~ ~ ~ ~ ~ ~ ~ ~

THE BEARS WELCOMED THE PACKERS TO CHICAGO
ON A DARK AND FRIGID SUNDAY NIGHT
AND AS MUCH AS THEY MAY HAVE WANTED TO
WEREN'T ABLE TO PUT UP MUCH OF A FIGHT

THE PACKERS DOMINATED IN THAT FOOTBALL GAME
AND THE OUTCOME NEVER REALLY WAS IN DOUBT
BY PLAYING SMART AND WITHOUT TURNOVERS
GREEN BAY TURNED A TOUGH GAME INTO A ROUT

NOW THE LIONS COME TO LAMBEAU FIELD
AS WISCONSIN'S WINTER GAINS A FIRM FOOTHOLD
IT SHOULDN'T HAVE TO BE MENTIONED HERE
HOW WELL GREEN BAY PLAYS WHEN IN THE COLD

BRETT FAVRE'S RECORD IS TWENTY-FIVE-AND-ZIP
WHEN THE TEMP IS LOWER THAN THIRTY-FOUR
DETROIT IS ABOUT TO BE REMINDED ONCE AGAIN
REAL FOOTBALL IS MEANT TO BE PLAYED OUTDOORS

THE LIONS' ROAD TO THE PLAYOFF GAMES
IS ABOUT TO GET A LITTLE LONGER
FOR WHILE THE PACKERS ARE RIDDLED BY INJURIES
OUT IN THE COLD THEY ARE JUST A LITTLE STRONGER

RESULTS:
Green Bay beat the
Detroit Lions 26-13

Minnesota lost to the
St Louis Rams 29-40

GB: 8-7
MN: 11-4

PACKERS "VERSES" VIKINGS

~ Carl Nelson

IT WAS THE WEEK BEFORE CHRISTMAS
AND DOWN IN THE 'DOME
PURPLE CREATURES WERE STIRRING
'TWAS DENNY GREEN AND HIS GNOMES

THE VIKES WERE IN FIRST PLACE
WITH HOME FIELD NEARLY THEIRS
A WIN OVER GREEN BAY
WOULD AVOID PLAYOFF CARES

MINNESOTA'S GOAL WAS SO SIMPLE
"JUST AVOID PLAYOFF TRAVEL"
BUT THEN THE GAME STARTED
AND THEIR PLAN STARTED TO UNRAVEL

THE PACK TOOK THE KICKOFF
AND MOVED THE BALL SO DARNED WELL
SOON "DAUNTE'S INFERNO"
LOOKED MORE LIKE "VIKING HELL"

NO ONE CAN SAY QUITE WHAT HAPPENED
PERHAPS TWAS THE SEASON
MINNESOTA NEVER STOPPED 'EM
FOR WHATEVER THE REASON

NOW THOSE VIKINGS MUST GO OUT
TO THE INDY COLTS' HOME
KNOWING THAT A LOSS THERE
REMOVES PLAYOFF GAMES FROM THE DOME

THE VIKES SHOULD BEAT INDY
BUT THAT'S A BET ONE MAY HEDGE
THAT DEFENSE COULDN'T STOP AHMAN GREEN
AND THE COLTS WILL HAVE "THE EDGE"

~ ~ ~ ~ ~ ~ ~ ~ ~ ~ ~ ~ ~ ~ ~ ~ ~

BUT FIRST UP TO LAMBEAU
JUMPS TAMPA BAY'S TEAM
WHERE THE AIR'S FILLED WITH SNOWFLAKES
AND THE TEMP'LL BE JUST THIRTEEN

IT'S NEARLY A LEGEND
HOW WHEN OUT IN THE COLD
BRETT FAVRE SEEMS UNBEATABLE
WHILE THE BUCS SIMPLY FOLD

NO MATTER WHAT HAPPENS FROM NOW ON
EACH TIME THE VIKINGS LOOK BACK
THEY'LL ALWAYS HAVE TO ADMIT TO
BEING SWEPT BY THE PACK

SINCE IT IS THIS TIME OF YEAR
LET'S FOR A MOMENT ALL THESE RIVALRIES BURY
I HOPE YOUR DAYS ARE FILLED WITH PEACE
AND MAY YOUR HOLIDAYS BE MERRY!!

MERRY CHRISTMAS!!

RESULTS:
Green Bay beat the
Tampa Bay Buccaneers 17-14

Minnesota lost to the
Indianapolis Colts 10-31

Final Standings
GB: 4-12
MN: 9-7

PACKERS "VERSES" VIKINGS ~ Carl Nelson

THE WINTER WIND WHISTLED ACROSS THE SNOW
ON A FRIGID CHRISTMAS EVE
CAUSING MANY A WARM-BLOODED BUCCANEER
TO WIPE HIS NOSE ACROSS HIS SLEEVE

THE PACKERS PLAYED THE ROLE OF SANTA CLAUS
DELIVERING THE CENTRAL CROWN TO DENNY'S VIKES
BY BEATING TAMPA'S BUCCANEERS
IN THE WINTER WEATHER THE PACKERS LIKE

GREEN BAY JUMPED OUT TO AN EARLY LEAD
CARRIED BY THE LEGS OF AHMAN GREEN
WHO THOUGH BEGINNING THIS YEAR AS A BACK-UP
HAS BEEN PLAYING LIKE A HEAD-COACHES' DREAM

WHILE FAVRE'S PASSES FOUND THEIR TARGETS
WHEN THERE REALLY WAS A NEED
THE PASSING GAME WAS NOT IN SYNCH
AND NEVER REALLY GOT UP TO SPEED

THE PACKERS' DEFENSE HOWEVER WAS IN CHARGE
UNTIL THE CLOSING MOMENTS OF THE GAME
THOUGH ONCE SHAUN KING BEGAN TO SCRAMBLE
THEY JUST DIDN'T LOOK THE SAME

TWO FOURTH-QUARTER TAMPA TOUCHDOWNS
LEFT THE BAYS TIED AS TIME WOUND DOWN
THIS IS ABOUT THE TIME THE TV LEFT
THANKS TO OUR LOCAL FOX NETWORK CLOWNS

DESPITE THE BLACKOUT WE DISCOVERED
GRAMMATICA HAD MISSED THE WINNING KICK
AND THAT GREEN BAY HAD DRIVEN DOWN THE FIELD
WHERE RYAN LONGWELL TURNED THE FINAL TRICK

WE'D HAD TO DEPEND ON "GAME UPDATES"
TO HEAR HOW THE OVERTIME PERIOD PROCEEDED
WHILE WATCHING THE INTROS OF THE VIKINGS
WHICH WAS SOMETHING THAT NOBODY NEEDED

AFTER ALL THE COLD-WEATHER HEROICS
-DUE TO THE RAMS' BEATING OF THE SAINTS
THOUGH THE PACK HAD A CHANCE TO MAKE THE PLAYOFFS
THE BRUTAL TRUTH IS THAT THEY AIN'T

THE GREEN BAY PACKERS MADE QUITE A RUN
IN THE PAST MONTH SWEEPING THEIR CENTRAL FOES
THERE'S A LOT THAT'S GOOD TO BUILD ON
AND A DIRECTION FOR NEXT YEAR'S TEAM TO GO

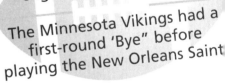

RESULTS:
The Green Bay Packers were edged from the playoffs

The Minnesota Vikings had a first-round 'Bye' before playing the New Orleans Saint

**Divisional
Playoffs
Jan. 6**

2001

PACKERS "VERSES" VIKINGS   ~ Carl Nelson

THE LAST MONTH OF THE SEASON
WASN'T KIND TO DENNY AND HIS CREW
REALLY TO PUT THE FACTS QUITE PLAINLY
THE VIKES WERE BEATEN BLACK AND BLUE

THE COLTS THE RAMS AND YES, THE PACK
TOOK IT TO MINNESOTA'S TEAM
AND FOR THE FIRST TIME THIS FOOTBALL SEASON
A CHAMPIONSHIP LOOKED LIKE JUST ANOTHER DREAM

ROBERT SMITH FOUND HIMSELF WITH A SORE KNEE
CULPEPPER GOT HIS ANKLE TWISTED
AND THE REST OF THE VIKINGS' FOOTBALL TEAM
WAS NOT AS GOOD AS DENNY HAD INSISTED

WHILE THE VIKINGS RECIEVED A COUPLE GIFTS
A BYE WEEK AND A HOME GAME AMONG THOSE
THE GRAND PLAN OF COACH DENNY GREEN
LOOKED MORE LIKE "THE EMPEROR'S NEW CLOTHES"

THE SAINTS FROM DOWN IN NEW ORLEANS
ARE PLAYING FAR FAR BETTER THAN THEY SHOULD
THIS TEAM THAT SHOULD BE CRIPPLED BY ITS INJURIES
INSTEAD THEY'RE LOOKING PRETTY GOOD

THE TEAM THE VIKINGS SEEMED TO FEAR MOST
THE ONCE CHAMPS—NOW "ALSO-RAMS"
WERE FOR ALMOST ALL OF LAST WEEK'S GAME
FORCED TO PLAY LIKE "SAINTLY LAMBS"

LED BY YOUNG QB AARON BROOKS
THE SAINTS DON'T KNOW THEY SHOULDN'T WIN
SO FAR THEY'VE WON SEVEN GAMES ON THE ROAD
THIS WEEK THEY MAY DO IT ONCE AGAIN

RESULTS:
Minnesota beat the
New Orleans Saints 34-16

This let them go to the NFC
Championship game,
where the New York Giants
crushed them 41-0.

FOR ONCE THERE MAY BE NO ADVANTAGE
TO A HOME GAME FOR DENNY'S BOYS
FOR THE SAINTS ARE FAMILIAR WITH INSIDE PLAY
INCLUDING PIPED-IN NOISE

WHO'LL SHOW UP FOR THIS WEEKEND'S PLAYOFF GAME
BETWEEN THE SAINTS AND MINNESOTA'S VIKES
WILL IT BE THE TEAM THAT WENT 0-FOR-DECEMBER
OR THE ONE THAT EVERYBODY LIKES

THAT QUESTION IS TOUGH TO ANSWER
WATCHING THIS GAME SHOULD BE QUITE A BALL
BUT UNLESS DENNY PULLS SOME MAGIC FROM HIS BUTT
IT SEEMS THE VIKES ARE DUE TO FALL

107

PACKERS
" VERSES "
VIKINGS

Green Bay Packers
Regular Season 12-4
Postseason 1-1

Minnesota Vikings
Regular Season 5-11
No Postseason

2 0 0 1

Carl "Gator" Nelson

~ Carl Nelson

PACKERS "VERSES" VIKINGS

DURING THE FIRST HALF OF LAST YEAR'S SEASON
THE VIKINGS PLAYED LIKE A TEAM POSSESSED
BUT AS THE SCHEDULE WAS WINDING DOWN
INTO MEDIOCRITY THEY REGRESSED

THIS IS A SEASON THAT WILL TELL MANY TALES
ABOUT HOW GOOD THE VIKINGS TRULY ARE
YES THEY STILL HAVE MOSS AND CARTER
DAUNTE CULPEPPER SEEMS A RISING STAR

ROBERT SMITH HOWEVER HUNG UP THE SPIKES
THE OFFENSIVE LINE IS TWO-THIRDS NEW
THERE'LL BE A ROOKIE AS THE FEATURE BACK
WHO KNOWS HOW HE WILL DO?

OH THE VIKINGS' OFFENSE WILL BE QUITE GOOD
PUTTING HUGE NUMBERS ON THE BOARD
TOO BAD THAT WITH THAT ALLEGED DEFENSIVE TEAM
THEY'LL BE LUCKY TO NOT FIND THEMSELVES OUTSCORED

THE SEASON OPENS WITH WHAT SHOULD BE
THE EASIEST GAME THE VIKES WILL FACE
THE PANTHERS, WITH A ROOKIE AT THE QB SPOT
WON'T BE ABLE TO KEEP UP THE PACE

~ ~ ~ ~ ~ ~ ~ ~ ~ ~ ~ ~ ~ ~ ~ ~ ~ ~

AS LAST SEASON WOUND DOWN TO ITS CLOSE
THE GREEN BAY PACKERS WERE ON A TEAR
WINNING ALL OF THE LAST FOUR GAMES
AGAINST THE LIONS VIKINGS BUCS AND BEARS

MIKE SHERMAN LOOKED OUT UPON THE TEAM
THAT HAD ACCOMPLISHED THIS AMAZING RUN
AND SAID "LET'S KEEP THIS BUNCH TOGETHER
AND NEXT YEAR WE'LL REALLY HAVE SOME FUN"

SO AHMAN IS BACK AND DORSEY TOO
OF COURSE BRETT FAVRE HAS MADE HIS RETURN
"FREE" IS HERE AND BRADFORD'S BACK
FINALLY GIVING THE PACK SOME SPEED TO BURN

THERE'S ONE BIG CHANGE IN THE DEFENSIVE LINE
A MUCH SLIMMER GILBERT BROWN HAS REAPPEARED
MAKING RUNNING PLAYS THAT GO UP THE MIDDLE
A ROUTE THAT WILL CAUSE MANY BACKS GREAT FEAR

LIKE EVERY TEAM THIS TIME OF YEAR
A PLAYOFF BERTH IS GREEN BAY'S GOAL
SUNDAY THE LIONS WILL BE THE FIRST OBSTACLE
OVER WHICH THE PACK WILL ROLL

GB: 0-0
MN: 0-0

RESULTS:
Green Bay beat the
Detroit Lions 28-6

Minnesota lost to the
Carolina Panthers 13-24

GB: 1-0
MN: 0-1

PACKERS "VERSES" VIKINGS ~ Carl Nelson

CAN IT ONLY BE TWO WEEKS AGO?
IT FEELS LIKE IT'S BEEN YEARS
THE EVENTS SUBSEQUENT TO FOOTBALL'S FIRST GAMES
HAVE CAUSED NO END OF PAIN AND TEARS

THE GAMES PEOPLE LOVE TOOK A WEEK OFF
NOT FROM FEAR- BUT TO SHOW RESPECT
THIS WEEK BEGINS THE JOURNEY BACK TO NORMALCY
PREPARING TO SHOW THE WORLD "YOU AIN'T SEEN NOTHIN' YET"

~ ~ ~ ~ ~ ~ ~ ~ ~ ~ ~ ~ ~ ~ ~ ~ ~ ~ ~

THE VIKINGS CRUISED INTO THE CAROLINA GAME
IN A MANNER THAT LEFT NO DOUBT
THEY FULLY EXPECTED TO NOT BE CHALLENGED
AND THEY'D TRY TO SHUT THE PANTHERS OUT

FOR THE VIKINGS' TEAM WAS SO MUCH IMPROVED
(OR AT LEAST THAT'S WHAT ALL THE PAPERS SAID)
MAYBE DENNY SHOULD BAN PAPERS FROM THE CLUBHOUSE
FOR THEY SURELY SWELLED THE VIKINGS' HEADS

"WE JUST DIDN'T TAKE THEM SERIOUSLY"
WAS THE WORD FROM MR MOSS
WHO INSTEAD OF DOMINATING OFFENSIVELY
CAUGHT JUST A SINGLE CULPEPPER TOSS

THAT WAS THE THEME OF THIS WHOLE GAME
AS THE VIKES MASSIVELY UNDERACHIEVED
IF THEY DON'T GET THEIR COLLECTIVE ACT TOGETHER
MINNESOTA FANS WILL FIND THEY'VE BEEN DECEIVED

IT'S OFF TO CHIGAGO THIS COMING WEEK
TO FACE A BEARS' TEAM LARGELY IN DISARRAY
UNLESS THE VIKES BEAT THIS TEAM DECISIVELY
LISTEN FOR THE SHOUTS OF TRUE DISMAY

110

A LIGHT RAIN FELL GENTLY TO LAMBEAU'S TURF
AS THIS SEASON GOT OFF TO ITS START
AFTER THREE FIRST-QUARTER PACKERS' SCORES
THE LIONS' TEAM JUST SIMPLY FELL APART

THE OFFENSE WAS HITTING ON ALL CYLINDERS
BRISK FAVRE PASSES WHISTLED THROUGH THE AIR
BUT IT WAS THE RUNNING OF AHMAN GREEN
THAT TRULY CAUSED THE LIONS TO DESPAIR

SEVENTEEN CARRIES FOR ONE-FIFTY SEVEN
THEN HE CAUGHT THREE BALLS FOR TWENTY MORE
AND THE PLAY OF THE DAY WAS WHEN HE WENT
FOR EIGHTY-THREE YARDS AND A SCORE

BUT GREEN ALONE DIDN'T WIN THIS GAME
THE DEFENSE PLAYED A LARGE PART AS WELL
TWO INTERCEPTIONS AND SEVEN SACKS
GAVE CHARLIE BATCH A GLIMPSE OF HELL

THIS WEEK THE REDSKINS COME TO THE SHRINE
A TEAM EMBARRASSED IN THE FIRST WEEK
UNFORTUNATELY FOR ANY REDSKINS FANS
THIS GAME'S OUTCOME LOOKS EQUALLY BLEAK

RESULTS:
Green Bay beat the
Washington Redskins 37-0

Minnesota lost to the
Chicago Bears 10-17

GB: 2-0
MN: 0-2

PACKERS "VERSES" VIKINGS ~ Carl Nelson

FEELING THEY HAD SOMETHING TO PROVE
LAST SUNDAY THE VIKES INVADED SOLDIER FIELD
NEVER DREAMING THAT BY THE GAME'S END
THEY'D BE WONDERING "HEY— JUST WHAT'S THE DEAL?"

FOR THE BEARS WHO AFTER ALL ARE STILL THE BEARS
HAD HANDED THE VIKINGS THEIR SECOND STRAIGHT LOSS
AND FOR A SECOND STRAIGHT WEEK THERE WERE NO BIG PLAYS
THROWN FROM CULPEPPER TO OL' RANDY MOSS

NOW IT'S THE BUCS FROM TAMPA BAY
COMING TO TAKE ON THE VIKES IN THE DOME
MAYBE CRIS CARTER WILL BEHAVE HIMSELF
AND JUST LEAVE HIS POOR TEAMMATES ALONE

FOR UNLESS THE VIKINGS PULL THEIR HEADS
FROM WHATEVER CAVITY IN WHICH THEY RESIDE
A PRETTY DARNED TOUGH TAMPA TEAM
WILL TAKE THEM FOR QUITE A RIDE

AFTER THE RESULTS OF THE FIRST TWO GAMES
VIKINGS' FANS ARE BEGINNING TO SCREAM
"WHO ARE THE GUYS IN THOSE PURPLE HATS
AND WHAT HAVE THEY DONE WITH OUR TEAM?"

~ ~ ~ ~ ~ ~ ~ ~ ~ ~ ~ ~ ~ ~ ~ ~ ~ ~ ~

THE DIFFERENCE BETWEEN A REALLY GOOD TEAM
AND ONE THAT ISN'T SO HOT
IS GOOD TEAMS DOMINATE THE GAMES THEY SHOULD
AND SELDOM LOSE THE ONES THEY SHOULD NOT

MONDAY NIGHT THE PACKERS WERE FAVORED
FOR THE GAME AGAINST GEORGE AND THE 'SKINS
MOST PEOPLE THOUGHT IT WOULD BE A TOUGH GAME
BUT ONE THE PACKERS WOULD EVENTUALLY WIN

WHO WOULD HAVE THOUGHT THIS PACKERS' TEAM
WOULD SO COMPLETELY DOMINATE THIS GAME?
OFFENSE DEFENSE AND SPECIAL TEAMS
ALL WERE AS INTENSE AS WHITE-HOT FLAME

GREEN BAY'S TEAM SCORED THIRTY-SEVEN POINTS
WHILE THE REDSKINS' TOTAL WAS NIL
EVERY PACKER FAN WHO WATCHED THAT GAME
WAS FILLED WITH THE AWE AND THE THRILL

THAT THRILL SHOULD CONTINUE THIS SUNDAY
THE PANTHERS ARE NEXT IN THE SIGHTS
THOUGH THEY BEAT UP THE VIKES IN THE OPENER
THEY'LL BE THE LOSERS COME THIS SUNDAY NIGHT

RESULTS:
Green Bay beat the
Carolina Panthers 28-7

Minnesota beat the
Tampa Bay Buccaneers 20-16

GB: 3-0
MN: 1-2

PACKERS "VERSES" VIKINGS

~ Carl Nelson

THE QUESTION GOING INTO SUNDAY'S GAME
WAS "WILL THE VIKINGS FINALLY WIN?"
OR WILL THEY MANAGE TO FALL APART
LIKE THEY HAVE TIME AND TIME AGAIN?

TAMPA'S BUCS WERE THE FIRST VICTIM
OF THE VIKES THIS FOOTBALL SEASON
AND WHILE MINNESOTA WASN'T OVERPOWERING
THEIR OFFENSE DID PROVIDE THE REASON

A LONG FLOATING BALL TO THE TIGHT END
AS AWAY THE GAME'S FINAL MINUTES TICKED
PROVIDED MINNESOTA THE CHANCE TO SCORE
AND FOR THE BUCCANNEERS TO JUST FEEL SICK

WHILE NOT IMPRESSIVE MINNESOTA'S TEAM
DID WHAT IT HAD TO GET IT DONE
THIS WEEK IT'S THE NEW ORLEANS' SAINTS
LOOKING FOR THEIR DAY IN THE SUN

HAVE THE VIKINGS PUT BEHIND THEM
THE REASONS FOR THEIR LOSING STREAK?
OR WILL UNREST AND INEPTITUDE
PLAGUE THEM YET AGAIN THIS WEEK?

~ ~ ~ ~ ~ ~ ~ ~ ~ ~ ~ ~ ~ ~ ~ ~ ~ ~ ~

GREEN BAY BROUGHT A TWO-GAME STREAK
TO SUNDAY'S CAROLINA PANTHER GAME
AND ALTHOUGH THE FIELD LOOKED FRESHLY PLOWED
THE PACKERS WON IT JUST THE SAME

THOUGH A LITTLE SLOW IN STARTING OFF
THE PACKERS NEVER LOST THEIR POISE
AND AFTER CAPITALIZING ON A COUPLE BREAKS
THEY SET ABOUT TO MAKE SOME NOISE

THREE TOUCHDOWNS WAS THE MARGIN
THAT BROUGHT THE WIN HOME FOR THE PACK
THEY'VE STARTED OFF AT THREE-AND-O
AND THERE'S NO REASON THEY'LL LOOK BACK

FRESH FROM LOSING TO THE VIKINGS
THE BUCCANNEERS ARE NEXT IN LINE
LOOK FOR A TOUGH HARD-FOUGHT CONTEST
IN WHICH BOTH DEFENSES WILL REALLY SHINE

SUNDAY'S GAME SHOULD BE A CLASSIC
AS THE "BATTLE OF THE BAYS" SO OFTEN IS
THE PACKERS WILL BE CHANTING "WE'RE NUMBER ONE"
WHILE TAMPA'S COMMENT WILL BE "GEE WHIZ"

RESULTS:
Green Bay lost to the
Tampa Bay Buccaneers 10-14

Minnesota lost to the
New Orleans Saints 15-28

113

GB: 3-1
MN: 1-3

PACKERS "VERSES" VIKINGS ~ Carl Nelson

"WHEN THE SAINTS GO MARCHING IN"
IS AN OLD SONG LOVED BY MANY
BUT AFTER WATCHING IT HAPPEN SEVEN TIMES
IT'S NOT TOO WELL-LIKED BY DENNY

THE OPENING PLAY SET THE TONE
FOR THE WAY THE VIKES' DAY WOULD GO
CULPEPPER DROPPED BACK TO THROW A PASS
AND DOWN ON HIS BUTT HE DID GO

THAT'S KIND OF THE WAY THE WHOLE GAME WENT
MINNESOTA NEVER GOT THEIR GAME ON TRACK
RANDY MOSS AT LAST GOT A TOUCHDOWN
BUT CRIS CARTER GAVE ONE RIGHT BACK

OPPORTUNITY PRESENTS ITSELF THIS WEEK
AS DETROIT PUSSYFOOTS INTO THE METRODOME
BATCH AND THE LIONS SHOULD BE AN EASY WIN
BUT THE VIKES HAVEN'T EVEN PLAYED WELL AT HOME

THERE'S JUST NOT A PHASE OF THIS VIKINGS' TEAM
THAT IS WORKING THE WAY THAT IT SHOULD
IF THEY CAN'T CRUSH THIS DETROIT TEAM
IT WILL BE CLEAR THAT THEY'RE JUST NO DARNED GOOD

~ ~ ~ ~ ~ ~ ~ ~ ~ ~ ~ ~ ~ ~ ~ ~ ~ ~

WHEN THE PACKERS TAKE ON THE BUCCANEERS
EVERYONE KNOWS JUST WHAT TO EXPECT
AN ALL-OUT WAR BETWEN THE TEAMS
EACH LOOKING TO EARN THE OTHER'S RESPECT

ON A SWELTERING FIELD IN TAMPA
BOTH TEAMS PLAYED JUST AS WELL AS THEY COULD
TAMPA'S OFFENSE MAY BE SOMEWHAT SHAKY
BUT THAT DEFENSE IS PRETTY DARNED GOOD

AN INTERCEPTION RETURNED FOR A SCORE
AND A LATE ALSTOTT TOUCHDOWN RUN
LEFT GREEN BAY BRUISED AND BEATEN
BY FOUR POINTS AT THE SOUND OF THE GUN

IT DOESN'T GET ANY EASIER THIS WEEK
BALTIMORE'S RAVENS ARE COMING TO CALL
THEY'LL BRING WITH THEM AN AWESOME DEFENSE
BUT THEY HAVE SOME TROUBLE MOVING THE BALL

BRETT AND THE BOYS WILL HAVE TO BE CAREFUL
AS THEY TAKE ON THE CHAMPIONS SUNDAY
IF THE GAME THEY PLAY IS MISTAKE-FREE
THEY CAN RETURN TO THEIR WINNING WAYS

RESULTS:
Green Bay beat the
Baltimore Ravens 31-23

Minnesota beat the
Detroit Lions 31-26

Week 6
Oct. 21
2 0 0 1

FOR THIRTY MINUTES OF SUNDAY'S GAME
MINNESOTA'S VIKINGS WERE LIVIN' LARGE
BUT THE SECOND HALF FOUND THEM STRUGGLING
TO DEFLECT THE LIONS' LAST-MINUTE CHARGE

MANY ARE WONDERING ABOUT THE VIKES
AND WHAT COULD HAVE HAPPENED TO THIS TEAM
IS THE WHOLE GROUP JUST UNDERACHIEVING
OR ARE THEY AS BAD AS IT WOULD SEEM?

~ ~ ~ ~ ~ ~ ~ ~ ~ ~ ~ ~ ~ ~ ~ ~ ~

THE PACKERS' RECORD WAS AT THREE AND ONE
WHEN THE BALTIMORE RAVENS CAME TO CALL
GREEN BAY HAD JUST LOST TO THE BUCCANNEERS
SURELY TO THE CHAMPIONS THEY WOULD FALL

HOWEVER BALTIMORE SOON LEARNED THE MEANING
OF "UNEASY RESTS THE HEAD THAT WEARS THE CROWN"
FOR BOTH OFFENSIVELY AND DEFENSIVELY
THE PACKERS TOOK CONTROL AND SHUT THEM DOWN

~ ~ ~ ~ ~ ~ ~ ~ ~ ~ ~ ~ ~ ~ ~ ~ ~ ~

SINCE THE SCHEDULE WAS FIRST PUBLISHED
AROUND THIS WEEK HAS BEEN DRAWN A CIRCLE
FOR IT IS THE FIRST MEETING OF THIS YEAR
BETWEEN THE CHEESEHEADS AND THE PURPLE

"THE BLACK HOLE OF PROFESSIONAL FOOTBALL"
IS HOW THE METRODOME HAS BEEN PERCEIVED
MANY TEAMS GO IN EXPECTING TO BEAT THE VIKES
AND FIND THAT THEY HAVE BEEN SELF-DECEIVED

THE PACKERS HAVE NOT BEEN IMMUNE TO THIS
FOR YEARS IT SEEMED THEY COULD NOT WIN IN THERE
SUCH WEIRD THINGS OCCURRED DURING THOSE GAMES
IT APPEARED A VIKINGS' CURSE HOVERED IN THE AIR

LAST YEAR HOWEVER IN THE DOME
THE PACKERS WON, MOVING THE BALL AT WILL
AND WHILE IT'S ALWAYS SWEET TO BEAT THE VIKES
IN THE 'DOME IT'S A SPECIAL KIND OF THRILL

RESULTS:
Green Bay lost to the
Minnesota Vikings 13-35

ON PAPER THIS WEEK SHOULD BE A LOT THE SAME
ONLY THIS VIKINGS' TEAM DOESN'T LOOK NEAR AS GOOD
THE DEFENSE IS ALMOST NONEXISTENT
AND THE OFFENSE ISN'T WORKING LIKE IT SHOULD

THE PACKERS ON THE OTHER HAND
ARE PLAYING LIKE A TEAM POSSESSED
AND FOR ONCE IT'S THE VIKES WHO MUST PLAY PERFECTLY
TO HAVE A HOPE OF STANDING UP TO THIS TEST

GB: 4-1
MN: 2-3

PACKERS "VERSES" VIKINGS ~ Carl Nelson

115

GB: 4-2
MN: 3-3

PACKERS "VERSES" VIKINGS ~ Carl Nelson

THE PACKERS ROLLED INTO THE METRODOME
LOOKING TO TAKE HOME THE EASY WIN
BUT WHATEVER DEMONS HAUNT THAT PLACE
DESCENDED ON GREEN BAY ONCE AGAIN

A WEEK AGO THE GREEN BAY PACKERS' TEAM
LOOKED TO TRULY BE ON A ROLL
THEN THEY TRAVELED TO THAT MINNESOTA DOME
BETTER KNOWN AS GREEN BAY'S "BLACK HOLE"

DESPITE MANY EARLY OPPORTUNITIES
THE PACKERS COULDN'T SEEM TO SCORE
AND ONCE THEIR CONFIDENCE BEGAN TO WAIVER
THE VIKINGS DOMINATED THEM ONCE MORE

EXCEPT FOR A GREAT RUN BY AHMAN GREEN
AND TOUCHDOWNS BY LEE AND BUBBA FRANKS
THE PACKERS LOOKED QUITE MISERABLE
AS IF THEY HAD NO GAS IN THEIR TANKS

THE PACKER TEAM LOOKED SO COMPLETELY BAD
IT'S EASY TO SEE THIS SIMPLY WAS A "GLITCH"
AND IN DECEMBER'S WANING DAYS
THE VIKES WILL FIND THAT PAYBACKS CAN BE QUITE RICH

~ ~ ~ ~ ~ ~ ~ ~ ~ ~ ~ ~ ~ ~ ~ ~ ~ ~ ~

THE VIKINGS THIS WEEK MUST TRAVEL SOUTH
FAR FROM THE FRIENDLY CONFINES OF THEIR HOME
FOR A REMATCH WITH TAMPA'S BUCCANEERS
WHOM THEY MANAGED TO BEAT IN THE 'DOME

THE BUCS ARE IN A PLACE MUCH THE SAME
AS THE VIKINGS WERE LAST WEEK
THEY'VE NOT PLAYED WELL AND ARE A LITTLE NICKED
AND WILL BE FACING A TEAM THAT'S AT ITS PEAK

THIS IS THE RECIPE FOR AN UPSET WIN
AS GREEN BAY'S PACKERS CAN WELL ATTEST
IT'S WHEN SOME TEAMS FEEL TRULY CORNERED
THAT OFTIMES THEY PLAY THEIR BEST

MINNESOTA MAY FINALLY BE AWAKENING
LAST WEEK THEIR EYES WERE SURELY OPEN WIDE
CAN THEY MAINTAIN THE SAME INTENSITY
AND NOT STUMBLE OVER THEIR PURPLE PRIDE?

THERE IS NO CLEAR FAVORITE IN THIS GAME
ONE WHICH EITHER TEAM COULD WIN
BUT THE BUCS HAVE WON FOUR OF THE LAST FIVE
AND WILL PROBABLY DO THAT ONCE AGAIN

RESULTS:
Green Bay was on their "Bye Week"

Minnesota lost to the Tampa Bay Buccaneers 14-41

GB: 4-2
MN: 3-4

PACKERS "VERSES" VIKINGS ~ Carl Nelson

LAST WEEK AT JUST ABOUT THIS TIME
THE VIKES WERE FEELING GOOD
THEY WERE FRESH FROM UPSETTING THE PACKERS' TEAM
AND WERE PLAYING LIKE THEY SHOULD

TAMPA BAY WAS THE NEXT OPPONENT
THAT MINNESOTA HAD LINED UP IN THEIR SIGHTS
THE BUCS WERE INJURED AND HAD NOT PLAYED WELL
IT SEEMED THE VIKINGS HAD THEM DEAD TO RIGHTS

BUT EVERY FOOTBALL TEAM HAS ITS BAD DAYS
ON SUNDAY THE VIKINGS HAD ONE OF THOSE
FROM THE KICKOFF TO THE FINAL GUN
THEY WERE AS FLAT AS DAUNTE'S NOSE

THE BUCCANEERS NEVER LET THEM INTO THE GAME
FROM THE BEGINNING THE VIKES WERE DOOMED
THE ONLY FIGHT THEY SHOWED WAS ON THE SIDELINES
ONTO WHICH THE TV CAMERAS ZOOMED

WHEN THE BLOODSHED WAS ALL FINISHED
THE VIKES HAD LOST FORTY-ONE TO FOURTEEN
DENNY WILL SPEND THIS UPCOMING BYE WEEK
FIGURING HOW TO SAVE THIS FOOTBALL TEAM

~ ~ ~ ~ ~ ~ ~ ~ ~ ~ ~ ~ ~ ~ ~ ~ ~ ~

THE PACKERS THIS WEEK FACE TAMPA'S TEAM
WHO WILL STILL BE FLUSHED FROM THE VIKINGS' WIN
EARLIER THIS YEAR TAMPA GOT PAST GREEN BAY
COULD IT POSSIBLY HAPPEN ONCE AGAIN?

MIKE ALSTOTT WAS THE STAR OF THAT GAME
COMING UP WITH THE LATE GAME SCORING RUN
AGAINST A TIRED GREEN BAY DEFENSE
WHO WERE DRAINED BY THE HEAT AND SUN

A REPEAT PERFORMANCE ISN'T LIKELY
GREEN BAY SHOULD BE FEELING QUITE REFRESHED
AND LET'S THROW IN ONE MORE FACTOR
THAT MAY PLAY INTO THIS WEEK'S TEST

IT MIGHT BE THE METRODOME OR RAYMOND JAMES
EVERY TEAM HAS TO PLAY IN A PLACE IT FEARS
FOR TAMPA'S BUCS IT'S LAMBEAU FIELD
WHERE THEY'VE NOT WON IN TWELVE LONG YEARS

AHMAN GREEN WILL GET BACK ON PACE
AND FRANKS SHOULD CATCH A COUPLE TD TOSSES
IT'S KIND OF A SHAME THIS RIVALRY HAS TO END
WITH THIRTEEN CONSECUTIVE TAMPA LOSSES

RESULTS:
Green bay beat the
Tampa Bay Buccaneers 21-20

Minnesota was on their
"Bye Week"

GB: 5-2
MN: 3-4

PACKERS "VERSES" VIKINGS ~ Carl Nelson

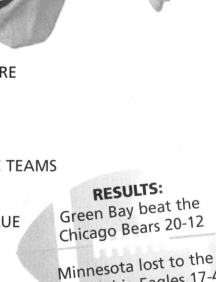

THE VIKINGS HAVE HAD A WEEK OFF
TO REFLECT ON WHAT HAPPENED IN TAMPA BAY
SOMEHOW THEY MUST PULL THEMSELVES TOGETHER
AND NOT ALLOW A REPEAT OF THAT DAY

DONOVAN MCNABB AND THE EAGLES' TEAM
ARE THE NEXT CHALLENGE THE VIKINGS MUST FACE
MINNESOTA IS STRIVING TO CLIMB TO FOUR AND FOUR
WHILE PHILLY'S TRYING TO STAY IN FIRST PLACE

LIKE CULPEPPER YOUNG MCNABB
IS A THREAT TO RUN AS WELL AS PASS
UNLIKE DAUNTE HOWEVER THE EAGLES' LINE
KEEPS DONOVAN'S BUTT UP OFF THE GRASS

DUCE STALEY AT THE RUNNING BACK
SHOULD GIVE THE VIKINGS' DEFENSE FITS
SPEAKING OF DEFENSE DON'T BE SURPRISED
TO SEE SOME VIKINGS TAKE BIG HITS

AS ROAD WARRIORS MINNESOTA'S TEAM
USUALLY MANAGE TO LOOK A LITTLE LAME
ALL OF THEIR LOSSES HAVE BEEN ON THE ROAD
LOOK FOR SUNDAY'S OUTCOME TO BE THE SAME

~ ~ ~ ~ ~ ~ ~ ~ ~ ~ ~ ~ ~ ~ ~ ~ ~ ~ ~

THE PACKERS THIS WEEK TRAVEL SOUTHWARD
TO RENEW THEIR MUCH-STORIED WAR
WITH CHICAGO'S BEARS AT SOLDIER FIELD
A PLACE WHERE THEY'LL PLAY NO MORE

SEVEN STRAIGHT TIMES GREEN BAY HAS GONE THERE
AND DEALT TO THE BEARS A BITTER DEFEAT
SOMEHOW THAT IS ONE PACKERS' VICTORY
THAT IS ALWAYS PARTICULARLY SWEET

THERE HAVE BEEN HARD FEELINGS BETWEEN THESE TEAMS
GOING BACK TO WHEN THE LEAGUE WAS NEW
THEY'LL BITE AND SCRATCH AND KICK AND GOUGE
AND GENERALLY BEAT EACH OTHER BLACK-AND-BLUE

RESULTS:
Green Bay beat the
Chicago Bears 20-12

Minnesota lost to the
Philadelphia Eagles 17-48

THE BEARS ARE CURRENTLY IN FIRST PLACE
HOLDING A FULL GAME LEAD OVER GREEN BAY
THE RECORD IS THE RESULT OF A LOT OF HARD WORK
AND A COUPLE UNBELIEVABLY LUCKY GAME-ENDING PLAYS

FOR THE BEARS TO WIN THIS UPCOMING SUNDAY
IT WILL TAKE A LOT MORE THAN THAT LUCK
THE PACK IS DOING QUITE WELL THEMSELVES
AND AS IT SAYS IN THE SONG— "THE BEARS STILL SUCK"

GB: 6-2
MN: 3-5

PACKERS "VERSES" VIKINGS ~ Carl Nelson

GENERAL CUSTER HAD A BETTER CHANCE
THAN THE VIKINGS HAD LAST WEEK
EVEN DURING THE LES STECKEL YEARS
THE VIKES HAVE NEVER LOOKED SO WEAK

A LITTLE MORE THAN A YEAR AGO
THE VIKES WERE RIDING HIGH
THEY HAD JUST POLISHED OFF THE SAINTS
AFTER A FIRST-ROUND PLAYOFF BYE

A QUICK TRIP OUT TO THE EAST COAST
AND THE SUPER BOWL BERTH WOULD BE ENSURED
THE GIANTS REALLY CAUSED NO WORRY
BUT WERE AN ANNOYANCE TO BE ENDURED

NO ONE REALLY UNDERSTANDS OR CAN EXPLAIN
WHAT HAPPENED TO MINNESOTA'S TEAM THAT DAY
BUT TRACES OF THAT GAME LINGER
AND ARE EVIDENT IN THE WAY THE VIKINGS PLAY

SO MONDAY NIGHT IS REVENGE TIME
AS THE GIANTS ROLL INTO THE 'DOME
IS EMOTION REALLY GOING TO BE ENOUGH
TO PREVENT THE VIKES BEING BLOWN OUT AT HOME?

~ ~ ~ ~ ~ ~ ~ ~ ~ ~ ~ ~ ~ ~ ~ ~ ~ ~ ~

CHICAGO'S BEARS HAD QUITE A CHANCE
TO CONTINUE THEIR SIX-GAME VICTORY RUN
BUT WHEN THE GAME WAS ON THE LINE
ONCE AGAIN THEY COULDN'T GET IT DONE

THE PACKERS TOOK AWAY THE "A-TRAIN"
AND WHILE DA BEARS CONTESTED EVERY YARD
AHMAN'S LEGS AND BRETT FAVRE'S ARM
COLLAPSED CHICAGO'S HOUSE OF CARDS

THE PACK NOW RETURNS TO LAMBEAU FIELD
TO TAKE ON ATLANTA'S "DIRTY BIRDS"
HOW STRANGE TO THINK THAT THREE YEARS AGO
GREEN BAY WOULD HAVE TREMBLED AT THOSE WORDS

BUT TOUGH TIMES HAVE BEFALLEN THE FALCONS
THEY'VE NOT DONE VERY WELL SINCE THEN
JAMAL HAS TWICE BLOWN OUT A KNEE
AND IT'S NOT IF THE QB GETS HURT—BUT WHEN

RESULTS:
Green Bay lost to the
Atlanta Falcons 20-23

Minnesota beat the
New York Giants 28-16

COMPLACENCY CAN BECOME THE ENEMY
WHEN PLAYING A SLUMPING TEAM OF THIS VERY TYPE
THE PACKERS HAVE TO MAINTAIN THEIR INTENSITY
TO LIVE UP TO ALL THE CURRENT PACKERS' HYPE

GB: 6-3
MN: 4-5

PACKERS "VERSES" VIKINGS ~ Carl Nelson

WAS REVENGE THE MOTIVATING FACTOR
IN THE VIKINGS' MONDAY WIN?
WAS IT DESIRE TO HONOR KOREY STRINGER
OR THE FEAR OF BEING CRUSHED ONCE AGAIN?

WHATEVER THE REASON THEY SHOWED UP BIG
AND ALTHOUGH THE GAME WASN'T VERY PRETTY
THEY PLAYED WELL ENOUGH TO BEAT NEW YORK
IN A PERFORMANCE THAT WAS DOWNRIGHT GRITTY

THIS WEEK COMES A CHANCE TO HELP THEMSELVES
BY KNOCKING OFF THE DIVISION-LEADING BEARS
ONCE BEFORE THIS SEASON THESE TEAMS HAVE PLAYED
WITH THE BEARS PULLING OUT THE WIN DOWN THERE

BUT THIS GAME WILL BE ON THE VIKINGS' HOME FIELD
IN THE HUBERT HUMPHREY "ROLLER-DOME"
WHILE THE BEARS ARE SHOWING THAT THEY'RE FOR REAL
THE VIKES ARE HARD TO BEAT AT HOME

FOR ONCE IN THEIR LIVES THEY'LL BE HEROES
TO THE BUCS AND GREEN BAY'S PACK
IF THEY CAN MANAGE TO GET PAST THE BEARS
AND DEAL CHIGAGO A MASSIVE SET BACK

~ ~ ~ ~ ~ ~ ~ ~ ~ ~ ~ ~ ~ ~ ~ ~ ~ ~ ~

ONCE AGAIN THIS GREEN BAY PACKERS' TEAM
TOOK THE FIELD SEEMINGLY UNPREPARED
STARTING THE GAME WITH A LACK OF FOCUS
LOOKING ALMOST AS IF NOBODY CARED

THE FALCONS MEANWHILE WERE "ON THE BEAM"
AND BROUGHT THEIR BEST GAME TO GREEN BAY
THEY BLOCKED AND RAN AND TACKLED HARD
AND TOOK THE WIN AT LAMBEAU LAST SUNDAY

PERHAPS THE PACKERS WERE COMPLACENT
BELIEVING THE THINGS WRITTEN IN THE PRESS
OR MAYBE THEY OVERLOOKED THE BIRDS
THINKING THAT ON THE FIELD THEY WERE THE BEST

NOW THE PACKERS FACE A MUCH TOUGHER TEST
THAN ON THE SURFACE IT WOULD SEEM
THEY MUST GO ON THE ROAD TO FACE THE LIONS
FOR WHOM THE FIRST WIN IS STILL A DREAM

GREEN BAY MUST PLAY THEM ON THANKSGIVING DAY
WHEN THE LIONS LOOK BETTER THAN IT SEEMS THEY COULD
GREEN BAY MUST SLAY SOME "DOME-GAME DEMONS"
IF THEY ARE TO PICK UP THE WIN THEY SHOULD

RESULTS:
Green Bay beat the
Detroit Lions 29-27

Minnesota lost to the
Chicago Bears 6-13

GB: 7-3
MN: 4-6

~ Carl Nelson

PACKERS "VERSES" VIKINGS

"THE VIKINGS ALWAYS PLAY BETTER IN THE 'DOME"
IS WHAT FOOTBALL ANALYSTS OFTEN SAY
WELL CHICAGO'S BEARS "DOME-INATED" THEM
IN THE EVENING GAME LAST SUNDAY

MINNESOTA'S DEFENSE IT MUST BE SAID
INSPIRED BY THE "GIANT" WIN LAST MONDAY NIGHT
TOOK THE FIELD SET TO DEFEND THEIR TURF
AND WEREN'T ABOUT TO YIELD WITHOUT A FIGHT

BUT ONCE AGAIN IT WAS THE VIKINGS' OFFENSE
THAT CAME UP SHORT IN THE FINAL TALLY
WHILE THE DEFENSE ONLY GAVE UP THIRTEEN POINTS
THE VIKES WERE UNABLE TO MOUNT AN OFFENSIVE RALLY

NOW IT'S ON THE ROAD TO PITTSBURGH
TO TAKE ON THE STEELERS WHO ARE EIGHT-AND-TWO
DENNY GREEN AND THE REST OF THE COACHING STAFF
HAVE TO BE WONDERING JUST WHAT THEY CAN DO

KORDELL STEWART IS FINALLY PLAYING WELL
AND DOWN THE FIELD "THE BUS" HAS BEEN A RUMBLIN'
UNLESS THE VIKES CAN PULL OFF A MIRACLE
ANY POST-SEASON DREAMS WILL BE A-CRUMBLIN'

~ ~ ~ ~ ~ ~ ~ ~ ~ ~ ~ ~ ~ ~ ~ ~ ~ ~

EXCEPT FOR THE LAST THREE MINUTES
AT THE SILVERDOME ON TURKEY DAY
GREEN BAY SEEMED TO HAVE THE GAME IN HAND
AND MOST THINGS WERE GOING THE PACKERS' WAY

BUT THEN THE DETROIT LIONS DID THEIR LEVEL BEST
TO RUIN THANKSGIVING FOR PACKER FANS
A LATE-GAME COMEBACK AND A PAIR OF SCORES
LEFT THE GAME'S OUTCOME SQUARELY IN THEIR HANDS

A YOUNG QUARTERBACK MADE A BAD CHOICE
ON A TWO-POINT CONVERSION TRY
WHICH IF SUCCESSFUL WOULD HAVE PROVIDED
THE LIONS WITH AN END-OF-GAME TIE

BUT IT DIDN'T HAPPEN QUITE THAT WAY
EVERYWHERE PACKERS' FANS SIGHED WITH RELIEF
AND HOPEFULLY THE GREEN BAY PLAYERS LEARNED
THAT AN "EASY WIN" IS A FAULTY BELIEF

THE JACKSONVILLE JAGUARS ARE UP NEXT
PROVIDING THE CHALLENGE FOR THIS WEEK
STAYING WITHIN STRIKING DISTANCE OF THE BEARS
SHOULD PROVIDE ANY MOTIVATION THE PACKERS SEEK

RESULTS:
Green Bay beat the
Jacksonville Jaguars 28-21

Minnesota lost to the
Pittsburgh Steelers 16-21

GB: 8-3
MN: 4-7

IN A SCENE THAT WAS ALL TOO FAMILIAR TO VIKES' FANS
A "WHIPPING" WAS GIVEN IN LAST SUNDAY'S GAME
THE DEFENSE HAD BEEN RUN DOWN BY "THE BUS"
BEFORE INJURIES FORCED HIM TO PULL UP QUITE LAME

CULPEPPER HIMSELF HAD SOUGHT THE BENCH
TO NURSE A SWOLLEN DAMAGED KNEE
TODD BOUMAN CAME ON TO FILL HIS SHOES
AND PUT ON A QUITE A SHOW TO SEE

MICHAEL BENNETT FINALLY HAD THE CHANCE
TO SHOWCASE HIS LIGHTNING-QUICK FEET
RANDY MOSS SEEMED TO COME ALIVE
BUT THE RALLY COULDN'T SAVE THEM FROM DEFEAT

TENNESEE'S TITANS ARE THIS WEEK'S FOE
BRINGING EDDIE GEORGE AND "AIR" MCNAIR
BUT LIKE THE VIKES THEY'VE BEEN DISAPPOINTING
SO MINNESOTA FANS SHOULD NOT FEEL DESPAIR

THE VIKINGS WILL STILL NEED A BIG GAME
FROM EVERYONE ON BOTH SIDES OF THE BALL
THE TITANS AREN'T GOING TO ROLL OVER AND DIE
AND WILL GIVE MINNESOTA THEIR ALL

~ ~ ~ ~ ~ ~ ~ ~ ~ ~ ~ ~ ~ ~ ~ ~ ~ ~ ~

THE FOOTBALL GODS MAY HAVE SMILED
ON THE PACKERS LAST MONDAY NIGHT
AND IT'S A DARNED GOOD THING THEY DID
AS THE JAGUARS PUT UP QUITE A FIGHT

MONDAY'S WIN KEPT THE PACKERS IN SECOND PLACE
A MERE HALF-GAME BEHIND THOSE DARNED BEARS
WHO INVADE THE TEMPLE OF LAMBEAU SUNDAY
NOT INTENDING THAT FIRST PLACE TO SHARE

THE BEARS HAVE BEEN WINNING SOME CLOSE GAMES
THOUGH IT COULD BE SAID THEIR OPPONENTS HAVE BEATEN THEMSELVES
BUT THIS GAME WON'T BE WON WITH TRICKERY
OR THE HELP OF MAGIC OR ELVES

THIS WILL BE A GAME FROM THE "OLD DAYS"
THAT WILL FEATURE THE RUN FAR MORE THAN THE PASS
LIKE GLADIATORS THEY WILL DO BATTLE
UNTIL ONE TEAM IS KNOCKED ON THEIR GRASS

AND WHILE THE SUN IS SETTING IN THE WEST
AND THE CHEESEHEADS HAVE FINISHED THE COLD BEER AND WURST
THEY WILL RETURN TO THEIR HOMES QUITE CONTENTED
KNOWING THE PACKERS ARE FIRMLY ENTRENCHED IN FIRS

PACKERS "VERSES" VIKINGS ~ Carl Nelson

RESULTS:
Green Bay beat the
Chicago Bears 17-7

Minnesota beat the
Tennessee Titans 42-24

PACKERS "VERSES" VIKINGS ~ Carl Nelson

LAST SUNDAY THE VIKINGS GAVE A DEMO
OF WHAT THAT OFFENSE IS SUPPOSED TO BE
ABLE TO SCORE SEEMINGLY AT WILL
AGAINST THE TITANS OF TENNESSEE

THE VIKINGS SPOTTED THEM AN EARLY LEAD
AS THEY HAVE DONE TO SO MANY TEAMS BEFORE
IT WASN'T LOOKING GOOD 'TIL THE TITANS FUMBLED
THEN TODD BOUMAN LED THEM TO THE SCORE

AND SCORE THEY DID IN MANY WAYS
THROUGH THE PASSING GAME AND THE RUN
CARTER WAS EVEN THROWING LATERALS
AND OVERALL THE VIKES WERE HAVING FUN

IT'S JUST TOO BAD IT'S COME TOO LATE
IN WHAT HAS BECOME A SEASON OF FRUSTRATION
NOW THE VIKINGS TRAVEL TO FACE THE LIONS
WHO HAVE HAD TO CARRY THEIR SHARE OF HUMILIATION

DETROIT'S TEAM MAY NOT BE AS BAD
AS THE WON-LOSS RECORD MAKES IT APPEAR
MINNESOTA MUST REMAIN ON THEIR TOES
OR THE LIONS WILL KNOCK THEM ON THEIR REARS

~ ~ ~ ~ ~ ~ ~ ~ ~ ~ ~ ~ ~ ~ ~ ~ ~ ~ ~

LIKE THE LAST TIME THAT THESE TWO TEAMS MET
CHICAGO BAFFLED GREEN BAY'S PACK
ALTHOUGH THEY HAVE THE ABILITY TO PASS
THEY CHOSE THE CHICAGO "WET-TOAST" ATTACK

THE PACKER "D" PROVED UP TO THE TASK
OF STOPPING THE VAUNTED "A-TRAIN" AND HIS RUNS
WHILE CHICAGO COULDN'T STOP AHMAN GREEN
WHO TORE THROUGH THEM LIKE A BULLET FROM A GUN

SO AT LEAST FOR THIS MOMENT
THE PACKERS ARE SITTING IN FIRST PLACE
WITH FOUR TO GO THERE'S NO ROOM FOR ERROR
IN THIS LATE STAGE OF THE RACE

WHILE THE BEARS DIDN'T TRY TO PASS THE BALL
TENNESSEE'S TITANS WON'T EVEN HESITATE
"AIR" MCNAIR WILL PUT IT UP
AND HOPE THE PACKERS GET THERE LATE

RESULTS:
Green Bay lost to the
Tennessee Titans 20-26

Minnesota lost to the
Detroit Lions 24-27

BUT THE TENNESSEE TITAN DEFENSE
MADE EVEN MINNESOTA'S OFFENSE LOOK PRETTY GOOD
AS LONG AS THE PACK DOESN'T LOOK PAST THIS TEAM
THEY'LL BRING HOME THE VICTORY THAT THEY SHOULD

GB: 9-4
MN: 5-8

PACKERS "VERSES" VIKINGS ~ Carl Nelson

LAST SUNDAY THE VIKINGS WERE AS BENEVOLENT
AS IS SANTA CLAUS WITH HIS ELVES
FOR ALTHOUGH THE LIONS HAD LOST A DOZEN GAMES
MINNESOTA MANAGED TO SAVE THEM FROM THEMSELVES

THIS GAME STARTED OUT PRETTY UGLY
WITH BOTH DEFENSES SCORING THE FIRST TDs
THEN THE LIONS STARTED ON A MINI-ROLL
THAT SEEM TO BRING THE VIKINGS TO THEIR KNEES

BUT EARLY IN THE SECOND HALF
THE VIKINGS WENT ON A SCORING TEAR
GAINING THE LEAD IN THE FOURTH QUARTER
BUT THE ABILITY TO HOLD IT JUST WASN'T THERE

THIS WEEK THE VIKES' HOME SEASON ENDS
WITH JACKSONVILLE COMING INTO THE 'DOME
MINNESOTA'S PLAYOFF HOPES HAVE EVAPORATED
BUT THEY'LL TRY FOR ONE LAST WIN AT HOME

AFTER LOSING TO BOTH CAROLINA AND DETROIT
FOR THEIR OWN PRIDE THEY MUST BEAT THE JAGS
BUT IF THE VIKINGS FALL BEHIND LATE IN THIS GAME
LOOK FOR THE FANS TO COVER THEIR HEADS WITH BAGS

~ ~ ~ ~ ~ ~ ~ ~ ~ ~ ~ ~ ~ ~ ~ ~ ~ ~ ~

THERE SHOULD NOT HAVE BEEN MUCH OF A CHALLENGE
PRESENTED TO THE PACKERS IN LAST WEEK'S GAME
BUT AFTER BIG GAMES THEY STRUGGLE WITH CONSISTENCY
AND ON SUNDAY THE STORY WAS THE SAME

THE TITANS WERE SO BATTERED AND INJURY-RIDDLED
THEY RESEMBLED THE AFGHANI TALIBAN
EARLY ON THE DEFENSE STYMIED THE PACK
AND "TERRORIZED" GREEN BAY'S OFFENSIVE PLAN

RESULTS:
Green Bay beat the
Cleveland Browns 30-7

Minnesota lost to the
Jacksonville Jaguars 3-33

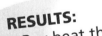

WHILE FAVRE AND THE PACKERS LABORED BRAVELY
FOR WHATEVER REASON THEY NEVER GOT IN SYNCH
THE RECEIVERS COULDN'T CATCH THE DOGGONE BALL
AND THE PACKERS' DEFENSE DROVE THE FANS TO DRINK

A PLAYOFF SPOT CAN BE CLINCHED THIS WEEK
WITH A VICTORY OVER THE CLEVELAND BROWNS
FORTUNATELY THIS GAME WILL BE PLAYED AT LAMBEAU
SO THERE SHOULD BE NO BOTTLES RAINING DOWN

THE PACKERS SIMPLY HAVE TO WIN THIS GAME
TO BECOME ONE OF THIS YEAR'S PLAYOFF CONTENDERS
IT'S TIME FOR THIS TEAM TO MAKE A STAND
AND TO SHOW THAT THEY AREN'T MERELY PRETENDERS

MERRY CHRISTMAS TO ONE AND ALL !!

124

GB: 10-4
MN: 5-9

~ Carl Nelson

PACKERS "VERSES" VIKINGS

WHILE "IT MAY BE BETTER TO GIVE THAN TO RECEIVE"
THE VIKINGS TOOK THE CONCEPT TO EXTREMES
GETTING WHIPPED AT HOME BY JACKSONVILLE
IN A GAME MORE LIKE A NIGHTMARE THAN A DREAM

AFTER BOUMAN WENT OUT IN THE FIRST QUARTER
MINNESOTA'S OFFENSE SPIRALED INTO THE TURF
WHILE THE VIKING DEFENSE WAS SO OUTMANNED
IT GAVE MOST FANS THE CHANCE TO CHANNEL SURF

~ ~ ~ ~ ~ ~ ~ ~ ~ ~ ~ ~ ~ ~ ~ ~ ~

THE CLEVELAND BROWNS CAME INTO LAMBEAU FIELD
HOPING TO PULL AN UPSET ON THE PACK
BUT AHMAN'S FIRST CARRY WENT FOR TWENTY-SEVEN
FROM THAT POINT ON THEY NEVER LOOKED BACK

ON A DAY THAT REALLY LOOKED LIKE LATE DECEMBER
COLD AND WINDY WITH SNOWFLAKES DRIFTING DOWN
GREEN BAY CLINCHED THEMSELVES A PLAYOFF SPOT
BY BLOWING OUT THOSE SELF-SAME BROWNS

~ ~ ~ ~ ~ ~ ~ ~ ~ ~ ~ ~ ~ ~ ~ ~ ~

THIS WEEK THE PACKERS HOST THAT VIKINGS' TEAM
WHICH HAS LOOKED SO BAD IN RECENT WEEKS
MINNESOTA'S TEAM WILL BE PLAYING FOR THEIR PRIDE
AND THE CHANCE TO BRAG ABOUT A VIKINGS' SWEEP

BUT THIS IS A TEAM WHOSE STARTING QUARTERBACK
IS A GUY WHOSE FIRST NAME SOUNDS LIKE A FISH
WHILE THE VIKES HAVE HAD LUCK WITH THEIR BACKUPS
TO THINK SPURGEON CAN "WYNN" IS JUST AN IDLE WISH

THEIR OFFENSIVE LINE IS POROUS
AND THE DEFENSIVE LINE IS EVEN WORSE
CRIS CARTER IS BADMOUTHING RANDI MOSS
AND THE RUNNING GAME NEEDS A NURSE

SO IT WOULD BE THE PERFECT SETUP
FOR THE PACKERS TO COME OUT FLAT
LIKE THE LAST TIME THESE TWO TEAMS PLAYED
WHEN THEY DID EXACTLY THAT

THIS TIME HOWEVER THE PACK'S AT HOME
PLAYING UNDER A SNOW-FILLED WISCONSIN SKY
BRETT FAVRE IS PERFECT UNDER THESE CONDITIONS
AND THIS TEAM IS FLYING HIGH

GREEN BAY WOULD ALSO LIKE SOME SMALL REVENGE
FOR THE VIKES LOSING TO CHICAGO NOT ONCE BUT TWICE
THE PACK IS SUPPOSED TO WIN BY ELEVEN POINTS
BUT THE TEN-POINTER WILL BE JUST AS NICE

MINNESOTA
The Land of
10,000 Lakes

How do
you think
they got
there?

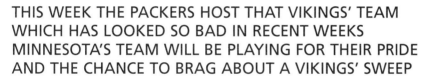

RESULTS:
Green Bay beat the
Minnesota Vikings 24-13

GB: 11-4
MN: 5-10

~ Carl Nelson

PACKERS "VERSES" VIKINGS

WHATEVER ELSE IS SAID ABOUT SUNDAY'S GAME
THE VIKINGS' DEFENSE MUST GET SOME "PROPS"
THEY PLAYED A FIRED-UP INTENSE GAME
AND BROUGHT THE PACKERS' OFFENSE TO A STOP

THE PACKERS' DEFENSE PLAYED WELL TOO
ALTHOUGH THEY HAD BIG PROBLEMS AGAINST THE RUN
BUT MOSS AND CARTER CONTRIBUTED ZERO TOUCHDOWNS
AND SPERGON DIDN'T HAVE A LOT OF FUN

THE PACKERS MAY HAVE THOUGHT THE VIKES
WOULD PLAY AS THEY HAD IN THE TWO WEEKS PAST
WHEN THEY STUMBLED AND FUMBLED AND LOOKED PRETTY BAD
BUT THE VIKES NEARLY KICKED THE PACKERS' ASS

MINNESOTA LED THIS GAME LATE
UP BY THREE WITH TEN MINUTES TO GO
BEFORE BRETT FAVRE FOUND HIS RHYTHM
AND HIS PASSES LED TO THE FINAL PACKERS' BLOW

~ ~ ~ ~ ~ ~ ~ ~ ~ ~ ~ ~ ~ ~ ~ ~ ~ ~

THE VIKINGS CLOSE THIS UNPLEASANT SEASON
BY FACING THE RAVENS MONDAY NIGHT
AT THE YEAR'S BEGINING IT SEEMED THIS GAME
WOULD BE A SIMPLY MARVELOUS SIGHT

BUT ALAS FORTUNE HASN'T SMILED MUCH
ON EITHER TEAM IN THIS CONTEST
BUT BALTIMORE IS STILL GRASPING FOR THE PLAYOFFS
AND IT SEEMS THE VIKINGS WON'T PASS THIS TEST

AND NOW UGLY RUMORS HAVE SURFACED
CAUSING MANY PEOPLE TO SCRATCH THEIR HEADS
IT SEEMS DENNY GREEN WILL BE FIRED NEXT WEEK
AT THE REQUEST OF THE OWNER, "BIG RED"

~ ~ ~ ~ ~ ~ ~ ~ ~ ~ ~ ~ ~ ~ ~ ~ ~ ~

THE PACKERS TRAVEL OUT TO THE EAST COAST
FOR A GAME WITH THE GIANTS THIS WEEK
AND WHILE NEW YORK WILL FINISH THEIR SEASON
A HOME PLAYOFF GAME IS WHAT GREEN BAY WILL SEEK

THE PACKERS' DEFENSE IS SPOTTY AND INJURED
AND THE RECEIVERS HAVE GROWN HANDS OF STONE
WHILE AHMAN GREEN IS GIVING EACH GAME HIS ALL
IT'S OFTEN UP TO BRETT FAVRE ALONE

BUT THIS GAME WILL BE PLAYED IN THE OPEN
ON GRASS IN THE COLD AND POSSIBLY SNOW
THE TABLE IS SET AND IT'S UP TO THE PACKERS
TO DECIDE JUST HOW THIS GAME WILL GO

RESULTS:
Green Bay beat the
New York Giants 34-25

Minnesota lost to the
Baltimore Ravens 3-19

126

GB: 12-4
MN: 5-11

~ Carl Nelson

PACKERS "VERSES" VIKINGS

WITH ONE OF THE UGLIEST GAMES EVER WITNESSED
THE VIKINGS CLOSED OUT THE SEASON MONDAY NIGHT
THERE WASN'T A LOT FOR VIKES FANS TO TAKE HOPE FROM
THANKFULLY FOR THIS YEAR THEY'VE TURNED OUT THE LIGHTS

NOW IT'S TIME FOR THE VIKINGS' POSTMORTEM
WHAT IN THE WORLD EVER HAPPENED TO THIS TEAM?
THEY ENTERED THIS SEASON FULL OF PROMISE
AND ENDED IT CAUGHT IN A VERY BAD SCENE

WHILE STRINGER'S DEATH MAY HAVE BEEN A PART
OF THE STRUGGLES IN THE EARLY GAMES
UNITY AND LEADERSHIP SEEMED TO BE LACKING
WITH SIDELINE BICKERING FANNING THE FLAMES

MICHAEL BENNETT WAS NOT THE NEEDED FILL-IN
FOR THE VOID LEFT BY ROBERT SMITH
AND ONCE CULPEPPER STARTED GETTING INJURED
THERE WASN'T A LOT FOR THE VIKINGS TO WORK WITH

ABOUT THE DEFENSE WHAT CAN BE SAID?
EXCEPT THAT THEY DIDN'T INSPIRE MUCH FEAR
ADD THESE FACTORS AND IT'S NO BIG SURPRISE
THE VIKES DIDN'T WIN MUCH THIS YEAR

NOW DENNY GREEN HAS BEEN SENT PACKING
A BEGINNING TO SOLVING THIS PUZZLE
THE FIRST ORDER OF BUSINESS FOR HIS REPLACEMENT
WILL BE TO FIND A "RANDY-PROOF" MUZZLE
~ ~ ~ ~ ~ ~ ~ ~ ~ ~ ~ ~ ~ ~ ~ ~ ~ ~ ~

THE PACKERS DEFEATED THE NEW YORK GIANTS
TO KEEP THEIR HOME PLAYOFF HOPES ALIVE
EARLY ON THEY DOMINATED NEW YORK
ALTHOUGH NEAR THE END BRETT DID TAKE A DIVE

BUT THIS WEEK THE POSTSEASON BEGINS ANEW
WITH THE PACK WELCOMING THE 'NINERS TO LAMBEAU
BE ASSURED THE PACKERS REMEMBER THE LAST PLAYOFF GAME
WHEN A LOSS LEFT THEM WITH NOWHERE TO GO

STEVE YOUNG IS GONE AND JERRY RICE TOO
THOUGH GARCIA AND OWENS HAVE TAKEN THEIR PLACE
GARRISON HEARST HAS RECOVERED FROM HIS INJURIES
AND IS RUNNING ALL OVER THE PLACE

AND THAT'S THE KEY FOR THIS PACKERS' TEAM
CONTROLLING THE 'NINERS GROUND GAME
EARLY ON GREEN BAY'S "D" WAS AWESOME
FOR SOME WEEKS THEY HAVE NOT BEEN THE SAME

RESULTS:
Green Bay beat the
San Francisco 49ers 25-15

SAN FRANCISCO'S DEFENSE IS ADEQUATE
AS LONG AS THEY ARE PLAYING A TEAM THAT'S BEHIND
AND ALLOWING THE PACKERS TO BE IN THAT POSITION
IS THE LAST THING ON OUR BRETT FAVRE'S MIND

IF THE RECEIVERS CAN STEP UP THEIR PLAY
AND AHMAN GIVES THE RUNNING GAME A STRONG SHOWING
THE PACKERS CAN GET PAST THIS 'NINER TEAM
AND IT'S OFF TO CHICAGO THEY'LL BE GOING!!

Playoff Record
GB: 1-0
St. Louis: 0-0

PACKERS "VERSES" VIKINGS ~ Carl Nelson

WHEN JEFF GARCIA TOOK THE SNAP
THAT STARTED LAST SUNDAY'S GAME
HE LOOKED UP AND SAW GILBERT BROWN
THEN THE STARS THAT FLASHED THROUGH HIS BRAIN

AND SO STARTED THE GAME WITH THE 'NINERS
A CONTEST THAT WAS TOUGH AND HARD-FOUGHT
ONE SAN FRANCISCO THOUGHT THEY SHOULD WIN
BUT AS HISTORY NOW SHOWS JUST COULD NOT

THE FIRST HALF BELONGED TO THE DEFENSIVE TEAMS
WITH NEITHER OFFENSE ABLE TO GET ON THE TRACK
HALFTIME FOUND THE SCORE SEVEN-TO-SIX
WITH A BLOCKED POINT BEGINNING TO HAUNT OUR PACK

BUT IN THE SECOND HALF THE GAME WAS DIFFERENT
WITH BOTH TEAMS FINDING WAYS TO MOVE THE BALL
THE PACK LED FIFTEEN TO EIGHT AT THE START OF THE FOURTH
AS GREEN BAY'S TEAM BEGAN TO ANSWER THE CALL

THE 'NINERS QUICKLY RETOOK THE LEAD
BUT GREEN BAY'S KICKER GOT IT BACK
AFTER A GREAT PLAY BY MIKE MCKENZIE
WHO CUT TERRELL OWENS NO SLACK

AHMAN GREEN WRAPPED UP THE SCORING
WITH A TOUCHDOWN NEAR THIS GAME'S END
THE LAMBEAU FIELD PLAYOFF STREAK IS STILL ALIVE
UNTIL THE PACKERS EXTEND IT AGAIN

WHAT'S THE REWARD FOR BEATING THE 'NINERS?
A CHANCE TO TAKE ON THE RAMS IN THEIR HOME
ST LOUIS HAS AN OFFENSE QUITE EXPLOSIVE
AND A TEAM THAT IS BUILT TO PLAY IN A DOME

KURT WARNER'S NATURAL QB SKILLS
HAVE BEEN DEVELOPED AND REFINED
NOT TO MENTION A GROUP OF RECEIVERS
THAT'S AS GOOD AS YOU'RE LIKELY TO FIND

RESULTS:
Green Bay lost to the
St Louis Rams 17-45

THE EXPERTS PICK THIS TEAM BY A WHOPPING TEN POINTS
OVER BRETT FAVRE AND OUR BELOVED PACK
BUT FAVRE AND THE TEAM DON'T SEEM WORRIED
AND HAVE WORKED OUT A PLAN OF ATTACK

THIS IS ANOTHER GAME THAT WILL DEMAND
THAT THE PACKERS PLAY FLAWLESS FOOTBALL
BUT IF THEY DON'T GET EXCITED AND MAKE DUMB MISTAKES
THERE'S A GOOD CHANCE THEY CAN ANSWER THIS CALL

A GOOD GAME IS NEEDED FROM GREEN AND FAVRE
AND THE DEFENSE MUST STEP UP TO THE LINE
IF THEY CAN HURRY AND RATTLE THE RAMS
THIS GAME'S OUTCOME SHOULD SUIT US JUST FINE

GB: 13-5
Final Season
Record

PACKERS "VERSES" VIKINGS ~ Carl Nelson

"IF YOU LIVE BY THE SWORD YOU'LL DIE BY THE SWORD"
IS THE WAY THE OLD SAYING GOES
THAT PROVED TO BE TRUE FOR THE PACKERS
AS A LOOK AT SUNDAY'S GAME SHOWS

IT WAS SUPPOSED TO BE A GAME FOR THE AGES
QUITE THE OFFENSIVE MASTERPIECE
HOWEVER IT DIDN'T WORK OUT QUITE THAT WAY
BECAUSE OF THE GROUP THAT WAS MENTIONED LEAST

AN EARLY PASS FROM BRETT TO BUBBA
WAS CAUGHT THEN DROPPED ON THE GROUND
A QUICK WHISTLE SAVED THE PACK THAT PLAY
AND THE PACKERS WERE GLAD FOR THAT SOUND

BUT THEN A MISREAD DEFENSIVE MOVE
AND AN ADJUSTMENT THAT WAS MADE FAR TOO QUICK
LED TO FAVRE'S PASS BEING INTERCEPTED
AND THE RAMS SCORING ON A TOO-EASY PICK

THAT'S THE WAY THAT THE WHOLE GAME WENT
WITH THE RAMS DEFENSE STEALING THE SHOW
SHOWING UP QUITE EFFICIENTLY
EVERYWHERE THE PACK WANTED THE BALL TO GO

IT WOULD BE EASY TO PUT THE BLAME ON BRETT FAVRE
OR BAD LUCK OR A FAULTY GAME PLAN
BUT IT WAS GREAT EFFORT BY THE ST LOUIS DEFENSE
MAKING GREAT PLAYS AGAIN AND AGAIN

THE RAMS' OFFENSE WAS GOOD ENOUGH
BUT NOT THE OVERWHELMING FORCE
THAT HAD BEEN PREDICTED BEFORE THE GAME
BY ALL OF THE MEDIA OF COURSE

THE PACK DEFENSE ACTUALLY PLAYED WELL ENOUGH
TO HAVE MADE A GAME OUT OF THIS ROUT
BUT ONCE THE TURNOVER FLOOD STARTED
THE OUTCOME REALLY WAS NEVER IN DOUBT

RESULTS:
The St Louis Rams beat the
Philadelphia Eagles 29-24

The New England Patriots beat the
Pittsburgh Steelers 24-17

SO THE PACKERS' SEASON ENDED
WITH A WHIMPER INSTEAD OF A BANG
BUT GREEN BAY'S TEAM DID WELL THIS SEASON
AND THERE'S NO REASON FOR THEIR HEADS TO HANG

SOME PLAYERS OF COURSE JUST WON'T BE BACK
AND THERE'S HOPE THAT NEW GUYS THOSE HOLES WILL FILL
THOUGH THIS YEAR THEY FELL SHORT OF THE CHAMPIONSHIP
NEXT YEAR I DON'T THINK THEY WILL

~ Carl Nelson

PACKERS "VERSES" VIKINGS

Super Bowl Record
Patriots: 0-2
Rams: 1-1

IT'S SUPER BOWL TIME ALREADY
HARDLY SEEMS THAT IT CAN BE SO
TWENTY ONE WEEKS SINCE THE KICKOFF
WHEREVER DID THAT TIME GO?

BUT NOW THIS COMING SUNDAY
WILL BE THE FINAL TEST
OF THE TWO TEAMS WHO HAVE PROVEN
THAT THEY STAND ABOVE THE REST

FROM THE AFC COMES THE PATRIOTS
A TEAM THAT IS SOMEWHAT OF A SURPRISE
WHOSE SUPERSTAR QUARTERBACK WENT OUT EARLY
AND HAD TRY ON THE BACKUP ON FOR SIZE

THAT MAN IS YOUNG TOM BRADY
HE'S PLAYED LIKE A MAN POSSESSED
AND WAS THE WINNER IN TEN OF FOURTEEN GAMES
FAR BETTER THAN COACHES COULD HAVE GUESSED

NOW BRADY AND THE PATRIOTS
FACE THE RAMS IN NEW ORLEANS
BRINGING A MOSTLY NO-NAME TEAM
WHO HAVE ACHIEVED FAR MORE THAN ANYONE DREAMED

THE SAINT LOUIS RAMS FOR A CONTRAST
WERE FAVORED SINCE THE SEASON'S START
THE ONLY THREAT TO THIS CHAMPIONSHIP RUN
WOULD HAVE BEEN IF SOMEHOW THEY FELL APART

BUT THAT SURELY DIDN'T HAPPEN
EVEN WITH A DEFENSE THAT WAS THREE-QUARTERS NEW
THE NFL LOOKED LIKE A FIELD OF WHEAT
THAT THE RAMS WENT SLICING THROUGH

KURT WARNER WON THIS YEAR'S MVP
WITH MARSHALL FAULK NOT FAR BEHIND
AND THAT MARVELOUS COMBINATION OF SKILL
IS THE BEST THAT ONE CAN BRING TO MIND

TO MAKE A CONTEST OUT OF THIS FOOTBALL GAME
THE PATS CANNOT AFFORD TO MAKE ANY MISTAKES
FOR AS WAS SHOWN AGAINST THE PACKERS
THE RAMS WON'T NEED TOO MANY BREAKS

RESULTS:
The New England Patriots
beat the St Louis Rams 20-17

UNLESS THE RAMS UNDERGO A MELTDOWN
THIS GAMES' OUTCOME SHOULDN'T BE IN DOUBT
BUT AS ALL OF US WHO LOVE THE UNDERDOGS KNOW
'TIL THE FINAL GUN, NO ONE SHOULD BE COUNTED OUT!

PACKERS

" VERSES "

VIKINGS

Green Bay Packers
Regular Season 12-4
Postseason 0-1

Minnesota Vikings
Regular Season 6-10
No Postseason

2002

Carl "Gator" Nelson

PACKERS "VERSES" VIKINGS ~ Carl Nelson

IT'S THE TIME OF YEAR LOVED BY FOOTBALL FANS
AS ANOTHER NEW SEASON IS SET TO BEGIN
AFTER SIX LONG MONTHS OF HOPE AND HYPE
WE'RE ALL EXPECTING OUR FAVORITES TO WIN

IT'S BEEN AN INTERESTING OFFSEASON
FOR BOTH THE PACKERS' AND VIKINGS' TEAMS
NEW DRAFT CHOICES AND SOME FREE AGENTS
FIGURE PROMINENTLY IN ALL OF THEIR SCHEMES

WHILE THE VIKINGS STARTED LAST YEAR WITH HIGH HOPES
REALITY SOON REARED ITS UGLY HEAD
WHILE THEY HAD HOPED TO REMAIN AMONG THE ELITE
IT WAS A "FIVE-AND-ELEVEN" TYPE SEASON INSTEAD

NOT A LOT WENT WELL FOR THE VIKINGS
WHOLESALE ROSTER CHANGES WERE SOON THE RESULT
FROM RETIREMENTS TO NON-RESIGNINGS
AND A FEW GUYS WHO WERE JUST TOLD "GET OUT"

THE VIKES PLAYED HEAVILY IN THE FREE AGENT POOL
SIGNING PLAYERS BOTH WELL-KNOWN AND OBSCURE
THERE'S TALK OF NINE NEW STARTERS ON THE DEFENSE
AND THE CHEMISTRY THERE MUST BE QUITE UNSURE

THE COLLEGE DRAFT DIDN'T TURN OUT MUCH BETTER
THE VIKES TOOK "REACHES" MORE OFTEN THAN NOT
SEVERAL OF THE NEW FACES IN PURPLE WERE CHOSEN
MUCH EARLIER THAN THE EXPERTS HAD THOUGHT

MOST OF THE STARS HOWEVER STILL REMAIN
CULPEPPER'S KNEE IS SEEMINGLY HEALED
AND WONDER OF WONDERS THE "MATURE SIDE"
OF RANDY MOSS IS ABOUT TO BE REVEALED

THE VIKES SAY BENNETT'S RUNNING BETTER
AND THAT THE OFFENSE HAS BEEN OVERHAULED
AND SINCE THEY KNOW THAT MOSS IS THEIR KEY
FOUR OF TEN PLAYS TO HIM WILL BE CALLED

THIS NEW PLAN WILL GET THE ACID TEST
THIS SUNDAY'S SEASON-OPENING GAME
WHEN THEY TAKE ON LAST YEAR'S DIVISION WINNER
AS THE BEARS WELCOME THE VIKES TO CHAMPAIGN

IT MAY BE A TASK THAT'S SIMPLY TOO LARGE
FOR A TEAM WITH SO MANY NEW FACES
MINNESOTA'S DEFENSE IS BOUND TO STRUGGLE
AS THE BEARS' OFFENSE GOES THROUGH ITS PACES

AND WHEN THE DUST HAS ALL SETTLED
ALTHOUGH THERE'LL BE BIG PLAYS FROM MOSS
THE BEARS WILL EMERGE VICTORIOUS
AND WILL HAVE HANDED THE VIKES THEIR FIRST LOSS

PACKERS "VERSES" VIKINGS ~ Carl Nelson

LAST YEAR'S GREEN BAY PACKERS TEAM
PUT TOGETHER A SEASON THAT MADE US QUITE PROUD
AND GOING INTO THE ST LOUIS PLAYOFF GAME
IT SEEMED THEY WERE SET TO STEP OUT OF THE CROWD

ALAS AS WE SAW THAT WAS NOT TO BE
IN A GAME THAT TURNED INTO A ROUT
WHILE OVERALL THE PACK DIDN'T PLAY BADLY
IT WAS SIX "PICKS" THAT KNOCKED GREEN BAY OUT

SO THE PACKERS TOO HAVE MADE CHANGES
STARTING WITH THE WIDE-RECEIVING CORPS
AS SCHROEDER BRADFORD AND FREEMAN
WERE SHOWN QUICKLY RIGHT OUT OF THE DOOR

MIKE SHERMAN THEN TOOK A LONG LOOK AROUND
AND SETTLED ON NEW ENGLAND'S TERRY GLENN
A PLAYER WITH TALENT BUT A CHECKERED PAST
WHICH HAS HURT HIM AGAIN AND AGAIN

THIS YEAR HOWEVER HE'S DEDICATED
TO REVIVING A CAREER IN DECLINE
ALTHOUGH HE'S BEEN HAMPERED WITH A SORE KNEE
HIS BEHAVIOR HAS BEEN NOTHING BUT FINE

THEN THE PACKERS DRAFTED YOUNG JAVON WALKER
WHOSE HANDS WERE RUMORED A LITTLE SUSPECT
BUT HIS PLAY IN PRACTICE AND DURING PRESEASON
HAS EARNED HIM A LOT OF RESPECT

JOE JOHNSON WAS THE NEXT BIG NAME
SHERMAN BROUGHT INTO THE PACKERS' FOLD
AND TEAMED WITH VONNIE GILBERT AND KGB
WILL PROVIDE A D-LINE TO BEHOLD

HARDY NICKERSON CAME NEXT FOR LEADERSHIP
BUT HE CAN SURELY STILL FLY TO THE BALL
ADDED TO THE REST OF THAT DEFENSIVE TEAM
WILL BE A BIG PART OF OPPONENT'S DOWNFALL

DONALD DRIVER BUBBA FRANKS AND AHMAN GREEN
WILL COMBINE WITH A DARNED GOOD O-LINE
TO MOVE THE BALL BEHIND OL' BRETT FAVRE
WHO IS IMPROVING WITH AGE LIKE FINE WINE

THIS WEEK FOR THE OPENER THE FALCONS
HAVE BEEN CHOSEN FOR THE FIRST SACRIFICE
ATALNTA BEAT THE PACKERS AT LAMBEAU LAST YEAR
SO THE PAYBACK WILL BE TWICE AS NICE

IN A WAY IT'S ALMOST TOO BAD FOR ATLANTA
OPENING DAY AT LAMBEAU IS A TOUGH START
WATCH FOR THE PACK'S DEFENSE TO FEAST ON "DIRTY BIRD"
WHILE FAVRE GREEN AND GLENN TAKE THE FALCONS APART

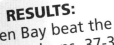

RESULTS:
Green Bay beat the
Atlanta Falcons 37-34

Minnesota lost to the
Chicago Bears 23-27

GB: 1-0
MN: 0-1

PACKERS "VERSES" VIKINGS ~ Carl Nelson

THE BEARS STARTED LAST WEEK'S GAME BELIEVING
THAT THEY WOULD BEAT THE VIKINGS EASILY
BUT MINNESOTA HAD SOME OTHER PLANS
THAT QUITE NEARLY CAME TO BE

FOR ABOUT THREE-AND-ONE-HALF QUARTERS
IT LOOKED LIKE MIKE TICE COULD BE RIGHT
THE VIKES TOOK THE GAME TO THE BEARS
AND REALLY PUT UP QUITE A FIGHT

BUT AS THE END OF THE GAME BEGAN TO CLOSE IN
THE VIKINGS' MACHINE BEGAN TO CRUMBLE
THE BEARS SCORED TWICE IN SIX MINUTES OR SO
AND IT ENDED WITH A CULPEPPER FUMBLE

THIS WEEK THE VIKES ARE AT THE HUMPHREYDOME
TAKING ON DREW BLEDSOE AND THE BILLS
BUFFALO HAS A SOLID RUNNING GAME
AND DREW WILL GIVE THE VIKES' D-BACKS CHILLS

THE VIKINGS' TEAM WILL HAVE TO REACH DOWN INSIDE
AND COME UP WITH A NEARLY PERFECT GAME
TO PREVENT A COLLAPSE OF THEIR CONFIDENCE
AND HAVING THIS WEEK WIND UP THE SAME

~ ~ ~ ~ ~ ~ ~ ~ ~ ~ ~ ~ ~ ~ ~ ~ ~ ~ ~

THE PACKERS' DEFENSE ALMOST LOOKED SILLY
AGAINST ATLANTA'S MICHAEL VICK
WHOSE STRONG ARM WAS OVERSHADOWED
BY THE FACT HIS FEET ARE SO DARNED QUICK

FORTUNATELY FOR PACKERS FANS
SOME FALCON DROPS PREVENTED TWO TDs
AND GAVE THE PACKERS A CHANCE TO REGROUP
AND WIN THEIR FIRST GAME IN OT

WHILE THE GREEN BAY DEFENSE STRUGGLED
THE OFFENSIVE TEAM SURELY DID THEIR PART
WITH GREEN AND MEALY RUNNING VERY WELL
AND THE RECEIVERS PULLING IN BRETT FAVRE'S DARTS

AARON BROOKS WILL LEAD NEW ORLEANS' SAINTS
AGAINST THE PACK SUNDAY DOWN IN THE SUPERDOME
THEY MANAGED TO GET BY THE BUCS LAST WEEK
AND WILL WANT TO LOOK SHARP AT HOME

SO BE PREPARED TO HEAR FANS SINGING
"OH WHEN THE SAINTS GO MARCHING IN"
BUT AS NEW ORLEANS LIMPS OFF AFTER THE GAME
GREEN BAY'S TEAM WILL HAVE ANOTHER WIN

RESULTS:
Green Bay lost to the
New Orleans Saints 20-35

Minnesota lost to the
Buffalo Bills 39-45

GB: 1-1
MN: 0-2

PACKERS "VERSES" VIKINGS ~ Carl Nelson

IT LOOKED LIKE THE VIKES MIGHT JUST DO IT
WITH HALF A MINUTE LEFT LAST WEEK
BUT THEY COULDN'T CONTAIN BLEDSOE'S PASSING ARM
AND DOWNFIELD THE BILLS DID STREAK

WITH A FIELD GOAL BOUNCING OVER
AND NO TIME LEFT ON THE CLOCK
THE GAME WENT INTO OVERTIME
AND THE VIKES WENT INTO SHOCK

WHAT'S GOING ON WITH THIS VIKINGS' TEAM
THAT THEY CAN'T SEEM TO HOLD A LEAD?
MAYBE IT'S A DEFENSE THAT CAN'T MAKE A TACKLE
BEING BUILT INSTEAD FOR "SPEED"

CAROLINA'S PANTHERS VISIT SUNDAY
HOPING FOR A REPEAT OF LAST YEAR'S GAME
WHEN THEY SURPRISED THE FAVORED VIKINGS' TEAM
WHO NEVER AGAIN LOOKED QUITE THE SAME

FOR THE VIKINGS TO LOSE THREE IN A ROW
WOULD SEEM TO BE MORE THAN A STUMBLE
THE PANTHERS SHOULD PICK UP THEIR FIRST LOSS
UNLESS THE GAME TURNS AGAIN ON DAUNTE'S FUMBLES

~ ~ ~ ~ ~ ~ ~ ~ ~ ~ ~ ~ ~ ~ ~ ~ ~ ~ ~ ~

"WHAT IN THE HECK IS GOING ON?"
IS THE BIG QUESTION IN THE PACKERS' MINDS
THE ANSWERS SEEM TO BE ELUSIVE
BUT IT'S ONE THAT THEY'LL HAVE TO FIND

LAST WEEK'S GAME PROVIDED CENTER STAGE
TO THE PROBLEMS THAT NOW PLAGUE THE PACK
TURNOVERS INJURIES AND BAD DEFENSE
HAVE COMBINED TO GET THIS TEAM OFF-TRACK

BUT IT'S NOT ALL BAD FOR PACKERS FANS
SOME THINGS REALLY ARE GOING PRETTY WELL
BRETT FAVRE IS LOOKING PRETTY GOOD
AND THE RECEIVER CORPS IS STARTING TO GEL

THEY'RE ON THE ROAD THIS COMING WEEK
TO TAKE ON THE LIONS OF DETROIT
A GROUP WHO IS FLOUNDERING IN EVERY WAY
AND IS COACHED BY A GROUP OF MALADROITS

RESULTS:
Green Bay beat the
Detroit Lions 37-31

Minnesota lost to the
Carolina Panthers 14-21

WHEN A TEAM IS HAVING PROBLEMS LIKE THE PACKERS
WITH SOME TROUBLES THAT DEFY DESCRIPTION
SOMETIMES A BIG WIN CAN HELP THEM TO GET WELL
"THE LIONS" ARE THE PERFECT GREEN BAY PRESCRIPTION

135

GB: 2-1
MN: 0-3

PACKERS "VERSES" VIKINGS ~ Carl Nelson

THE VIKES WERE FEELING FRUSTRATED
AFTER TAKING TWO GAMES ON THE CHIN
SURELY THEY COULD PLAY WELL ENOUGH
TO KEEP THAT FROM HAPPENING ONCE AGAIN

BUT LAST SUNDAY THE CAROLINA PANTHERS
BEAT THE VIKINGS IN THEIR OWN HOUSE
NOT BY OVERWHELMING THEM
BUT BY PLAYING A GAME OF "CAT" AND MOUSE

GOOD FUNDAMENTAL FOOTBALL
TACKLING AND RUNNING AND THE REST
USUALLY WINS OVER "RATIO"' AND FLASHY PLAYS
AS THE VIKES WERE FOUND LACKING IN THIS TEST

NOW IT'S OFF TO PLAY THE SEAHAWKS
A CONTEST WITH ANOTHER STRUGGLING TEAM
THE 'HAWKS ALSO ARE AN ONGOING ENIGMA
WHO CAN'T BE AS BAD AS IT WOULD SEEM

THE GOOD NEWS IS THAT ONE TEAM
WILL NO LONGER BE IN THE WINLESS RANKS
THE BAD NEWS IS THAT THE LOSER
WILL FIND THEIR SEASON'S GONE INTO THE TANK

~ ~ ~ ~ ~ ~ ~ ~ ~ ~ ~ ~ ~ ~ ~ ~ ~ ~

THE PACKERS WILL FACE A "CAT-NAMED" TEAM
FOR THE SECOND TIME IN AS MANY WEEKS
HOWEVER UNLIKE THE "MOTOR-CITY KITTIES"
THE PANTHERS ARE LOOKING ANYTHING BUT WEAK

WHILE THE PACKERS HAD TO HANG ON
AGAINST A LAST-MINUTE DETROIT LIONS' CHARGE
THE PANTHERS WERE BEATING UP THE VIKINGS
HAVING FUN AND LIVIN' LARGE

THEY PLAYED THEIR GAME PLAN ALL DAY LONG
WINNING WITH GOOD DEFENSE AND RUNNING GAME
THE STUFF WE EXPECTED TO SEE FROM THE PACKERS
THOUGH IT'S NOT WORKED OUT QUITE THE SAME

RESULTS:
Green Bay beat the
Carolina Panthers 17-14

Minnesota lost to the
Seattle Seahawks 48-23

THE PACKERS' DEFENSE HAS ITS WORK CUT OUT
HEAVEN KNOWS THEY'VE HAD SOME TROUBLE
INJURIES HAVE FORCED SOME ROOKIE PLAYERS
TO LEARN THEIR POSITIONS ON THE DOUBLE

ALTHOUGH NAJEH DAVENPORT FILLED IN QUITE WELL
FORTUNATELY THIS WEEK AHMAN SHOULD BE BACK
AND WITH FAVRE THROWING DARTS TO GLENN AND DRIVER
SUNDAY'S WINNER WILL BE THE PACK

GB: 3-1
MN: 0-4

PACKERS "VERSES" VIKINGS ~ Carl Nelson

THERE'S NOT A LOT TO SAY ABOUT THE VIKINGS
WHO WERE SIMPLY POUNDED LAST SUNDAY NIGHT
THEY HAVE TO TAKE THIS COMING BYE WEEK
AND COME UP WITH A WAY TO PUT THINGS RIGHT

MIKE TICE AND CREW HAVE A LOT TO FIX
TO MAKE THIS GROUP LOOK LIKE A TEAM ONCE AGAIN
AND HE ONLY HAS THIS ONE EXTRA WEEK
OR ON HIM ALL THE BLAME WILL BE PINNED

~ ~ ~ ~ ~ ~ ~ ~ ~ ~ ~ ~ ~ ~ ~ ~ ~ ~ ~

THE PACKERS NEEDED A LITTLE GOOD FORTUNE
TO MAKE THE WIN OVER THE PANTHERS STICK
CAROLINA WAS READY TO TIE IT AT GAME'S END
BUT SOMEHOW MANAGED TO MISS ON THE KICK

THIS WEEK RENEWS AN ANCIENT RIVALRY
ONE THAT GOES BACK TO THE LEAGUE'S EARLY DAYS
AS THE PACKERS TRAVEL TO MEET THE BEARS
ON THEIR "HOME FIELD" THIS COMING MONDAY

IN PRESEASON PREDICTIONS THE PACK AND BEARS
WERE TOUTED AS CHAMPIONSHIP CONTENDERS
WHILE THESE TEAMS HAVE HAD SOME GOOD MOMENTS
AT OTHER TIMES BOTH HAVE APPEARED PRETENDERS

BOTH TEAMS ARE BATTERED AND WOUNDED
AND HAVE FOUND THE GOING A LITTLE TOUGHER THAN PLANNED
BUT THIS GAME IS A FOOTBALL LOVER'S CLASSIC
AS BOTH TEAMS STRIVE TO GET THE UPPER HAND

THESE GAMES ARE PORTRAITS OF THE DISLIKE
THAT EXISTS BETWEEN THESE TWO OLD-TIME FOES
AND A PLAY THAT SEEMS A SIMPLE TACKLE
VERY OFTEN ENDS WITH A PUNCH TO THE NOSE

THE BEARS ARE HAVING SOME PROBLEMS
GETTING ENOUGH POINTS UP ON THE BOARD
THEY CAN'T SEEM TO GET THE "A-TRAIN" ON-TRACK
AND THE PASSING GAME SIMPLY HASN'T SOARED

THE PACKERS ARE SCORING MORE EASILY
IT'S THE DEFENSE THAT GIVES MIKE SHERMAN GRAY HAIR
THEY HAVEN'T PUT A GREAT GAME TOGETHER AS YET
DESPITE THE TALENT THE PACKERS HAVE THERE

THE HOME TEAM SHOULD HAVE THE ADVANTAGE
BUT HISTORY SHOWS THAT ISN'T THE CASE
NINE TIMES ON THE BEARS' FIELD IN THE LAST DECADE
GREEN BAY HAS PUT THEM IN THEIR PLACE

ON MONDAY NIGHT THE BATTLE BEGINS AGAIN
AS THOSE BEARS TRY TO NOT FALL FURTHER BEHIND
BUT AS THE LIGHTS ARE TURNED OUT IN CHAMPAIGN
THE PACK WILL HAVE BEATEN THEM AT HOME ONE MORE TIME

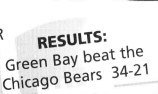

RESULTS:
Green Bay beat the Chicago Bears 34-21

Minnesota was on their "Bye" Week

137

GB: 4-1
MN: 0-4

PACKERS "VERSES" VIKINGS ~ Carl Nelson

THE VIKINGS' YEAR HAS SIMPLY SUCKED
AT LEAST UP TO THIS POINT IN TIME
THEY'VE STUMBLED FUMBLED AND LOST FOUR GAMES
FOR REASONS AS YET UNDEFINED

AS THE VIKINGS' TEAM RETURNS TO WORK
FROM A WELL-TIMED BYE-WEEK'S REST
HOPEFULLY MIKE TICE AND HIS COACHING STAFF
HAVE FOUND THE ANSWERS TO THIS MESS

AT LEAST THIS WEEK THEY PLAY AT HOME
WHERE THEY SHOULD GET A BOOST FROM THE HOME CROWD
BUT UNLESS THE VIKES START OFF QUICKLY IN THIS GAME
IT'S THE "BOO-BIRDS" WHO WILL BE THE MOST LOUD

DETROIT'S LIONS WILL HAVE THE CHANCE
TO DRIVE A NAIL INTO THE COFFIN OF MIKE TICE
THE LIONS ARE COMING OFF THEIR FIRST WIN
AND THEY'VE DISCOVERED THAT FEELS PRETTY NICE

LAST YEAR THE LIONS SURPRISED THE VIKES
BY BEATING THEM WHEN IT WAS UNEXPECTED
WILL THE OUTCOME BE DIFFERENT THIS COMING WEEK
WHEN THE VIKINGS ARE FEELING SO DISRESPECTED?

~ ~ ~ ~ ~ ~ ~ ~ ~ ~ ~ ~ ~ ~ ~ ~ ~ ~

BRETT FAVRE SHOWED EVERYONE THIS WEEK
WHY HE'S ALONE AT THE TOP OF THE CLASS
WHEN LAST MONDAY NIGHT IN CHAMPAIGN
HE WAS KEY IN KICKING CHICAGO'S ASS

THE REST OF THE TEAM PLAYED WELL OF COURSE
BUT BRETT FOUND HIMSELF IN "THE ZONE"
AND IT LOOKED FOR AWHILE DURING THAT GAME
THAT HE COULD HAVE WON IT ALL ALONE

THAT'S NOT THE CASE NOR SHOULD IT BE
IT'S TEAMWORK THAT BRINGS SUCCESS
IF ONLY THERE HADN'T BEEN SO MANY INJURIES
THAT SEEMED TO COME IN AN EXCESS

MIKE SHERMAN IS JUGGLING PLAYERS
AND HOPEFULLY THE ANSWERS WILL BE FOUND
BEFORE SUNDAY'S GAME IN NEW ENGLAND
ON THE PATRIOTS' HOME GROUND

GREEN BAY TOPPED THEM IN A SUPER BOWL
AND DID IT ONCE AGAIN SINCE THEN
IT WON'T BE EASY BUT A WIN'S IN STORE
ALONG WITH REVENGE FOR TERRY GLENN

RESULTS:
Green Bay beat the
New England Patriots 28-10

Minnesota beat the
Detroit Lions 31-24

GB: 5-1
MN: 1-4

PACKERS "VERSES" VIKINGS ~ Carl Nelson

AS THE VIKINGS PREPARE FOR THE NEW YORK JETS
THEY ARE FEELING PRETTY DOGGONE GOOD
FINALLY THEY PLAYED A FOOTBALL GAME
AND WON IT LIKE THEY THOUGHT THEY SHOULD

FOR MIKE TICE TO PICK UP HIS FIRST WIN
MUST HAVE FELT LIKE REALIZING A DREAM
WITH ALL THE STRIFE THAT'S BEEN GOING ON
IN AND AROUND THIS FOOTBALL TEAM

SO WITH A WIN UNDER THEIR BELTS
THE VIKINGS HEAD OUT ON THE ROAD
THEY'VE DROPPED THIRTEEN STRAIGHT AWAY-GAMES
WHICH MUST FEEL LIKE QUITE A HEAVY LOAD

THE JETS ALSO HAVE FOUND IT TOUGH
ALSO HAVING A RECORD OF ONE-AND-FOUR
SO THEY ARE STARTING A FRESH YOUNG QUARTERBACK
IN HOPES THAT HE CAN FIND A WAY TO SCORE

THIS GAME SHOULD BE A CLOSE ONE
WHO'LL BE THE WINNER REMAINS TO BE SEEN
BUT WITH THE JETS AT HOME AND FRESH FROM A BYE
LOOK FOR THE VIKINGS' STREAK TO HIT FOURTEEN

~ ~ ~ ~ ~ ~ ~ ~ ~ ~ ~ ~ ~ ~ ~ ~ ~ ~ ~

WITH A DEFENSE SEEMINGLY HELD TOGETHER
WITH DUCT TAPE AND BALING WIRE
GREEN BAY ENGAGED THE PATRIOTS
WITH SURPRISING GRIT AND FIRE

AS AHMAN GREEN GROUND OUT THE YARDS
AND FAVRE THREW AS MANY PASSES AS WERE NEEDED
THE CHAMPION PATS LEFT THE BALL ON THE GROUND
AND AS A RESULT WOUND UP BEING DEFEATED

THIS WEEK THE 'SKINS BRING THE "FUN 'N GUN"
TO LAMBEAU'S HALLOWED TURF
IT PROMISES TO SCORE MORE TOUCHDOWNS
THAN JOE THEISMAN AND THE "SMURFS"

RESULTS:
Green Bay beat the
Washington Redskins 30-9

Minnesota lost to the
New York Jets 7-20

THINGS HAVE NOT WORKED OUT SO WELL
FOR COACH SPURRIER AND HIS CREW
BUT THAT REDSKINS' DEFENSE HAS SO MUCH TALENT
ANY MISTAKES AND THE PACKERS WILL BE SCREWED

A WELL-PLAYED GAME CAN BEAT THE 'SKINS
AND IF ONE THROWS IN THAT OLD "LAMBEAU MYSTIQUE"
BRETT AHMAN AND THE PACKERS' TEAM
SHOULD GO VICTORIOUS TO THE BYE WEEK

GB: 6-1
MN: 1-5

PACKERS "VERSES" VIKINGS ~ Carl Nelson

MIKE TICE LOOKED SOMEWHAT DISTRAUGHT
AS HE TALKED TO THE PRESS ON SUNDAY NIGHT
HIS TEAM HAD LOST TO THE NEW YORK JETS
WITHOUT PUTTING UP MUCH OF A FIGHT

AT TIMES THE VIKINGS WOULD LOOK OK
AND AT OTHERS THEY LOOKED KIND OF SICK
THEY'D MOVE THE BALL AND START SOME DRIVES
BUT THEY ENDED WITH FUMBLES OR PICKS

WHILE TICE TALKED OF NEEDING CONFIDENCE
AND OF THE EXECUTION THAT HE'S DESIRED
ONE WOULD ALMOST HAVE TO WONDER
IF THIS CONTINUES WILL "MIKIE" BE FIRED?

THIS WEEK IT'S THE BEARS WHO COME CALLING
A TEAM WITH PROBLEMS OF THEIR OWN
THEY WERE SUPPOSED TO BE CONTENDERS
BUT THAT LEVEL OF PLAY'S NOT BEEN SHOWN

THE BEARS HAVE BEEN CRIPPLED BY INJURIES
WHILE THE VIKINGS HAVE JUST CRIPPLED THEMSELVES
CHICAGO SHOULD "BEAR-LY" PULL OUT A WIN HERE
UNLESS THE VIKES HAVE HELP FROM THE "DOME ELVES"

~ ~ ~ ~ ~ ~ ~ ~ ~ ~ ~ ~ ~ ~ ~ ~ ~ ~

IN THE THIRD QUARTER OF LAST SUNDAY'S GAME
GREEN BAY FANS GAVE A COLLECTIVE GASP
AS THE FUTURE OF THIS YEAR'S PACKERS' TEAM
WAS IN TWO WASHINGTON LINEBACKERS' GRASPS

FAVRE WENT DOWN AND IT DIDN'T LOOK GOOD
WHEN HE WAS DRIVEN FROM THE FIELD ON A CART
BUT THE NEWS THAT BRETT'S KNEE WASN'T HURT BADLY
LIGHTENED THE DARKNESS IN PACKERS FANS' HEARTS

THE PACKERS WENT ON TO WIN THAT GAME
BRINGING THE GAMES THEY'VE WON TO SIX
THIS WEEK IS THE "BYE"—A LITTLE TIME OFF
AND A CHANCE TO HEAL BRUISES AND NICKS

RESULTS:
Green Bay was on their "Bye Week"

Minnesota beat the Chicago Bears 25-7

GREEN BAY'S TEAM IS DOING QUITE WELL
EACH WEEK THIS GROUP IS IMPROVING
FAVRE AND THE WIDEOUTS ARE DEEP IN THE GROOVE
AND THE RUNNING GAME KEEPS THE CHAINS MOVING

THE DEFENSE IS PEERLESS AT STRIPPING THE BALL
WATCHING THEM HAS REALLY BEEN FUN
AND THEY SHOULD ALL BE HEALTHY AFTER THIS WEEK
AS GREEN BAY ENTERS THE SECOND HALF RUN

GB: 6-1
MN: 2-5

PACKERS "VERSES" VIKINGS ~ Carl Nelson

WHILE THE MINNESOTA VIKINGS' TEAM
HAS HAD MORE THAN ITS SHARE OF TROUBLES
JUDGING BY THE WAY THEY BEAT THOSE BEARS
CHICAGO MUST FEEL THAT THEIR'S ARE DOUBLE

THE VIKING'S GAME PLAN WORKED OUT QUITE WELL
ALLOWING THE VIKES TO AVOID LOSING SUNDAY'S GAME
THEY TOOK THE BALL OUT OF DAUNTE'S HANDS
AND "GROUND" IT OUT IN A MANNER QUITE PLAIN

WHILE THAT GAME PLAN MAY HAVE BEEN EFFECTIVE
AGAINST THE SLUMPING CHIGAGO BEARS
IT MAY NOT WORK OUT QUITE THAT WAY THIS WEEK
WHEN THE VIKES PLAY TAMPA DOWN THERE

THE ROAD ISN'T GOOD FOR THE VIKINGS' TEAM
AND THE BUCCANEERS AREN'T EXACTLY NICE
IN THE PAST TWO GAMES DOWN IN THE FLORIDA SUN
TAMPA'S SCORED FORTY-ONE NOT ONCE BUT TWICE

NOW THE BUCS MAY HAVE QUESTIONS AT QUARTERBACK
AND THE RUNNING GAME SEEMS TO HAVE FALTERED
BUT THE VIKES HAVEN'T HAD A ROAD WIN IN FOURTEEN TRIES
IT WOULD SEEM A SHAME TO HAVE THAT STREAK ALTERED

~ ~ ~ ~ ~ ~ ~ ~ ~ ~ ~ ~ ~ ~ ~ ~ ~ ~ ~ ~

DURING THE GAME AGAINST THE REDSKINS
EVERY PACKERS FAN'S HEART CAME TO A STOP
WHEN BRETT FAVRE WENT DOWN AWKWARDLY
AND HEARD HIS KNEE GO "SNAP CRACKLE POP"

BUT THE DAMAGE WAS LESS THAN IT FIRST APPEARED
HE SHOULD BE ABLE TO PLAY IN A BRACE
FORTUNATELY HE COULD REST IT DURING THE BYE WEEK
AND THE PACK SHOULD BE ABLE TO STAY IN FIRST PLACE

NEXT MONDAY NIGHT IT BEGINS AGAIN
AS THE DOLPHINS VISIT LAMBEAU FIELD
GREEN BAY'S OFFENSE WILL HAVE CHANGED SOMEWHAT
AS FAVRE'S LEG THEY WILL STRIVE TO SHIELD

IT WON'T BE EASY AGAINST MIAMI'S "D"
IT'S A TOUGH GROUP STRONG AND FAST
THE PACKERS MUST BE UP TO THE CHALLENGE
OF KEEPING BRETT ON HIS FEET AND OFF THE GRASS

MIAMI WILL BRING THE BEST GAME THEY'VE GOT
RICKY WILLIAMS WILL TEST THAT PACKERS' "D"
BUT THIS GAME IS DESTINED TO BE BRETT FAVRE'S
WHILE THE DOLPHINS PICK UP LOSS NUMBER THREE

RESULTS:
Green Bay beat the
Miami Dolphins 24-10

Minnesota lost to the
Tamp Bay Buccaneers 24-38

GB: 7-1
(Best record
in the NFL!)
MN: 2-6

PACKERS "VERSES" VIKINGS

~ Carl Nelson

THE VIKINGS WENT DOWN TO TAMPA BAY
HOPING TO REVERSE THEIR RECENT TREND
OF GIVING "CAREER DAYS" TO THE OPPOSITION
BUT CAME UP A LITTLE SHORT ONCE AGAIN

HOWEVER "HOPE SPRINGS ETERNAL" OR SO IT'S SAID
AND MINNESOTA'S TEAM IS NO EXCEPTION
THEY'VE FINALLY SIGNED THEIR FIRST ROUND PICK
HOPING HE'LL BRING DAUNTE SOME BETTER PROTECTION

FACING A ROOKIE WHO MANAGED TO MISS TRAINING CAMP
MUST HAVE THE NEW YORK GIANTS LICKING THEIR CHOPS
YOU CAN BET STRAHAN AND THE REST OF THAT DEFENSE
WILL HAVE A LARGE NUMBER OF QUARTERBACK DROPS

KERRY COLLINS AND HIS OFFENSIVE TEAM
THIS YEAR HAVE STRUGGLED FROM TIME TO TIME
BUT THE PROSPECT OF FACING MINNESOTA'S TEAM
HAS TO HAVE THEM FEELING THAT THEY'LL BE JUST FINE

WILL THIS BE THE WEEK THAT THE VIKINGS' TEAM GELS?
THEY TEND TO PLAY BETTER WHEN THEY'RE IN THE 'DOME
BUT UNLESS UNFORSEEN CIRCUMSTANCES INTERVENE
IT LOOKS LIKE A BAD LOSS FOR THEM AT HOME

~ ~ ~ ~ ~ ~ ~ ~ ~ ~ ~ ~ ~ ~ ~ ~ ~ ~

THE BIG QUESTIONS ON THE MINDS OF ALL
AS THE PACK OPENED THE GAME LAST MONDAY NIGHT
WERE "HOW IS BRETT'S KNEE GOING TO HOLD UP?"
"DO YOU SUPPOSE THAT IT'S REALLY ALL RIGHT?"

THE ANSWERS WERE OBVIOUS FROM THE FIRST PLAY
AS BRETT ROLLED OUT AND THREW THAT FIRST PASS
WHILE THE DOLPHINS GAVE IT ALL THAT THEY HAD
IN THE END THEY WERE SIMPLY OUTCLASSED

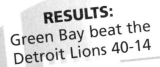

RESULTS:
Green Bay beat the
Detroit Lions 40-14

Minnesota lost to the
New York Giants 20-27

THE LIONS COME TO VISIT LAMBEAU THIS WEEK
AFTER PULLING OUT THIS YEAR'S THIRD WIN
THE PACKERS BARELY WON THE LAST MEETING
WILL THIS GAME BE THAT CLOSELY CONTESTED AGAIN?

WHILE THE LIONS ARE TAKING SOME FORWARD STEPS
(THEY'VE ALREADY WON MORE GAMES THAN LAST YEAR)
SOMEHOW JOEY HARRINGTON AND THE LIONS' TEAM
JUST DON'T SEEM TO BE INSPIRING A LOT OF FEAR

IT MIGHT WELL BE THAT DREADED "COMPLACENCY"
WILL BE WHAT THE PACKERS HAVE TO FEAR MOST
THE LIONS MIGHT BE ABLE TO MOUNT A CHALLENGE
IF THROUGH THIS GAME GREEN BAY TRIES TO COAST

GB: 8-1
(Still the Best!)
MN: 2-7

PACKERS "VERSES" VIKINGS ~ Carl Nelson

TODD BOUMAN FINALLY GOT HIS CHANCE LAST WEEK
AS THE VIKES WERE STUMBLING TO ANOTHER LOSS
ALTHOUGH HE DIDN'T PRODUCE A HEROIC VICTORY
HE SHOWED HE COULD AT LEAST GET THE BALL TO MOSS

SO...DOES BOUMAN GET THE START THIS WEEK?
LEAVING DAUNTE'S BUTT PLANTED FIRMLY ON THE PINE?
MIKEY TICE HAS DECIDED THAT IDEA ISN'T GOOD
AND THAT CULPEPPER WILL DO JUST FINE

THE WISDOM OF THAT REMAINS TO BE SEEN
LOOK FOR HIM TO BE QUICKLY YANKED
IF AS USUAL HE STARTS MAKING TURNOVERS
AND THE GAME STARTS HEADING TO THE TANK

IT'S A LARGE TASK THE VIKINGS HAVE THIS WEEK
AS GREEN BAY'S PACKERS COME INTO THE 'DOME
AND WHILE ABYSMAL WHILE PLAYING ON THE ROAD
THEY'VE BEEN SOMEWHAT TOUGHER WHEN AT HOME

MICHAEL BENNETT HAS BEEN RUNNING WELL
BUT MOE WILLIAMS IS THE GUY WHO SCORES
NOW IF ONLY THE VIKINGS' DEFENSE COULD STOP
GETTING TURNED AROUND LIKE REVOLVING DOORS...

~ ~ ~ ~ ~ ~ ~ ~ ~ ~ ~ ~ ~ ~ ~ ~ ~ ~ ~

GREEN BAY'S PACKERS ON THE OTHER HAND
ARE PLAYING LIKE A TEAM THAT'S EIGHT-AND-ONE
AND WILL PRESENT PROBLEMS FOR THE VIKINGS' TEAM
THAT WILL KEEP THE VIKES FROM HAVING TOO MUCH FUN

FRESH FROM A STOMPING OF DETROIT'S LIONS
THE PACK IS FEELING STRONG AND STEADY
BRETT FAVRE HAS THE OFFENSE FLOWING
AND THAT DEFENSE IS ALWAYS MORE THAN READY

DONALD DRIVER HAS STEPPED UP HIS GAME
THE RUNNING BACKS ARE LOOKING MIGHTY FINE
AND AFTER SERVING MAINLY AS A DECOY
TERRY GLENN WILL SHOW THIS WEEK'S HIS TIME

AFTER A START THAT LOOKED A LITTLE SHAKY
THE PACKERS' DEFENSE HAS NOW TURNED UP THE HEAT
MINNESOTA'S PASS-BLOCKERS WILL BE HARD PRESSED
TO KEEP DAUNTE STANDING ON HIS FEET

RESULTS:
Green Bay lost to the
Minnesota Vikings 21-31

IT MAY BE TRUE THAT IN SEASONS PAST
THE PACK'S HAD PROBLEMS IN THAT DOME
THIS YEAR HOWEVER GREEN BAY'S ON TRACK
AND WON'T BE BOTHERED BY THE "METRO-GNOMES"

GB: 8-2
MN: 3-7

PACKERS "VERSES" VIKINGS ~ Carl Nelson

AAARRRGGGHHH!!!! IT'S HAPPENED ONCE AGAIN THIS YEAR
THE ANNUAL NIGHTMARE IN THE METRODOME
THE VIKES REARED UP AND BEAT GREEN BAY
AS THEY HAVE SO OFTEN DONE THERE AT THEIR HOME

WHILE THE PACKERS GAVE THIS GAME THEIR ALL
MISTAKES AND INJURY STOPPED THE WINNING ROLL
MINNESOTA GOT INTO BRETT FAVRE'S HEAD
SOON THE GAME WAS IN THE VIKES' CONTROL

TO GIVE THE VIKINGS' TEAM THEIR DUE
THEY PLAYED LIKE THEY WERE POSSESSED
IF THAT INTENSITY WAS AVAILABLE EVERY WEEK
MINNESOTA'S RECORD WOULDN'T BE SUCH A MESS

THE PACKERS HAVE TO RIGHT THEMSELVES
AND KEEP THIS LOSS IN A PROPER PERSPECTIVE
IT'S A SIMPLE LOSS AND NOTHING MORE
AND DOES NOT MEAN THAT THE PACK'S DEFECTIVE

~ ~ ~ ~ ~ ~ ~ ~ ~ ~ ~ ~ ~ ~ ~ ~ ~ ~ ~

THIS WEEK THE VIKES FACE THEIR OWN NIGHTMARE
A ROAD GAME PLAYED OUTSIDE UNDER AN OPEN SKY
IT'S BEEN TWO LONG YEARS SINCE THEY'VE WON ONE
NO MATTER HOW MIGHTILY THEY HAVE TRIED

THE PATS POSSESS AN OUTSTANDING AIR GAME
AND A RUNNING GAME THAT CAN PRODUCE
THE DEFENSE HAS BIG-PLAY CAPABILITY
AND IS JUST WAITING TO BE TURNED LOOSE

THE VIKES MAY FIND LAST SUNDAY'S VICTORY
WON'T DO MUCH TO EASE THE STING
OF BEING HANDED CONSECUTIVE-ROAD-LOSS FIFTEEN
BY THE TEAM WEARING THE SUPER BOWL RING

~ ~ ~ ~ ~ ~ ~ ~ ~ ~ ~ ~ ~ ~ ~ ~ ~ ~ ~

GREEN BAY GOES FROM THE FRYING PAN TO THE FIRE
WITH THE GAME UPCOMING THIS SUNDAY
AS THE TEAMS TIED WITH THE LEAGUE'S BEST RECORD
WILL GO HEAD TO HEAD DOWN IN TAMPA BAY

THE BUCS ARE A TEAM THAT IS A MYSTERY
FOR THEIR OFFENSE IS NOTHING TO INSPIRE SHOUTS
WARREN SAPP AND THE TAMPA DEFENSE
IS ALL ANYONE CARES TO TALK ABOUT

THAT LACK OF OFFENSE WILL DOOM THE BUCS
AS FAVRE AND GREEN FORCE THE "D" TO YIELD
THE WIN GREEN BAY PICKS UP ON SUNDAY
WILL HELP BRING THE PLAYOFF GAMES TO LAMBEAU FIELD

RESULTS:
Green Bay lost to the
Tampa Bay Buccaneers 7-21

Minnesota lost to the
New England Patriots 17-24

144

GB: 8-3
MN: 3-8

PACKERS "VERSES" VIKINGS ~ Carl Nelson

THE PATRIOTS JOINED A LONG LIST OF TEAMS
THAT HAVE BEATEN THE VIKINGS AT THEIR HOMES
AS IT'S BEEN MORE THAN TWO FULL CALENDAR YEARS
SINCE MINNESOTA WON AWAY FROM THE METRODOME

NEW ENGLAND DID NOTHING REALLY SPECIAL
THEY JUST TOOK AN EARLY LEAD AND WAITED
KNOWING THEN EVEN IF THE VIKINGS MADE A RUN
ANOTHER ROAD LOSS PROBABLY WAS FATED

THE FALCONS VISIT THE VIKES THIS WEEK
FOR THE FIRST TIME IN FOUR LONG YEARS
LAST TIME THEY FOILED A SUPER BOWL RUN
AND CAUSED A FLOOD OF MINNESOTA TEARS

THIS TIME THEY BRING IN QB MICHAEL VICK
THIS YEAR'S "YOUNG PHENOMENON"
A TERM ONCE APPLIED TO CULPEPPER AND MOSS
THOUGH THOSE DAYS HAVE COME AND GONE

BECAUSE THIS GAME IS AT THAT METRODOME
THERE IS A CHANCE THAT THE VIKINGS WILL LOOK GREAT
HOWEVER THE FALCONS HAVEN'T LOST IN SEVEN WEEKS
AND THIS GAME SHOULD MAKE IT NUMBER EIGHT

~ ~ ~ ~ ~ ~ ~ ~ ~ ~ ~ ~ ~ ~ ~ ~ ~ ~ ~

THE PACKERS TOOK A LOSS LAST SUNDAY
IN A GAME OVERSHADOWED BY WARREN SAPP'S HIT
WHILE THE LEAGUE SAID THAT IT WAS LEGAL
IT STILL APPEARED TO PURELY BE CHICKENS_IT

MORE IMPORTANTLY IT WAS THE SECOND LOSS
IN JUST THE SAME NUMBER OF WEEKS
MAKING MORE THAN ONE PACKERS FAN WONDER
IF THIS TEAM HAS ALREADY PEAKED

THAT MIGHT STILL BE A LITTLE PREMATURE
THOUGH THE GAME PLAN COULD USE SOME REPAIR
THIS WEEK WILL PROVIDE THEM JUST THAT CHANCE
IN THE FORM OF CHICAGO'S BEARS

A TRAGEDY IN THEIR OWN RIGHT
THE BEARS DEFINE THE TERM "COLLAPSE"
THEY'D LOST EIGHT STRAIGHT BEFORE LAST WEEK
WHEN DETROIT PUT THE WIN IN THEIR LAPS

WHILE THE BEARS COME INTO THIS WEEK'S GAME
HOPING TO AVOID COMPLETE HUMILIATION
GREEN BAY WILL DEMONSTRATE CONVINCINGLY
THE PAST TWO WEEKS WERE AN ABERRATION

RESULTS:
Green Bay beat the
Chicago Bears 30-20

Minnesota lost to the
Atlanta Falcons 24-30

145

GB: 9-3
MN: 3-9

PACKERS "VERSES" VIKINGS ~ Carl Nelson

ONE HAS TO GIVE THE VIKINGS CREDIT
FOR COMING UP WITH SUCH CREATIVE WAYS
OF SNATCHING DEFEAT FROM THE JAWS OF VICTORY
IN NEARLY EVERY GAME THEY PLAY

LAST WEEK IT LOOKED LIKE THE FALCONS' TEAM
WOULD BE THE ONES THAT TOOK THE LOSS
UNTIL AN ILLEGAL FORMATION CALL
NULLIFIED A MOSS-TO-CULPEPPER SCORING TOSS

THAT SET UP A CHANCE FOR OVERTIME
WHERE MICHAEL VICK PROVED TO BE TOO MUCH
FOR A VIKINGS' OFFENSE THAT COULDN'T MOVE THE BALL
AND THEIR DEFENSE WHO CHOKED UP IN THE CLUTCH

~ ~ ~ ~ ~ ~ ~ ~ ~ ~ ~ ~ ~ ~ ~ ~ ~

GREEN BAY'S PACKERS SEIZED AN OPPORTUNITY
AS WELL AS A CHICAGO FUMBLE
AND USED THAT PLAY TO RIGHT THEMSELVES
AND END THE PAST TWO WEEKS' STUMBLE

ALTHOUGH THE PACK STARTED A LITTLE SLOWLY
ALLOWING "DA BEARS" TO TAKE AN EARLY LEAD
MIKE SHERMAN GAVE A HALFTIME SPEECH
THAT MADE HIS TEAM SIT UP AND TAKE HEED

ROOKIE TONY FISHER FILLED IN WELL
FOR AN INJURED AHMAN GREEN
HE RUNS QUITE WELL AND HAS NIFTY MOVES
AND HIS FULL POTENTIAL HAS YET TO BE SEEN

~ ~ ~ ~ ~ ~ ~ ~ ~ ~ ~ ~ ~ ~ ~ ~ ~ ~

SUNDAY NIGHT WISCONSIN'S WINTER WINDS
WILL WHISTLE PAST OUR TEAMS AS THEY MEET
IN THE REMATCH OF THE EARLIER GAME
THAT SENT THE GREEN BAY PACKERS TO DEFEAT

THIS GAME WILL BE A DIFFERENT ONE
AS THE VIKES ARE FORCED FROM THEIR COMFY DOME
AND WILL HAVE TO OVERCOME THE ELEMENTS
AND A PACKERS' TEAM THAT'S HARD TO BEAT AT HOME

THE PACK WON'T TAKE THE VIKINGS LIGHTLY
DESPITE THE TWO-YEAR ROAD LOSS STREAK
FOR THOUGH GREEN BAY HAS BECOME DIVISION CHAMPS
THEY HAVE TO REGAIN THAT EARLY-SEASON PEAK

THE VIKES ARE ABOUT TO FIND OUT
HOW PAINFUL A LOSS IS IN THE COLD
FOR THE PACKERS RARELY LOSE AT HOME
AND IN DECEMBER BRETT'S GOOD AS GOLD

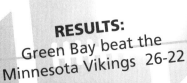

RESULTS:
Green Bay beat the
Minnesota Vikings 26-22

GB: 10-3
(2002 North
Champions)
MN: 3-10

PACKERS "VERSES" VIKINGS ~ Carl Nelson

AT THE END OF THE PACKERS-VIKINGS GAME
ON A COLD AND WINTRY LAMBEAU NIGHT
OCCURED A MOST EMBARASSING THING
AS BOTH TEAMS WOUND UP IN A FIGHT

THE VIKES CONTINUED THEIR ROAD GAME MISERIES
AS THEY BLEW A NEARLY GAME-LONG LEAD
AND WHILE THE OFFICIALS MAY HAVE PLAYED A PART
THERE WERE NO BIG PLAYS IN THEIR TIME OF NEED

THE PACKERS AGAIN STARTED SLOWLY
WITHOUT THE ABILITY TO SUSTAIN A DRIVE
BUT THIS WAS LAMBEAU IN DECEMBER
THE TIME WHEN BRETT FAVRE SEEMS TO THRIVE

THE PACKERS MANAGED TO WIN THIS GAME
BEHIND FISHER AND FERGUSON'S BREAKOUT GAMES
WHICH WERE TARNISHED SOMEWHAT BY THAT FIGHT
ALL INVOLVED SHOULD HANG THEIR HEADS IN SHAME

~ ~ ~ ~ ~ ~ ~ ~ ~ ~ ~ ~ ~ ~ ~ ~ ~ ~ ~

THE VIKES WILL HAVE TO COMPOSE THEMSELVES
IN ORDER TO GIVE THEIR TEAM A CHANCE
AGAINST THE SAINTS OF NEW ORLEANS
WHO ARE LOOKING TO ENTER THE PLAYOFF DANCE

THE SAINTS REALLY LIKE TO RUN THE BALL
ALTHOUGH AARON BROOKS LIKES TO PASS AS WELL
AND UNLESS THE SECONDARY STEPS IT UP
FOR THE VIKES IT COULD BE A DAY IN HELL

WHILE BENNETT IS RUNNING VERY WELL
MINNESOTA'S AIR ATTACK IS INCONSISTENT
AND SINCE THE SAINTS' DEFENSE IS PRETTY GOOD
THE ROAD-LOSS STREAK SHOULD REMAIN PERSISTENT

~ ~ ~ ~ ~ ~ ~ ~ ~ ~ ~ ~ ~ ~ ~ ~ ~ ~ ~

THE SAN FRANCISCO FORTY-NINERS' TEAM
WHO OWN THE "WEST" DIVISION CROWN
EAGERLY AWAIT THE GREEN BAY PACKERS
WHO ARE THIS WEEK COMING TO THEIR TOWN

BOTH TEAMS HAVE PLAYED THROUGH INJURIES
THAT WOULD HAVE CRUSHED MOST OTHER TEAMS
AND STILL MANAGED TO HAVE THE KIND OF YEAR
OF WHICH OTHER TEAMS CAN ONLY DREAM

THERE'S A LOT OF HISTORY BETWEEN THESE TEAMS
MORE OFTEN THAN NOT GREEN BAY GETS THE WIN
MOST OF THE INJURED PACKERS RETURN THIS WEEK
THAT SHOULD BE ENOUGH TO BEAT THE 'NINERS YET AGAIN

RESULTS:
Green Bay beat the
San Francisco 49ers 20-14

Minnesota beat the
New Orleans Saints 32-31

GB: 11-3
(NFCN Champs)
MN: 4-10

PACKERS "VERSES" VIKINGS ~ Carl Nelson

THE VIKES FINALLY WON OUT ON THE ROAD
DEFEATING THE NEW ORLEANS SAINTS LAST WEEK
WITH A GUTSY MOVE BY COACH MIKE TICE
LETTING DAUNTE SCORE TWO ON A QUARTERBACK SNEAK

TO BE SURE IT WASN'T A PRETTY PLAY
AS CULPEPPER DRIBBLED THE BALL FOR A WHILE
ALL VIKING FANS HELD THEIR BREATH AT THAT POINT
BEFORE THEY FINALLY STARTED TO SMILE

MINNESOTA'S OFFENSE HUNG IN WITH THE SAINTS
AND THEY LED FOR MOST OF THE GAME
THE VIKINGS' DEFENSE ROSE TO THE CALL
AND SURPRISINGLY DIDN'T LOOK LAME

SO... CAN THE VIKE'S NEW-FOUND CONFIDENCE
CARRY OVER INTO THIS WEEK'S GAME WITH THE 'FINS?
MIAMI BRINGS RICKY WILLIAMS AND A KILLER DEFENSE
AND CRIS CARTER RETURNS TO THE 'DOME ONCE AGAIN

IT WOULD BE NICE TO BE ABLE TO HAZARD THE GUESS
THAT THE VIKES HAVE A CHANCE WITH MIAMI
BUT THE 'FINS ARE PLAYING FOR A HOME FIELD SLOT
AND THE CHANCES FOR A VIKES' WIN ARE TOO SMALL TO SEE

~ ~ ~ ~ ~ ~ ~ ~ ~ ~ ~ ~ ~ ~ ~ ~ ~ ~

COMING FROM THE DEPTHS OF WISCONSIN'S WINTER
THE WIND AND RAIN IN 'FRISCO SEEMED A LITTLE MILD
AND ALTHOUGH THIS GAME ALSO STARTED A LITTLE SLOWLY
THE FINISH REALLY TURNED OUT TO BE QUITE WILD

AT GAME'S END THE 'NINERS DROVE DOWN THE FIELD
WHILE TRAILING THE PACKERS BY SIX
BUT THE PACKERS' DEFENSE SHUT OWENS AND GARCIA DOWN
AND PREVENTED ANY GAME-WINNING TRICKS

THE PACKERS CLOSE OUT THIS SEASON'S HOMESTANDS
AGAINST DREW BLEDSOE AND THE BUFFALO BILLS
WHO ALTHOUGH THEY'VE LATELY STRUGGLED
HAVE THE ABILITY TO PROVIDE MANY THRILLS

THE BILLS HAVE A GOOD RECEIVING CORPS
AND A BUDDING SUPERSTAR AT RUNNING BACK
THE DEFENSE MAY NOT BE RATED HIGHLY
BUT THEY'LL NOT CUT THE PACKERS MUCH SLACK

THE PACKERS HAVE A GOLDEN OPPORTUNITY
TO FINISH THE SEASON UNBEATEN AT LAMBEAU FIELD
MIKE SHERMAN WILL USE THIS AS THE MOTIVATION
AND THE PACK WILL FORCE BUFFALO'S BILLS TO YIELD

RESULTS:
Green Bay beat the
Buffalo Bills 10-0

Minnesota beat the
Miami Dolphins 20-17

GB: 12-3
(NFCN Champs)
MN: 5-10

PACKERS "VERSES" VIKINGS ~ Carl Nelson

IN A MANNER THAT WAS MOST IMPROBABLE
THE VIKES NETTED THE DOLPHINS IN LAST WEEK'S GAME
BY HAVING ANDERSON CONVERT A FIELD-GOAL TRY
THAT WAS SO LONG, EVEN TRYING IT SEEMED QUITE INSANE

EVEN CRIS CARTER'S METRODOME RETURN
COULDN'T SAVE THE 'FINS LAST SATURDAY
AS ANDERSON'S KICK BARELY CROSSED THE BAR
THE FINS' PLAYOFF BERTH GUARANTEE SLIPPED AWAY

THE VIKINGS NOW HAVE A TWO-GAME WINNING STREAK
AND THIS WEEK THEY'LL TRY TO MAKE IT THREE
BUT THIS GAME WILL BE PLAYED OVER IN DETROIT
AND SHOULD BE AN INTERESTING CONTEST TO SEE

GOING SIMPLY BY THE LIONS' RECORD
IT WOULD SEEM THE VIKINGS SHOULD HAVE SOME FUN
BUT THE LAST TIME THAT THESE TWO TEAMS MET
THE LIONS LED TILL THE GAME'S FINAL GUN

THE VIKES MAY BE A LITTLE COMPLACENT THIS WEEK
ASSUMING THEY ARE FAR SUPERIOR FOR WHATEVER REASON
THE LIONS HOWEVER WON'T ROLL OVER FOR THEM
AND MAY WELL CARRY A WIN INTO THE OFFSEASON

~ ~ ~ ~ ~ ~ ~ ~ ~ ~ ~ ~ ~ ~ ~ ~ ~ ~ ~

THE BILLS STILL CARRIED PLAYOFF HOPES
AS THEY WENT THROUGH LAST WEEK'S GAME PREPARATION
HOWEVER AS THEY TOOK THEIR SPOT ON LAMBEAU FIELD
THEY BECAME PART OF GREEN BAY'S "HOLLIDAY" CELEBRATION

WHILE THE CHILLY WIND BLEW ACROSS THE TURF
MAKING THE PASSING GAME TREACHEROUS AT BEST
THE PACKERS' DEFENSE SIMPLY ENGULFED THE BILLS
AND EMERGED VICTORIOUS FROM THE TEST

ANOTHER FOE WITH POST-SEASON ASPIRATIONS
IS ON THE PACKERS' SLATE THIS WEEK
A WIN BY THE JETS ALONG WITH A LITTLE HELP
COULD GET THEM THE PLAYOFF SPOT THEY SEEK

CHAD PENNINGTON IS THE QUARTERBACK
WHO WILL TRY LEADING THE JETS TO THE WIN
HE IS A GOOD YOUNG FIELD GENERAL
WHO'S PULLED THE JETS OUT TIME AND AGAIN

BUT HE WILL BE UP AGAINST THE MASTER
BRETT'S SEEN YOUNG GUYS COME AND GO
AND ON A MUDDY FIELD IN NEW JERSEY SUNDAY
THE JETS' HOPES WILL RECEIVE THE FINAL BLOW

RESULTS:
Green Bay lost to the
New York Jets 17-42

Minnesota beat the
Detroit Lions 38-36

GB: 12-4
(NFCN Champs)
MN: 6-10

PACKERS "VERSES" VIKINGS ~ Carl Nelson

IN A GAME WHERE DEFENSE WASN'T FEATURED
AND BOTH TEAMS SCORED TIME AND AGAIN
THE VIKINGS HELD OFF THE DETROIT LIONS
AND ENDED THE SEASON AT SIX-AND-TEN

THE RECORD AT LEAST IS AN IMPROVEMENT
OVER LAST SEASON'S FIVE-AND-ELEVEN FINAL TALLY
ALTHOUGH THE VIKES ONLY HAD THREE WINS
UNTIL THE FAMOUS LATE-SEASON RALLY

TRUTH BE TOLD THE VIKING TEAM MADE SOME STRIDES
FOR EXAMPLE IN THEIR RUNNING GAME
BUT THE PASSING GAME DID NOT KEEP UP WITH THAT
AND TURNOVERS BECAME DAUNTE'S CLAIM TO FAME

WE'LL NOT TALK MUCH ABOUT THE DEFENSIVE TEAM
BECAUSE QUITE FRANKLY IT JUST WOULD NOT BE NICE
LET IT SUFFICE TO SAY IT MUST BE A HIGH PRIORITY
FOR THE VIKES AND THEIR HEAD COACH MIKEY TICE

SO INTO THE OFFSEASON GO RED'S BUNCH
WITH A HIGH DRAFT CHOICE AND FREE AGENT CASH TO BURN
MAYBE THIS YEAR THEY'LL CHECK QUALITY NOT PRICE
OR PERHAPS THEY JUST NEVER WILL LEARN....

~ ~ ~ ~ ~ ~ ~ ~ ~ ~ ~ ~ ~ ~ ~ ~ ~ ~ ~

THE PACKERS HAD A SIMPLE GOAL IN MIND
AS THEY TOOK THE FIELD IN NEW YORK LAST WEEK
"JUST BEAT THE JETS AND WE'LL HAVE HOME FIELD—
THAT WILL GIVE US THE EDGE THAT WE SEEK"

ALAS THE JETS HAD OTHER PLANS
AND IT SEEMED THE PACK DID TOO
FOR NEW YORK TOOK THE GAME AWAY
AND BEAT THE PACKERS BLACK-AND-BLUE

SO NOW INSTEAD GETTING A WEEK OFF
IT'S THE FALCONS AT LAMBEAU SATURDAY NIGHT
THE SAME TWO TEAMS THAT STARTED THIS SEASON
IN A GAME THAT BECAME AN OVERTIME FIGHT

MICHAEL VICK AGAIN FACES THE PACK
AND HIS IS A FACE THAT SHOULD CAUSE SOME CONCERN
FOR HE CAN THROW THE FOOTBALL VERY WELL
AND MORE THAN ONE DEFENSE HIS QUICK FEET HAVE BURNED

THE PACKERS ARE BATTERED THAT MUCH IS SURE
AND WHILE THE FALCONS WON'T LIE DOWN AND PLAY DEAD
IT'S ATLANTA WHO WILL PACK UP AND GO HOME WITH A LOSS
WHILE THE PACKERS PREPARE FOR THE NEXT GAME AHEAD

RESULTS:
Green Bay lost to Atlanta 7-27

Minnesota missed out on the postseason

PACKERS "VERSES" VIKINGS ~ Carl Nelson

GB: 0-1
(Wild Card Loser)
Final Record: 12-5

MORE THAN VAGUELY REMINISCENT OF LAST YEAR
THE SEASON ENDED UGLY FOR SHERMAN AND THE GANG
AND SO YET AGAIN THE PACK GOES INTO THE OFFSEASON
WITH A WHIMPER INSTEAD OF A BANG

WHATEVER HAPPENED TO THIS PACKERS' TEAM
WHO EARLY ON SEEMED TO BE THE ONES TO BEAT?
HOW IN THE WORLD COULD THEY BE SO HUMBLED
IN A FIRST-EVER LAMBEAU PLAYOFF GAME DEFEAT?

THAT THE FALCONS WERE NOT INTIMIDATED
BECAME QUITE OBVIOUS FOR ALL TO SEE
THEY JUST CAME IN AND OUTPLAYED THE PACK
DESPITE LAMBEAU'S WEATHER AND HISTORY

MICHAEL VICK IS ONE OF THOSE AMAZING GUYS
THAT ARE SO DIFFICULT TO BRING DOWN
MANY TIMES PACKER HANDS WERE UPON HIM
ONLY TO BE UNABLE TO PULL HIM TO THE GROUND

THE PACKER DEFENSE TO ITS CREDIT
GAVE THE GAME EVERYTHING THEY HAD
BUT INJURIES HAVE SO LIMITED THAT GROUP
THAT THEY SIMPLY WOUND UP LOOKING BAD

THE PACKERS' OFFENSE IN A LIKE FASHION
CAME INTO THIS GAME PIECED AND TAPED TOGETHER
DONALD DRIVER GAVE IT HIS BEST SHOT
AND CAUGHT A SCORE BEFORE LEAVING ALTOGETHER

AHMAN GREEN REBRUISED A KNEE
GLENN TOOK ANOTHER SHOT TO THE HEAD
WHEN THOSE THREE PLAYERS LEFT THE GAME
PACKER FANS FELT AN IMPENDING DREAD

WHILE FISHER AND JAVON WALKER
MADE SOME GOOD PLAYS IN THIS GAME
BRETT FAVRE'S LOSS OF HIS MAIN WEAPONS
FORCED THE OFFENSE TO APPEAR A LITTLE LAME

TOSS IN A COUPLE OF COACHING GAFFES
A SPECIAL TEAMS' GOOF AND TWO KICKS LONGWELL MISSED
AND IT REALLY SHOULD COME AS NO SURPRISE
THAT "GOOD-BYE" GREEN BAY'S PLAYOFF HOPES WERE KISSED

SO NOW COMES THE TIME FOR GREEN BAY'S FANS
TO REFLECT ON THE GOOD THINGS THE PACKERS DID
THEY WOUND UP TIED WITH THE LEAGUE'S BEST RECORD
AND FOUND A NEW STAR IN THAT WALKER KID

IT'S THE TIME WHEN SOME PLAYERS ARE TOLD "GOOD-BYE"
AND OTHERS ARE WELCOMED TO THE PACKER FOLD
THERE IS THE NUCLEUS OF A GOOD TEAM HERE
WHO NEXT SEASON AGAIN WILL CONTEND FOR THE GOLD....

NFC
Philedelphia: 13-4
Tampa Bay: 13-4
AFC
Oakland: 12-5
Tennessee: 12-5

PACKERS "VERSES" VIKINGS   ~ Carl Nelson

THE TIME HAS COME TO FINALLY DETERMINE
WHO WILL PLAY IN THIS YEAR'S SUPER BOWL
NEXT SUNDAY THE LAST FOUR FOOTBALL TEAMS
WILL DECIDE JUST WHO WILL FILL THOSE ROLES

PHILLY HAS SIMPLY CRUSHED THE BUCS
THE PAST FEW TIMES THEY'VE COME TO VISIT
AND GRUDEN AND THE BUCCANEERS
ARE TIRED OF THE QUESTION "WHY IS IT?"

IT'S GOING TO BE DARK AND COLD IN PHILLY
AND THE EAGLES' "D" WON'T CUT 'EM ANY SLACK
UNLESS THE TAMPA OFFENSIVE LINE IS FLAWLESS
BRAD JOHNSON WILL SPEND THE NIGHT ON HIS BACK

MIKE ALSTOTT WILL HAVE TO RUN WITH SPEED
AND NOT PUT THE FOOTBALL ON THE GROUND
THE BUCS' RECEIVERS HAVE TO PLAY TOUGH
AND NOT LET THE EAGLES PUSH THEM AROUND

AS FAR AS SAPP AND THE TAMPA DEFENSE
CHANCES ARE GOOD THAT THEY WILL BE EXPOSED
AS A TEAM THAT'S GOOD WHEN THEY'RE AHEAD
BUT WHEN TRAILING ARE EASILY HOSED

~ ~ ~ ~ ~ ~ ~ ~ ~ ~ ~ ~ ~ ~ ~ ~ ~ ~ ~

IT'S SOMEWHAT SURPRISING TO SEE THE TITANS
PLAYING IN THIS YEAR'S CHAMPIONSHIP GAME
OTHER THAN EDDIE GEORGE AND STEVE MCNAIR
NONE OF THE PLAYERS HAVE WELL-KNOWN NAMES

THE TITANS HAVEN'T HAD AN EASY ROAD
IN MAKING IT TO THIS WEEKEND'S TEST
AND THIS WEEK THEY CARRY A LONG LIST OF INJURIES
INTO A GAME AGAINST THE TEAM THAT MAY WELL BE THE BEST

THE RAIDERS ON THE OTHER HAND HAVE A ROSTER
THAT LOOKS A LOT LIKE A FOOTBALL "WHO'S WHO"
AMONG THOSE NAMES ARE GANNON, RICE AND TIM BROWN
AND IT'S WELL-KNOWN JUST WHAT THOSE GUYS CAN DO

BACK WHEN THE SEASON WAS JUST BEGINNING
LA PUT UP FIFTY-TWO AGAINST THIS TITAN TEAM
SINCE THAT TIME THE RAIDERS HAVE REFINED THEIR GAME
AND IN THE PAST WEEKS HAVE JUST BEEN GAINING STEAM

THEY'VE REACHED THAT MAGICAL PLATEAU
WHERE THE GAME LOOKS MORE LIKE A DANCE
WITH EVERY MOVE ALMOST SO CHOREOGRAPHED
THAT NO PLAY LOOKS LIKE A WAYWARD CHANCE

THE TITANS HOWEVER CAN WIN THIS GAME
ALTHOUGH IT MAY TAKE A BREAK OR TWO
BUT IF THE RAIDERS BREAK ON TOP EARLY
THE "FLAMING THUMBTACKS" WILL BE SCREWED

THERE IS A REASON THEY PLAY THESE GAMES
FOR SOMETIMES AN UNDERDOG HITS ITS PEAK
REARING UP AND BEATING THE FAVORITE
BUT IT'S NOT GOING TO HAPPEN THIS WEEK

RESULTS:
The Tampa Bay Buccaneers beat
the Philadelphia Eagles 27-10

The Oakland Raiders beat the
Tennessee Titans 41-24

PACKERS "VERSES" VIKINGS ~ Carl Nelson

BACK IN THE SUNNY WARMTH OF SEPTEMBER
THIRTY-TWO TEAMS FIRST TOOK THE FIELD
EACH CARRYING DREAMS OF THE CHAMPIONSHIP
AND HIGH HOPES OF WHAT THIS YEAR WOULD YIELD

AS THE WEEKS WORE ON FOR ALL OF THE TEAMS
COMPETITION LEFT MOST OF THOSE DREAMS BEREFT
AS ATTRITION WHITTLED DOWN THE CONTENDERS
UNTIL NOW WHEN ONLY THESE TWO ARE LEFT

IT'S THE OAKLAND RAIDERS' TEAM
A GROUP THAT ALL JUST LOVE TO HATE
THAT THE TAMPA BAY BUCCANEERS
FIND HEAPED UPON THEIR PLATE

JON GRUDEN LEADS THE BUCCANEERS' TEAM
(THOUGH LAST YEAR HE COACHED THE SILVER-AND-BLACK)
HE LEAPT AT THE CHANCE TO MOVE OUT EAST
AND NEVER ONCE HAS LOOKED BACK

THE RESULT IS A TEAM FROM FLORIDA
THAT FOR ONCE IS AN OFFENSIVE THREAT
LAST WEEK THEY SHOWED THEY CAN RUN THE BALL
AND BRAD JOHNSON MAY NOT HAVE PEAKED YET

BUT AS ALWAYS IT'S THE TAMPA DEFENSE
COMING FOREMOST TO EVERYONE'S MIND
THEY PLAY THE DREADED "COVER TWO"
THAT MAKES SCORING OPPORTUNITIES HARD TO FIND

WARREN SAPP IS THE VOCAL LEADER
ALTHOUGH HIS PLAY HAS DIMINISHED OF LATE
INSTEAD IT'S THE SECONDARY AND 'BACKERS
THAT REALLY SHOULD BE REGARDED AS GREAT

FACING THEM IS RICH GANNON OF OAKLAND
WHOSE TALENT AND PRESENCE HAVE STEADILY GROWN
UNTIL THIS YEAR HE'S THE LEAGUE'S MVP
AS HIS PLAY HAS REPEATEDLY SHOWN

HIS OFFENSIVE WEAPONS ARE MANY FOLD
INCLUDING TIMMY BROWN AND JERRY RICE
TOSS IN THE TALENTS OF CHARLIE GARNER
AND THE WHOLE PACKAGE TURNS OUT PRETTY NICE

OAKLAND ALSO HAS AN OFFENSIVE LINE THAT'S HUGE
AND SHOULD BE ABLE TO HANDLE WHAT THE BUCS CAN BRING
WHILE THE RAIDERS' DEFENSE HAS SOME MEMBERS
THAT ALREADY HAVE A SUPER BOWL RING

SO WHO'LL BE THE TEAM THAT HOISTS THE PRIZE
AND CARRIES THE "CHAMPION" TAG INTO NEXT YEAR?
MIKE ALSOTT WILL LOSE A FUMBLE LATE IN THE GAME
BRINGING TAMPA BAY FANS TO TEARS....

Super Bowl Record
Oakland: 3-1
Tampa Bay: 0-0

RESULTS:
The Tampa Bay Buccaneers beat
the Oakland Raiders 48-21

PACKERS

" VERSES "

VIKINGS

Green Bay Packers
Regular Season 10-6
Postseason 1-1

Minnesota Vikings
Regular Season 9-7
No Postseason

2003

Carl "Gator" Nelson

IT HARDLY SEEMS IT CAN BE TIME
FOR ANOTHER FOOTBALL SEASON TO BEGIN
YET HERE IT IS AS SUMMER WANES
AND THE DAYS GROW SHORTER ONCE AGAIN

THE SUPER BOWL SEEMS SO LONG AGO
THAT THE DETAILS HAVE BEGUN TO FADE
THE OFFSEASON TIME HAS COME AND GONE
BRINGING FREE AGENTS AND AN OCCASIONAL TRADE

NOW STADIUM CREWS ARE HARD AT WORK
MOWING GRASS AND PAINTING LINES
KNOWING THAT SOON IT ALL WILL BEGIN
AND THAT IT'S GOT TO LOOK BETTER THAN FINE

FOR EVERY HOME FIELD HAS THE POTENTIAL
OF SEEING THAT LOCAL TEAM GO ALL THE WAY
AT LEAST UNTIL THE SEASON STARTS
AND THOSE DREAMS BEGIN TO SLIP AWAY

~ ~ ~ ~ ~ ~ ~ ~ ~ ~ ~ ~ ~ ~ ~ ~ ~

GREEN BAY'S PACKERS ENTER THIS SEASON
IN A FRESHLY REMODELED LAMBEAU FIELD
THE PLACE WHERE LAST SEASON ENDED
AS THE FALCONS FORCED THE PACK TO YIELD

SINCE THAT GAME THERE'VE BEEN CHANGES
AS THE PACKERS ATTEMPT TO FILL SOME HOLES
LAST YEAR THE INJURY LIST WAS FAR TOO LONG
AND BY YEAR'S END REALLY TOOK A TOLL

BUT "TIME HEALS ALL WOUNDS" AS THEY SAY
AND MOST OF THE VICTIMS HAVE RETURNED
BOTH OF THE BIG BOOKEND TACKLES ARE BACK
AND THE DEFENSE NOW HAS SPEED TO BURN

BRETT FAVRE RETURNS TO LEAD THE OFFENSE
WHICH INCLUDES DONALD DRIVER AND AHMAN GREEN
BUT WHO ELSE WILL STEP UP AS RECEIVER
IS SOMETHING THAT RIGHT NOW CANNOT BE FORSEEN

THE ADDITION OF OL' WESLEY WALLS WILL HELP
INCREASE PRODUCTION FROM THE TIGHT END
AND NICK LUCHEY AND NAJEH DAVENPORT
WILL PROVIDE THE POWER RUSHING ONCE AGAIN

NICK BARNETT WILL LEAD THE 'BACKERS
SWARMING BEHIND GILBERT, HUNT AND KGB
WHILE SHARPER, MCKENZIE AND AL HARRIS
WILL PROVIDE A BULLETPROOF PASSING "D"

PACKERS "VERSES" VIKINGS ~ Carl Nelson

GB: 0-0
MN: 0-0

~ Carl Nelson

PACKERS "VERSES" VIKINGS

THE VIKINGS THINK THEY'VE FOUND THE KEYS
THAT WILL OPEN RESPECTABILITY'S DOORS THIS YEAR
IMPROVEMENTS ON THE BALL'S DEFENSIVE SIDE
MIGHT WELL MEAN THOSE DAYS ARE NEAR

FRESH FROM DETROIT MISTER CHRIS CLAIRBORNE
STEPS INTO THE VIKINGS' LINEBACKERS' MIX
ALONG WITH ROOKIE EJ HENDERSON
WHO'LL BE LEARNING SOME OF OL' BIEKERT'S TRICKS

ON THE DEFENSIVE LINE CHRIS HOVAN IS THOUGHT
TO TRULY BE A RISING YOUNG FOOTBALL STAR
IF HE JUST PLAYS HALF AS WELL AS HE TALKS
THERE IS A CHANCE THIS YOUNG MAN COULD GO FAR

BUT THE SECONDARY IS AGAIN THE SPOT
THAT WILL BE CONSIDERED THE VIKES' ACHILLES HEEL
ONLY IF THE FREE AGENT CORNERS CAN BE HEALTHY
CAN THEIR SIGNING BE CONSIDERED A GOOD DEAL

MOSS AND CULPEPPER WILL LEAD THE VIKES
AGAIN THEY'LL PASS AND CATCH THE BALL
PROVIDED AGAIN THAT RANDY WILL RUN HIS ROUTES
AND DAUNTE DOESN'T FUMBLE WHEN HE FALLS

BUT IT'S THE LOSS OF MICHAEL BENNETT
THAT WILL PUT A DENT IN THE VIKINGS' DREAMS
WHILE THE BACKS BEHIND HIM MAY BE ADEQUATE
HE HAD THE SPEED TO EXPLOIT DEFENSIVE SEAMS

~ ~ ~ ~ ~ ~ ~ ~ ~ ~ ~ ~ ~ ~ ~ ~ ~ ~ ~

AND AS THE SEASON OPENS SUNDAY
WHY WHAT A MIRACLE TO SEE
IT'S THE VIKINGS AT THE PACKERS
TO OPEN THIS YEAR'S FOOTBALL SPREE

RESULTS:
Green Bay lost to the
Minnesota Vikings 25-30

WHILE BOTH TEAMS WILL BE BRINGING A LOT OF HOPE
AND ALL THE TALENT THAT THEY POSSESS
THIS IS GOING TO BE A HARD-FOUGHT GAME
AND NO ONE COULD POSSIBLY EXPECT ANY LESS

WHO WILL TRIUMPH IN THIS GAME OF WILLS?
AND WHO WILL HAVE THEIR HOPES DEALT A MIGHTY BLOW?
WHICH TEAM WILL HAVE REPAIRED THE PROBLEMS BEST?
LATE SUNDAY WE WILL KNOW

BUT HERE'S A HINT AS TO THE OUTCOME
THAT WILL MOST PROBABLY BE SEEN
THE COLOR OF UNI WORN BY THE WINNERS
WILL BE PREDOMINANTLY GREEN....

~ Carl Nelson

PACKERS "VERSES" VIKINGS

GB: 0-1
MN: 1-0

THE DAY SHOULD HAVE BEEN RIPE WITH RAW EMOTION
BUT GREEN BAY'S PACKERS APPEARED PANCAKE-FLAT
AS IF THEY THOUGHT A WIN WAS ASSURED
BY MERELY DONNING THAT FAMOUS YELLOW HAT

NO ONE SEEMED TO BE ON THE SAME PAGE
DURING THE FIRST HALF OF THAT GAME
THE OFFENSE STUMBLED—THE DEFENSE DRAGGED
THE WHOLE TEAM DESERVES THE BLAME

WHILE THE VIKES SEEMED TO HAVE THE PACKERS' NUMBER
GREEN BAY DIDN'T DO THEMSELVES MUCH GOOD
EARLY ON THEY TRIED TO PASS ALMOST EXCLUSIVELY
INSTEAD OF RUNNING THE BALL LIKE THEY SHOULD

TO THEIR CREDIT THE MINNESOTA VIKINGS' TEAM
SEEMED VERY WELL PREPARED TO PLAY THE PACK
BEHIND CULPEPPER'S LEGS THEY KEPT THOSE CHAINS A-MOVING
SCORED EARLY AND NEVER DID LOOK BACK

RANDY MOSS HAD YET ANOTHER BIG DAY
WHICH IS GETTING TO BE TOO FAMILIAR A REFRAIN
BUT ON THIRD AND LONG IT WAS DAUNTE'S RUNS
CAUSING THE BULK OF THE PACKERS' PAIN

EVEN THOUGH IN HALF NUMBER TWO
THE PACKERS STARTED TO FIND THEIR STRIDE
INJURIES TO FERGIE AND DONALD DRIVER
PUSHED ANY COMEBACK HOPES ASIDE

~ ~ ~ ~ ~ ~ ~ ~ ~ ~ ~ ~ ~ ~ ~ ~ ~

KORDELL STEWART TOOK THE FIELD LAST WEEK
IN HIS FIRST GAME AS CHICAGO'S QUARTERBACK
THE ONLY NUMBER LARGER THAN HIS INTERCEPTIONS
WAS HOW MANY TIMES THAT HE WAS SACKED

THE VIKINGS CAN ALMOST MARK THIS ONE DOWN
AS A WIN EVEN BEFORE THE GAME BEGINS
FOR UNLESS SOMETHING DRAMATIC HAPPENS TO THE BEARS
THEY'LL BE HUMILIATED THIS WEEK ONCE AGAIN

~ ~ ~ ~ ~ ~ ~ ~ ~ ~ ~ ~ ~ ~ ~ ~ ~

THE PACKERS WILL HOST DETROIT'S LIONS
WHO ARE COMING OFF A BIG WIN OF THEIR OWN
BUT IT CAME AGAINST THE CARDINALS
SO ITS VALUE MAY YET BE UNKNOWN

RESULTS:
Green Bay beat the
Detroit Lions 31-6

Minnesota beat the
Chicago Bears 24-13

GREEN BAY'S TEAM WILL FEEL THE PRESSURE
OF NEEDING TO GET THAT FIRST HOME-FIELD WIN
LOOK FOR AHMAN TO RUN WILD ON THE LIONS
AS THE PACKERS BRING DETROIT BACK TO EARTH AGAIN

157

GB: 1-1
MN: 2-0

PACKERS "VERSES" VIKINGS ~ Carl Nelson

AFTER WATCHING THE SEASON OPENER
PACKERS FANS FELT SOMEWHAT ILL-AT-EASE
"SURELY THIS GREEN BAY TEAM CAN PLAY BETTER"
WAS THE THINKING IN THE LAND OF CHEESE

THEN FATE LET THE LIONS CHARGE INTO LAMBEAU
FEELING GREAT AFTER SHUFFLING ARIZONA'S "CARDS"
MAYBE THEY COULD PULL OFF ANOTHER UPSET
EVEN IF IT IS GREEN BAY'S HOME YARD

WE ALL SAW WHAT HAPPENED SUNDAY
AFTER AHMAN TOOK IT TO THE HOUSE
AND THE LIONS WHO CAME A-ROARING IN
CREPT BACK OUT QUIETLY AS A MOUSE

THIS WEEK IT'S WESTWARD THAT THE PACKERS GO
TO CHALLENGE THE CARDINALS IN THE DESERT SUN
AND REALLY THE WAY THOSE CARDS HAVE PLAYED
THIS GAME COULD BE A LOT OF FUN

THIS WILL BE A CHANCE FOR THE PACK TO DISPLAY
ALL OF THE WEAPONS THAT THEY POSSESS
AND IF GREEN BAY CAN SIMPLY KEEP ITS FOCUS
THEY WON'T BE THE MOST POLITE OF GUESTS

~ ~ ~ ~ ~ ~ ~ ~ ~ ~ ~ ~ ~ ~ ~ ~ ~ ~ ~

AFTER GETTING OVER ON THE PACKERS
MINNESOTA'S TEAM WAS FEELING PRETTY GOOD
NEXT UP WAS THE CHICAGO BEARS
A VIKINGS' WIN WAS SIMPLY UNDERSTOOD

THE BEARS SURELY DIDN'T PLAY VERY WELL
AND WERE PUSHED AROUND MOST OF THE DAY
BUT IT TOOK 'TIL LATE IN THE FOURTH QUARTER
BEFORE THE VIKES COULD PUT THOSE BEARS AWAY

THIS WEEK THE VIKINGS HIT THE ROAD
TO CHALLENGE THE DETROIT LIONS' TEAM
WHO CAN BE SOMEWHAT HARD TO BEAT
IF ONE LETS THEM BUILD UP A HEAD OF STEAM

RESULTS:
Green Bay lost to the
Arizona Cardinals 13-20

Minnesota beat the
Detroit Lions 23-13

WHILE "CULPEPPER TO MOSS FOR THE SCORE"
IS THE CALL THAT VIKINGS FANS LOVE TO HEAR
"HARRINGTON TO ROGERS" MAY BE THE NEXT COMBO
THAT DEFENSIVE COACHES WILL COME TO FEAR

WITH THE SECONDARY OF THE VIKINGS
STILL LEARNING HOW TO WORK TOGETHER WELL
IT WILL BE UP TO A QUESTIONABLE VIKINGS' OFFENSE
TO KEEP MINNESOTA'S TEAM FROM FOOTBALL HELL

GB: 1-2
MN: 3-0

PACKERS "VERSES" VIKINGS ~ Carl Nelson

THE PACKERS WENT INTO THE "PHOENIX PHURNACE"
AND MELTED LIKE A WISCONSIN CHEESE FONDUE
AFTER COLLAPSING LIKE A "HOUSE OF CARDS"
WHATEVER CAN THOSE GREEN BAY PACKERS DO?

THERE'S A LOT OF DIFFERING OPINIONS
ON WHAT IS LEADING THE PACK ASTRAY
IS IT THE QB OR PERHAPS THE COACHES?
DEPENDS ON WHO YOU HEAR TODAY

WHATEVER THE CAUSE THE CURE MUST BE FOUND
BEFORE THE PACKERS FALL TOO FAR BEHIND
EARLY LOSSES CAN BE EXPENSIVE
WHEN IT COMES TO LATE-SEASON TIME

ON MODAY NIGHT THE GREEN BAY PACKERS' TEAM
FACE THE CHICAGO BEARS IN A STADIUM UNUSED AS YET
AS THEY HELP OPEN THE NEW SOLDIER FIELD
WHICH LOOKS SOMEWHAT LIKE AN "X-FILES" TV SET

DESPITE THE NEW SURROUNDINGS
THE BEARS REMAIN AS A TEAM ABYSMAL
UNLESS THEY ARE TRULY INSPIRED MONDAY
THEIR CHANCES TO WIN WILL REMAIN QUITE DISMAL

~ ~ ~ ~ ~ ~ ~ ~ ~ ~ ~ ~ ~ ~ ~ ~ ~ ~ ~

THE VIKINGS WENT INTO THE LIONS' DEN
AND FOUND THE GOING A LITTLE TOUGH
BUT THE CHALLENGE MOUNTED BY DETROIT
JUST WASN'T QUITE ENOUGH

MINNESOTA WAS ABLE TO PULL THE "BIG PLAYS"
FROM THEIR BAG WHEN THEY WERE NEEDED
AND EVEN KNOCKING CULPEPPER FROM THE GAME
COULDN'T SAVE THE LIONS FROM WINDING UP DEFEATED

CULPEPPER SUFFERED SOME FRACTURED BONES
AS THE RESULT OF AN ENDZONE SHOT
BUT DON'T DESPAIR YOU VIKINGS FANS
FOR ON YOUR BENCH IS GUS FEROTTE!

TERELL OWENS AND THE 'NINERS VISIT THIS WEEK
A TEAM THAT'S A MIRROR IMAGE OF THE VIKES
DOWN TO A QB WITH A SORE BACK
AND A RECEIVER THAT NO ONE SEEMS TO LIKE

THE 'NINERS BRING A POUNDING STYLE OF RUNNING GAME
THAT MAY JUST MAKE THE VIKES A LITTLE HUMBLE
WHILE THIS WILL BE A GOOD GAME TO WATCH
THE VIKINGS' SEASON MAY TAKE JUST A LITTLE STUMBLE

RESULTS:
Green Bay beat the
Chicago Bears 38-23

Minnesota beat the
San Francisco 49ers 35-7

PACKERS "VERSES" VIKINGS ~ Carl Nelson

IN A NIGHTMARISH SCENARIO FOR PACKERS FANS
IT APPEARS THIS YEAR'S VIKES MAY BE FOR REAL
WITH THEIR RECORD OF 0-AND-FOUR
THE PURPLE HAS IMMENSE BANDWAGON APPEAL

WHILE MINNESOTA'S DEFENSE IS QUITE SURPRISING
THE OFFENSIVE TEAM HAS REALLY BEEN QUITE HOT
ESPECIALLY SINCE CULPEPPER HAS BEEN SIDELINED
AND THE REINS GIVEN OVER TO OL' GUS FEROTTE

THE FORTY-NINERS WHOSE RECORD STOOD AT ONE AND TWO
WERE STILL REGARDED AS A TEAM STANDING ON THE BRINK
HOWEVER CONSIDERING HOW BAD THEY LOOKED LAST SUNDAY
IT'S MORE LIKELY THAT THEY'LL DRIVE THEIR FANS TO DRINK

THIS WEEK MINNESOTA FACES ATLANTA'S FALCONS' TEAM
WHO LAST YEAR EASILY "GOT OVER" ON THE VIKES
UNFORTUNATELY THIS YEAR MIKE VICK HAS A BROKEN LEG
SETTING A MATCHUP THAT MIKE TICE HAS TO LIKE

FOR THE FALCONS WITHOUT HIM ARE JUST A SHELL
OF WHAT SEEMED TO BE AN UP-AND-COMING FOOTBALL TEAM
TO THINK THAT THEY'LL GET PAST THE VIKINGS
MAY WELL BE JUST A SWAMP-FEVER INDUCED DREAM

~ ~ ~ ~ ~ ~ ~ ~ ~ ~ ~ ~ ~ ~ ~ ~ ~ ~ ~ ~

THE PACKERS LIVED UP TO THE TRADITION
OF THE "ACME MEAT PACKING COMPANY"
DISMEMBERING THOSE POOR CHICAGO BEARS
ON MONDAY NIGHT FOR THE WHOLE WORLD TO SEE

BUT LET'S REMEMBER—IT WAS JUST "DA BEARS"
A TEAM THE PACK ALWAYS BEATS EASILY
NONETHELESS IT LOOKED GOOD TO SEE THE PACKERS
AVOID SLIPPING TO A RECORD OF ONE AND THREE

THIS SUNDAY WILL FEEL LIKE OLD HOME WEEK
AS MIKE HOLMGREN BRINGS THE 'HAWKS TO TOWN
COACHES AND RUNNERS AND QUARTERBACKS
ARE AMONG THE FOLK THESE TEAMS HAVE PASSED AROUND

SEATTLE BRINGS A POTENT TEAM TO LAMBEAU
WITH HASSELBECK RETURNING TO WHERE HE STARTED
AT RUNNING BACK, SHAUN ALEXANDER IS STRONG
POSSESSING GOOD SPEED AND IS BRAVE-HEARTED

WHILE THE SEAHAWKS WILL BRING ALL THE PACK CAN HANDLE
MIKE SHERMAN'S TASK IS A LITTLE DIFFERENT SORT
HE HAS TO MAKE HIS PACK BELIEVE IN THEMSELVES
AND THAT THEY CAN MAKE THE 'HAWKS FALL SHORT—-

RESULTS:
Green Bay beat the
Seattle Seahawks 35-13

Minnesota beat the
Atlanta Falcons 39-26

GB: 3-2
MN: 5-0

PACKERS "VERSES" VIKINGS ~ Carl Nelson

THE FALCONS WERE LOOKING FOR SOME "SOUTHERN COMFORT"
AS THEY WELCOMED THE VIKINGS TO THE GEORGIADOME
BUT THE COMFORT THAT FLOWED LAST SUNDAY AFTERNOON
DIDN'T WIND UP GOING TO THE TEAM THAT WAS AT HOME

THOUGH THE VIKINGS SHOWED THAT THEY HAVEN'T FORGOTTEN
EXACTLY HOW THEY PLAYED THE GAME LAST SEASON
THEY WERE GOOD ENOUGH TO GET PAST ATLANTA
BUT A COUPLE OF BREAKS WERE A BIG PART OF THE REASON

THE VIKINGS' DEFENSE GAVE UP SOME BIG PLAYS
AND MORE THAN THREE HUNDRED YARDS THOUGH THE AIR
BUT WHEN THE OPPORTUNITY CAME TO WIN THE GAME
THOSE DEFENSIVE PLAYERS MANAGED TO BE RIGHT THERE

THOUGH IT TOOK A BIG BOUNCE OF A DUNN FUMBLE
AND A FALCONS' PASS BOUNCING OFF A VIKINGS' HEAD
THE "GUS TO RANDY" CONNECTION TURNED THE TIDE
AND AT GAME'S END ATLANTA'S UPSET HOPES WERE DEAD

SO FOR NOW THE VIKES STAY UNBEATEN
AFTER THIS BYE WEEK DAUNTE'S BACK SHOULD BE FIXED
AND THE VIKINGS WILL COME BACK FROM A WELL-EARNED REST
IN PURSUIT OF WIN NUMBER SIX

~ ~ ~ ~ ~ ~ ~ ~ ~ ~ ~ ~ ~ ~ ~ ~ ~ ~ ~

THE PACKERS FACED LAST WEEK WITH SOME WORRY
AS THE SEAHAWKS CAME TO VISIT IN GREEN BAY
AFTER ALL THEY WERE STILL UNDEFEATED
AND WERE HOPING TO LEAVE WISCONSIN THAT WAY

MIKE HOLMGREN FIGURED TO KNOW THE PACK
ABOUT AS WELL AS ANYONE COULD
BUT THE PACKERS' COACHES CAME UP WITH A PLAN
THAT MADE BRETT LOOK BETTER THAN GOOD

WHILE THE PACKERS DIDN'T HAVE A LOT OF THOSE "BIG" PLAYS
THEY MADE MOST EVERYTHING THEY CALLED WORK OUT WELL
DEMONSTRATING PLAYS THAT WORKED SO EFFICIENTLY
SEATTLE'S COACHES MUST HAVE SAID "WHAT THE HELL..."

THIS WEEK THE CHALLENGE SEEMS FAMILIAR
AS PRIEST HOLMES AND THE CHIEFS COME TO TOWN,
ANOTHER TEAM THAT IS UNBEATEN AS YET
AND ANOTHER THAT THE PACK WILL PUT DOWN

WHILE THIS GAME WILL BE FAR FROM EASY TO WIN
AS LAMBEAU SHINES IN THE OCTOBER SUN
THE PACKERS WILL CHOOSE TO GRASP THEIR DESTINY
AND SEND THE CHIEFS HOME CARRYING LOSS NUMBER ONE

RESULTS:
Green Bay lost to the
Kansas City Chiefs in overtime 34-40

Minnesota was on their
"Bye Week"

161

PACKERS "VERSES" VIKINGS

~ Carl Nelson

THE VIKES HAVE SURELY BEEN ON A TEAR
UP TO THIS POINT OF THE FOOTBALL SEASON
AND WHILE BETTER PLAY HAS HELPED A LOT
"WINNER'S MAGIC" IS ANOTHER IMPORTANT REASON

WHILE BREAKS AND BOUNCES ARE PART OF THE GAME
WHEN YOU'RE WINNING THEY GO YOUR WAY
AND SOMETIMES THAT CAN BE THE DIFFERENCE
IN A CLOSE GAME ON ANY GIVEN SUNDAY

AS THE VIKINGS RETURN FROM "BYE WEEK"
THAT MAGIC IS STILL OBVIOUSLY IN FORCE
AS DENVER'S QUARTERBACK HOPPED OUT OF BED
AND BROKE HIS FOOT OF COURSE

BUT THE BRONCOS HAVE A RUNNING GAME
THAT MAY WELL MAKE THE VIKINGS PAUSE
AND THE BRONCOS' DEFENSE IS ROUGH AND TOUGH
AND WILLING TO HELP OUT THE CAUSE

DAUNTE CULPEPPER WILL FINALLY MAKE HIS RETURN
MINNESOTA'S DEFENSE SHOULD BE WELL-RESTED
WHICH IS GOOD, FOR EVEN WITH BEUERLEIN AT THE HELM
THE VIKINGS TEAM WILL BE SEVERELY TESTED

~ ~ ~ ~ ~ ~ ~ ~ ~ ~ ~ ~ ~ ~ ~ ~ ~ ~ ~

PACKERS FANS ALL AROUND THE WORLD
LAST WEEK LET OUT A COLLECTIVE SIGH
WHEN AHMAN PUT THE BALL ON THE GROUND
AFTER THE PACKERS BLOCKED KC'S FIELD-GOAL TRY

WHILE THE PACKERS HAD PLAYED VERY WELL
FOR MORE THAN THREE QUARTERS OF LAST WEEK'S GAME
THEY LET THE MOMENTUM GET AWAY FROM THEM
AND THE RESULT CAUSED ALL OF THOSE FOLKS' PAIN

NOW GOING TO PLAY THE SAINT LOUIS RAMS
THE PACKERS REALLY NEED A WIN
WHAT HAPPENED THE LAST TIME GREEN BAY WENT THERE
CAN'T BE ALLOWED TO OCCUR ONCE AGAIN

THE RAMS WILL BE WITHOUT MARSHALL FAULK
BUT ARE STILL FORMIDIBLE TO SAY THE LEAST
THEIR RECEIVERS ARE STILL TOP-NOTCH
AND THE RAMS' DEFENSE STILL CAN BE A BEAST

GOING INTO THIS YEAR'S BYE WEEK
THE PACKERS CAN'T AFFORD TO STUMBLE YET AGAIN
AND JUST THINK HOW MUCH FUN IT'S GOING TO BE
TO WATCH MIKE MARTZ TAKE ONE ON THE CHIN....

RESULTS:
Green Bay lost to the
St Louis Rams 24-34

Minnesota beat the
Denver Broncos 28-20

GB: 3-4
MN: 6-0

PACKERS "VERSES" VIKINGS ~ Carl Nelson

THE VIKINGS CONTINUE THE SEASON UNBEATEN
AS LAST WEEK THE BRONCOS' TEAM TO THEM FELL
BUT IS THIS TEAM A FAVORITE TO BE THE CHAMPIONS?
IT SEEMS FAR TOO EARLY TO TELL

WHILE IT'S PLAIN THAT THE VIKES ARE AN IMPROVED TEAM
WITH A RECORD THAT SHOWS THAT THEY'VE YET TO BE BESTED
SOMEHOW THERE'S A FEELING AMONG MANY FOLKS
THAT AGAINST A GOOD TEAM THEY'VE YET TO BE TESTED

THIS WEEK THE GIANTS PROBABLY WON'T BE THAT TEAM
AS THEY ARE FLOUNDERING JUST A BIT EARLY THIS YEAR
BUT THEN AGAIN THIS COULD JUST BE THE SETUP
TO MAKE VIKINGS' FANS MOAN AND CRY INTO THEIR BEER

THE GIANTS JUST AREN'T THE TEAM THEY USED TO BE
AND LIKE SO MANY OTHERS JUST DON'T UNDERSTAND WHY
THIS YEAR'S TALENT ISN'T SO DIFFERENT IT SEEMS
AND THE PLAYERS ARE GIVING IT THE OL' COLLEGE TRY

BUT ALAS THAT PROBABLY WON'T BE ENOUGH
THOUGH THE GIANTS WILL SURELY GIVE IT A GO
FOR RIGHT NOW THE VIKES BIGGEST FEAR
WILL BE FALLING VICTIM TO THEIR OWN INFLATED EGOS

~ ~ ~ ~ ~ ~ ~ ~ ~ ~ ~ ~ ~ ~ ~ ~ ~ ~ ~

AS THE PACKERS HEAD INTO THE BYE WEEK
THE TIMING COULD NOT HAVE BEEN MUCH BETTER
FOR GREEN BAY'S TEAM HAS TO USE THIS TIME
TO AS A GROUP GET THEIR ACT TOGETHER

THEY STARTED OUT FINE AGAINST THE RAMS
AND LOOKED FOR A TIME LIKE THEY MIGHT WIN
BUT INCONSISTENCY TURNOVERS AND MISTAKES
SPELLED GREEN BAY'S DOOM YET AGAIN

RESULTS:
Green Bay was on their
"Bye Week"

Minnesota lost to the
New York Giants 17-29

EVEN THOUGH BRETT FAVRE WAS ON TARGET
WITH THE MAJORITY OF HIS FORWARD PASSES
THE RAMS KNEW THAT WITHOUT AHMAN GREEN
THE PACKERS OFFENSE WOULD FALL ON THEIR ASSES

THAT WAS THE PLAN AND IT WAS A GOOD ONE
AS GREEN PUT THE BALL ON THE GROUND MORE THAN ONCE
GIVING THE RAMS MORE CHANCES TO SCORE
AND MAKING THE DEFENSE LOOK LIKE A COLLECTION OF DUNCES

SO AS THE PACKERS TAKE A FEW DAYS OF REST
LET'S ALL HOPE THAT THEY ARE ALL SEARCHING THEIR SOULS
AND WILL COME BACK WITH THE ANSWERS TO "HOW TO WIN"
BEFORE THEY LOSE SIGHT OF THEIR POST-SEASON GOALS

GB: 3-4
MN: 6-1

PACKERS "VERSES" VIKINGS ~ Carl Nelson

THE VIKINGS HAVE SEEMED ALMOST INVULNERABLE
FOR THE FIRST HALF OF THIS FOOTBALL SEASON
THEY'VE BEEN PLAYING BETTER THAN IN YEARS PAST
WHICH IS A BIG PART OF THE REASON

BUT ANOTHER FACTOR NEEDS TO BE CONSIDERED
"WHEN YOU'RE HOT THE BREAKS WILL GO YOUR WAY"
AND SOMETIMES THE BOUNCES THAT THE BALL TAKES
ARE AS IMPORTANT AS THE NUMBER OF GOOD PLAYS

THE GIANTS CAME TO THE METRODOME
CONSIDERED A MEDIOCRE TEAM AT BEST
YET WHEN THE FINAL GUN SOUNDED LAST SUNDAY
THEY HAD MANAGED TO STAND UP TO THE TEST

IT WASN'T THAT THE VIKES PLAYED BADLY
OR THAT NEW YORK PLAYED OVER THEIR HEAD
IT SIMPLY CAME DOWN TO WHO GOT THE BREAKS
THIS WEEK THE GIANTS RECEIVED THEM INSTEAD

SO NOW VIKES FANS HAVE GOT TO WONDER
IF THIS WAS A FLUKE OR THE START OF A TREND
CAN MINNESOTA'S TEAM RECOVER THEIR POISE
OR HAVE THE HIGH HOPES SUDDENLY COME TO AN END?

~ ~ ~ ~ ~ ~ ~ ~ ~ ~ ~ ~ ~ ~ ~ ~ ~ ~ ~

THE PACK HAS LEARNED SOME PAINFUL LESSONS
OVER THE PAST EIGHT FOOTBALL SUNDAYS
THEY'VE LOST TWO GAMES THAT THEY SHOULDN'T HAVE
AND LET TWO CLOSE ONES SLIP SLOWLY AWAY

SO WHAT WILL THE PACKERS BRING BACK WITH THEM
AFTER THE BYE WEEK'S MID-YEAR VACATION?
WILL MIKE SHERMAN AND THE COACHING STAFF
HAVE DEVISED SOME NEW FOOTBALL VARIATION?

WHATEVER THE PLAN IT MUST BE A GOOD ONE
FOR THE FIRST GAME BACK COULD BE A KILLER
AS THE PACKERS TRAVEL TO MINNESOTA
TO CHALLENGE THE VIKES IN WHAT SHOULD BE A THRILLER

BRETT AND THE BOYS STRUGGLE IN THAT DARNED DOME
(ALTHOUGH THEY MANAGE TO PULL OUT THE OCCASIONAL WIN)
THE PLACE IS LIKE PRO FOOTBALL'S "BLACK HOLE"
GOOD TEAMS GO IN AND FOR HOURS AREN'T SEEN AGAIN

THIS GAME SHOULD BE A MUCH CLOSER ONE
THAN WOULD HAVE BEEN PREDICTED TWO WEEKS AGO
AND WE ALL KNOW THE PACKERS WON'T DISAPPOINT US
THOSE FANS LUCKY ENOUGH TO GO!!

WHILE THE VIKES WILL DO THEIR LEVEL BEST
GREEN BAY'S PACKERS WILL SURELY DO THE SAME
AND THIS TIME THAT SHOULD BE JUST ENOUGH
FOR THE VISITORS TO WIN THIS FOOTBALL GAME

RESULTS:
Green Bay beat the
Minnesota Vikings 30-27

164

GB: 4-4
MN: 6-2

PACKERS "VERSES" VIKINGS ~ Carl Nelson

LAST SUNDAY NIGHT THE VIKINGS LEARNED
WHAT SO MANY TEAMS HAVE LEARNED BEFORE
THAT KEEPING ON THE WINNING TRACK
TAKES MORE THAN THE ABILITY TO SCORE

THE PACKERS USED WHAT HAD BEEN SHOWN
BY THE VIKES' OPPONENTS IN RECENT WEEKS
NAMELY THAT IF YOU CAN RUN THE BALL OUTSIDE
THE VAUNTED VIKINGS' "D" IS FULL OF LEAKS

NOW MINNESOTA'S TEAM HEADS OUT ON THE ROAD
SEEKING THE ANSWERS TO THE LOSING STREAK
DEFENSIVE SOLUTIONS WHICH MUST BE FOUND
BEFORE THEY RISK TAKING A THIRD LOSS THIS WEEK

FOR THERE IS ANOTHER OF THOSE RUNNING BACKS
RESIDING IN THE CHARGERS' GOLD-AND-BLUE
WHO RUNS WITH SPEED AND CAN GET OUTSIDE
WHICH IS WHAT THE VIKES CAN'T LET HIM DO

IT WILL BE FUN TO WATCH THIS WEEK'S GAME
TO SEE IF TICE AND CREW CAN SAVE THE DAY
FOR THE LOSING STREAK WILL REACH THREE GAMES
IF SAN DIEGO PULLS THE UPSET ON SUNDAY

~ ~

TYPICALLY THE PACKERS STRUGGLE
IN THAT ACCURSED METRODOME
THIS WEEK HOWEVER WAS A LITTLE DIFFERENT
IT LOOKED AS IF THEY FELT QUITE AT HOME

BRETT FAVRE BROUGHT HIS BROKEN THUMB
AND AHMAN SHOWED HIS BLAZING SPEED
AND COUPLED WITH THE WAY THE DEFENSE PLAYED
PROVIDING A WIN THAT FILLED THE PACKERS' NEED

THAT WIN BROUGHT THEM BACK TO FOUR AND FOUR
AND BACK INTO THE NORTH DIVISION RACE
WITH THE WHEELS FALLING FROM THE VIKES' BANDWAGON
IT'S NOT SO FARFETCHED TO SEE THE PACKERS IN FIRST PLACE

THE PHILADELPHIA EAGLES ARE THIS WEEK'S FOE
COMING TO PLAY ON A COLD WISCONSIN NIGHT
ANOTHER TEAM THAT STARTED A LITTLE SLOWLY THIS YEAR
BUT STILL CAPABLE OF GIVING THE PACKERS QUITE A FIGHT

THIS SHOULD BE A CLASSIC GAME TO SEE
AS BOTH TEAMS ARE HITTING THEIR STRIDE
WHILE MCNABB AND THE EAGLES WILL KEEP IT CLOSE
THE DECIDING FACTOR WILL BE OLD-TIME PACKERS' PRIDE

RESULTS:
Green Bay lost to the
Philadelphia Eagles 14-17

Minnesota lost to the
San Diego Chargers 42-28

GB: 4-5
MN: 6-3

PACKERS "VERSES" VIKINGS ~ Carl Nelson

THERE'S A CERTAIN MAGIC IN MINNESOTA THESE DAYS
THE LIKES OF WHICH MAY NOT HAVE BEEN SEEN BEFORE
AS THE VIKINGS HAVE TURNED FROM A DOMINANT TEAM
TO ONE ON THE SHORT END OF THE SCORE

IT'S NOT QUITE CLEAR WHY THIS HAS OCCURRED
FOR AN ANSWER MIKE TICE IS SEARCHING HIGH AND LOW
BUT THE VIKES HAVE FORGOTTEN HOW TO PLAY DEFENSE
AND YOU CAN'T WIN THAT WAY YOU KNOW

LAST WEEK THE SAN DIEGO CHARGERS' TEAM
(WHO DON'T EVEN REMOTELY RESEMBLE THEIR NAME)
GAVE FORTY-ONE-YEAR-OLD DOUG FLUTIE THE START
AND HE MADE THE VIKINGS' TEAM APPEAR QUITE LAME

BESIDES THE MISMATCHES IN THE PASSING "D"
TOMLINSON COULD RUN ON THE VIKES AT WILL
SHOWING THAT CONTRARY TO POPULAR VIKINGS' "PR"
THOSE LINEBACKERS ARE OVER THE HILL

FORTUNATELY FOR MINNESOTA'S FANS
THEY PLAY THE RAIDERS THIS COMING WEEK
A TEAM WITHOUT ANY OFFENSIVE THREATS
WHO MIGHT BE THE PATSIES THE VIKINGS SEEK

~ ~ ~ ~ ~ ~ ~ ~ ~ ~ ~ ~ ~ ~ ~ ~ ~ ~

THE PACKERS LOST A TOUGH GAME MONDAY
WHEN IT LOOKED LIKE THEY HAD IT WELL IN HAND
AND THE RUMBLES AND GRUMBLES OF FAN UNREST
ARE ECHOING THROUGHOUT PACKERLAND

TRUTH BE TOLD IT LOOKED LIKE A MISERABLE NIGHT
WITH COLD AND ICY RAIN JUST POURING DOWN
THE BALL WAS MORE SLIPPERY THAN IT LOOKED
AND SIX TIMES THE PACKERS PUT IT ON THE GROUND

BUT STILL AND ALL AS THE GAME WOUND DOWN
AHMAN GREEN ONCE AGAIN HANDED THEM THE LEAD
BUT THE OFFENSE COULDN'T GET THE ONE FIRST DOWN
WHICH WOULD HAVE BEEN THE PACKERS' GREATEST NEED

SO NOW THEY'VE BUNDLED UP AND HEADED SOUTH
FOR A GAME AGAINST THE WORLD CHAMPION BUCCANEERS
WHO DESPITE THE TALK OF BEING AN "UPCOMING DYNASTY"
HAVE STRUGGLED JUST A BIT THIS YEAR

THE PACKERS HAVE A REALLY GOOD CHANCE
OF GAINING REVENGE ON SAPP AND CREW
WITH BOTH TEAMS COMING IN AT FOUR-AND-FIVE
IT'S UP TO WHAT BRETT AND THE PACK CAN DO

TIME TO CHECK WHAT'S DEEP INSIDE
AND TO PLAY A GAME THAT'S ERROR-FREE
FOR THE PACKERS CAN'T AFFORD MORE LOSSES
IF THEY HOPE TO SEE THE POST-SEASON IN 2K3

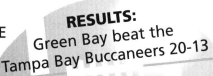

RESULTS:
Green Bay beat the
Tampa Bay Buccaneers 20-13

Minnesota lost to the
Oakland Raiders 18-28

GB: 5-5
MN: 6-4

PACKERS "VERSES" VIKINGS ~ Carl Nelson

AFTER WINNING SIX CONSECUTIVE FOOTBALL GAMES
THE VIKES HAVE DROPPED FOUR IN A ROW
AND IT'S BECOMING QUITE THE QUESTION
JUST HOW LONG THIS STREAK WILL GO

THE RAIDERS WOULD HAVE SEEMED JUST THE TEAM
TO LET THE VIKINGS GET BACK ON TRACK
BUT CULPEPPER TOSSED AN EARLY INTERCEPTION
AND THE RAIDERS NEVER ONCE LOOKED BACK

BUT THE VIKINGS WOULDN'T GIVE UP—
AND THEY TURNED THE BALL OVER FIVE MORE TIMES
THIS WEEK MOSS WAS BLAMING THE COACHES
AND DESPITE WHAT TICE IS SAYING—EVERYTHING IS NOT "JUST FINE"

THIS WEEK MAY BE THE VIKES' BEST CHANCE
TO REGAIN THE STATUS OF "CONTENDERS"
FOR THIS WEEK IT'S THE LIONS' TURN TO VISIT THE 'DOME
AND THEY NICELY FIT THE DESCRIPTION OF "PRETENDERS"

THERE IS NO REASON THE VIKINGS SHOULDN'T OWN THIS TEAM
AND SIMPLY BEAT THEM TOTALLY BLACK-AND-BLUE
BUT THAT'S WHAT THEY THOUGHT ABOUT THE GIANTS
AND THE PACKERS CHARGERS AND RAIDERS TOO

~ ~ ~ ~ ~ ~ ~ ~ ~ ~ ~ ~ ~ ~ ~ ~ ~ ~

THERE WAS A LOT OF ATTENTION IN THE PRESS
REGARDING THE PACKERS' GRUDGE AGAINST WARREN SAPP
AND WHILE NO ALTERCATIONS EVOLVED
THEY SURELY MADE HIM SHUT HIS YAP

FOR THE PACKERS DOMINATED TAMPA'S DEFENSIVE LINE
ON A DAY WHEN BRETT FAVRE'S ARM WAS NOT THE KEY
IT WAS THE WAY GREEN BAY RAN BEHIND THE O-LINE
THAT LET THE PACKERS RUN DOWN THE FEARED BUCS' "D"

AND WITH THAT LITTLE BIT OF BUSINESS NOW BEHIND THEM
THE PACKERS MUST LOOK AHEAD TO THEIR NEXT FEW FOES
FOR SUDDENLY THEY ARE BACK IN THE PLAYOFF CHASE
AND FROM THERE WHO KNOWS HOW FAR THEY'LL GO?

THIS WEEK THE 'NINERS COME TO LAMBEAU FIELD
A GAME THAT USUALLY MAKES THE PACKERS WEAR A SMILE
BUT THIS YEAR SAN FRAN BRINGS A FRESH NEW QUARTERBACK
WHO SEEMS TO PLAY WITH BOTH "SMARTS" AND STYLE

BUT THIS SHOULD TURN OUT A CLASSIC GAME
WITH THE GROUND GAME DETERMINING WHO WILL WIN
AND WITH AHMAN RUNNING BEHIND THE PACK'S O-LINE
GREEN BAY SHOULD EMERGE VICTORIOUS ONCE AGAIN

RESULTS:
Green Bay beat the
San Francisco 49ers 20-10

Minnesota beat the
Detroit Lions 24-14

167

GB: 6-5
MN: 7-4

PACKERS "VERSES" VIKINGS ~ Carl Nelson

WELL, THE VIKINGS STOPPED THE LOSING STREAK
AVOIDING A LOSS THAT WOULD HAVE LEFT THEM HAUNTED
THOUGH IT TOOK NOT ONE BUT TWO DEFENSIVE SCORES
MAKING IT NOT AS CONVINCING AS THEY'D HAVE WANTED

THE LIONS GAVE IT ALL THEY HAD
(AND THEIR RECORD SHOWS THAT'S TRUE)
AND AS INEPT AS DETROIT'S OFFENSE IS
MORE THAN THE UNIFORMS SHOULD BE BLUE

THE VIKES DIDN'T OVER-RUN THIS TEAM
AS THE LIONS' DEFENSE TOOK THEIR MEASURE
AND IT WAS THE FACT HARRINGTON THREW TWO BAD PICKS
THAT GAVE MINNESOTA THIS WIN WHICH THEY SO TREASURE

THIS WEEK THE VIKES HEAD OUT TO ST LOUIS
TO PLAY THE RAMS ON THEIR HOME FIELD
MIKE TICE SAYS THE VIKES ARE "EXCITED" FOR THIS MATCHUP
WHILE MANY WOULD WONDER "IS THIS GUY FOR REAL?"

WHILE THE RAMS HAVE STRUGGLED SOMEWHAT THIS YEAR
THEY'RE THE BEST TEAM THE VIKES HAVE FACED FOR SOME TIME
UNLESS MINNESOTA CAN HOLD DOWN FAULK AND BRUCE
LOOK FOR THEM TO COME UP SHORT AT THE FINISH LINE

~ ~ ~ ~ ~ ~ ~ ~ ~ ~ ~ ~ ~ ~ ~ ~ ~ ~ ~

THE 'NINERS CAME TO LAMBEAU FIELD
ON A COLD AND WET NOVEMBER DAY
CONFIDENT THAT THEY COULD CONTAIN
THE REDESIGNED OFFENSE OF GREEN BAY

FOR WITH A STYLE REMINISCENT OF YEARS PAST
THE PACKERS' PERSONALITY HAS COMPLETELY CHANGED
NO LONGER ARE THEY CONTENT TO RIDE BRETT'S ARM
BUT NOW THRIVE WITH A POWER-RUNNING GAME

THE FINESSE OF THE "PURE" WEST COAST OFFENSE
COULDN'T KEEP UP WITH THE PACK'S BRUTE FORCE
WHICH COMBINED WITH A GREAT DEFENSIVE GAME
GAVE GREEN BAY THE BIG WIN OF COURSE

THIS WEEK WHILE THE TURKEY IS IN THE OVEN
THE PACKERS WILL FACE ANOTHER DIVISION FOE
PLAYING THE LIONS IN DETROIT ON THANKSGIVING
WHICH OFTEN IS AN EASY GAME TO BLOW

THE LIONS TURN UP THEIR GAME A NOTCH
WHEN THE NATION TUNES IN ON TURKEY DAY
FOR THEM UNFORTUNATELY IT WON'T BE ENOUGH
AS THEY BECOME THE LATEST VICTIM OF GREEN BAY

RESULTS:
Green Bay lost to Detroit 14-22

Minnesota lost to the St Louis Rams 17-48

168

Week 14
Dec. 7
2003

GB: 6-6
MN: 7-5

PACKERS "VERSES" VIKINGS

~ Carl Nelson

FOR A FEW SHINING MOMENTS ON SUNDAY IT SEEMED
THE VIKES HAD A CHANCE AGAINST THE RAMS
BUT THEN TICE ROLLED OUT THE FAKE FIELD GOAL PLAY
AND THE SCORE NEVER GOT CLOSE AGAIN

WHAT IN THE WORLD HAS HAPPENED TO THESE GUYS
WHO ONCE SEEMED TO BE LEADING THE ELITE?
EVERYTHING THAT USED TO WORK FOR THEM
IS NOW LEADING THEM TO A DEFEAT

THE OFFENSIVE LINE IS SIMPLY THAT
AS SHOWN BY LAST WEEK'S EIGHT CULPEPPER SACKS
AND THE DEFENSIVE TEAM SEEMS TO BE COMPLETELY BLIND
TO THE OPPOSITION'S RECEIVERS AND RUNNING BACKS

THIS WEEK IT'S THE SEATTLE SEAHAWKS' TEAM
THAT WILL INVADE THE METRODOME
THEY CARRY A RECORD OF EIGHT AND FOUR
BUT IT SEEMS THEY CAN WIN ONLY AT HOME

THIS MAY BE THE LAST CHANCE FOR MIKE AND THE BOYS
TO SALVAGE SOME OF THIS SEASON'S EXPECTATIONS
IF THEY DON'T THERE WILL BE HELL TO PAY
FROM A VERY DISGRUNTLED VIKINGS' NATION

~ ~ ~ ~ ~ ~ ~ ~ ~ ~ ~ ~ ~ ~ ~ ~ ~ ~ ~

IN THE EARLY AFTERNOON OF THANKSGIVING DAY
AS THE CLOCK'S HANDS WERE APPROACHING ONE
IT BECAME EVIDENT THAT LIKE MILLIONS OF OTHER TURKEYS
THE GREEN BAY PACKERS WERE GETTING NICELY DONE

THE LIONS PULLED OFF ANOTHER UPSET ON THANKSGIVING
WHICH REALLY SHOULDN'T BE AN UPSET ANY MORE
FOR VERY OFTEN A TEAM THAT LOOKS MUCH BETTER COMES IN
JUST TO WATCH THE LIONS RUNNING UP THE SCORE

SO NOW IT'S TIME FOR THOSE GREEN BAY PACKERS
TO REALIZE THAT THEIR BACKS ARE AGAINST THE WALL
AS THEY WELCOME THE BEARS TO LAMBEAU FIELD
IN A GAME THAT COULD DEFINE THIS FALL

FOR THE PACKERS SHOULD FIND THE CHICAGO BEARS
MUCH LIKE THEY HAVE IN THE PAST FEW YEARS
A TEAM THAT SIMPLY CAN'T COMPETE WITH THEM
AND JUST DOESN'T INSPIRE A LOT OF FEAR

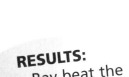

RESULTS:
Green Bay beat the
Chicago Bears 34-21

Minnesota beat the
Seattle Seahawks 34-7

BUT CHICAGO'S WON A COUPLE OF GAMES IN A ROW
AND HAS NOW BECOME A BULLET THAT MUST BE DODGED
THE PACK CAN DO THAT IF THEY JUST PULL THEIR HEADS
FROM WHICHEVER ORIFICE WHEREIN THEY MAY BE LODGED

169

GB: 7-6
MN: 8-5

PACKERS "VERSES" VIKINGS ~ Carl Nelson

LAST SUNDAY THE MINNESOTA VIKINGS' TEAM
KICKED THE LIVING STUFFING OUTTA SEATTLE
AND FOR ONCE THE THINGS THAT TICE HAD SAID
DIDN'T SOUND LIKE IDLE MEDIA PRATTLE

FOR ABOUT THREE HOURS THERE IN THE METRODOME
IT MUST HAVE FELT LIKE THE SEASON'S FIRST FEW WEEKS
AS THE NATURAL ABILITIES OF THESE VIKINGS PLAYERS
MESHED IN THE WAY THAT ALL FOOTBALL COACHES SEEK

THIS WEEK THE VIKES TRAVEL TO FACE THE BEARS
HOPING TO SECURE THE NORTH'S DIVISION CROWN
THEY ONLY MUST GET PAST THE CHICAGO TEAM
WHO AFTER LAST WEEK'S LOSS MUST BE FEELING DOWN

BUT THIS IS ONE OF THOSE FOOTBALL GAMES
WHERE THE RECORD CAN BE MOSTLY DISCOUNTED
FOR WHEN THE BEARS AND VIKINGS CLASH
SOME MIGHTY STRUGGLES HAVE BEEN MOUNTED

THE FACT THE BEARS WILL START A ROOKIE QUARTERBACK
SHOULD BE MAKING THE MINNESOTA'S DEFENSE WEAR A GRIN
BUT WE MUST REMEMBER THAT THESE ARE THE VIKES
WHO ARE VERY CAPABLE OF SCREWING UP YET AGAIN

~ ~ ~ ~ ~ ~ ~ ~ ~ ~ ~ ~ ~ ~ ~ ~ ~ ~ ~ ~

LAST WEEK THOSE BEARS CAME UP TO LAMBEAU FIELD
TO VISIT THE LONG-TIME RIVAL PACKERS' TEAM
WHEN THE PACK GRACIOUSLY SPOTTED THEM FOUTEEN POINTS
THE BEARS MUST HAVE THOUGHT THEY WERE LIVING A DREAM

UNFORTUNATELY FOR THEM THERE WAS A WAKE-UP CALL
AND THE PACKERS' TEAM WAS ON THE LINE
ROLLING OFF THIRTY-FOUR UNANSWERED POINTS
AND LEAVING THE BEARS QUITE FAR BEHIND

THE SAN DIEGO CHARGERS WILL BE THE FOE THIS WEEK
PLAYING AT HOME UNDER THE CALIFORNIA SUN
THERE'S SOME QUESTION OF WHO MAY BE THE QUARTERBACK
BUT THERE'S NO QUESTION THAT THE CHARGERS LIKE TO RUN

THIS SHOULD BE AN INTERESTING MATCHUP TO WATCH
FEATURING TWO OF THE LEAGUE'S BEST RUNNING BACKS
AHMAN GREEN AND THE CHARGER'S LADAINIAN TOMLINSON
WILL BOTH CARRY THEIR TEAMS' HOPES ON THEIR BACKS

THIS GAME CARRIES GREAT IMPORTANCE TO GREEN BAY
AS IT ONE OF THE THREE GAMES THEY SIMPLY HAVE TO WIN
IF THEY ARE TO HAVE ANY HOPE OF GETTING INTO THE PLAYOFFS
WHERE THEY SO DESPERATELY WANT TO GO AGAIN

RESULTS:
Green Bay beat the
San Diego Chargers 38-21

Minnesota lost to the
Chicago Bears 10-13

Week 16
Dec.
20 & 22
2003

GB: 8-6
MN: 8-6

PACKERS "VERSES" VIKINGS ~ Carl Nelson

THE BEARS HAVE SPENT MOST OF THIS PAST SEASON
BEING GENERALLY ABUSED AND KICKED AROUND
HOWEVER LAST WEEK THEY TOOK ON THE VIKINGS
AND MANAGED TO RUN THEM RIGHT INTO THE GROUND

THE VIKINGS HAVE GOT TO BE WONDERING
"JUST WHAT THE HELL IS GOING ON??"
ONCE THEY HAD A RECORD THAT SEEMED INSURMOUNTABLE
AND JUST A FEW WEEKS LATER FIND THAT LEAD IS GONE

RANDI MOSS AND THE REST OF HIS TEAMMATES
HAVE TO FIGURE OUT JUST WHAT IT'S GOING TO TAKE
FOR THEM TO THINK ANYTHING HAS BEEN ASSURED
WOULD BE A TRAGIC AND EXPENSIVE MISTAKE

THE CHIEFS WHO'LL VISIT FROM KANSAS CITY
ARE THE NEXT OBSTACLE TO A VIKINGS' PLAYOFF BERTH
KC HAS PLAYED QUITE WELL ALL SEASON LONG
WHILE THE VIKES HAVE GONE FROM GOOD TO BAD TO WORSE

PRIEST HOLMES COULD WELL REPRESENT THE VERY THINGS
THAT HAVE CAUSED THE VIKINGS SUCH DISTRESS
AND UNLESS MINNESOTA'S OFFENSE GETS IN GEAR
THEIR SEASON COULD WIND UP IN A DREADFUL MESS

~ ~ ~ ~ ~ ~ ~ ~ ~ ~ ~ ~ ~ ~ ~ ~ ~ ~

THERE HAVE BEEN TIMES THIS FOOTBALL SEASON
WHEN IT HAS SEEMED LIKE THE PACK WAS DONE
BUT JUST WHEN IT APPEARS THAT ALL HOPE HAS FLED
AT DAY'S END—THE PACKERS HAVE SOMEHOW WON

LAST WEEK IT WAS THE CHARGERS' TEAM
THAT LOOKED LIKE THEY'D FINISH OFF GREEN BAY
MAKING A RUN TO COME FROM BEHIND
UNTIL THE PACK STEPPED UP AND SAVED THE DAY

BOTH THE OFFENSE AND THE DEFENSE
PLAYED LARGE PARTS IN THE 'BOLTS DEMISE
AND TURNING FAVRE LOOSE TO USE HIS ARM
WAS A COACHING MOVE QUITE WISE

IT WAS VERY NICE TO SEE THE DOWNFIELD PASS
COME BACK OUT OF THE PACKERS' BAG OF TRICKS
FOR AT THE TIME WHEN RUNNING YARDS ARE HARD TO GET
HOW WONDERFUL TO SEE THEM THROW FOR SIX

MONDAY NIGHT IT'LL BE THE OAKLAND RAIDERS
WHO WILL TRY TO SLOW THE PACKERS' TEAM
BUT WOE BE THE TEAM WHO GETS IN THE WAY
WHEN GREEN BAY STARTS TO BUILD A HEAD OF STEAM....

RESULTS:
Green Bay beat the
Oakland Raiders 41-7

Minnesota beat the
Kansas City Chiefs 45-20

171

GB: 9-6
MN: 9-6

THE VIKINGS CHANGED THEIR "STYLE" A BIT
AS THEY WERE RUNNING TO AND "FRO"
TRYING ANYTHING THAT MIGHT INFLUENCE
JUST HOW THE CHIEFS' GAME WOULD GO

AND WHETHER IT WAS FROM LETTING THEIR HAIR "DOWN"
OR FROM A COUPLE FORTUITOUS EARLY CALLS
MINNESOTA PLAYED THEIR BEST GAME IN WEEKS
SOME MIGHT EVEN SAY THE BEST SINCE EARLY FALL

TO GIVE THEM THEIR DUE MINNESOTA'S VIKINGS' TEAM
HAS BATTLED BACK FROM A HORRIBLE MIDSEASON SLUMP
GOING THREE AND SIX AFTER SIX STRAIGHT WINS
AND GENERALLY LOOKING LIKE A BUNCH OF CHUMPS

BUT THAT CAN BE DIFFERENT AFTER SUNDAY'S GAME
PROVIDED THE VIKINGS CAN DEFEAT THE CARDS
WHO WOULDN'T SEEM TO PROVIDE MUCH OF A THREAT
BUT THOSE ARE THE WINS THE VIKES SEEM TO FIND SO HARD

A CHANCE TO WIN THE NORTH DIVISION CROWN
AWAITS THE VIKES IN THE DESERT SUNDAY AFTERNOON
MINNESOTANS MUST HOPE THAT THE VIKES DON'T SCREW THIS UP
AND END THE VIKINGS' SEASON FAR TOO SOON....

~ ~ ~ ~ ~ ~ ~ ~ ~ ~ ~ ~ ~ ~ ~ ~ ~ ~ ~

THE OAKLAND RAIDERS MAY HAVE THOUGHT
THAT BRETT FAVRE MIGHT BE A LITTLE OFF HIS GAME
AND THAT SUCH A SHORT TIME AFTER HIS FATHER'S DEATH
HIS DESIRE TO WIN COULDN'T BE QUITE THE SAME

BUT BRETT STEPPED UP AND TOOK THEM ON
MUCH LIKE HIS DAD WOULD HAVE SURELY WANTED
AND PLAYED SO WELL THE RAIDERS HAD TO THINK
THAT THE COLISEUM MIGHT WELL BE HAUNTED

BUT THERE WAS NO SPIRIT HOVERING NEAR
OTHER THAN THE SPIRIT OF THE PACKERS' TEAM
AND THE WAY IN WHICH THEY PLAYED LAST WEEK
WAS THE STUFF OF WHICH MOST COACHES DREAM

THIS WEEK WITH A PLAYOFF BERTH ON THE LINE
THE PACKERS STEP BACK ONTO THE LAMBEAU GRASS
TO TAKE ON AN INJURED DENVER BRONCOS' TEAM
WHO WILL BE FORCED TO RELY MOSTLY ON THE PASS

THE LOSS OF PORTIS WILL SOMEWHAT SLOW THE BRONCS
AND MAKE IT A LITTLE HARDER TO STOP THE PACKERS' WIN
WHICH IS WHAT THE GREEN BAY TEAM WILL HAVE TO DO
TO ENTER THE POST-SEASON ONCE AGAIN

PACKERS "VERSES" VIKINGS ~ Carl Nelson

RESULTS:
Green Bay beat the
Denver Broncos 31-3

Minnesota lost to the
Arizona Cardinals 17-18

172

**Wild Card
Week
Jan. 4
2004**

PACKERS "VERSES" VIKINGS

~ Carl Nelson

IT SEEMED THE VIKINGS HAD IT ALL GOING THEIR WAY
BEFORE THE HOUSE OF "CARDS"CAME CRASHING DOWN
AND IT WAS NO "CARD-SHARP" WHO WAS TO BLAME
BUT A SECOND-STRINGER NAMED JOSH MCCOWN

WHILE IT SEEMED THAT THE DIVISION CROWN
WAS FIRMLY IN THE VIKINGS' GRASP
THE GAME'S NOT OVER 'TIL THE FAT LADY'S SUNG
AND YOUR OPPONENT HAS BREATHED HIS LAST

FOR THAT LAST GASP TURNED THE FOOTBALL GAME
INTO A NIGHTMARE FOR THE VIKINGS' FANS
AS A DESPERATION PASS SETTLED FROM THE AIR
INTO A THIRD-STRING RECEIVER'S HANDS

THE VIKINGS HOWEVER MADE HUGE GAINS
FROM THE DISASTER THEY WERE LAST YEAR
THERE WERE SOME SIGNS OF THE TEAM THEY CAN BE
THOUGH SURPRISINGLY MIKE TICE STILL WILL BE HERE

WHEN THE VIKINGS LEARN THAT NOTHING COMES FREE
AND THE EFFORT FOR EACH CONTEST MUST BE THE SAME
NEXT SEASON THEY MAY BE A FORCE TO CONSIDER
WITH THE TERM "WINNER" ATTACHED TO THEIR NAME

~ ~ ~ ~ ~ ~ ~ ~ ~ ~ ~ ~ ~ ~ ~ ~ ~ ~ ~

WHILE THE PACKERS WERE TROUNCING THE BRONCOS' TEAM
THEIR THOUGHTS WERE FOCUSED FAR TO THE WEST
FOR IT SEEMED THERE WAS NO HOPE FOR A PLAYOFF SPOT
ALHTOUGH THEY WERE PLAYING THEIR VERY BEST

WHILE AHMAN GREEN WAS RUNNING FREE
AND THE DEFENSE WAS HOLDING THEIR OWN
IT SEEMED IT WOULD ALL BE FOR NAUGHT
'TIL A CERTAIN TOUCHDOWN PASS WAS THROWN

THE PACKERS FOUND THEMSELVES DIVISION CHAMPS
PREPARING FOR THE HOME PLAYOFF GAME THEY'VE EARNED
AS SHERMAN'S OLD BOSS MIKE HOLMGREN COMES TO TOWN
TO FACE THE PACKERS AND A'BACK THAT HE ONCE SPURNED

THE 'HAWKS ARE FAMILIAR WITH THE GREEN BAY SCHEME
RECYCLING BOTH THE COACH AND A QUARTERBACK
THEY BRING WITH THEM A TOUGH DEFENSE
AS WELL AS ANOTHER VERY GOOD RUNNING ATTACK

SO THERE'LL BE NO SLACKING AT PRACTICE THIS WEEK
AS THE PACKERS PREPARE FOR THIS MAJOR TEST
THE LESSON FROM LAST YEAR'S LOSS HAS SUNK IN
"IT TAKES HARD WORK TO BE THE BEST"

GB: 10-6
(Defending
NFCN Champs)
MN: 9-7
(Home on the
Couch)

RESULTS:
Green bay beat the
Seattle Seahawks 33-27
in overtime

Minnesota missed out
on the postseason

173

~ Carl Nelson

PACKERS "VERSES" VIKINGS

GB: 1-0
Philadelphia: 0-0

WITH THE ABRUPTNESS OF A CAR WRECK
SEATTLE'S SEASON CAME TO AN END
AS AL HARRIS STEPPED IN FRONT OF A PASS
THAT HASSELBECK WISHED HE HAD BACK AGAIN

BUT TO THAT POINT—WHAT A GREAT FOOTBALL GAME
AS BOTH TEAMS MATCHED UP PRETTY WELL
BUT WHEN IT CAME DOWN TO THE GAME'S LAST PLAYS
IT WAS EXPERIENCE WHICH SEEMED TO TELL

NOW IT'S OFF TO PHILADELPHIA
KNOWN AS THE "CITY OF BROTHERLY LOVE"
A NAME THAT WOULD BE MORE BELIEVABLE
WITHOUT FANS THROWING DEBRIS FROM UP ABOVE

THE EAGLES HAVE HAD A WEEK OFF
TO REFLECT REWIND AND GET RESET
AND THIS MORE THAN THE PHILLY HOME GAME
WOULD MAKE A PACKERS' WIN SEEM AN UPSET

BUT THIS EAGLE TEAM HAS SOME NOTED WEAKNESSES
ONE OF WHICH HAPPENS TO BE WHAT GREEN BAY DOES BEST
AHMAN GREEN AND THE PACK'S O-LINE
WILL PUT PHILLY'S RUN DEFENSE TO ITS FINAL TEST

MCNABB IS A PRETTY GOOD YOUNG QUARTERBACK
THERE IS NO WAY TO DENY THAT'S TRUE
AND "DUCE" AGAIN IS THE GUY ON THE GROUND
BUT THE PACKERS KNOW HIS NUMBER TOO

BACK IN NOVEMBER SIX PACKER FUMBLES
LET THE EAGLES EKE OUT A LAST-SECOND WIN
BUT THE PACK HAS LEARNED TO RETAIN THE BALL
AND WON'T BE GIVING UP THOSE GIFTS AGAIN

FOR THAT NIGHT MARKED THE LAST TIME
AHMAN PUT THE BALL ON THE GROUND FOR GRABS
AND SINCE BRETT'S GROWN ACCUSTOMED TO HIS SORE THUMB
HE'LL BE MORE THAN A MATCH FOR YOUNG MCNABB

THE PACKERS' DEFENSE HAS STEPPED UP ITS GAME
AND THE RECEIVING CORPS HAS ALSO DONE ITS PART
SHERMAN AND THE COACHES HAVE GOT THE PLAN
AND THE PLAYERS WILL SUPPLY THE HEART

RESULTS:
Green Bay lost to the
Philadelphia Eagles 17-20

SO WHILE THE PHILLY TEAM WILL BE FAVORED
ONCE SUNDAY'S FINAL GUN HAS SOUNDED
THE PACKERS' TEAM WILL BE MOVING ON
WHILE THE EAGLE'S FLIGHT WILL HAVE BEEN GROUNDED

THE PACKERS FOUND THEIR SEASON ENDING
MUCH AS DID SEATTLE THE WEEK BEFORE
AS THE RESULT OF AN ILL-THROWN PASS
THAT LED TO AN OVERTIME-ENDING SCORE

WHILE THE SITUATION IS FILLED WITH "WHAT-IFS"
AND "COULDA/SHOULDA-BEENS"
THE PACK COULDN'T MAKE THE PLAYS THEY NEEDED
AND AS A RESULT THEY DIDN'T WIN

TO BE SURE IT'S CAUSED MUCH PACKER-FAN PAIN
ANGER DESPAIR AND SOME FRUSTRATION
BUT REALITY SHOWS THEY HAD A PRETTY GOOD YEAR
IF ONE CAN LOOK AT AN OVERALL SUMMATION

EARLY LOSSES REALLY COST THIS TEAM
A LEGITIMATE SHOT AT THEIR FOURTH LOMBARDI
DROPPING GAMES LIKE THE ONE IN ARIZONA
DID MUCH TO FORESTALL THAT VICTORY PARTY

BUT DESPITE PUTTING THEMSELVES DEEP IN A HOLE
THE PACKERS' TEAM NEVER ONCE CONCEDED
FIGHTING, SCRATCHING AND CLAWING BACK
AND FINALLY GETTING THE WINS THEY NEEDED

FREE AGENT PICKUPS TURNED A STRUGGLING DEFENSE
INTO A FORMIDABLE LATE-SEASON FORCE
AND NICK BARNETT SHOWED HIMSELF TO BE A LEADER
(HE WAS THE FIRST-ROUND CHOICE OF COURSE)

EACH TIME HE TROTS OUT TO THE HUDDLE
BRETT FAVRE REWRITES A PAGE IN THE RECORD BOOK
AND THE FACT THAT HE LEADS THE LEAGUE IN TD PASSES
KEEPS HIM PLAYING MUCH YOUNGER THAN HE LOOKS

AHMAN GREEN AGAIN PROVED HIS WORTHINESS
OF BEING CONSIDERED AMONG THE LEAGUE'S ELITE
AND THE LINE THAT BLOCKS FOR HIS TREMENDOUS RUNS
CAN BEST BE DESCRIBED AS "SWEET"

JAVON WALKER LOOKS LIKE THE NEXT BIG-PLAY GUY
WHEN IT'S TIME FOR THE PACKERS TO TAKE TO THE AIR
AND WHAT A COMFORT FOR BRETT TO KNOW
THAT FERGUSON AND DRIVER ARE ALSO THERE

WHILE IT WAS SURPRISING TO MOST OF THE PACKERS FANS
THAT THEY REPEATED AS "NORTH" DIVISION CHAMPS THIS YEAR
BUT KEEP THE FAITH YOU TRUE BELIEVERS
THIS WILL BE AN EVEN BETTER TEAM NEXT YEAR

GB: 11-7
(Divisional Playoff
loss to the Eagles)
MN: 9-7

ON A SUNDAY EARLY LAST SEPTEMBER
THIRTY-TWO TEAMS BEGAN THIS FOOTBALL SEASON
FOR MONTHS THESE MEN HAVE SWEATED AND BLED
THIS WEEK'S GAME IS THE FINAL REASON

WHILE IT MAY BE TOUGH TO GET TOO ENTHUSED
THIS YEAR'S SUPER BOWL IS NOW AT HAND
AS CAROLINA'S PANTHERS AND THE NEW ENGLAND PATS
STRIVE TO BE THE BEST TEAM IN THE LAND

THOUGH SUNDAY WILL DAWN QUIETLY IN HOUSTON
TENSION AND EXCITEMENT SOON WILL FILL THE AIR
AND WHEN IT'S FINALLY TIME FOR KICKOFF
IT'S WON'T REALLY MATTER WHO IS THERE

WHILE THERE AREN'T A LOT OF HOUSEHOLD NAMES
ON THE ROSTERS OF THESE TWO TEAMS
THAT DOESN'T CHANGE THE FACT THAT THIS GAME
IS THE REALIZATION OF THOSE PLAYERS' DREAMS

WHILE IT WOULD SEEM THAT NEW ENGLAND'S TEAM
IS THE BOOKIES' EARLY CHOICE TO WIN
LET'S NOT FORGET THE PATS' FIRST BOWL VISIT
COULD ANOTHER UPSET HAPPEN ONCE AGAIN?

THE PATS ARE A VERY GOOD FOOTBALL TEAM
AND DESERVE TO BE THE NUMBER-ONE CONTENDER
PUTTING TOGETHER A FOURTEEN-GAME WINNING STREAK
AND NEVER ONCE TRAILING SINCE MID-NOVEMBER

TOM BRADY HAS ONCE AGAIN SHOWN US ALL
THAT TO BE A WINNER DOESN'T TAKE GREAT THEATRICS
BUT IT HELPS TO HAVE A VERY GOOD TEAM AROUND HIM
AND COACHES WHO UNDERSTAND EFFECTIVE TACTICS

CAROLINA'S TEAM HAS HAD TO FIGHT
EACH AND EVERY STEP ALONG THE WAY
WINNING MANY CLOSE GAMES WITH DETERMINATION
AND SOLID MISTAKE-FREE FOOTBALL PLAY

JAKE DELHOMME BEGAN THE YEAR AS A SECOND-STRINGER
THE MAIN RUNNING BACK WAS CAST OFF BY THE 'SKINS
BUT ADD THE RIGHT AMOUNT OF "D" AND EMOTION
AND THE RECIPE IS RIGHT FOR ABOUT FOURTEEN WINS

THAT THE PANTHERS ARE GOING TO RUN THE BALL
IS A STONE-COLD CERTAINTY
AND WHETHER THE PATS CAN STOP THOSE RUNS
WILL BE THIS GAME'S WINNING KEY

IF THE PANTHERS' PASS RUSH CAN GET TO BRADY
AND MAKE SOME OF HIS PASSES GO AWRY
THEN THERE MAY BE HOPE FOR CAROLINA
TO WIN THE LOMBARDI ON THEIR FIRST TRY

BUT THE PATS ARE JUST TOO SOLID A TEAM
TO LET CAROLINA'S EMOTION GET IN THE WAY
THE LOMBARDI WILL BE HEADED FOR NEW ENGLAND
WHILE THE "CATS" PLAN FOR ANOTHER DAY

PACKERS "VERSES" VIKINGS   ~ Carl Nelson

RESULTS:
The New England Patriots
beat the Carolina Panthers 31-29

PACKERS

" VERSES "

VIKINGS

Green Bay Packers
Regular Season 10-6
Postseason 0-1

Minnesota Vikings
Regular Season 8-8
Postseason 1-1

2004

Carl "Gator" Nelson

GB: 0-0
MN: 0-0

PACKERS "VERSES" VIKINGS ~ Carl Nelson

NOW THAT SUMMER'S NEARLY OVER
WITH NO MORE HOT WEATHER AND ALL THAT CRAP
IT'S TIME FOR FOOTBALL OUR OWN TRUE LOVE
AND WE'RE AWAITING THIS YEAR'S FIRST SNAP

BOTH OF THE LOCAL FAVORITE TEAMS
ENTER THIS SEASON WITH HOPES VERY HIGH
AND IN THE FASHION OF TRUE FOOTBALL FANS
WE ALL CAN GIVE THE REASONS WHY

WHETHER IT WAS DRAFTING A DEFENSIVE END
OR BRINGING IN A "LOCKDOWN" CORNERBACK
EVERY FAN IS TRULY CONVINCED THOSE PLAYERS
ARE JUST WHAT THEIR TEAM LACKED

BUT IT'S NEVER QUITE THAT EASY
AND MANY TEAMS CAN ATTEST THAT'S TRUE
THE WHOLE TEAM HAS TO COMBINE SKILL AND LUCK
TO HAVE THOSE WINS COME THROUGH

~ ~ ~ ~ ~ ~ ~ ~ ~ ~ ~ ~ ~ ~ ~ ~ ~ ~ ~

THE VIKES FOUND OUT THE HARD WAY
THAT UNTIL THE FINAL GUNSHOT SOUNDS
EVEN A TEAM THAT SHOULDN'T BE ABLE TO
CAN COMPLETE A TOUCHDOWN PASS IN BOUNDS

THEY STARTED THE YEAR WITH SIX STRAIGHT WINS
THEN THEY DROPPED SEVEN OF THE NEXT TEN
CRUSHING THE HEARTS OF THOSE VIKINGS' FANS
HOPING TO SEE THE PLAYOFFS ONCE AGAIN

THE VIKES WELCOME THE COWPOKES SUNDAY
ONTO THE NEW TURF OF THE METRODOME
WHAT BETTER PLACE TO SHOW WHAT THEY CAN DO
THAN IN THE FRIENDLY CONFINES OF THEIR HOME

BUT THIS ISN'T THE "POKES" GROUP OF YEARS PAST
WHO TREMBLED AT THE SIGHT OF AN OFFENSIVE TEAM
THESE COWBOYS MADE THE PLAYOFFS THEMSELVES
AND SHARE IN THE VIKINGS' POST-SEASON DREAMS

BILL PARCELLS HAS BEEN WORKING MAGIC HERE
WITH TESTAVERDE AND CREW UNDER HIS SPELL
TERRY GLENN AND KEYSHAWN WILL BE CATCHING THE BALLS
THAT VINNY CAN THROW DOWN THE FIELD SO WELL

BUT THE VIKING "D" SHOULD HAVE NO TROUBLE HERE
ON PAPER THEY ARE VERY IMPROVED
BUT WHAT SHOWS ON PAPER SOMETIMES DOESN'T WORK OUT
AS HISTORY OFTEN HAS PROVED

TO TELL THE TRUTH, THE VIKES SHOULD WIN
ALTHOUGH THE COWBOYS WILL PUT UP A FIGHT
IF THAT DEFENSE CAN'T CONTAIN RANDY MOSS
DALLAS WILL BE IN FOR A VERY LONG NIGHT

~ Carl Nelson

PACKERS "VERSES" VIKINGS

THE PACKERS PUT A RUN TOGETHER
DURING LAST SEASON'S WANING DAYS
THE EAGLES HOWEVER SENT THEM HOME
BY CONVERTING AN INFAMOUS FOURTH-DOWN PLAY

SO WHAT DID THE TEAM FROM GREEN BAY DO?
THE TEAM THEY'D FIELDED DIDN'T LOOK ALL THAT BAD
SO MIKE SHERMAN FIRED THE DEFENSIVE BOSS
AND MOSTLY PRESERVED THE TEAM THAT HE HAD

BRETT FAVRE WILL STILL BE FLINGING TDs
TO "J-WALK" "FERGY" AND "DOUBLE-D"
STANDING SAFE BEHIND AN OFFENSIVE LINE
THAT OPENS HUGE HOLES FOR AHMAN GREEN

IT'S THE DEFENSE THAT HOLDS THE MOST QUESTIONS
AS THERE HAVE BEEN MORE CHANGES EVIDENT THERE
WITH A NEW SAFETY AND A CORNERBACK REPLACEMENT
FOR MIKE MCKENZIE AND HIS NOW-FAMOUS HAIR

THE PACKERS OPEN OUT ON THE ROAD
IN THE FIRST MONDAY-NIGHTER THIS YEAR
GOING TO VISIT CAROLINA'S PANTHERS
A TEAM ON THE CHAMPIONSHIP-LEVEL TIER

DELHOMME HAS EMERGED AS A LEGIT QB
STEVEN DAVIS IS A GOOD RUNNING BACK
BUT THAT DEFENSE IS THE MAIN FACTOR CONSIDERED
WHEN FIGURING HOW TO BLUNT CAROLINA'S ATTACK

THE PACKERS' O-LINE WILL HAVE TO BE TOP-NOTCH
BUYING TIME FOR THE PASSES OF BRETT FAVRE
AHMAN GREEN WILL ALSO NEED THEIR HELP
AS CHUNKS OF YARDAGE HE TRIES TO CARVE

THE PACKERS' WIDE RECEIVERS MAY BE THE KEY
IF THEIR PATTERNS CAN BE CLEANLY RUN
FOR WITH THE WAY PASS DEFENSE IS BEING CALLED
THE FAST WIDEOUTS WILL HAVE SOME REAL FUN

IN A WAY IT'S GOOD FOR THE PACKERS
TO BEGIN THE SEASON WITH THIS SORT OF TEST
FOR IF THEY WANT TO GET DEEP INTO THE PLAYOFFS
THEY HAVE TO BEAT TEAMS REGARDED AS THE BEST

~ ~ ~ ~ ~ ~ ~ ~ ~ ~ ~ ~ ~ ~ ~ ~ ~ ~ ~ ~

TUESDAY MORNING'S SPORTS PAGE
WILL SHOW US WHAT WE ALREADY KNOW
THE PACK AND VIKINGS WILL BE TIED FOR FIRST
WITH THE SAME RECORDS OF ONE-AND-O

RESULTS:
Green Bay beat the
Carolina Panthers 24-14

Minnesota beat the
Dallas Cowboys 35-17

179

GB: 1-0
MN: 1-0

PACKERS "VERSES" VIKINGS ~ Carl Nelson

"THE MORE THINGS CHANGE..." THE ADAGE GOES
"...THE MORE THEY STAY THE SAME"
DESPITE THE TALK ABOUT THE "NEW" VIKES
ALL THAT'S DIFFERENT ARE SOME NAMES

OFFENSIVELY THE VIKES ARE MONSTERS
AND TRULY FEARSOME WHILE ATTACKING
BUT THE WAY DALLAS MOVED THE BALL LAST WEEK
SHOWED THE VIKES' DEFENSE MIGHT BE A LITTLE LACKING

THEIR DEFENSIVE LINE WAS SOMEWHAT POROUS
THE PASS RUSH WAS NOT A FORCE
THE SECONDARY WAS SIMPLY ATROCIOUS
AND HOVAN DISAPPEARED AGAIN OF COURSE

THIS WEEK THE VIKES MUST WAIT 'TIL MONDAY
TO SEE THE FACES OF AN OPPOSING TEAM
FINDING OUT THAT IT'S PHILLY'S EAGLES
MUST LOOK A LOT LIKE A BAD DREAM

MCNABB TO OWENS MIGHT BE THE PAIR
TO CHALLENGE CULPEPPER TO MOSS IN SCORING
THOUGH THE EAGLES WILL PULL THIS GAME OUT LATE
NO ONE OUT IN "TV-LAND" WILL BE A-SNORING

~ ~ ~ ~ ~ ~ ~ ~ ~ ~ ~ ~ ~ ~ ~ ~ ~

THE CLOUD OF DOUBT THAT FOLLOWED GREEN BAY
INTO LAST MONDAY'S GAME WAS SOON DISPELLED
ONCE THE PACKERS' OFFENSE WHICH HAD BEEN DORMANT
WAS EXPLOSIVELY RELEASED FROM ITS SHELL

THE DEFENSE ANSWERED ANOTHER QUESTION
STEPPING SQUARELY UP TO THE PLATE
AND SQUELCHING THE PANTHER OFFENSE
WHICH SEALED CAROLINA'S FATE

IN THIS WEEK'S OPENER AT LAMBEAU FIELD
THE CHICAGO BEARS PROVIDE A WELL-KNOWN FOE
RENEWING A RIVALRY STARTED BACK IN 'TWENTY-ONE
EIGHTY-THREE LONG YEARS AGO

SOME OF THOSE GAMES HAVE BEEN GREAT ONES
AND IN ALL OF THEM SOME BLOOD HAS BEEN SPILLED
BUT IN THE LAST DECADE THE PACK'S GONE EIGHTEEN-AND-TWO
WHICH HAS REMOVED A LITTLE OF THE THRILL

NONETHELESS THIS WILL BE QUITE A TUSSLE
IF NOT AN OUTRIGHT FOOTBALL BRAWL
BUT TO NO AVAIL FOR POOR CHICAGO
WHO REALLY HAVE NO CHANCE AT ALL....

~ ~ ~ ~ ~ ~ ~ ~ ~ ~ ~ ~ ~ ~ ~ ~ ~

THIS WEEKEND'S WEATHER SHOULD BE GREAT
WITH LOTS OF WARMTH AND AUTUMN SUN
WE'LL ENJOY IT AS THE PACKERS GO TWO-AND-O
WHILE THE VIKES FALL TO ONE-AND-ONE

RESULTS:
Green Bay lost to the
Chicago Bears 10-21

Minnesota lost to the
Philadelphia Eagles 16-27

180

PACKERS "VERSES" VIKINGS ~ Carl Nelson

THE EAGLES WERE WAITING FOR DAUNTE AND THE VIKES
WHEN THEY CAME TO PHILLY LAST MONDAY NIGHT
AND FROM THE THINGS STATED IN THE PRESS
IT LOOKED LIKE MOSS AND "T.O." WOULD HAVE QUITE A NIGHT

BUT AS SO OFTEN HAPPENS IN FOOTBALL GAMES
THOSE THINGS JUST NEVER CAME TO BE
THEY WERE MORE VALUABLE AS HIGH-PRICED DECOYS
THOUGH EACH DID SCORE A LATE TD

MINNESOTA STRUGGLED GETTING INTO THE ENDZONE
WHICH WAS A FUNCTION OF THE PHILLY "D"
WHILE THE EAGLES WERE ABLE TO CROSS THE LINE
AND THAT DOOMED THE VIKES YOU SEE

THIS WEEK CHICAGO'S BEARS COME TO "MINNY"
FRESH FROM A TROUNCING OF GREEN BAY
THE VIKES WOULD DO WELL TO BEWARE
OF THE GAME THAT THOSE BEARS CAN PLAY

BOTH OF THESE TEAMS ARE PRETTY BATTERED
WITH A NUMBERS OF BIG NAMES HAVING TO SIT OUT
BUT THE VIKES ARE STILL THE HEAVY FAVORITES
ALTHOUGH THIS GAME'S OUTCOME IS VERY MUCH IN DOUBT

~ ~ ~ ~ ~ ~ ~ ~ ~ ~ ~ ~ ~ ~ ~ ~ ~ ~ ~

WHEN LOVIE SMITH TOOK HIS JOB
ON A COLD AND WINTERY CHICAGO DAY
HE HUNG HIS HAT ON A SINGLE HOOK
"I KNOW HOW TO BEAT GREEN BAY"

THE BEARS MUST HAVE TAKEN HIS WORD AS TRUTH
PLAYING THEIR "A GAME" AGAINST THE PACK
SCORING ON AHMAN'S FUMBLE PLAY
AND THEREAFTER NEVER LOOKING BACK

THE PACKERS DIDN'T MAKE IT EASY
BUT NEITHER DID THEY SAVE THE DAY
AND LOSING TO THE BEARS AT LAMBEAU
MADE THIS WEEK SEEM PRETTY DARK AND GRAY

THE PACK NEEDS TO PULL OUT OF THOSE DOLDRUMS FAST
FOR THIS WEEK THEY HEAD OFF TO PLAY THE COLTS
AND WHILE INDY MAY HAVE LOST THEIR "EDGE"
MANNING STILL CAN THROW THOSE LIGHTNING BOLTS

WHEN PEYTON AND BRETT START THROWING DOWNFIELD
LOOK FOR THE SCOREBOARD NUMBERS TO START A-SPINNING
BUT NO MATTER HOW MANY PASSES GO FOR SCORES
AHMAN GREEN WILL BE THE KEY TO WINNING

THE BEARS WILL GIVE THE VIKINGS' TEAM
A VALIANT STRUGGLE BEFORE CONCEEDING
WHILE THE PACKERS WILL HAVE TO CATCH A BREAK
TO PICK UP THE WIN THAT THEY ARE NEEDING

RESULTS:
Green Bay lost to the
Indianapolis Colts 31-45

Minnesota beat the
Chicago Bears 27-22

PACKERS "VERSES" VIKINGS ~ Carl Nelson

TO VIKINGLAND NOW COMES THE "BYE WEEK"
THAT TEAMS LOOK FORWARD TO ALL YEAR LONG
WHICH LETS THE PLAYERS REST AND HEAL
AND KNOW THAT THEY CAN DO NO WRONG

THE CHICAGO BEARS PUT UP QUITE A FIGHT
LAST WEEK WHILE VISITING THE METRODOME
BUT THE VIKINGS' TEAM MANAGED TO PREVAIL
JUST LIKE THEY USUALLY DO WHEN AT HOME

SOME THINGS ARE BECOMING EVIDENT HERE
AS THE SEASON REALLY GETS UNDERWAY
ONE OF THOSE IS THAT THE VIKING TEAM
IS SHORT OF GUYS HEALTHY ENOUGH TO PLAY

OFFENSIVELY THE VIKES ARE PERFORMING
AT THE LEVEL THAT MOST PEOPLE EXPECTED
BUT DESPITE "IMPROVEMENTS" AND WITH THE WOUNDS
THAT DEFENSE IS A LITTLE LESS THAN HIGHLY RESPECTED

BUT WITH MIKEY BENNETT'S KNEE READY TO GO
(ONCE O SMITH DOES HIS TIME FOR SMOKIN' DOPE)
AND AS LONG AS CULPEPPER CAN CONNECT WITH MOSS
VIKINGS' FANS CAN HOLD ON TO THEIR HOPES

~ ~ ~ ~ ~ ~ ~ ~ ~ ~ ~ ~ ~ ~ ~ ~ ~

THE COLTS-PACKERS' GAME WAS JUST LIKE EXPECTED
A PASSING BONANZA AS THE PASSING STATS SHOW
FOR A WHOLE QUARTER THERE WAS NO GROUND GAME
AS MANNING AND FAVRE JUST DROPPED BACK AND LET GO

UP AND DOWN THE FIELD THEY WENT
WITH HARDLY A PAUSE IN BETWEEN
WHILE ALL THE SCORING WAS ENTERTAINING TO WATCH
DEFENSIVE FANS WERE LETTING OUT SCREAMS

THE PROBLEMS IN THE SECONDARY OF GREEN BAY
SEEMED EXCEPTIONALLY EVIDENT LAST WEEK
BUT THURSDAY'S PRACTICE HAD KNOCKED 3 DBs OUT
ALLOWING THE COLTS THE CHANCES THEY WOULD SEEK

THIS WEEK THE GIANTS COME TO LAMBEAU FIELD
BRINGING A TEAM PLAYING NOT UNLIKE GREEN BAY
SHOWING FLASHES OF BOTH GREAT TALENT AND INEPTITUDE
DEPENDING ON WHICH TEAM SHOWS UP EACH SUNDAY

BUT IT'S EARLY IN THE SEASON YET
AND WHILE THE GIANTS HAVE HAD SOME EARLY STUMBLES
KURT WARNER CAN PASS EFFECTIVELY
AND BARBER RUNS WELL (UNLESS OF COURSE HE FUMBLES)

~ ~ ~ ~ ~ ~ ~ ~ ~ ~ ~ ~ ~ ~ ~ ~ ~ ~

WHILE THE VIKES' FANS CAN USE THIS WEEK
TO GET THAT LATE-SUMMER YARD WORK COMPLETED
GREEN BAY FANS WILL WATCH AND CHEW THEIR NAILS
UNTIL THE NEW YORK GIANTS ARE DEFEATED

RESULTS:
Green Bay lost to the
New York Giants 7-14

Minnesota was on their
"Bye Week"

GB: 1-3
MN: 2-1

PACKERS "VERSES" VIKINGS ~ Carl Nelson

THE VIKINGS COME BACK FROM THE BYE WEEK
IN WORSE SHAPE THAN WHEN THEY WENT IN
WITH BENNETT'S NEW INJURY AND O.SMITH SITTING OUT
AT RUNNING BACK THEY'RE LOOKING VERY THIN

TICE AND CREW MUST BE SCRATCHING THEIR HEADS
AND WONDERING WHY THE INJURIES JUST KEEP ON MOUNTING
ADD CLAIRBORN, HENDERSON, AND ALL THE REST
THAT LIST'S QUITE LONG, BUT HEY-WHO'S COUNTING?

THE "CULPEPPER TO MOSS STRATEGY" REPRESENTS THE GOAL
THAT FORMS THE VIKINGS' OFFENSIVE BASE
THE QUESTION IS WITHOUT A RUNNING GAME
WILL THAT BLOW UP IN MINNESOTA'S FACE?

THE TEXANS ARE A TEAM ON THE RISE
PUTTING TOGETHER TWO BIG WINS IN A ROW
THEY'LL TRY TO FOCUS ON RANDY MOSS
AND MAKE THE VIKES BEAT 'EM WITH MWELDE AND MOE

THE VIKES' D-BACKS WILL HAVE QUITE AN IMPACT
IN DETERMINING HOW THE FINAL SCORE WILL READ
FOR THE TEXANS, UNLIKE MINNESOTA
HAVE ALL THE GOOD HALFBACKS THEY'LL NEED

~ ~ ~ ~ ~ ~ ~ ~ ~ ~ ~ ~ ~ ~ ~ ~

EVEN THE MOST STEADFAST OF PACKERS FANS
HAVE TO WONDER "WHAT THE HELL'S GOING ON?"
GREEN BAY'S TEAM SITS AT ONE-AND-THREE
WHILE THE LAMBEAU MYSTIQUE IS APPARENTLY GONE

THOSE WHO'VE BEEN CHANTING "MIKE SHERMAN MUST GO"
ARE PUFFING THEIR CHESTS AND STRUTTING AROUND
BUT COACH MIKE'S NOT MISSED ANY TACKLES
NOR HAS HE PUT THE BALL ON THE GROUND

THERE ARE SO MANY THINGS GOING ON WITH THIS TEAM
THAT THERE'S NO ONE PLACE TO POINT A FINGER
THE COACHES AND PLAYERS MUST MOVE ON FROM HERE
IF THESE DOLDRUMS AREN'T GOING TO LINGER

LIKE THE PACKERS, THE TITANS HAVE HAD THEIR WOES
HERE AGAIN INJURY HAS PLAYED A BIG PART
TAKING SEVERAL FIRST LINE TITAN PLAYERS
BUT NEVER DAUNTING STEVE MCNAIR'S LION HEART

RESULTS:
Green Bay lost to the
Tennessee Titans 27-48

Minnesota beat the
Houston Texans 34-28

THIS IS GOING TO BE A HEAD-KNOCKING GAME
WITH BOTH TEAMS FIGHTING FOR SURVIVAL
NEITHER CAN STAND DROPPING BELOW ONE-AND-THREE
AND BOTH OF THEM NEEDING QUITE THE REVIVAL

~ ~ ~ ~ ~ ~ ~ ~ ~ ~ ~ ~ ~ ~ ~ ~ ~

THE VIKES WILL PREVAIL IN SUNDAY'S GAME
THE TEXANS REALLY DON'T STAND MUCH CHANCE OF WINNING
AND ON MONDAY THE PACKERS SHOULD WIN AS WELL
PROVIDED THAT FAVRE'S HEAD HAS FINALLY STOPPED SPINNING

GB: 1-4
MN: 3-1

PACKERS "VERSES" VIKINGS ~ Carl Nelson

THE VIKES LEAPT OUT TO AN IMPRESSIVE LEAD
AGAINST HOUSTON LAST SUNDAY
HOWEVER AS THE GAME WOUND DOWN TO THE END
THEY SAW THAT ADVANTAGE SLIP AWAY

THE TEXANS TOOK THEM INTO OVERTIME
AND THOUGH THE VIKES EKED OUT THE WIN
THE COACHES AND FANS AS WELL WERE WORRIED
THAT MINNESOTA HAD BLOWN IT YET AGAIN

BUT "A WIN'S A WIN" OR SO THEY SAY
AND "M ROB" PULLED IN THE FINAL SCORE
WHILE ANOTHER RISING STAR WAS UNCOVERED
IN VIKINGS' HALFBACK MWELDE MOORE

THIS WEEK AARON BROOKS WILL LEAD THE SAINTS
AS IT'S THE VIKES WHO'LL COME MARCHING IN
TO ENGAGE A SAINTS' TEAM THAT IS SOMEWHAT REELING
FROM TAKING TWO BAD LOSSES ON THE CHIN

BUT THE SAINTS WILL HAVE A NEW DEFENDER
WHO'S MOST FAMILIAR WITH WHAT THE VIKES CAN DO
AS EX- PACKER MIKE " PREDATOR" MCKENZIE
WILL MAKE HIS NEW ORLEANS' SAINTS DEBUT

~ ~ ~ ~ ~ ~ ~ ~ ~ ~ ~ ~ ~ ~ ~ ~ ~

AT LEAST THE PACKERS DIDN'T WASTE MUCH TIME
FOR THOSE OF US WONDERING HOW THEY'D LOOK
AFTER CHRIS BROWN TORE OFF HIS SECOND TOUCHDOWN RUN
GREEN BAY'S GOOSE WAS TOTALLY COOKED

THE TITANS CAME AND SAW AND CONQUERED
LIKE THE GIANTS DID THE WEEK BEFORE
GREEN BAY'S DEFENSE JUST COULDN'T STOP 'EM
AND THE OFFENSE COULDN'T MATCH THE SCORE

WHY DOES THE PACK SEEM TO BE FALLING APART?
THE ANSWERS AREN'T OUT THERE IN PLAIN VIEW
WHILE THE COACHES ARE GETTING MOST OF THE BLAME
THE PLAYERS ARE SOMEWHAT RESPONSIBLE TOO

THIS WEEK THE PACK HEADS OFF TO THE LIONS' DEN
TO FACE A DETROIT TEAM THAT IS RESURGENT
WHILE FROM THE PERSPECTIVE OF THE PACKERS
A WIN THIS WEEK HAS BECOME QUITE URGENT

FOR THE FIRST TIME IN RECENT MEMORY
THE LIONS ARE SITTING IN FIRST PLACE
AND THEY'LL DO WHATEVER THEY CAN MANAGE
TO AVOID A LOSS AND THE LOSS OF FACE

~ ~ ~ ~ ~ ~ ~ ~ ~ ~ ~ ~ ~ ~ ~ ~ ~

EVEN WITH THE HELP OF MIKE MCKENZIE
A SAINTS WIN WOULD JUST BE A FLUKE
WHILE PACKERS FANS JUST HAVE TO HOPE THEIR PLAY
DOESN'T MAKE US WANT TO PUKE!

RESULTS:
Green Bay beat the
Detroit Lions 38-10

Minnesota beat the
New Orleans Saints 38-31

GB: 2-4
MN: 4-1

PACKERS "VERSES" VIKINGS ~ Carl Nelson

MINNESOTA'S TEAM IS ON QUITE A ROLL
WITH CULPEPPER PLAYING LIKE HE'S POSSESSED
AND AS A RESULT THAT VIKING TEAM IS DOING BETTER
THAN MOST PEOPLE WOULD HAVE GUESSED

THE SAINTS WERE THE LATEST VICTIM
OF THE VIKINGS' OFFENSIVE HOLOCAUST
NOT INCIDENTALLY IT WAS ALSO THE THIRD GAME THIS YEAR
IN WHICH FIVE TOUCHDOWNS DANTE HAS DEFTLY TOSSED

YES IT ALL SEEMS TO BE GOING MINNY'S WAY
BUT IN MIKE TICE MUST BE A GNAWING FEAR
AFTER WATCHING WHAT HAPPENED TO HIS TEAM
FOLLOWING THE SIX-AND-0 START JUST LAST YEAR

THE TITANS JUST AREN'T THE SORT OF TEAM
THAT SHOULD REALLY CAUSE THE VIKES TO WORRY
ALTHOUGH WITH RANDY'S HAMSTRING SLOWING HIM DOWN
THAT COULD CHANGE IN QUITE A HURRY

THE TENNESSEE QUARTERBACK IS STEVE MCNAIR
AS TOUGH AND ACCURATE AS HE CAN BE
AND FRANKLY THE WAY THE VIKINGS' DEFENSE PLAYS
THIS MIGHT BE QUITE A GAME TO SEE

~ ~ ~ ~ ~ ~ ~ ~ ~ ~ ~ ~ ~ ~ ~ ~ ~

DETROIT'S TEAM CAME OUT ON THEIR HOME FIELD SUNDAY
FOR A GAME THAT SHOULD HAVE BEEN AN EASY WIN
BUT THE GREEN BAY PACKERS FLAT SURPRISED 'EM
AND THEY LOOKED LIKE "PAPER LIONS" ONCE AGAIN

FOR WHAT IT'S WORTH THE PACKERS PLAYED
WITH SOME PASSION AND DESIRE
PERHAPS THE FEAR OF GOING ONE AND FIVE
POURED SOME EXTRA FUEL ON THAT FIRE

NOW IT'S BACK TO LAMBEAU'S GRASS
TO TUSSLE WITH THEIR SECOND-MOST HATED TEAM
BUT GAMES AT HOME FOR THIS YEAR'S PACKERS
HAVE BEEN MORE A NIGHTMARE THAN A DREAM

THOSE COWBOYS WILL BRING ALL THEY HAVE
RIDING ON THE ARM OF TESTAVERDE
WHILE THE PACKERS CARRY A "COWPOKE" GRUDGE
SO THIS GAME MIGHT GET DOWNRIGHT DIRTY

THIS WON'T BE A REPEAT OF THE PLAYOFF YEARS
WHEN DALLAS SIMPLY OWNED FAVRE AND THE PACK
THAT COWBOYS' MAGIC HAS FADED AWAY
AND AT LEAST THIS WEEK—IT'S JUST NOT COMING BACK

~ ~ ~ ~ ~ ~ ~ ~ ~ ~ ~ ~ ~ ~ ~ ~ ~ ~

THE TITANS' DEFENSE WILL BE THE REASON FOR THE LOSS
THAT THE VIKINGS SHOULD PILE ON THAT TEAM
WHILE THE PACKERS' "WHUPPIN'" OF THE COWBOYS
WILL HELP GREEN BAY KEEP UP THEIR HEAD OF STEAM

RESULTS:
Green Bay beat the
Dallas Cowboys 41-20

Minnesota beat the
Tennessee Titans 20-3

185

GB: 3-4
MN: 5-1

PACKERS "VERSES" VIKINGS ~ Carl Nelson

MINNESOTA'S VIKINGS MET THE TITANS
AND QUICKLY CUT THEM DOWN TO SIZE
KEEPING TENNESSEE'S RUNNING GAME FROM WORKING
AND PUTTING STARS IN FRONT OF MCNAIR'S EYES

THIS WEEK IT'S THE NEW YORK GIANTS' CHANCE
TO COME TAKE THEIR TURN IN THE METRODOME
FACING A TEAM ON A ROLL JUST LIKE LAST YEAR
WHEN THEY CAME IN AND BEAT THOSE VIKES AT HOME

COULD REVENGE BE A MOTIVATOR
FOR MIKE TICE AND HIS VIKING BAND?
OR WILL THEY PLAY THEM LIKE ANY OTHER TEAM
SHOWING THEY HAVE THE SITUATION WELL IN HAND?

THE VIKE'S OFFENSE REALLY IS CLICKING
LIKE A WELL-OILED SCORING MACHINE
AND THE WAY THAT GROUP CAN PUT UP POINTS
TO THE DEFENSIVE MIND LOOKS PURELY OBSCENE

BUT IF THE VIKES THINK THIS WILL BE AN EASY GAME
OR THAT MOSS' RETURN WILL HAVE THE "G-MEN" SHAKIN'
TAKE ANOTHER LOOK AT THIS NEW YORK TEAM
AND YOU'LL SEE THAT ASSUMPTION MAY WELL BE MISTAKEN

~ ~ ~ ~ ~ ~ ~ ~ ~ ~ ~ ~ ~ ~ ~ ~ ~ ~ ~ ~

WHEN THE COWBOYS CAME TO LAMBEAU
THERE WAS SOME SWAGGER IN THEIR STRIDE
BUT THE PACKERS PRETTY MUCH ROUGHED THEM UP
THEN SIMPLY KICKED THE 'POKES ASIDE

SOMETHING'S GOING ON IN GREEN BAY
THOUGH WHAT IT IS ISN'T EXACTLY CLEAR
IS THIS SUCCESS MERELY AN ILLUSION
OR HAVE THE ANSWERS SUDDENLY BECOME CLEAR?

WITH MIKE SHERMAN CALLING THE PLAYS
THE OFFENSE REALLY HAS TAKEN FLIGHT
AND WITH GRADY JACKSON'S TRIUMPHANT RETURN
THE PACKERS' DEFENSE JUST MIGHT BE ALL RIGHT

FOR THE FIRST TIME IN A QUARTER-CENTURY
THE PACK GOES TO PLAY IN WASHINGTON DC
THE REDSKINS HAVE BEEN WORKING HARD
BUT ARE STILL LOOKING FOR WIN NUMBER THREE

THE SKINS HAVE LOST TWICE AS MANY AS THEY'VE WON
THOUGH BRUNELL AND PORTIS ARE GIVING IT THEIR ALL
PERHAPS JOE GIBBS SHOULD HAVE CONTINUED RACING CARS
FOR HE DOESN'T SEEM TO HAVE KEPT UP WITH FOOTBALL

~ ~ ~ ~ ~ ~ ~ ~ ~ ~ ~ ~ ~ ~ ~ ~ ~ ~ ~

THE VIKES MAY PULL THIS GAME OUT SUNDAY
BUT IT SEEMS MORE LIKELY THEY'LL TASTE DEFEAT
WHILE THE PACKERS WILL PULL SOME TRICKS FROM THE BAG
AND ENSURE THAT HALLOWEEN ENDS WITH A TREAT

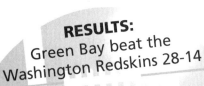

RESULTS:
Green Bay beat the
Washington Redskins 28-14

Minnesota lost to the
New York Giants 13-34

186

Week 9
Nov. 7-8
2004

GB: 4-4
MN: 5-2

PACKERS "VERSES" VIKINGS ~ Carl Nelson

IT MUST HAVE BEEN THE HALLOWEEN SPIRIT SUNDAY
CAUSING THE VIKES TO HAND OUT THOSE "TRICKS AND TREATS"
AS THEIR FANS WERE TREATED TO DANTE'S FIRST MELTDOWN
WHILE THE GIANTS WERE TRICKING THEM INTO DEFEAT

THERE WASN'T MUCH THAT WENT MIKE TICE'S WAY
WITH TURNOVERS AND MISSED TACKLES ABOUNDING
AND WHEN THE FANS LEFT BEFORE THE THIRD QUARTER ENDED
THE METRODOME SILENCE BECAME QUITE RESOUNDING

THIS WEEK MINNESOTA'S TEAM HAS AN EXTRA DAY
BEFORE VISITING THE COLTS NEXT MONDAY NIGHT
A MATCHUP SPOTLIGHTING TWO OFFENSES THAT CAN EXPLODE
AND DEFENSES WHO ARE UNABLE TO PUT UP A FIGHT

PEYTON MANNING AND EDGERRIN JAMES OF THOSE COLTS
ARE TWO REASONS THE VIKES' COACHES WILL WORRY
BECAUSE A COUPLE SECONDS INATTENTION TO THEM
CAN LEAD TO BIG TOUBLE IN QUITE A HURRY

SINCE NEITHER TEAM WILL BE ABLE TO STOP THE OTHER
EXPECT THIS GAME TO BECOME A SHOOTOUT
WITH THE VIKES' "M ROB" HURT AND MOSS IN QUESTION
THE OUTCOME SHOULD BE VERY MUCH IN DOUBT

~ ~ ~ ~ ~ ~ ~ ~ ~ ~ ~ ~ ~ ~ ~ ~ ~ ~

"DR JEKYLL AND MR HYDE" DESCRIBES THE PACKERS SUNDAY
AS THE TEAMS' TWO FACES WERE DISTINCTLY ON DISPLAY
THE FIRST PROVIDED A "MONSTEROUS" FIRST HALF OF THE GAME
BY GAME'S END THE OTHER NEARLY GAVE IT ALL AWAY

MARK BRUNELL SHOWED EVERONE WHY, AS BRETT'S BACKUP
HE NEVER WAS A THREAT TO UNSEAT "NUMBER FOUR"
THE YEARS HAVE ROBBED MARK OF HIS MOBILITY AND SPEED
AND FRANKLY RIGHT NOW HIS ARM IS LOOKING PRETTY POOR

BUT BEHIND BY SEVENTEEN POINTS AT HALFTIME
THE 'SKINS MOUNTED A STRONG COMEBACK BID
BUT IT WAS STOPPED BY A FLAG THAT HURT ALMOST AS MUCH
AS THE "DREADED" PICKOFF BY AL HARRIS DID

THE REFRAIN SEEMS FAMILIAR BUT STILL RINGS TRUE
"THIS BYE WEEK COULDN'T COME AT A BETTER TIME"
AS MANY PACKERS NEED A CHANCE TO REST AND TO HEAL
THINGS LIKE FAVRE'S RIGHT HAND AND PERHAPS HIS MIND

THE PACK HAS ENGINEERED QUITE THE COMEBACK
AFTER STRUGGLING THROUGH THE FIRST FOUR WEEKS
BUT NOW THE PACKERS' TEAM IS STEADILY IMPROVING
AND ARE BUILDING TOWARDS THE USUAL LATE-SEASON PEAK

~ ~ ~ ~ ~ ~ ~ ~ ~ ~ ~ ~ ~ ~ ~ ~ ~ ~

RESULTS:
Green Bay was on their
"Bye Week"

Minnesota lost to the
Indianapolis Colts 28-31

THE PACKERS WILL CLOSELY WATCH THE SCOREFEST
AS MINNESOTA GOES DOWN NEXT MONDAY NIGHT
AND WOE TO THOSE VIKINGS FOR THERE WILL BE NO REST—
NEXT WEEK GREEN BAY HAS THEM SQUARELY IN THEIR SIGHTS

187

GB: 4-4
MN: 5-3

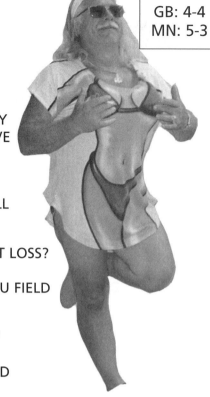

PACKERS "VERSES" VIKINGS ~ Carl Nelson

IT LOOKED MONDAY NIGHT LIKE THE STAGE WAS SET
FOR MINNESOTA'S DOWNWARD SPIRAL TO BEGIN
MOSS WAS OUT AND CULPEPPER HAD STRUGGLED
WOULD THE VIKES EMBARRASS THEMSELVES YET AGAIN?

BUT TO THE SURPRISE OF ALL THE FOOTBALL PUNDITS
THE VIKINGS CAME OUT AND WERE QUITE COMPETITIVE
THOUGH FOR WHATEVER REASON TICE DIDN'T PASS EARLY
AND THE VIKES' RUNNING BECAME SOMEWHAT REPETITIVE

MANNING AND CREW TOOK AN EARLY LEAD
USING BOTH THE RUN AND THE PASS AS EXPECTED
BUT WHEN THE VIKES FINALLY STARTED MOVING THE BALL
IT TURNED OUT THAT LEAD WAS BARELY PROTECTED

SO WHERE ARE THE VIKES AFTER THEIR SECOND STRAIGHT LOSS?
WHILE NOT GREAT—THEY'RE NOT CRASHING IN FLAMES
BUT THEY'RE TRAVELLING THIS WEEK TO FAMED LAMBEAU FIELD
TRYING TO AVOID A THIRD WEEK OF THE SAME

IT WON'T BE EASY THIS WEEK FOR CULPEPPER AND CREW
AS THE PACK IS RESTED COMING OFF THEIR "BYE"
FAVRE'S HAND IS BETTER AND SMALL HURTS HAVE HEALED
AND GREEN BAY WILL HAVE BLOOD IN THEIR EYE

FOR IT'S NOT "JUST A GAME" AS MANY WOULD SAY
BUT A TIE FOR FIRST PLACE THAT'S AT STAKE
AND TO SAY THESE TEAMS DON'T DISLIKE EACH OTHER
WOULD QUITE CLEARLY BE A MISTAKE

~ ~ ~ ~ ~ ~ ~ ~ ~ ~ ~ ~ ~ ~ ~ ~ ~ ~

THE PACKERS ARE MOUNTING A STRONG COMEBACK BID
RECOVERING FROM A DISASTEROUS EARLY SEASON
WHILE PLAYERS RETURNING FROM INJURY HAVE HELPED
FAVRE AND HIS RECEIVERS ARE THE MAIN REASON

DONALD DRIVER'S RE-EMERGED AS A "GO TO"GUY
AND JAVON WALKER IS LIVING UP TO HIS FIRST-ROUND BILLING
AND WHEN THE PASSING GAME IS GOING SO WELL
THAT LETS AHMAN GREEN BECOME HIS MOST THRILLING

GREEN BAY'S DEFENSE HAS LAGGED SOMEWHAT BEHIND
BUT HASN'T PRECLUDED THE PACKERS' SURVIVAL
THE HEALTH AND DEVELOPMENT OF THE DEFENSIVE TEAM
WILL BE SOMETHING QUITE CRUCIAL TO THIS REVIVAL

THAT DEFENSE WILL BE SORELY TESTED
FOR EVEN "MOSSLESS" THE VIKES MOVE THE BALL
GREEN BAY HOWEVER WILL BE UP TO THE TASK
AS MINNESOTA STARTS ITS ANNUAL FREE FALL

~ ~ ~ ~ ~ ~ ~ ~ ~ ~ ~ ~ ~ ~ ~ ~ ~ ~

IT SEEMED THE VIKES WOULD BE DOMINANT
JUDGING BY THE WAY THEY PLAYED THE FIRST SIX WEEKS
BUT NOW IS THE TIME THAT GREEN BAY HITS THEIR STRIDE
AND THEY'LL SHOW THAT WITH A BIG WIN THIS WEEK

RESULTS:
Green Bay beat the
Minnesota Vikings 34-31

188

WHEN THE DUST HAD SETTLED SUNDAY NIGHT
THE PACKERS HAD WON ANOTHER GAME
UNFORTUNATELY THE WAY THAT THEY CHOSE TO DO THIS
HAS BECOME SO FAMILIAR IT'S NEARLY LAME

GREEN BAY LEAPED OUT TO A SUBSTANTIAL LEAD
AND FOR THE REST OF THE GAME PLAYED PRETTY WELL
RUNNING AND PASSING THE BALL EFFICIENTLY
WHILE THE DEFENSE WAS GENERALLY RAISING HELL

BUT ONCE AGAIN THE HABIT RETURNED TO GREEN BAY
OF NOT LETTING ANYBODY HEAD FOR HOME TOO EARLY
AND LETTING THE VIKES MAKE QUITE A RUN AT AN UPSET
CAUSING MOST PACKERS' FANS TO GROW QUITE SURLY

YET IN THE END THE GOOD GUYS WON
AND THAT'S REALLY ALL THAT MATTERS
EVEN IF ALL OUR HAIRS TURNED GRAY
AND OUR NAILS ARE ALL CHEWED TO TATTERS

IT'S OFF TO TEXAS FOR A SUNDAY NIGHT GAME
AGAINST A TEAM THAT THE PACKERS HAVE NEVER BEAT
OF COURSE THAT IS PURELY A FUNCTION OF THE FACT
THIS IS THE FIRST TIME EVER THESE TEAMS WILL MEET!

~ ~ ~ ~ ~ ~ ~ ~ ~ ~ ~ ~ ~ ~ ~ ~ ~ ~

LAST SUNDAY THE VIKINGS CAME TO LAMBEAU
READY TO MIX IT UP WITH BRETT AND THE PACK
BUT GREEN BAY JUMPED OUT TO AN EARLY LEAD
AND SQUELCHED A LATE VIKES' TRY AT A COMEBACK

OFFENSIVELY THE MINNESOTA VIKINGS' TEAM
GAVE THE PACKERS' "D" ALL THAT THEY COULD HANDLE
BUT THAT VIKINGS' DEFENSE NEEDS A DIFFERENT SCHEME
OR PEHAPS A COUPLE PLAYERS MORE LIKE OL' JOHNNY RANDLE

THIS WEEK THE LIONS COME TO VISIT
AND THIS IS A GAME THE VIKINGS MUST WIN
FOR THOUGH ONCE ALMOST DEAD AND BURIED
THE LIONS ARE JUST ONE GAME BEHIND THE VIKES AGAIN

"UNFULFILLED POTENTIAL" IS THE TERM DECRIBING DETROIT
FOR ALTHOUGH ONCE AGAIN IT LOOKED LIKE THEY HAD THE TOOLS
THEY'RE SOMEHOW FLOUNDERING IN MEDIOCRITY
LEAVING THE LIONS' FANS FEELING THAT THEY'VE BEEN FOOLS

MIKE TICE INSISTS THAT THE VIKES AREN'T SLUMPING
BUT MOST FOLK WILL CHOOSE TO WAIT AND SEE
BECAUSE IF MINNESOTA DROPS ONE TO DETROIT'S LIONS
SOME WILL START TO QUESTION MIKE'S CREDIBILITY

~ ~ ~ ~ ~ ~ ~ ~ ~ ~ ~ ~ ~ ~ ~ ~ ~ ~

MIKE'S WORD SHOULD BE GOOD AS GOLD WITH SUNDAY'S WIN
THE LIONS DON'T HAVE THE SKILL TO BEAT THE VIKES IN THEIR DOME
AND WHILE THE TEXANS MAY PUT UP A GOOD FIGHT SUNDAY
THE STEADILY-IMPROVING PACKERS' TEAM WILL BEAT THEM AT HOME

GB: 5-4
MN: 5-4

PACKERS "VERSES" VIKINGS ~ Carl Nelson

RESULTS:
Green Bay beat the
Houston Texans 16-13

Minnesota beat the
Detroit Lions 22-19

GB: 6-4
MN: 6-4

~ Carl Nelson

PACKERS "VERSES" VIKINGS

THE LIONS WENT INTO THE VIKINGS' DEN
IN A TWIST OF THE OLD BIBLE TALE
AND PUT UP QUITE A FIGHT LEADING MOST OF THE TIME
UNTIL THE VIKES MANAGED AT LAST TO PREVAIL

NOW AFTER SPENDING A MONTH SITTING ON THE BENCH
NURSING A SORE AND DAMAGED "WHEEL"
THIS WEEK RANDY MOSS IS SUPPOSED TO RETURN
IF HIS TORN HAMSTRING HAS SUFFICIENTLY HEALED

WHILE MOSS HAS BEEN ON THE INJURY LIST
THE VIKINGS' LOSSES HAVE BEEN STEADILY MOUNTING
IN FACT AFTER STARTING OFF FIVE AND ONE
THEY WENT ONE AND THREE IF ANYONE'S COUNTING

BUT THE VIKES HOWEVER ARE A BETTER TEAM NOW
FOR ALL OF THE STUGGLES THEY'VE RECENTLY HAD
CULPEPPER'S BECOME A MORE COMPLETE QB
AND WITH HIS TALENT THAT CAN'T BE ALL BAD

THE JAGUARS WHO ARE THIS WEEK'S OPPONENT
HAVE PLAYED THROUGH INJURIES THEY DON'T WANT TO RE-LIVE
BUT IF BYRON LEFTWICH CAN RETURN TO THE LINEUP THIS WEEK
THE VIKES' DEFENSE ONCE AGAIN WILL RESEMBLE A SIEVE

~ ~ ~ ~ ~ ~ ~ ~ ~ ~ ~ ~ ~ ~ ~ ~ ~ ~

THE TEXANS WELCOMED GREEN BAY'S PACKERS
BY KNOCKING AHMAN GREEN RIGHT OUT OF THE GAME
SO THE PACKERS INSERTED YOUNG WALT WILLIAMS
AND HOUSTON'S TEAM TREATED HIM JUST THE SAME

WITHOUT HIS BACKS, BRETT FAVRE TOOK THE LOAD
SQUARELY ONTO HIS BIG BROAD SHOULDERS
THE DEFENSE KEPT THE TEXANS WITHIN TEN POINTS
AND LONGWELL GOT A BIG LIFT FROM HIS HOLDER

WITH ONLY FOUR SECONDS LEFT ON THE CLOCK
LONGWELL'S FIELD GOAL JUST CLEARED THE BAR
LIFTING GREEN BAY TO THEIR FIFTH STRAIGHT WIN
OVER A GOOD TEAM LED BY YOUNG DAVID CARR

NOW IT'S BACK TO LAMBEAU FIELD FOR MONDAY NIGHT
FACING THE RAMS IN THE WEEK'S SHOWCASE GAME
AS BRETT MAKES CONSECUTIVE START TWO HUNDRED
CELEBRATING THE TOUGHNESS THAT'S HIS CLAIM TO FAME

THE PACK WILL NEED AHMAN TO RETURN
AND THE DEFENSE TO STEP UP TO THE PLATE
IF THEY'RE GOING TO BEAT THIS ST LOUIS TEAM
THAT WILL TRY TO TAKE OFF RIGHT OUT OF THE GATE

~ ~ ~ ~ ~ ~ ~ ~ ~ ~ ~ ~ ~ ~ ~ ~ ~ ~

A HOME VIKING WIN OVER THE JAGS NEXT SUNDAY
ISN'T GOING TO BE ONE OF THEIR EASIEST TRICKS
WHILE THE ENERGY AND EXCITEMENT OVER IN GREEN BAY
SHOULD EXTEND THE WIN STREAK TO SIX

RESULTS:
Green Bay beat the
St Louis Rams 45-17

Minnesota beat the
Jacksonville Jaguars 27-16

GB: 7-4
MN: 7-4

PACKERS "VERSES" VIKINGS ~ Carl Nelson

THE JAGUARS CAME INTO THE METRODOME LAST WEEK
AND FOR A HALF KEPT THE SCORING TIGHT
BUT IN THEY END THEY CAME UP SOMEWHAT SHORT
BECAUSE BYRON LEFTWICH JUST COULDN'T GET IT RIGHT

THE VIKINGS WELCOMED RANDY MOSS BACK INTO THE FOLD
WITH A TOUCHDOWN PASS IN LAST SUNDAY'S GAME
AND THOUGH HE PROVIDED A KEY RECEPTION
SOMEHOW HIS MOVEMENTS DIDN'T QUITE LOOK THE SAME

THE BEARS WHO WILL HOST THE VIKES ON SUNDAY
WILL HOPE THOSE LIMITS PROVIDE DISTRESS
FOR THE BEARS' DEFENSE ALWAYS PLAYS MOSS TOUGH
AND WILL SURELY TRY TO PUT HIM TO THE TEST

FOR THE BEARS THERE'S NOT A LOT TO LOOK FORWARD TO
AS THEIR POSTSEASON HOPES HAVE CLEARLY DIMINISHED
LIKE MOST TEAMS IN THAT SPOT THEY MOSTLY HOPE TO LOOK BACK
AND FEEL PRIDE IN THEIR PLAY AS THE SEASON FINISHED

THE VIKINGS' TEAM MUST GATHER ITSELF FOR THE LATE-SEASON RUN
AND THE BEARS REPRESENT A TRAP THEY MUST AVOID
THEIR LAST TWO TRIPS TO SOLDIER FIELD HAVE BEEN LOSSES
AND A THIRD WOULD LEAVE THE BEARS SIMPLY OVERJOYED

~ ~ ~ ~ ~ ~ ~ ~ ~ ~ ~ ~ ~ ~ ~ ~ ~ ~

THE PACKERS' WIN STREAK REACHED TO SIX GAMES
IN A MILESTONE GAME LAST MONDAY NIGHT
BRETT FAVRE STARTED HIS TWO HUNDREDTH GAME
AND BEATING THE RAMS ALWAYS FEELS SO RIGHT

AHMAN'S ABSENCE DIDN'T KEEP THE PACK FROM RUNNING
AS NAJEH RAN AT WILL EVEN WITH SORE HAMSTRINGS
THREE TIMES FAVRE PASSES WENT FOR TOUCHDOWNS
AND SHOWED THE WORLD HE STILL THROWS WITH "ZING"

RESULTS:
Green Bay lost to the Philadelphia Eagles 17-47

Minnesota lost to the Chicago Bears 14-24

ANOTHER GHOST FROM GREEN BAY'S RECENT PAST
LOOMS IN FRONT OF THE PACKERS' TEAM THIS WEEK
AND AS THEY TRAVEL TO "THE CITY OF BROTHERLY LOVE"
IT'S REVENGE FOR LAST YEAR'S PLAYOFF GAME THEY SEEK

MCNABB AND THE EAGLES HAVE BEEN MOST IMPRESSIVE
SOARING ABOVE THE OTHER TEAMS THAT THEY HAVE FACED
TERRELL OWENS' ADDITION FILLED PHILLY'S MOST GLARING NEED
AND HE'S HELPED THEM LOCK UP THE FIRST PLAYOFF SPACE

BUT THIS IS A PACKERS' TEAM THAT BELIEVES STRONGLY IN ITSELF
AND BELIEVES THEY HAVE A MISSION TO COMPLETE
SUNDAY'S GAME SHOULD BE A HARD-FOUGHT BATTLE
IT'S A SHAME THAT ONE TEAM MUST GO DOWN IN DEFEAT

~ ~ ~ ~ ~ ~ ~ ~ ~ ~ ~ ~ ~ ~ ~ ~ ~ ~

THE VIKES SHOULD NEARLY HAVE A "WALK-OVER" GAME
AS THEY BEAT THE BEARS DOWN IN ILLINOIS
THE PACK CANNOT TAKE THE EAGLES LIGHTLY
BUT THAT SEVENTH WIN WILL BRING GREAT JOY

GB: 7-5
MN: 7-5

PACKERS "VERSES" VIKINGS ~ Carl Nelson

LIKE THE ETERNAL PASSING OF THE SEASONS
SOME THINGS HAPPEN EACH AND EVERY YEAR
FOR THE VIKES THE YEARLY TRIP TO PLAY CHICAGO
MUST BE STARTING TO PRODUCE JUST A LITTLE FEAR

FOR WHATEVER REASON THE BEARS HAVE THEM DIALED IN
AND RETAIN A FIRM HOLD ON THE VIKINGS' NUMBER
AND THOUGH THE BEARS HAVEN'T LOOKED VERY GOOD THIS YEAR
MINNESOTA MANAGED TO WAKE THEM FROM THEIR SLUMBER

THE SEAHAWKS WILL VISIT FROM SEATTLE'S SHORES
SMARTING FROM A BIG COLLAPSE ON MONDAY NIGHT
MIKE HOLMGREN WILL BE CHEWING BUTTS THIS WEEK
IN PREPARATION FOR NEXT SUNDAY'S FIGHT

THE SEAHAWKS BRING A TEAM BOTH YOUNG AND OLD
WITH SHAUN ALEXANDER AND JERRY RICE
AND A DEFENSE THAT CAN PLAY WELL AT TIMES
BUT LATELY HAS BEEN AS COLD AS ICE

THE VIKES THEMSELVES WILL HAVE TO FIND THE WAY
TO MAKE A TEAM WITH A HAMSTRUNG MOSS PERFORM
BECAUSE UNLESS MINNESOTA CAN SCORE FORTY POINTS
LAST WEEK'S RESULTS WILL BECOME THE NORM

~ ~ ~ ~ ~ ~ ~ ~ ~ ~ ~ ~ ~ ~ ~ ~ ~

THERE'S NOT A LOT THAT CAN BE SAID
ABOUT THE LAST GREEN BAY PACKERS' GAME
OTHER THAN "THANK GOODNESS IT'S FINALLY OVER"
THOUGH IT'S CAUSED NO END OF PAIN

THE OUTCOME REALLY SHOULD HAVE COME AS NO SURPRISE
THE EAGLES ARE ONE OF THE TOP TEAMS IN THE LEAGUE
WHILE GREEN BAY HAS BEEN PLAYING WITH SO MUCH EMOTION
THAT THEY WERE BOUND TO FINALLY BECOME FATIGUED

BUT IT'S NOW TIME TO PUT THAT GAME BEHIND THEM
AND THERE'S NO BETTER WAY THAN WITH A SOLID WIN
LO AND BEHOLD—HERE COME THE DETROIT LIONS
READY TO HELP START THE WINNING ONCE AGAIN

RESULTS:
Green Bay beat the
Detroit Lions 16-13

Minnesota lost to the
Seattle Seahawks 23-27

THE LIONS' TEAM HAS MADE SOME NOISE OF LATE
BUT THE PATH TO WINNING SEEMS ALWAYS TO GO WRONG
THE LIONS' DEFENSE HAS BEEN THE ONLY PART OF THE TEAM
THAT COULD POSSIBLY BE REGARDED AS STRONG

WHILE THE LIONS HAVE SHOWN FLASHES OF ADEQUACY
THEY ARE JUST WHAT THE PACK NEEDS AS THEIR NEXT FOE
A TEAM THAT'S LOST EVERY GAME PLAYED IN WISCONSIN
SINCE FAVRE WAS A ROOKIE WITH ATLANTA THIRTEEN YEARS AGO

~ ~ ~ ~ ~ ~ ~ ~ ~ ~ ~ ~ ~ ~ ~ ~ ~ ~

MINNESOTA'S DEFENSE MUST STOP THE RUN THIS WEEK
OR THE VIKE'S SEASON COULD BE HEADING DOWN THE DRAIN
WHILE THE PACKERS HOPE THE LIONS' EXPLOITATION
CAN PUT THEM ON THE WINNING TRACK ONCE AGAIN

GB: 8-5
MN: 7-6

PACKERS "VERSES" VIKINGS ~ Carl Nelson

A STRONG FOURTH-QUARTER COMEBACK BID
BROUGHT MINNESOTA'S VIKINGS OH SO CLOSE
UNTIL A CALL THAT WAS SO FLAT-OUT WEIRD
MADE MOST VIKINGS' FANS CURL UP THEIR TOES

IT WAS FIRST DOWN AT THE TWENTY
WITH TWO SIXTEEN LEFT IN THE DAY
THE VIKINGS COULD HAVE RAN THE BALL
BUT CHOSE A PASS BY MOSS TO BE THE CRUCIAL PLAY

AS THE 'HAWKS SNATCHED THE BALL FROM THE AIR
THE VIKES SAW HOPES OF VICTORY EVAPORATE
ANOTHER VICTIM OF COACH MIKE TICE'S CHOICES
WHICH HAVE BEEN QUESTIONABLE OF LATE

THE LIONS WILL BE SMARTING FROM A TOUGH LOSS
IN A GAME THEY COULD HAVE AS EASILY WON
AND AS THEY WELCOME THE VIKES TO FORD FIELD
IT'S DOUBTFUL THEY'LL BE IN THE MOOD FOR FUN

DETROIT HAS REDISCOVERED THEIR RUNNING GAME
THOUGH THE QUARTERBACK HAS BEEN IN A SLUMP
BUT THAT LIONS' DEFENSE HAS PLAYED WELL
AND WILL TRY MAKING THE VIKINGS LOOK LIKE CHUMPS

~ ~ ~ ~ ~ ~ ~ ~ ~ ~ ~ ~ ~ ~ ~ ~ ~

LAST SUNDAY THE GREEN BAY PACKERS WON
BEATING BOTH THE LIONS AND THE WEATHER
THE FIRST HALF WAS JUST UGLY FOR BOTH TEAMS
BUT IN THE SECOND THINGS BEGAN COMING TOGETHER

BOTH QUARTERBACKS WERE THROWING CURVEBALLS
ALTHOUGH THAT WAS SURELY NOT THEIR TRUE INTENTION
AND EVEN THE KICKERS FOUND CATCHING THE LONG SNAPS
DEMANDED EVERY BIT OF THEIR ATTENTION

BUT IN THE END GREEN BAY PERSERVERED
AND OPENED A ONE-GAME DIVISION LEAD
TO GAIN A BERTH IN THIS YEAR'S PLAYOFFS
A WIN SUNDAY IS THE ONLY THING THEY'LL NEED

THE JAGUARS ARE THE CHOSEN ONES THIS WEEK
AS THEY JOURNEY TO LAMBEAU'S WINTER CHILL
THEY'RE A TEAM THAT HAS BEEN UP AND DOWN
BUT HAVE THE ABILITY TO PROVIDE SOME THRILLS

AS JACKSONVILLE'S OFFENSE COULD PRESENT SOME PROBLEMS
THE PACKERS' DEFENSE MUST RISE TO THIS WEEK'S TASK
HOPEFULLY THEY'LL DO IT WITHOUT ALL THE PENALTIES
WHICH DOESN'T SEEM TO BE TOO MUCH TO ASK

RESULTS:
Green Bay lost to the
Jacksonville Jaguars 25-28

Minnesota beat the
Detroit Lions 28-27

~ ~ ~ ~ ~ ~ ~ ~ ~ ~ ~ ~ ~ ~ ~ ~ ~ ~

AS MIKE TICE PONDERS HIS VIKINGS' FUTURE
HIS TEAM MAY WELL LET THE LIONS HAVE THEIR WAY
WHILE THE PACKERS WILL HAVE TO WORK VERY HARD
BUT SHOULD CLINCH A PLAYOFF SPOT SUNDAY

GB: 8-6
MN: 8-6

PACKERS "VERSES" VIKINGS ~ Carl Nelson

DESPITE THREE TOUCHDOWN RECEPTIONS
BY NATE BURLESON AND RANDY MOSS
THE VIKES' INEPTITUDE ON DEFENSE
LED TO A LIONS' LAST-SECOND TD TOSS

IT TOOK A BAD SNAP BY A ROOKIE CENTER
BEFORE DETROIT'S LIONS WERE PUT AWAY
AFTER THROWING AN ALMIGHTY SCARE
INTO MINNESOTA'S VIKINGS LAST SUNDAY

~ ~ ~ ~ ~ ~ ~ ~ ~ ~ ~ ~ ~ ~ ~ ~ ~ ~

THE WISCONSIN WINTER SHOULD HAVE HELPED
AGAINST A TEAM USED TO FLORIDA'S HEAT
BUT IT DIDN'T HELP AGAINST THE JAGUARS
WHO DEALT THE PACK A SOUND DEFEAT

THE COLD SEEMED TO HURT THE PACK
AS THREE BRETT FAVRE PASSES WENT AWRY
AND BOTH HE AND AHMAN FUMBLED AWAY THE BALL
IT WAS ENOUGH TO CAUSE A GROWN MAN TO CRY

~ ~ ~ ~ ~ ~ ~ ~ ~ ~ ~ ~ ~ ~ ~ ~ ~ ~

BOTH THE PACK AND VIKES ARE PUZZLING TEAMS
EACH UNDERACHIEVING IN THEIR OWN WAY
AT TIMES THEY BOTH LOOK LIKE WORLD-BEATERS
OTHER TIMES SEEMING TO HAVE LOST THEIR WAY

SO NOW ON CHRISTMAS EVE AFTERNOON
THESE TEAMS MEET FOR A "DOME-FIELD" RUMBLE
WITH THE NORTH DIVISION CROWN AT STAKE
NEITHER OF THEM CAN AFFORD TO STUMBLE

IN WHAT SHOULD BE AN OFFENSIVE SHOOTOUT
(DUE TO THE LACK OF EFFECTIVE DEFENSIVE SCHEMES)
ONE OF THESE TEAMS WILL EARN A HOME FIELD PLAYOFF GAME
WHICH LOOKED A FEW SHORT WEEKS AGO LIKE A FUTILE DREAM

THE VIKES THINK THAT THEY HAVE THE EDGE
AFTER ALL "FAVRE CAN'T PLAY IN A DOME"
BUT THIS YEAR GREEN BAY'S DONE BETTER ON THE ROAD
THAN WHEN THEY'VE PLAYED AT HOME

THERE WILL BE A LOT OF TALENT TO COMPARE
WITH CULPEPPER AND FAVRE OR SMITH AND GREEN
WALKER AND MOSS SHOULD BOTH PUT ON A SHOW
THE LIKES OF WHICH HAVE BEEN RARELY SEEN

BUT WHILE THE "'FLASH AND DASH" APPROACH
MIGHT MAKE THE SCOREBOARD NUMBERS SPIN
IT STILL COMES DOWN TO THE GUYS IN THE TRENCHES
WHO DETERMINE JUST WHICH TEAM WILL WIN

RESULTS:
Green Bay beat the
Minnesota Vikings 34-31

SO WHO WILL WIN THIS IMPORTANT GAME?
WE'LL JUST HAVE TO WAIT AND SEE
BUT SATURDAY MORNING THERE SHOULD BE A CROWN
UNDERNEATH THE PACKERS' CHRISTMAS TREE!

194

GB: 9-6
(North Champs)
MN: 8-7

PACKERS "VERSES" VIKINGS ~ Carl Nelson

SANTA CLAUS CAME A LITTLE EARLY CHRISTMAS EVE
VISITING THE GAME IN THE METRODOME
BESTOWING ON GREEN BAY A DIVISION CROWN
AND GIVING LUMPS OF COAL TO THE "METROGNOMES"

THERE WERE SOME THINGS THE VIKINGS DID
THAT REALLY WORKED QUITE WELL
BUT PLAYING DEFENSE JUST WASN'T ONE OF THEM
AS THEY LOST THE GAME AT THE FINAL BELL

THIS WEEK THEY HEAD OUT UPON THE ROAD
TO TAKE ON JOE GIBBS AND THE REDSKINS
WITH THE MOST DIRECT ROUTE TO THE PLAYOFFS AT STAKE
IF THEY JUST WIN THIS GAME THEY WILL BE IN

THE 'SKINS HAVE BEEN AN ABYSMAL TEAM
LOSING TWICE AS MANY GAMES AS THEY HAVE WON
FACING A VIKINGS' TEAM WITH BENNETT AND MOSS
ISN'T GOING TO PROVIDE A LOT OF FUN

THE VIKES SHOULD BE ABLE TO SCALP THE 'SKINS
AND NOT EVEN REALLY BREAK A SWEAT
BUT AFTER LOSING SEVEN OF THE LAST TEN
WAITING TO BUY THOSE PLAYOFF TIX MAY BE THE BEST BET

~ ~ ~ ~ ~ ~ ~ ~ ~ ~ ~ ~ ~ ~ ~ ~ ~ ~

THE PACKERS EARNED THE DIVISION CROWN
IN EVERY TRUE SENSE OF THE WORD
AFTER STARTING OFF IN A HORRIFIC STYLE
WITH MANY "D'OHs" AND "OOPSes" CLEARLY HEARD

THE PACKERS FOUND THEMSELVES AS A TEAM
AND WERE ABLE TO MOVE TOWARD A COMMON GOAL
AND MOST IMPORTANTLY WORKING TOGETHER
TO DIG THEMSELVES OUT FROM THAT DEEP DARK HOLE

THIS WEEK THEY TRAVEL TO MEET THE BEARS
WHO WILL WELCOME THEM TO THE "NEW" SOLDIER FIELD
LAST YEAR IN THE BEARS' FIRST GAME THERE
THE PACKERS OF COURSE FORCED THEM TO YIELD

THE BEARS GOT OVER ON GREEN BAY
EARLIER THIS SEASON AT THE LAMBEAU GAME
THE PACKERS OWE THE BEARS FOR THAT SURPRISE
SO DON'T LOOK FOR THIS WEEK TO TURN OUT THE SAME

~ ~ ~ ~ ~ ~ ~ ~ ~ ~ ~ ~ ~ ~ ~ ~ ~ ~

WHILE THE VIKES MAY FEEL THEIR PLAYOFF ROAD IS SET
THEY SHOULD REMEMBER LAST YEAR AGAINST THE CARDS
WHILE THE BEARS MAY THINK THE PACK WILL BE COASTING
IN REALITY GREEN BAY WILL BE PLAYING HARD

RESULTS:
Green Bay beat the
Chicago Bears 31-14

Minnesota lost to the
Washington Redskins 18-21

FOR YEARS NUMBER NINETY-TWO PROWLED LAMBEAU FIELD
RARELY ALLOWING OPPOSING PLAYERS ROOM TO ROAM
NOW WE MUST SAY "GOOD-BYE" TO THE GREAT REGGIE WHITE
WHO FROM HIS SLEEP UNEXPECTEDLY WAS CALLED HOME....
—REST WELL BIG GUY—WE'LL ALL MISS YOU—
Reggie White—1961-2004

GB: 10-6
(2004 NFCN
Champs)
MN: 8-8
(Wild Card)

PACKERS "VERSES" VIKINGS ~ Carl Nelson

THE VIKINGS TRAVELED EAST TO WASHINGTON
TO CLOSE THE REGULAR SEASON OUT
AND THEY NOT ONLY LOST TO THE 'SKINS
THE GAME NEARLY BECAME A ROUT

FROM THE OPENING KICKOFF TO THE GAME'S END
THE VIKINGS REALLY NEVER HAD A CHANCE TO WIN
THE REDSKINS ARE JUST NOT VERY GOOD
BUT TICE'S TEAM COLLAPSED YET ONCE AGAIN

BUT NO MATTER TO THIS VIKINGS' TEAM
FOR THE PLAYOFF DOOR WAS OPEN JUST A CRACK
AND THROUGH NO DOING OF THEIR OWN
THEY MANAGED TO SLIP IN THROUGH THE BACK

SO THIS WEEK IT'S BACK TO GREEN BAY
THE SITE OF AN EARLIER DEFEAT
THINKING THAT WINNING A PLAYOFF GAME AT LAMBEAU
WOULD BE NOTHING LESS THAN "SWEET"

~ ~ ~ ~ ~ ~ ~ ~ ~ ~ ~ ~ ~ ~ ~

AND AS THE PACK PREPARES TO WELCOME THEM
ABOVE THEIR HEADS IMPORTANT QUESTIONS HOVER
"CAN THE OFFENSIVE LINE PROTECT BRETT FAVRE?"
AND "HAS THE DEFENSE FINALLY LEARNED TO COVER?"

LAST WEEK THE PACKERS POLISHED OFF THE BEARS
IN THE LAST GAME BEFORE THE PLAYOFFS BEGIN
GAINING A MEASURE OF REVENGE FOR THE EARLY LOSS
THAT SEEMED TO START THE PACKERS' DOWNWARD SPIN

IT TOOK A MONTH TO PULL OUT OF THAT DIVE
AND WHEN GREEN BAY DID IT WAS ALMOST TOO LATE
BUT THEY TOOK THE BIT BETWEEN THEIR TEETH
AND STARTED BY WINNING SIX GAMES STRAIGHT

FOR THE LAST HALF OF THE SEASON THEY'RE AT SIX-AND-TWO
WHILE THE RECORD IS THREE AND FIVE FOR THE VIKES
THOUGH FACING A TEAM THREE TIMES PRESENTS A CHALLENGE
THE MATCHUP IS ONE THAT GREEN BAY HAS TO LIKE

THEY SEEM TO HAVE THE VIKINGS' NUMBER THIS YEAR
WHILE THAT VIKING TEAM IS SURELY UNDERACHIEVING
NO MATTER HOW MUCH "POTENTIAL" THAT TEAM MAY HAVE
UNTIL THEY PLAY UP TO IT NO ONE WILL BE BELIEVING

WHILE THE PACKERS' "D" WILL HAVE ITS HANDS FULL
WITH A MINNESOTA OFFENSE THAT CAN REALLY MOVE THE BALL
THE VIKES' DEFENSE IS AT BEST A BIT QUESTIONABLE
SO CAN THEY SLOW THE PACKERS DOWN AT ALL?

~ ~ ~ ~ ~ ~ ~ ~ ~ ~ ~ ~ ~ ~ ~ ~ ~

WHEN ALL IS SAID AND DONE NEXT SUNDAY NIGHT
THE VIKES WILL FLY OFF BEATEN TO THEIR HOMES
WHILE THE PACKERS ENJOY THEIR VICTORY
AND START PLANNING FOR THE GEORGIADOME

RESULTS:
Green Bay lost to the
Minnesota Vikings 17-31

CONGRATULATIONS TO THE VIKINGS AND THEIR FANS
FOR AN IMPRESSIVE WIN IN GREEN BAY LAST SUNDAY
MINNESOTA SURELY WANTED TO WIN MORE
AT LEAST IT SURELY LOOKED THAT WAY

GB: 0-1
MN: 1-0

WHAT WAS THE PRIZE FOR THIS VIKINGS' FOOTBALL TEAM
WHO PICKED OFF THE HEAVILY-FAVORED GREEN BAY PACKERS?
WHY IT'S A TRIP TO PHILADELPHIA PA
TO FACE A TEAM WHO ARE NOT EXACTLY SLACKERS

WHILE THE EAGLES ARE MISSING TERRELL OWENS
WESTBROOK AND MCNABB STILL ARE FORCES TO BE RESPECTED
AND IT'S THE PHILLY DEFENSE THAT GETS THE HEADLINES
BECAUSE THEY'RE BETTER THAN EVEN THEY EXPECTED

THE VIKES WILL HAVE TO BE READY TO FIGHT
FOR EVERY INCH OF TURF THEY WILL TRAVERSE
AND AS ROUGH AS THE GAME IS ON THE FIELD
VIKES' FANS IN THE STANDS WILL FIND IT EVEN WORSE

BUT WHO KNOWS ABOUT THIS SUNDAY'S GAME?
STRANGER THINGS THAN A VIKINGS' WIN COULD HAPPEN
IF THEY TAKE THE LEAD AND MAKE NO MISTAKES
THEY COULD POSSIBLY CATCH THOSE EAGLES NAPPING

BUT OPTIMISTIC AS THE VIKINGS FEEL
PHILADELPHIA IS THE FAVORITE FOR A REASON
UNLESS MIKE TICE HAS SOME SURPRISES IN STORE
THIS COULD WELL BE THE END OF THE VIKINGS' SEASON

~ ~ ~ ~ ~ ~ ~ ~ ~ ~ ~ ~ ~ ~ ~ ~ ~ ~

YET AGAIN THE GREEN BAY PACKERS' DEFENSE
TOOK THE FIELD LOOKING JUST A BIT CONFUSED
AND SINCE THE DEFENSE NEVER REALLY KNEW WHAT TO DO
IT'S NO WONDER THAT THEY WERE SO EASILY ABUSED

GREEN BAY NEVER GOT THEIR GAME ON TRACK
AND THE STAR PLAYERS SEEMED TO GET HURT EARLY ON
BY THE TIME THAT DEFENSE FINALLY MADE SOME STOPS
THE CHANCE FOR A PACKERS' COMEBACK WAS GONE

THE FEELING IS GROWING FAR TOO FAMILIAR
AS THE PACKERS AND THEIR FANS ARE ONCE AGAIN
LEFT SMARTING FROM A BAD PLAYOFF LOSS
AND ARE ON THE OUTSIDE THE BIG GAME LOOKING IN

RESULTS:
Minnesota lost to the
Philadelphia Eagles 14-27

IS IT THE PLAYERS OR PERHAPS THE COACHING?
MAYBE IT'S THE WAY THE STARS HAVE BEEN ALIGNED
WE'LL HAVE TO WAIT 'TIL SPRING TO SEE HOW IT ALL TURNS OUT
AND WHO'S BEEN DRAFTED OR BEEN RE-SIGNED....

BUT NEXT FALL HOPE AGAIN WILL SPRING AS IT ALWAYS DOES
IN THE HEART OF EVERY GREEN BAY PACKERS FAN
FOR WE'LL ALL KNOW THAT OUR TEAM IS GREAT
AND THAT BRETT FAVRE IS STILL THE MAN....

PACKERS "VERSES" VIKINGS   ~ Carl Nelson

197

PACKERS "VERSES" VIKINGS

~ Carl Nelson

GB: 10-7
(0-1 in postseason)
MN: 9-9
(1-1 in postseason)

THE VIKINGS WENT INTO PHILADELPHIA
FULLY BELIEVING THEY COULD COME OUT ON TOP
HOWEVER THE EAGLES HAD SOME OTHER PLANS
AND THE VIKES' PLAYOFFS CAME TO A SUDDEN STOP

WHEN IT COMES DOWN TO POSTSEASON GAMES
TEAMS NEED TO BOND AND BECOME INDIVISIBLE
LAST WEEK THE VIKES'S DEFENSE LOOKED A LITTLE FLAT
WHILE RANDY MOSS WAS NEARLY INVISIBLE

THOUGH IT WAS JUST TWO SHORT WEEKS AGO
THAT THE VIKES SENT THE PACKERS TO DEFEAT
THE QUICK EXITS OF BOTH THOSE TEAMS
PROVES THEY'RE NOT AMONG THE LEAGUE'S "ELITE"

WINNING GAMES AT PLAYOFF TIME
REQUIRES MORE THAN THE ABILITY TO THROW
A TEAM HAS TO BE ABLE TO RUN AND TACKLE
AS WELL AS PLAY OUT IN THE SNOW

~ ~ ~ ~ ~ ~ ~ ~ ~ ~ ~ ~ ~ ~ ~ ~ ~ ~

THE FOUR TEAMS IN THIS WEEK'S CHAMPIONSHIPS
RESEMBLE EACH OTHER IN THAT MOST IMPORTANT SENSE
WHILE THEIR PASSING GAME IS MORE THAN ADEQUATE
THEY ALL CAN RUN AND PLAY DEFENSE

ATLANTA WILL BRING SOME "FLASH AND DASH"
WITH THE ARM AND LEGS OF MICHAEL VICK
AND THE FALCONS' DEFENSE CAN BE QUITE NASTY
THEY LOVE TO HIT AND ARE REALLY QUICK

THE EAGLES AS WE'VE RECENTLY SEEN
CAN GRIND A WIN OUT ON THE GROUND
AND THAT EAGLES' DEFENSE IS A FORCE UNTO ITSELF
AND DARNED HARD TO GET AROUND

THE STEELERS HOLD HOME FIELD ADVANTAGE
LARGELY BECAUSE THEY COULD "RIDE THE BUS"
AND WHILE THE "STEEL CURTAIN" MAY NOT BE REINCARNATED
THE STEELERS' DEFENSE HAS MADE MANY OPPONENTS CUSS

THE PATS HAVE A GREAT YOUNG QUARTERBACK
BUT IT'S COREY DILLON WHO MAKES THE PLAYS
AND THE PATRIOTS PLAY DEFENSE LIKE THOSE TEAMS
REMEMBERED FROM THE "GOOD OLD DAYS"

BOTH OF THESE GAMES WILL BE PLAYED OUTSIDE
AND BOTH CITIES ARE PREDICTED TO GET SNOW
WHAT A TREAT IT WILL BE TO WATCH THESE GAMES
AS THE SNOWFLAKES WHIRL AND BLOW

WHO WILL WIN? IT SHOULD BE OBVIOUS
BUT LET'S CUT THROUGH THE SUSPENSE
IT WILL BE THE EAGLES AGAINST THE PATS
IN JACKSONVILLE TWO WEEKS HENCE

RESULTS:
The Philadelphia Eagles beat
the Atlanta Falcons 27-10

The New England Patriots beat
the Pittsburgh Steelers 41-27

PACKERS "VERSES" VIKINGS ~ Carl Nelson

Super Bowl Record
Philadelphia: 0-1
NE Patriots: 2-2

AS SEASONS GO THIS ONE WAS A LITTLE UNUSUAL
IN HOW QUICKLY THE ELITE TEAMS WERE SORTED OUT
AND WHILE THE AFC HELD SOME MYSTERY 'TIL THE END
THE EAGLES' BERTH NEVER REALLY WAS IN DOUBT

THE EAGLES SIMPLY TORE THROUGH THE NFC
LIKE TERRELL OWENS TEARS THROUGH DEFENSIVE TEAMS
AND UNLIKE THE PAST YEARS WHEN THEY MISSED THE DANCE
THIS YEAR THEY'LL LIVE OUT THOSE "SUPER" DREAMS

MCNABB IS MIGHTY IMPRESSIVE AT QUARTERBACK
WHILE WESTBROOK AND LEVENS CHURN OUT YARDS
AND EVEN THOUGH HE HELPED GET THE EAGLES HERE
BEING A MAJOR FACTOR JUST ISN'T IN OWENS' CARDS

ALTHOUGH HE SAYS THAT HE'S BEEN "HEALED"
AND HAS EVEN MANAGED TO TAKE TO THE PRACTICE FIELD
HIS BIGGEST CONTRIBUTION MAY BE AS "DECOY"
AS THE PATRIOTS POUND HIM AND TRY TO MAKE HIM YIELD

IT'S THE "D" WHICH IS THE JEWEL IN THE EAGLES' CROWN
THIS GROUP IS ALWAYS RATED AMONG THE BEST
AND THE NEW ENGLAND PATRIOTS ARE ABOUT
TO PROVIDE THEM WITH THEIR TOUGHEST TEST
~ ~ ~ ~ ~ ~ ~ ~ ~ ~ ~ ~ ~ ~ ~ ~ ~ ~ ~

THE PATRIOTS ARE IN DANGER OF BECOMING THE TEAM
THAT EVERYBODY JUST LOVES TO HATE
BUT AFTER TAKING TWO OF THE LAST THREE LOMBARDIS HOME
IT'S BECOMING EVIDENT THEY'RE TRULY GREAT

TOM BRADY HAS TO BE THE BIGGEST KEY
TO THE SUCCESS OF THIS NEW ENGLAND TEAM
FOR A YOUNG MAN WHO STARTED AS A BACKUP
HIS CAREER PATH IS TRULY EVERY PLAYER'S DREAM

COREY DILLON CAME OVER FROM THE BENGALS
TO CARRY THE BALL IN TIMES OF NEED
AND BEHIND THE BLOCKING OF THAT PATS' LINE
HE DOES IT VERY WELL, INDEED

THE RECIEVERS AND THE TIGHT ENDS
ARE KIND OF AN ORDINARY LOT
BUT STILL ARE CAPABLE OF PLAYING PRETTY WELL
IF IT HAPPENS THAT BRADY GETS WHITE-HOT

THE PATS' DEFENSE IS VERY GOOD
WHEN THEY SET THEIR MINDS TO BE
AND WHAT THE MINDSET IS ON SUNDAY EVENING
IS WHAT EVERYONE WILL WATCH TO SEE

WHAT'S SO AMAZING ABOUT THIS PATRIOT TEAM
IS THEY'RE NOT LOADED WITH "STARS" AND ALL THAT STUFF
BUT WHAT HAS LET THEIR RECORD BECOME SO GOOD
IS THAT THEY CAN ALWAYS DO "JUST ENOUGH"

RESULTS:
The New England Patriots beat
the Philadelphia Eagles 24-21

SO LATE SUNDAY EVENING AS THE CHAMPAGNE FLOWS
WHO WILL TAKE HOME THE TROPHY FROM THIS GAME?
VINCE LOMBARDI THE NAMESAKE WON TWO IN A ROW
LOOK FOR NEW ENGLAND TO DO THE SAME

PACKERS

" VERSES "

VIKINGS

Green Bay Packers
Regular Season 4-12
No Postseason

Minnesota Vikings
Regular Season 9-7
No Postseason

2005

Carl "Gator" Nelson

PACKERS "VERSES" VIKINGS ~ Carl Nelson

THE SEASONS ARE CHANGING ALL AROUND US
SUNLIGHT HOURS ARE SHORTER EVERY DAY
AND THE CAREFREE LAZY DAYS OF SUMMER
HAVE SOMEHOW ALL GOTTEN CLEAN AWAY

BUT DON'T BE SAD AS AUTUMN NEARS
FOR IT'S THE TIME SO MANY OF US TREASURE
WHERE TIME COMES IN FIFTEEN-MINUTE QUARTERS
AND IT'S FIRST DOWNS WE WANT TO MEASURE

YES IT'S TIME AGAIN FOR FOOTBALL GAMES
THOUGH THEY SOMETIMES CAUSE DOMESTIC STRESS
ALMOST EVERYBODY LOVES TO WATCH
AND ARGUE ABOUT WHOSE FAVORITE TEAM IS BEST

AROUND HERE THAT CONFLICT IS A SIMPLE ONE
AS FANS OF BOTH THE PACKERS AND VIKINGS ABOUND
WHILE THE PACK'S LOOKED BETTER FOR THE PAST FEW YEARS
IN LAST YEAR'S PLAYOFFS THE VIKES KICKED THEM AROUND

~ ~ ~ ~ ~ ~ ~ ~ ~ ~ ~ ~ ~ ~ ~ ~ ~

THE WINDS OF CHANGE BLEW THROUGH VIKINGLAND—
RED'S "PURPLE PRIDE" CRY WILL BE HEARD NO MORE
AND IN A MOVE SOME FELT LONG OVERDUE
RANDY MOSS WAS FINALLY SHOWN THE DOOR

NOW COMES THE TIME THE VIKES HAVE AWAITED
AS DAUNTE FINALLY WILL GET TO BE "THE MAN IN CHARGE"
AND JUDGING BY HIS RESPONSE DURING PRESEASON
THIS MAY BE THE YEAR HE STARTS "LIVING LARGE"

THE DRAFT BROUGHT IN SEVERAL NEW FACES
AS THE COACHES PLAYED OUT THEIR HUNCHES
MINNESOTA ALSO INDULGED THEIR CURRENT VICE
AND THE VETERAN FREE AGENTS CAME IN BUNCHES

THOUGH SOME OF THOSE KIDS LOOK PRETTY GOOD
AND SOME OF THE FREE AGENTS DO AS WELL
THEIR CONTRIBUTIONS TO ANY TEAM SUCCESS
IS DEPENDENT ON HOW QUICKLY THIS TEAM CAN GEL

MINNESOTA GOT LUCKY THIS OPENING WEEK
AS THE VIKES PLAY IN THEIR COMFY METRODOME
WELCOMING THE BUCS OF TAMPA BAY
WHO'LL BE WISHING THAT THEY WERE BACK HOME

THOSE BUCS WON THE SUPER BOWL A FEW YEARS AGO
BUT THEN FELL QUICKLY FROM THE LEAGUE'S ELITE
AS PLAYERS JUMPED SHIP LEFT AND RIGHT
AND "CHUCKY" GRUDEN GREW FAMILIAR WITH DEFEAT

WHILE THE BUCS HAVE TAKEN THREE OF THE LAST FOUR
THE VIKINGS WILL WANT TO START THE SEASON STRONG
UNLESS TAMPA PLAYS LIKE A TEAM POSSESSED
BETTING ON THE BUCS IS JUST GOING TO BE WRONG

PACKERS "VERSES" VIKINGS ~ Carl Nelson

THE PACKERS TOO HAVE MADE SOME CHANGES
MOST NOTABLY AT MANAGEMENT'S TOP END
WHERE TED THOMPSON WAS MADE GM
LEAVING SHERMAN "JUST" HEAD COACH ONCE AGAIN

BUT IT'S NOT BEEN AN EASY TIME FOR "OUR TED"
AS CONTRACT DISPUTES AND HOLDOUTS ABOUNDED
BRETT FAVRE HIMSELF THOUGHT OF HANGING 'EM UP
WHICH WOULD HAVE LEFT THE PACKERS' OFFENSE GROUNDED

SOME KEY FREE AGENTS WERE ALLOWED TO LEAVE
MOST NOTABLY BOTH OF THE STARTING GUARDS
THAT'S NOT GOING TO HELP THE PASSING GAME
AND FINDING RUNNING LANES IS GOING TO BE HARD

HOWEVER BRETT'S RETURNED IN OUTSTANDING SHAPE
AND THE WIDE RECIEVERS ARE TUNED AND READY
AHMAN GREEN IS ANXIOUS TO RUN THE BALL
AND IF BUBBA'S NOT SPECTACULAR—HE'LL BE STEADY

THE OFFENSE IS GOING TO BE JUST FINE
OF THAT PACK FANS SHOULD HAVE NO FEAR
IT'S THE DEFENSIVE SIDE OF THE BALL
THAT MAY MAKE US ALL SHED A TEAR

THE PACKERS TRIED TO DRAFT FOR "D"
BUT THAT'S NEVER AN EASY TASK
HOPEFULLY SOME OF THESE KIDS WILL BE ABLE
TO DO THE THINGS THAT GREEN BAY WILL ASK

ENGAGING THE LIONS OVER AT FORD FIELD
IS NOT A BAD WAY TO START THE FOOTBALL SEASON
DETROIT SEEMS TO THINK THEY'E QUITE IMPROVED
BUT IT'S HARD TO UNDERSTAND THE REASON

HARRINGTON JUST DOESN'T SEEM TO HAVE THE GIFT
ALTHOUGH HE'S GOT RECEIVERS THAT ARE TO DIE FOR
AND KEVIN JONES IS A BRIGHT YOUNG STAR
WHO IS ALWAYS A THREAT TO TAKE THE BALL AND SCORE

THAT THE PACKERS ARE GOING TO WIN THIS GAME
IS WHAT PRETTY MUCH EVERYONE IS SAYING
THOUGH THIS YEAR'S SUPER BOWL WILL BE IN DETROIT
THIS WILL SHOW WHY THE LIONS WON'T BE PLAYING

~ ~ ~ ~ ~ ~ ~ ~ ~ ~ ~ ~ ~ ~ ~ ~ ~

WHILE IT'S VERY EARLY IN THE SEASON
IT'S NEVER TOO EARLY TO CLAIM BRAGGING RIGHTS
AND THEY WILL BE IN POSSESSION OF THE PACKERS
ONCE THE GAMES ARE OVER SUNDAY NIGHT

RESULTS:
Green Bay lost to the
Detroit Lions 3-17

Minnesota lost to the
Tampa Bay Buccaneers 13-24

GB: 0-1
MN: 0-1

PACKERS "VERSES" VIKINGS

~ Carl Nelson

THE MARGIN IS VERY SMALL IN THE NFL
BETWEEN A BITTER LOSS AND A VICTORY SWEET
BOTH OUR VIKINGS AND GREEN BAY PACKERS FOUND
IT SOMETIMES COMES DOWN TO ONLY HANDS AND FEET

THE VIKES SAW THE BALL LEAVE CULPEPPER'S HANDS
RATHER MORE OFTEN THAN THEY'D INTENDED
AND IT'S PRETTY SURE THAT IT WASN'T TAMPA BAY
FOR WHOM MOST OF THOSE PLAYS WERE INTENDED

ONCE PROJECTED TO BE THE VIKINGS' STRENGTH
THE OFFENSIVE LINE JUST COULDN'T GET IT DONE
THERE WERE NO LANES FOR THE RUNNING BACKS
WHILE TAMPA'S DEFENSE KEPT DAUNTE ON THE RUN

AND WHILE THE DEFENSE LOOKED SOMEWHAT IMPROVED
DID THEY REALLY LIVE UP TO THE EXCESSIVE BILLING?
IT DIDN'T LOOK LIKE THEY COULD STOP THIRD AND LONG
THOUGH SHARPER'S PICKOFF RETURN WAS THRILLING

NOW THE VIKES MUST HIT THE ROAD TO "THE NATTI"
THAT ISN'T SOMETHING THAT THEY DO TOO WELL
TRYING TO AVOID A SECOND EARLY-SEASON LOSS
WHICH COULD THROW THE TEAM INTO FOOTBALL HELL

THE BENGALS' STRENGTHS ARE THE VERY THINGS
THAT GIVE MINNESOTA'S VIKINGS FITS
A STRONG RUNNING BACK, A GOOD QB
AND A DEFENSE THAT NEVER QUITS
~ ~ ~ ~ ~ ~ ~ ~ ~ ~ ~ ~ ~ ~ ~ ~ ~

THE PACKERS DISCOVERED THAT THE SEASON
CAN DEPEND ON WHERE A PLAYER PLANTS ONE FOOT
LIKE THE RIGHT FOOT OF JAVON WALKER WAS PLANTED
JUST BEFORE HIS ANTERIOR CRUCIATE WENT "KAPUT"

THIS WILL HURT THE GREEN BAY TEAM
AT LEAST IN THE EARLY PART OF THIS SEASON
ANOTHER PERSONNEL CHANGE AMONG SO MANY
OCCURRING WITH WHAT SEEMS NO RHYME OR REASON

BRETT FAVRE FOUND HIMSELF DOING THE "BOB AND WEAVE"
ALMOST EVERY TIME HE DROPPED BACK TO PASS
AND WITH THE CHANCY PLAY OF THE "NEW" OFFENSIVE LINEMEN
HE WAS TOO OFTEN KNOCKED DOWN UPON HIS "GRASS"

WITHOUT THE PLAY OF A GOOD OFFENSIVE LINE
AHMAN GREEN HAS TROUBLE GETTING UP TO SPEED
AND IT'S JUST A LITTLE MORE PROTECTIVE TIME
THAT BRETT FAVRE IS GOING TO NEED

BUT THIS WEEK CLEVELAND'S TEAM COMES TO VISIT
LICKING THEIR OWN WOUNDS FROM AN OPENING LOSS
THE PACKERS ARE COUNTING ON A SURPRISING DEFENSE
TO SHUT DOWN THE BROWNS AT ANY COST
~ ~ ~ ~ ~ ~ ~ ~ ~ ~ ~ ~ ~ ~ ~ ~ ~

IN WEEK TWO OF THE "POST-MOSS ERA"
THE VIKES WILL AGAIN BE SHOWN A LITTLE LACKING
WHILE A RETURN TO THE VENUE OF LAMBEAU FIELD
SHOULD HELP THE PACKERS GIVE THE BROWNS A SHELLACKING

RESULTS:
Green Bay lost to the
Cleveland Browns 24-26

Minnesota lost to the
Cincinnati Bengals 8-37

GB: 0-2
MN: 0-2

PACKERS "VERSES" VIKINGS ~ Carl Nelson

"IT WAS ONLY AN ANOMALY" SAID MIKE TICE
WHEN SPEAKING OF THE LOSS TO TAMPA BAY
"WE'VE JUST GOT A COUPLE OF THINGS TO WORK OUT
AND WE'LL BE MUCH BETTER COME NEXT SUNDAY"

WELL LAST SUNDAY WAS THE DAY IN QUESTION
AS THE BENGALS HUNG THE VIKINGS OUT TO DRY
AND IT DOESN'T SEEM LIKE IT WILL GET BETTER
NO MATTER WHAT THE COACHING STAFF MAY TRY

THE OFFENSE SEEMS TO BE GETTING BLAMED
WHILE THE DEFENSE SURELY NEEDS TO TAKE IT'S SHARE
FOR THEY CAN'T SEEM TO STOP THE OPPOSING TEAM
ON THE GROUND OR EVEN THROUGH THE AIR

THIS WEEK THE SAINTS WILL COME A-MARCHIN' IN
A TEAM THAT DOESN'T EVEN HAVE A HOME
BEING A SYMBOL OF THOSE FOLKS FROM NEW ORLEANS
TO TAKE ON THOSE VIKES IN THE METRODOME

AARON BROOKS, JOE HORN AND DEUCE MCALLISTER
WILL BRING IN A SAINTS' TEAM THAT'S FILLED WITH DESIRE
TO TAKE THOSE STRUGGLING VIKINGS ON
AND SHOULD SIMPLY SET THAT BUNCH ON FIRE

~ ~ ~ ~ ~ ~ ~ ~ ~ ~ ~ ~ ~ ~ ~ ~ ~

ON A DAY WHEN REGGIE WHITE WAS HONORED
AND HIS NUMBER JOINED THOSE ON THE "RING OF FAME"
THE LOWLY BROWNS CAME TO LAMBEAU FIELD
AND PUT THE GREEN BAY PACKERS' TEAM TO SHAME

THE FANS IN TITLETOWN ARE GROWING RESTLESS
AS THE MYSTERY OF THE "DISAPPEARING PACKERS" GROWS
"THOSE UNIFORMS SURELY MUST BE FILLED WITH IMPOSTERS-
FOR THIS TEAM CAN NEITHER RUN NOR THROW"

BRETT FAVRE IS LOOKING A LITTLE UPTIGHT
AND HE'S NOT APPEARING TO HAVE MUCH FUN
BUT INCONSISTENT RECEIVERS AND A PATCHWORK LINE
ARE KEEPING HIM CONSTANTLY ON THE RUN

THIS WEEK THE BUCS COME TO LAMBEAU FIELD
IN A REMATCH OF WHAT WAS ONCE A CLASSIC GAME
TAMPA HASN'T WON IN GREEN BAY SINCE 'EIGHTY-NINE
IF ONLY THIS WEEK COULD WORK OUT THE SAME

THIS YEAR THE BUCS ARE COMING IN UNDEFEATED
WHILE THE PACK IS YEARNING FOR THE FIRST BIG WIN
"CADILLAC" WILLIAMS GRIESE, AND THE REST OF THAT TEAM
WILL DO THEIR BEST TO DENY THE PACK AGAIN

~ ~ ~ ~ ~ ~ ~ ~ ~ ~ ~ ~ ~ ~ ~ ~ ~ ~

THIS WEEK THE VIKES HAVE A BETTER CHANCE TO WIN
KICKING AROUND A HEARTSICK TEAM THAT HAS NO HOME
WHILE UNLESS THE PACKERS CAN PERFORM A MIRACLE
THEY MAY WELL FIND LAST PLACE IS THE ONLY THING THEY OWN

RESULTS:
Green Bay lost to the
Tampa Bay Buccaneers 16-17

Minnesota beat the
New Orleans Saints 33-16

Week 4
Oct. 2-3
2 0 0 5

GB: 0-3
MN: 1-2

PACKERS "VERSES" VIKINGS

~ Carl Nelson

MINNESOTA KICKED IT INTO HIGH GEAR
AND ROLLED OVER THE SAINTS OF NEW ORLEANS
OF COURSE SINCE THOSE SAINTS ARE HOMELESS
SOME MIGHT SAY THE VIKES WERE A LITTLE MEAN

THE SAINTS FUMBLED THE KICKOFF RETURN
AND REALLY HAD NO CHANCE AFTER THAT TIME
AS TRAVIS TAYLOR CAUGHT A TOUCHDOWN PASS
(ONLY APPEARING TO HAVE A TOE ON THE LINE!)

IT WON'T BE SO EASY IN THE GEORGIADOME
AGAINST A TEAM HATED BY EVERY VIKINGS' SON
FOR THE TIME THE FALCONS KEPT THEM FROM THE SUPER BOWL
THOUGH THE VIKES' RECORD WAS A COOL FIFTEEN AND ONE

AND VIKINGS FANS HAVE NIGHTMARES OF A FEW YEARS LATER
SEEING FORTY-SIX YARDS PASSING UNDER MIKE VICK'S FEET
IN A GAME THE VIKES HAD TAKEN INTO OVERTIME
ONLY TO SEE THAT GAME ENDING IN DEFEAT

THE VIKES WILL DO WHATEVER THEY CAN
TO AVOID THE STING OF GOING ONE AND THREE
BUT UNLESS THE FALCONS MAKE SOME HUGE MISTAKES
THAT PAIN IS SIMPLY MEANT TO BE

~ ~ ~ ~ ~ ~ ~ ~ ~ ~ ~ ~ ~ ~ ~ ~ ~ ~ ~

IT LOOKS AT TIMES LIKE THE PACK
JUST DOESN'T HAVE A CLUE
THINGS JUST DON'T SEEM TO BE WORKING RIGHT
NO MATTER WHAT THEY DO

THINGS ARE SO BAD THAT RYAN LONGWELL
WHO IS USUALLY STEADY AS CAN BE
NOT ONLY MISSED A FIELD GOAL TRY
HE ALSO MISSED A P-A-T

WHILE THE BUCCANEERS FOUND LAMBEAU FIELD
A TOUGH PLACE TO COME AND PLAY
THEY STILL MANAGED TO EKE OUT A ONE-POINT WIN
AT THE END OF THE GAME SUNDAY

MONDAY NIGHT THE PANTHERS HOST THE PACKERS
IN THE FINAL GAME OF THE FOURTH WEEK
WITH BOTH TEAMS HOPING THIS WILL BE THE START
OF AN EXTENDED WINNING STREAK

GAMES PLAYED ON MONDAY NIGHT ARE SUCH A CIRCUS
IT'S REALLY TOUGH TO MAKE A WINNER'S CALL
BUT IT WON'T BODE WELL FOR THE GREEN BAY TEAM
IF FAVRE KEEPS THROWING AWAY THE FREAKIN' BALL

MIKE VICK WILL USE BOTH HIS ARM AND LEGS
TO LEAD THE "DIRTY BIRDS" TO ANOTHER WIN
WHILE THE STRANGE THINGS THAT HAPPEN MONDAY NIGHTS
SHOULD HELP LEAD THE PACKERS TO THEIR FIRST WIN

RESULTS:
Green Bay lost to the
Carolina Panthers 29-32

Minnesota lost to the
Atlanta Falcons 10-30

PACKERS "VERSES" VIKINGS ~ Carl Nelson

GB: 0-4
MN: 1-3

THE VIKES HAD FINALLY FULFILLED SOME EXPECTATIONS
AFTER THEY HAD PUSHED THE SAINTS AROUND
THEN LAST WEEK THEY WENT TO PLAY THE FALCONS
AT THE GEORGIADOME IN ATLANTA THEIR HOMETOWN

CULPEPPER WAS DROPPED AN AMAZING TEN TIMES
(THOUGH A PENALTY NULLIFIED ONE OF THOSE SACKS)
THE VIKES HADTO PUNT TWICE IN THE FIRST QUARTER
WHILE THE FALCONS SCORED AND NEVER LOOKED BACK

SO THE VIKES WELCOME THE CHANCE TO HAVE A WEEK OFF
AFTER BEING THOROUGHLY BEATEN ONCE AGAIN
WHATEVER IS HAPPENING TO THIS TEAM
MUST BE CAUSING MIKE TICE'S HEAD TO SPIN

THE OFFENSE—SUPPOSEDLY UNSTOPPABLE—
HASN'T BEEN ABLE TO DO MUCH WITH THE BALL
WHILE THE BIG INVESTMENT IN THE DEFENSE
HAS PAID NO DIVIDENDS AT ALL

OWNER ZYGI WILF SAYS HE'LL STICK WITH MIKE
AND DO WHATEVER TICE SAYS IT'LL TAKE TO WIN
BUT WHY HAS HE BROUGHT EX-COACH CONSULTANTS
FOGE FAZIO AND JERRY RHOME BACK AGAIN??

HOPEFULLY COACH MIKE HAS AN UNDERSTANDING
THAT HIS JOB UPON THE TEAM'S RESULTS DEPEND
AND UNLESS THE VIKES START BUYING WHAT HE'S SELLING
HIS DAYS IN MINNESOTA WILL SOON BE COMING TO AN END

FOR A TIME EARLY IN THE MONDAY NIGHT GAME
GREEN BAY LOOKED LIKE THEY WERE OVERWHELMED
BUT THEN THE PACKERS TRIED TO MAKE A COMEBACK
WITH NUMBER FOUR FIRMLY AT THE HELM

WITH AHMAN GREEN AMONG THE INJURED
THE ONLY CHANCE WAS THROUGH THE AIR
SOMEHOW FAVRE PICKED APART THE PANTHER DEFENSE
ALMOST AS IF IT WASN'T THERE

ALAS THE COMEBACK ATTEMPT FELL A LITTLE SHORT
WITH DONALD DRIVER UNABLE TO BRING IN A LAST PASS
BUT OH WHAT A RUN THE PACKERS MADE
BEFORE THEY SEEMINGLY JUST RAN OUT OF GAS

THIS WEEK IT'S BACK TO LAMBEAU FIELD
TO TAKE ON THE SAINTS OF NEW ORLEANS
WHO ARE IN THE UNENVIABLE POSITION
OF ALWAYS PLAYING AS THE VISITING TEAM

THE SAINTS OF COURSE ARE HAVING TROUBLES
BUT THEY'VE WON MORE GAMES THAN HAS GREEN BAY
PERHAPS THE PACKERS CAN REGAIN THEIR FOOTING
AND FINALLY BEGIN TO MAKE SOME PLAYS

~ ~ ~ ~ ~ ~ ~ ~ ~ ~ ~ ~ ~ ~ ~ ~ ~ ~ ~

THE VIKES AT LEAST ARE ON THE BYE WEEK
SO DISASTER SHOULD BE A WEEK REMOVED
WHILE THE PACKERS HAVE TO WIN THIS WEEK
TO GET BACK INTO THEIR NORMAL GROOVE

RESULTS:
Green Bay beat the
New Orleans Saints 52-3

Minnesota was on their
"Bye Week"

PACKERS "VERSES" VIKINGS

~ Carl Nelson

THE VIKES WERE SUPPOSED TO TAKE A WEEK OFF
TO TRY TO FIND AND FIX WHATEVER AILS 'EM
BUT IN A FASHION THAT'S GROWN FAR TOO FAMILIAR
SOME PLAYERS CHOSE TO SCREW UP AND ACT LIKE SCUM

THIS WAS A SITUATION WHEN THE COACH WOULD ASK
THE SIMPLE QUESTION..."WHATEVER WERE THEY THINKING...?"
A CRUISE ON LOVELY LAKE MINNETONKA'S WATER
THAT INCLUDED STRIPPERS HOOKERS AND LOTS OF DRINKING?

WHAT A TREAT TO DROP ON THEIR COACH MIKE TICE
WHO'S FINDING JOB SECURITY FADING QUICKLY AWAY
AND APPARENTLY CAN'T MAKE HIS TEAM BEHAVE
ANY BETTER THAN THEY PLAY

THIS WEEK THE VIKES HAVE A CHANCE TO GET AWAY
AS THEY TRAVEL TO FACE CHICAGO'S BEARS
A TEAM THAT HAS WON AS MANY AS THE VIKINGS HAVE
AND USUALLY BEATS MINNESOTA IN GAMES DOWN THERE

THE VIKES ARE STILL TRYING TO FIGURE OUT
JUST WHAT THEY CAN DO SINCE RANDY LEFT
THE OFFENSIVE LINE HASN'T HELPED OUT MUCH
NOR HAS DAUNTE'S BECOMING MUCH LESS THAN DEFT

THE BEARS' DEFENSE HAS ALWAYS BEEN THAT TEAM'S HEART
AND THIS YEAR IS SURELY NO EXCEPTION
CULPEPPER WILL HAVE TO PLAY A VERY GOOD GAME
TO AVOID THROWING A BUNCH MORE INTERCEPTIONS

~ ~ ~ ~ ~ ~ ~ ~ ~ ~ ~ ~ ~ ~ ~ ~ ~

WHEN THE SAINTS CAME INTO LAMBEAU FIELD
THEY HAD TO HAVE BEEN FEELING PRETTY GOOD
GREEN BAY HADN'T BEEN PLAYING VERY WELL
AND THERE WAS NO REASON TO BELIEVE THAT THEY WOULD

THE SAINTS GAVE THE GAME ALL THEY HAD
BUT IT WAS ALL UNFORTUNATELY TO NO AVAIL
IT WAS THE SORT OF GAME THAT LEFT NO DOUBT
THAT GREEN BAY'S PACKERS WOULD CLEARLY PREVAIL

WHILE THE PACKERS STARTED OUT A LITTLE SLOWLY
IT DIDN'T LOOK LIKE THEY WERE DOING TOO MUCH WRONG
AFTER NAJEH SCORED THE FIRST RUSHING TOUCHDOWN
AL HARRIS JUMPED A PATTERN AND THEN THE ROUT WAS ON

WHAT A DAY WAS HAD BY GOOD OL' BRETT FAVRE
ON THE DAY BEFORE HE TURNED THIRTY-SIX
TOSSING THREE SCORES FOR THE SECOND STRAIGHT WEEK
AND MAKING THE PACKERS' OFFENSE LOOK LIKE IT HAD BEEN FIXED

~ ~ ~ ~ ~ ~ ~ ~ ~ ~ ~ ~ ~ ~ ~ ~ ~ ~ ~

THE PACK WILL GET TO SPEND THE DAY
WATCHING THE GAMES WITHOUT TOO MANY CARES
AND ALMOST CHEERING (BUT NOT QUITE...)
AS THE "VIKINGS' SHIP" GETS TORPEDOED BY THE BEARS

RESULTS:
Green Bay was on their
"Bye Week"

Minnesota lost to the
Chicago Bears 3-28

GB: 1-5
MN: 1-5

~ Carl Nelson

PACKERS "VERSES" VIKINGS

THE VIKINGS WENT FACE-DOWN AGAINST CHICAGO'S BEARS
AT SOLDIER FIELD LAST SUNDAY AFTERNOON
AND NO MATTER HOW "ENCOURAGED" MIKE TICE SAYS HE IS
THE OWNER'S SINGING A VERY DIFFERENT TUNE

"A NEW DAY IN MINNESOTA" IS WHAT HE'S SELLING
TO PRETTY MUCH EVERYBODY WHO MIGHT GIVE HIM A LISTEN
BUT WHEN TRYING TO GET THE PUBLIC TO FUND A STADIUM
THERE'S NO LIMIT TO THE BUTT OUT THERE FOR KISSIN'

~ ~ ~ ~ ~ ~ ~ ~ ~ ~ ~ ~ ~ ~ ~ ~ ~

BUT NOW IT'S "CHEESE WEEK IN VIKING LAND"
AS THE PACKERS COME TO THE 'DOME THIS WEEK
THE COACHES FEEL THIS WILL PROVIDE SOME FOCUS
WHICH MIGHT LEAD TO THE BETTER PLAY THEY SEEK

DAUNTE CULPEPPER HASN'T LOOKED LIKE THIS IN YEARS
HE AND THE COACHES ARE LOOKING FOR THE REASON
WHY MOSTLY OPPOSING DEFENSES CATCH HIS PASSES
AND SO FAR HAVE DONE SO A DOZEN TIMES THIS SEASON

BUT TO BE FAIR IT'S NOT JUST THE PASSING GAME
THAT'S NOT QUITE UP TO THE "CHAMPIONSHIP CONTENDER" BILLING
NEITHER THE RUNNING GAME NOR THE DEFENSE
HAVE BEEN WHAT ONE COULD CALL TRULY THRILLING

ALTHOUGH THEIR RECORDS ARE THE SAME
AT A PRETTY POOR ONE AND FIVE
PACKERS FANS ARE BEGINNING TO BELIEVE
AND THEIR TEAM IS STARTING TO COME ALIVE

BRETT FAVRE IS SHOWING THAT THIRTY-SIX ISN'T OLD
FIRING BALLS FASTER THAN THE EYE CAN TRACK
AND A REDISCOVERED PREDISPOSITION TO SCRAMBLING
IS LETTING HIM AVOID THE PASS RUSH AND THE SACK

THE PACKERS' DEFENSE APPEARS REBORN
AS EVEN THE PAST COUPLE OF LOSSES HAVE BEEN TIGHT
THE YOUNG PLAYERS ARE FINALLY LEARNING TO BE A TEAM
AND THAT FOLLOWING THE PLAN WILL MAKE IT RIGHT

ONCE UPON A TIME THE 'DOME GAME WAS A NIGHTMARE
AS BRETT AND THE PACKERS WOULD JUST MELT DOWN
BUT SINCE THEY'VE NOT LOST THERE SINCE '02
GREEN BAY HAS TURNED THAT TREND AROUND

GREEN BAY WILL HAVE TO BE ABLE TO RUN THE BALL
AND STOP THE GROUND GAME OF THE VIKES
IN ORDER FOR THE OUTCOME OF THIS GAME
TO BE THE ONE THAT CHEESEHEADS WILL LIKE

~ ~ ~ ~ ~ ~ ~ ~ ~ ~ ~ ~ ~ ~ ~ ~ ~ ~

THE PACKERS WON'T LET THEMSELVES BE USED
TO HELP SHAKE OFF THE VIKINGS' DREADFUL FUNK
BETWEEN AHMAN'S LEGS AND BRETT FAVRE'S BOMBS
THE VIKINGS' SHIP WILL ONCE AGAIN BE SUNK

RESULTS:
Green Bay lost to the
Minnesota Vikings 20-23

EARLY ON IT REALLY LOOKED LIKE LAST WEEK'S GAME
WAS PROCEEDING ACCORDING TO THE SCRIPT—
FOR THE FIRST HALF THE PACKERS DOMINATED
LEAVING THE HOME FANS FEELING THEY'D BEEN "GYPPED"

BUT THEN IN QUARTERS THREE AND FOUR
THE VIKINGS TURNED THAT GAME AROUND
PASSING THE BALL PRETTY DARNED WELL
AND EVEN MOVING IT ON THE GROUND

STILL AT THE END GREEN BAY BATTLED BACK
TYING THE GAME AS THE CLOCK NEARED THE FINAL CLICK
THAT'S WHEN A BAD PLAY BY A YOUNG CORNERBACK
SET UP EX-BEAR EDINGER'S GAME-WINNING KICK

SO TICE'S FACE (AND JOB) WAS SAVED AGAIN
FOR AT LEAST ANOTHER WEEK
ALTHOUGH THE FACT THE VIKES COULD BEAT GREEN BAY
PERHAPS ISN'T AS POSITIVE A SIGN AS THEY MIGHT SEEK

THIS WEEK THE VIKES HEAD OUT ON THE ROAD
TO PLAY THE PANTHERS UNDER A SOUTHERN SKY
WHICH DOESN'T BODE WELL FOR THE PURPLE TEAM
FOR WHOM OUTDOOR GAMES MAKE THEM WANT TO CRY

~ ~ ~ ~ ~ ~ ~ ~ ~ ~ ~ ~ ~ ~ ~ ~ ~

DURING THE PACKERS' NEWS CONFERENCE MONDAY
IN WHAT HAD BECOME QUITE A FAMILIAR SCENE
IT WAS ANNOUNCED THAT ANOTHER PLAYER WENT TO "I-R"
THIS TIME IT WAS RUNNING BACK AHMAN GREEN

THE ONLY CONSTANT IN GREEN BAY THIS YEAR
IS THE PLAY OF THE "OLD MAN" BRETT LORENZO FAVRE
WHO IS PLAYING BETTER THAN HE HAS IN YEARS
AS OPPOSING DEFENSES HIS BLAZING PASSES CARVE

THIS WEEK IT'S OFF TO PLAY CINCINNATI'S BENGALS
A TEAM THAT ON THE SURFACE IS LOOKING PRETTY GOOD
BUT SEVERAL OF THE EARLY OPPONENTS WERE PUSHOVERS
AND THEY'RE NOT BEATING SOME OF THE TEAMS THEY SHOULD

THERE IS SOME HISTORY OF NOTE HOWEVER
SOMETHING THAT HAPPENED THIRTEEN YEARS AGO
WHEN THE BENGALS KNOCKED OUT DON MAJIKOWSKI
GIVING FAVRE THE CHANCE FOR HIS FIRST TOUCHDOWN THROW

THEY ARE GOING TO BE A HANDFUL FOR GREEN BAY
AS CHAD AND RUDI JOHNSON COME OUT OF THE TUNNEL
QB CARSON PALMER TRAILS ONLY BRETT IN SCORING PASSES
WHILE THE BENGALS DEFENSE IS ALWAYS SET TO RUMBLE

~ ~ ~ ~ ~ ~ ~ ~ ~ ~ ~ ~ ~ ~ ~ ~ ~ ~

WHILE VIKINGS MAY THINK THEY'VE TURNED THE CORNER
THE PANTHERS WILL GLADLY SHOW THEM THE TRUTH
WHILE THE BIGGEST SOURCE OF GREEN BAY PACKERS' HOPE
IS THIS TEAM HAS ALL THE CONFIDENCE OF YOUTH

GB: 1-5
MN: 2-4

~ Carl Nelson

PACKERS "VERSES" VIKINGS

RESULTS:
Green Bay lost to the
Cincinnati Bengals 14-21

Minnesota lost to the
Carolina Panthers 13-38

GB: 1-6
MN: 2-5

PACKERS "VERSES" VIKINGS ~ Carl Nelson

THE QUESTION HAS TO BE IN ZYGI WILF'S MIND
"ARE THE VIKINGS SUFFERING FROM SOME SORT OF CURSE?"
JUST WHEN IT APPEARS THINGS ARE AS BAD AS THEY CAN BE
SUDDENLY THEY GET A WHOLE LOT WORSE

WHEN DAUNTE CULPEPPER RAN FOR A FIRST-DOWN
THE VIKINGS' SIDELINE WAS CHEERING AND FILLED WITH GLEE
UNFORTUNATELY WHEN HE WAS TACKLED ON THE PLAY
MOST OF THE LIGAMENTS WERE TORN IN HIS RIGHT KNEE

SO THE BRAD JOHNSON ERA BEGINS ANEW
WITH A TOTALLY DIFFERENT PASSING STYLE
IT TOOK TAMPA BAY TO A SUPER BOWL WIN
ALTHOUGH GRANTED—THAT'S BEEN A WHILE

THIS WEEK THE DETROIT LIONS COME TO TOWN
A TEAM NOT SURE WHO'LL BE THE QUARTERBACK
WILL IT BE THE DISAPPOINTING JOEY HARRINGTON
OR JEFF GARCIA—WHO'S SORT OF AN OLD HACK?

THE LIONS CAN PLAY GOOD DEFENSE THOUGH
AND THE VIKINGS' LINE IS SOMEWHAT SUSPECT
UNLESS THEY CAN TURN THEIR GAME UP A NOTCH
THEY MAY GET ANOTHER QUARTERBACK'S BODY WRECKED

~ ~ ~ ~ ~ ~ ~ ~ ~ ~ ~ ~ ~ ~ ~ ~ ~

THE PACKERS LOST ANOTHER CLOSE ONE LAST WEEK
AS THE BENGALS HELD ON WHILE TIME RAN OUT
BRETT FAVRE HAD HIS TEAM ON THE MOVE AT THE END
UNTIL A FAN GRABBED THE BALL AND RAN ABOUT

THE BREAK IN THE ACTION GAVE THE BENGALS TIME
TO GAIN THEIR EQUILIBRIUM ONCE AGAIN
STOPPING THE PACKERS ON THE NEXT TWO PLAYS
AND HOLDING ON FOR A SINGLE-TOUCHDOWN WIN

THESE GAMES ARE SO DARNED FRUSTRATING
ALTHOUGH "MORAL VICTORIES" COULD BE CLAIMED
BUT A LOSS IS STILL A LOSS
NO MATTER WHAT IT'S NAMED

THIS WEEK THE PACKERS FACE THE STEELERS
WHO ARE FEELING A LITTLE BEATEN UP THEMSELVES
WITH ROTHLISBERGER AND BETTIS HAVING SORE KNEES
BRINGING BACK-UPS BATCH AND STALEY FROM THE SHELVES

RESULTS:
Green Bay lost to the
Pittsburgh Steelers 10-20

Minnesota beat the
Detroit Lions 27-14

A NOVEMBER GAME AT LAMBEAU FIELD
AGAINST AN OPPONENT NEARLY AS BEAT UP AS THE PACK
SHOULD GIVE GREEN BAY A CHANCE TO TAKE THE LEAD
AND HOPEFULLY NEVER GIVE IT BACK

~ ~ ~ ~ ~ ~ ~ ~ ~ ~ ~ ~ ~ ~ ~ ~ ~

IF THE VIKES CAN'T GET PAST DETROIT THIS WEEK
THEY SHOULDN'T SHOW THEIR FACES BACK IN THE TWIN CITIES
AND WHILE THERE'S SLIM CHANCE FOR GREEN BAY THIS WEEK
IT PROBABLY WON'T BE ENOUGH— AND ISN'T THAT A PITY ?

Week 10
Nov. 13
2 0 0 5

GB: 1-7
MN: 2-6

PACKERS "VERSES" VIKINGS ~ Carl Nelson

DESPITE A LAPSE EARLY IN THE THIRD QUARTER
MINNESOTA GOT OVER ON THE "MOTOR CITY" TEAM
AND WHILE BRAD JOHNSON DIDN'T HURT THE VIKES
HE DIDN'T QUITE RE-ESTABLISH TICE'S PLAYOFF DREAMS

IT TOOK FAR TOO LONG TO PUT THE LIONS AWAY
CONSIDERING THAT DETROIT'S TEAM IS REALLY PRETTY BAD
YET THEY MANAGED TO TAKE A RUN AT MINNESOTA
BUT A WIN WOULD HAVE TAKEN MORE TALENT THAN THEY HAD

IT DOESN'T GET ANY BETTER FOR THE VIKES
AS THEY PREPARE FOR ANOTHER NIGHTMARISH TRIP
TO THE EAST COAST TO FACE A NEW YORK GIANTS' TEAM
THAT ALWAYS SEEMS THE VIKINGS' WINGS TO CLIP

SINCE BEATING THE VIKINGS FORTY-ONE TO ZERO
FIVE YEARS AGO IN THE CHAMPIONSHIP GAME
THE GIANTS HAVE HAD MINNESOTA'S NUMBER
AND AFTERWORD THE VIKES ARE NEVER QUITE THE SAME

PERHAPS IT WILL BE DIFFERENT THIS TIME
MAYBE THE VIKINGS CAN PULL OUT A VICTORY
ALTHOUGH IT WOULD BE AN EXTREME UPSET
AND THE CONCEPT IS VERY DIFFICULT TO SEE

~ ~ ~ ~ ~ ~ ~ ~ ~ ~ ~ ~ ~ ~ ~ ~ ~

THE REVOLVING DOOR OVER IN GREEN BAY
CONTINUES SPINNING EVERY SINGLE WEEK
AS INJURIES AND UNEVEN PLAY ROB THE PACK
OF THE OFFENSIVE CONSISTENCY THEY SEEK

THESE NEW FACES WEARING GREEN AND GOLD
ARE PLAYERS WHO ARE BEST KNOWN BY THEIR MOTHERS
YET THEY'VE BEEN SIGNED AND GIVEN THE CHANCE
TO PLAY ALONGSIDE THEIR MORE FAMOUS PACKER BROTHERS

WHILE THE PACKERS PLAYED THE STEELERS TOUGH
WITH TRUE GRIT AND FIRE AND EMOTION
UNFORTUNATELY THAT WASN'T ENOUGH TO OVERCOME
INTERCEPTIONS FUMBLES AND ILLEGAL MOTION

RESULTS:
Green Bay beat the
Atlanta Falcons 33-25

Minnesota beat the
New York Giants 24-21

IT'S BECOMING CLEAR TO THE STAUNCHEST PACKER FAN
THIS TEAM ISN'T PLAYING LIKE WE HOPED THEY WOULD
THEY'RE NOT LOSING FOR LACK OF TRYING
BUT ON THE FIELD THEY'RE JUST NOT VERY GOOD

THE TRIP TO ATLANTA DOESN'T BODE TOO WELL
FOR THOSE GUYS ARE CHASING THE PLAYOFF DREAM
THE WHOLE FALCONS' TEAM HAS COME TOGETHER AROUND MIKE VICK
AND THEY ARE VERY MUCH AN UP-AND-COMING TEAM

~ ~ ~ ~ ~ ~ ~ ~ ~ ~ ~ ~ ~ ~ ~ ~ ~

THE GIANTS SHOULD POUND THE VIKES AGAIN
THERE'S NO WAY THOSE WORDS TO SWEETEN
AS FOR THE PACKERS AGAIN THEY'LL GIVE THEIR ALL
HOPEFULLY MONDAY WON'T FIND THEM BRUISED AND BEATEN

GB: 2-7
MN: 4-5

~ Carl Nelson

PACKERS "VERSES" VIKINGS

THOUGH THE RUNNING GAME SIMPLY DID NOT EXIST
AND THE PASSING GAME WAS LESS THAN THRILLING
MINNESOTA'S VIKINGS STEPPED INTO THE "DAVID" ROLE
AND DID SOME DRAMATIC GIANT-KILLING

A PICK A PUNT AND A KICKOFF WERE RETURNED
PROVIDING THE VEHICLE FOR THE VIKINGS' WIN
DESPITE THE GIANTS' LATE TD AND TWO-POINTER
A LAST-SECOND KICK LET MINNESOTA WIN A GAME AGAIN

IT'S NOT QUITE CLEAR HOW THIS COULD HAPPEN
FOR NO ONE GAVE THE VIKES A CHANCE IN HELL
THE GIANTS NEVER COULD GET THEIR GAME ON TRACK
THE REASON WHY IS IMPOSSIBLE TO TELL

DOES THIS GAME MARK A NEW BEGINNING FOR THE VIKES?
OR DOES IT ONLY REPRESENT A ONE-GAME REPRIEVE?
THE PROOF WILL BE SEEN OVER THE NEXT SEVEN WEEKS
UNLESS MIKE TICE'S OPTIMISM CAN BE BELIEVED

~ ~ ~ ~ ~ ~ ~ ~ ~ ~ ~ ~ ~ ~ ~ ~ ~ ~

THE PACKERS WENT INTO THE GEORGIADOME LAST SUNDAY
FEELING LIKE A PLAIN GIRL AT A FORMAL DANCE
FACING A STRONG AND TALENTED FALCONS' TEAM
WHILE NO ONE GAVE THEM EVEN HALF A CHANCE

EARLY ON HOWEVER SOMETHING HAPPENED
AS THE PACKERS WENT ON AN EARLY TOUCHDOWN DRIVE
THEY THEN PROMPTLY STRIPPED THE BALL FROM ATLANTA
SCORED AGAIN—AND THEN THEY REALLY CAME ALIVE

FROM THAT POINT ON THE GAME WAS PRETTY EVEN
WITH BOTH TEAMS PLAYING SOME GIVE AND TAKE
WHILE THE FALCONS CAME BACK TO TIE THE GAME
THE PACKERS' "D" NEVER MADE THE BIG MISTAKE

AND AS HAPPENS IN THE LEAGUE FROM TIME TO TIME
A NEW HERO HAS MADE HIS PRESENSE FELT SUNDAY
HE'S A YOUNG RUNNING BACK NAMED SAMKON GADO
WHO SCORED THREE TIMES ON HIS TWENTY-THIRD BIRTHDAY

A MONTH AGO WHEN THESE TEAMS MET IN MINNESOTA
GREEN BAY SIMPLY OWNED THE GAME'S FIRST HALF
BUT SOMEHOW MINNESOTA REVERSED THAT DOMINATION
AND MANAGED TO WIND UP WITH THAT WEEK'S LAST LAUGH

IN A GAME FAR MORE IMPORTANT THAN IT MIGHT SEEM
AT LAMBEAU FIELD THIS COMING MONDAY NIGHT
THESE TEAMS WON'T BE COMPETING FOR FIRST PLACE
BUT FOR THEIR FANS' "BORDER BRAGGING RIGHTS"

~ ~ ~ ~ ~ ~ ~ ~ ~ ~ ~ ~ ~ ~ ~ ~ ~ ~

WHILE IT'S IMPOSSIBLE TO KNOW WHO'LL WIN
THE PACKERS WILL PROBABLY DELIVER THE FINAL BLOW
AND GET PAST THE VIKINGS OF MINNESOTA
EVEN IF IT TAKES AN "ACT OF GADO"

RESULTS:
Green Bay lost to the
Minnesota Vikings 17-20

212

GB: 2-8
MN: 5-5

~ Carl Nelson

PACKERS "VERSES" VIKINGS

IT WAS A LOT LIKE WATCHING "THE TWILIGHT ZONE"
AS THE GAME UNFOLDED LAST MONDAY NIGHT
GREEN BAY PLAYED WELL DURING THE FIRST HALF
BUT WENT DOWN IN THE SECOND HALF WITHOUT A FIGHT

GIVE SOME CREDIT TO THE VIKINGS' TEAM
THEY EARNED THIS WIN OVER THE PACK
BY PLAYING STUBBORN AGGRESSIVE DEFENSE
AND POUNDING THE BALL WITH THEIR RUNNING BACK

TICE AND HIS BOYS ARE FEELING PRETTY GOOD
AFTER LOOKING AT THE GAMES OF THE PAST FEW WEEKS
FOR THEY'VE NOW WON THREE GAMES IN A ROW
AND THEIR PLAY IS BUILDING TOWARD A PEAK

THIS WEEK THOUGH THE VIKES WILL BE ONE DAY SHORT
AS THEY PREPARE FOR THE NEXT TEAM THAT COMES TO TOWN
A GROUP THAT'S A REINCARNATION OF A FOUNDING TEAM
BETTER KNOWN AS THE CLEVELAND BROWNS

MUCH LIKE THE VIKES THE BROWNS STARTED SLOWLY
BUT HAVE IMPROVED DRAMATICALLY OF LATE
HOLDING THE DOLPHINS SCORELESS LAST WEEK
WITH A PERFORMANCE THAT WAS IMPRESSIVE IF NOT GREAT

THE VIKES MUST WORK HARD TO REMAIN GROUNDED
AND KEEP REALITY A PART OF THEIR SCHEMES
FOR IT'S AT ABOUT THIS TIME EVERY SEASON
WHEN OVERCONFIDENCE SHOOTS DOWN THE VIKINGS' DREAMS

~ ~ ~ ~ ~ ~ ~ ~ ~ ~ ~ ~ ~ ~ ~ ~ ~ ~ ~

THE PACKERS ONCE AGAIN GAVE IT ALL THEY HAD
AND AGAIN FOUND OUT THAT IT WASN'T QUITE ENOUGH
WHEN YOUR TEAM JUST DOESN'T HAVE THE TALENT
EVERY GAME BECOMES EXTRA ROUGH

IN YEARS PAST THE GREEN BAY PACKERS' TEAM
WOULD HAVE RELISHED THIS WEEK'S GAME
AGAINST AN EAGLES' TEAM THAT'S SO DEPLETED
THAT ONLY THEIR NAME REMAINS THE SAME

"T.O." IS OUT AND MCNABB AS WELL
ALONG WITH A FEW OF THE DEFENSIVE GUYS
THE LIST OF THEIR "INJURED AND INACTIVES" HAS GROWN
UNTIL IT RESEMBLES GREEN BAY'S LIST IN SIZE

THESE ARE THE TEAMS THAT WILL PLAY ON SUNDAY
AND WHILE NEITHER ARE STRANGERS TO DEFEAT
THE PACKERS WILL PLAY PHILLY PRETTY TOUGH
AS LONG AS BRETT FAVRE IS ON HIS FEET

~ ~ ~ ~ ~ ~ ~ ~ ~ ~ ~ ~ ~ ~ ~ ~ ~ ~

IF THE VIKINGS DON'T TAKE THIS GAME SERIOUSLY ENOUGH
THE BROWNS HAVE A GOOD CHANCE OF COMING OUT THE WINNER
WHILE THE PACKERS WILL TRY TO STUFF THE EAGLES
LIKE THE TURKEY FROM THANKSGIVING'S DINNER!

RESULTS:
Green Bay lost to the
Philadelphia Eagles 14-19

Minnesota beat the
Cleveland Browns 24-12

HAPPY THANKSGIVING !!

213

PACKERS "VERSES" VIKINGS ~ Carl Nelson

MINNESOTA'S AMAZING WINNING STREAK CONTINUES
NO MATTER HOW UNLIKELY IT MAY SEEM
AND EVEN THE MOST BITTER AND CYNICAL OF VIKINGS FANS
ARE DUSTING OFF ABANDONED PLAYOFF DREAMS

IT MAY BE INCUMBANT TO REMIND THESE FANS
THE WAY MINNESOTA GOT PAST CLEVELAND AND TRENT DILFER
AND THAT IT WASN'T SO MUCH OFFENSIVE EXCELLENCE
BUT A FUNCTION OF THOSE THREE PASSES THAT THEY PILFERED

A MONTH AGO THE VIKES PLAYED THE LIONS IN THE METRODOME
ON A DAY FILLED WITH ENDINGS AND BEGINNINGS
AS DAUNTE'S INJURY ENDED HIS PLAYING FOR THE YEAR
WHILE THE VIKINGS SOMEHOW STARTED WINNING

THE LIONS ARE A TEAM IN TURMOIL THIS WEEK
AFTER COACH MARIUCCI (DESERVEDLY) GOT THE AX
AND THE DEFENSE IS MOUTHING OFF ABOUT THE OFFENSE
WHILE THE FILL-IN COACH SWITCHES QUARTERBACKS....

ATHOUGH IT LOOKS LIKE THIS TEAM HAS COLLAPSED
TAKING THEM TOO LIGHTLY COULD BE A MISTAKE
FOR ALL THOSE LIONS' PLAYERS ARE GOING TO PLAY VERY HARD
KNOWING NEXT YEAR'S ROSTER SPOT MAY WELL BE AT STAKE

~ ~ ~ ~ ~ ~ ~ ~ ~ ~ ~ ~ ~ ~ ~ ~

IT'S TRULY BECOMING TIRESOME TO WATCH EACH WEEK
AS GREEN BAY LETS ALL THOSE CLOSE GAMES SLIP AWAY
DEMONSTRATING THEY ARE A LITTLE SHORT OF TALENT
NO MATTER HOW HARD OR WELL THE REMAINING FELLOWS PLAY

IT LOOKED LIKE THERE MIGHT BE A BRIGHT SPOT LAST SUNDAY
AND THAT IN SPITE OF THEMSELVES THE PACKERS MIGHT JUST WIN
BUT THEIR OLD HABITS RESURFACED IN QUARTER NUMBER FOUR
AND A FUMBLED KICKOFF SPELLED DEFEAT FOR THEM ONCE AGAIN

THIS WEEK MAY PROVIDE A RESPITE OF SORTS FOR GREEN BAY FANS
AS THEIR PACKERS TRAVEL SOUTH TO ENGAGE THE HATED BEARS
WHILE IT WOULD SEEM TO BE A STRANGE GAME TO LOOK FORWARD TO
ELEVEN STRAIGHT TIMES GREEN BAY HAS WON DOWN THERE

THESE BEARS RESEMBLE THEIR FEARSOME PREDECESSORS
THE ONES KNOWN AS THE "MOSTERS OF THE MIDWAY" IN YEARS PAST
WITH THE DEFENSE ONCE AGAIN THE STRENGTH OF THE TEAM
WHILE THE OFFENSE WINS WITH A LESS IMPRESSIVE CAST

URLACHER ALEX BROWN AND ADWALE OGUNLEYE APPEAR
THROWBACKS TO AN EARLIER TOUGHER TIME
ALTHOUGH KYLE ORTON AND JONES SCORE ENOUGH TO WIN
IT ALL BEGINS WITH THIS IMPENETRABLE DEFENSIVE LINE

~ ~ ~ ~ ~ ~ ~ ~ ~ ~ ~ ~ ~ ~ ~ ~ ~

AT GAME'S END THE VIKES WILL FIND THE LIONS WERE TOUGHER
THAN THE "MOTOR CITY KITTYS" THEY REMEMBERED
WHILE GREEN BAY WILL CARRY THE FIGHT INTO CHICAGO
KNOWING THAT THEY RARELY LOSE GAMES DURING DECEMBER

RESULTS:
Green Bay lost to the
Chicago Bears 7-19

Minnesota beat the
Detroit Lions 21-16

Week 14
Dec. 11
2005

GB: 2-10
MN: 7-5

PACKERS "VERSES" VIKINGS ~ Carl Nelson

SINCE DAUNTE'S RIGHT KNEE WENT "KA-BLOOIE"
THE VIKES HAVEN'T BEEN QUITE THE SAME
THEY DIDN'T GO IN THE DUMPER AS EXPECTED
BUT HAVE MANAGED SOMEHOW TO WIN ALL THEIR GAMES

LAST WEEK, THOUGH THE LIONS SHOULD HAVE BEEN EASY
WHILE IT DIDN'T QUITE WORK OUT THAT WAY
THE LIONS LOOKED READY TO SCORE AND GO AHEAD
BEFORE A VIKES' INTERCEPTION SAVED THE DAY

THE RAMS WHO THIS WEEK COME TO VISIT
ARE HAVING LOTS OF PROBLEMS OF THEIR OWN
WITH MANY PLAYERS AND THE COACH MISSING GAMES
AND A NEW QUARTERBACK WHO'S NEARLY UNKNOWN

BECAUSE THE RAMS USUALLY EMBARRASS THE VIKES
MINNESOTA'S PLAYERS CAN'T WAIT TO START THIS GAME
FEELING THEY'VE BECOME NEARLY UNBEATABLE
AND THINK THE RAMS ARE LOOKING PRETTY LAME

BUT THE VIKES' DEFENSE ISN'T BULLETPROOF YET
AND IT'S TOUGH TO KNOW WHAT A ROOKIE CAN DO
UNLESS THE VIKES CAN CONTAIN BOTH FITZPATRICK AND THE RUN
THEY COULD FIND THEMSELVES THOROUGHLY SCREWED

~ ~ ~ ~ ~ ~ ~ ~ ~ ~ ~ ~ ~ ~ ~ ~

WHEN IT CAME TO LAST SUNDAY'S FOOTBALL GAME
THE PACK WAS JUST WHAT THE BEARS' TEAM DESIRED
AN OPPONENT WHOSE TALENT IS PRETTY THIN
AND IN ABJECT MISERY SEEMS HOPELESSLY MIRED

MIKE SHERMAN AND HIS COACHING STAFF
CAN'T SEEM TO FIND THE PLAYER COMBINATION
THAT WILL ALLOW THE PACK TO WIN ONCE MORE
AND IT'S CAUSING WIDESPREAD CONSTERNATION

THIS SUNDAY NIGHT IN A PRIME-TIME GAME
(DON'T YOU THINK THOSE TV GUYS ARE MAD!)
THE LIONS VISIT GREEN BAY TO TAKE ON THE PACK
IN A GAME THAT MAY BE FRANKLY QUITE SAD

BOTH OF THE QB'S ARE BATTLE-SCARRED VETS
WHO HAVE SAMPLED THEIR FAIR SHARE OF WINS
NOW THEY ARE TRYING TO CARRY THEIR TEAMS
AND HELP THEM FIND SUCCESS ONCE AGAIN

GREEN BAY AND DETROIT HAVE BOTH UNDERACHIEVED
AND FOR EACH THERE'S A LONG LIST OF REASONS
FOR NOW, ALL THEY ARE REALLY TRYING TO DO
IS GRACEFULLY PLAY OUT THE REST OF THE SEASON

~ ~ ~ ~ ~ ~ ~ ~ ~ ~ ~ ~ ~ ~ ~ ~ ~

THE VIKINGS MUST NOT OVERLOOK THIS WEEK'S GAME
OR THE RAMS WILL LAY A LOSS ON THAT BUNCH
WHILE THE PACKERS WILL TRY TO SHOW DETROIT
THEY CAN STILL THROW A GOOD KNOCKOUT PUNCH

RESULTS:
Green Bay beat the Detroit Lions 16-13

Minnesota beat the St Louis Rams 27-13

215

GB: 3-10
MN: 8-5

PACKERS "VERSES" VIKINGS ~ Carl Nelson

THE RAMS TRIED HARD TO CHALLENGE THE VIKES
BUT WHEN THEIR SCORING CHANCES AROSE
ST LOUIS COULDN'T SEEM TO AVOID THE INTERCEPTION
AND THEIR YOUNG QUARTERBACK THREW FIVE OF THOSE

THERE'S AN OUTLOOK BASED ON "CARPE DIEM"
WHICH OF COURSE MEANS TO "SEIZE THE DAY"
LATELY THE VIKINGS' MOTTO IS "CARPE FOOTBALL"
AS THEY GATHER TURNOVERS EACH SUNDAY

THE VIKINGS' DEFENSE AND SPECIAL TEAMS
ARE WHAT'S KEEPING MINNESOTA'S STREAK ALIVE
BUT THAT OFFENSE WILL HAVE TO STEP IT UP
IN ORDER FOR THIS TEAM TO THRIVE

THIS WEEK THE STEELERS COME TO TOWN
THEY'RE A ROUGH-AND-TUMBLE SORT OF BUNCH
AND LAST WEEK FOLLOWING BEHIND "THE BUS"
THEY HANDED THE CHICAGO BEARS THEIR LUNCH

THE STEELERS WILL BRING MORE THAN A RUNNING GAME
ROTHLISBERGER'S PASSES ARE TOUGH TO BAT DOWN
BUT IT'S WHAT'S CALLED THE "BLITZBURGH DEFENSE"
THAT HAS BROUGHT THIS STEELERS' TEAM RENOWN

~ ~ ~ ~ ~ ~ ~ ~ ~ ~ ~ ~ ~ ~ ~ ~ ~

WHEN THE PACKERS AND THE LIONS MET
IT WASN'T THE PRETTIEST OF FOOTBALL GAMES
AND THE REF'S OBSCURE CALL MAY HAVE HELPED
BUT GREEN BAY TOPPED DETROIT JUST THE SAME

AT FIRST GLANCE IT MAY APPEAR TO OBSERVERS
THAT THE PACKERS HAVE HURT THEMSELVES YET AGAIN
BY MOVING DOWNWARD IN NEXT SPRING'S FOOTBALL DRAFT
BUT OH IT FELT SO GOOD TO WATCH THEM WIN

THE BALTIMORE RAVENS ARE THE HOST THIS WEEK
AS THE PACKERS TAKE THEIR LAST ROAD TRIP
AND THIS MAY PROVIDE A WINNING OPPORTUNITY
PROVIDED THE PACKERS' GAME DOESN'T SLIP

THE RAVENS HAVE BEEN HAUNTED BY INCONSISTENCY
NEITHER THE BACKS OR RECEIVERS OFTEN SCORE
AND AS FAR AS THE ONCE-VAUNTED DEFENSE GOES
THEY DOMINATE THAT FIELD "...NEVERMORE..."

JUST A FEW YEARS AGO BOTH THESE TEAMS
WERE THOUGHT AMONG THE LEAGUE'S ELITE
BUT THE PENDULUM HAS SWUNG FOR BOTH OF THEM
AND THEY'VE BOTH BECOME TOO FAMILIAR WITH DEFEAT

~ ~ ~ ~ ~ ~ ~ ~ ~ ~ ~ ~ ~ ~ ~ ~ ~

THE STEELERS JUST POUNDED CHICAGO'S BEARS
AND PLAN TO STOP ANOTHER WINNING STREAK
WHILE THE PACKERS WILL DO EVERYTHING THEY CAN
TO USHER IN A RAVENS' FALL THIS WEEK

RESULTS:
Green Bay lost to the Baltimore Ravens 3-48

Minnesota lost to the Pittsburgh Steelers 3-18

THE VIKINGS BROUGHT A SIX-GAME WIN STREAK
INTO LAST SUNDAY'S GAME AT THE METRODOME
BUT THE STEELERS BEAT DOWN THE VIKINGS TEAM
AND PRETTY MUCH MADE THE PLACE THEIR HOME

GB: 3-11
MN: 8-6

THESE STEELERS ARE THE KIND OF TEAM
THAT USUALLY GIVES THE VIKINGS FITS
ONE THAT DOESN'T GET BEHIND THE VIKINGS EARLY
GET FRUSTRATED AND THEN QUIT

SO THE VIKES MUST PUT THIS LOSS BEHIND THEM
FOR THIS WEEK THE CHALLENGE IS NO LESS
AS THEY FACE A FIRED-UP BALTIMORE RAVENS' TEAM
THAT RIGHT NOW IS PLAYING AT THIS SEASON'S BEST

Green Bay PACKERS Fan Fest 2006

FINALLY—KYLE BOLLER LOOKS LIKE A QUARTERBACK
AS HE IS TOSSING SCORING PASSES TO TODD HEAP
AND JAMAL LEWIS IS RUNNING WELL ENOUGH
TO CAUSE OPPOSING LINEBACKERS TO LOSE SLEEP

THE DEFENSE MUST SWARM LIKE BEES AROUND A HIVE
FOR THE VIKES TO BEAT BALTIMORE THIS WEEK
MIKE TICE SHOULD FIND IT EASY TO MOTIVATE THEM
FOR IT'S A PLAYOFF BERTH HIS TEAM SEEKS

~ ~ ~ ~ ~ ~ ~ ~ ~ ~ ~ ~ ~ ~ ~ ~ ~ ~

NOT CONTENT TO SIMPLY BEAT THE PACKERS MONDAY
THE RAVENS CONTINUED TO "HEAP" IT ON
AND NO MATTER WHAT THE PACK TRIED TO COUNTER WITH
IT SURE LOOKED LIKE THEY WERE GUESSING WRONG

THE RAVENS TOOK CHARGE EARLY IN THAT GAME
AND THE PACKERS JUST SEEMED TO DEFLATE
A LONG RETURN OF A FIRST QUARTER PUNT
FORETOLD THE PACKERS' FINAL FATE

THIS WEEK WON'T BE ANY EASIER TO TAKE
AS CHICAGO'S BEARS INVADE GREEN BAY
THEY WON'T BE GIVING THE PACKERS ANY GIFTS
THOUGH THE GAME IS PLAYED ON CHRISTMAS DAY

THE BEARS HAVE LIVED ON THEIR DEFENSE
AND MOSTLY MOVED THE BALL ON THE GROUND
NOW WITH REX GROSSMAN RETURNING FROM HIS INJURY
THE BEARS CAN ALSO THROW THE BALL AROUND

RESULTS:
Green Bay lost to the
Chicago Bears 17-24

Minnesota lost to the
Baltimore Ravens 23-30

GREEN BAY'S DEFENSE CAN'T SEEM TO TACKLE
AND NOW SAMKON HAS JOINED THE INJURED LIST
THAT PACKERS' TEAM IS TOTALLY IN TATTERS
FULFILLING THE BEARS' NUMBER ONE CHRISTMAS WISH

~ ~ ~ ~ ~ ~ ~ ~ ~ ~ ~ ~ ~ ~ ~ ~ ~ ~

ALTHOUGH IT'S NOT LIKELY TO HAPPEN THIS WEEK
THE PERFECT CHRISTMAS GIFT WOULD BE A PACKERS' WIN
AND WILL THE VIKES KEEP THEIR PLAYOFF HOPES ALIVE
OR MORE LIKELY BREAK THEIR FANS' HEARTS ONCE AGAIN?

MERRY CHRISTMAS ho-ho-ho !!

PACKERS "VERSES" VIKINGS ~ Carl Nelson

217

GB: 3-12
MN: 8-7

PACKERS "VERSES" VIKINGS ~ Carl Nelson

ON CHRISTMAS DAY THE PACKERS LOOKED
LIKE A FIGHTER BATTERED ONTO THE ROPES
COUNTER-PUNCHING AND REMAINING ALIVE
AND STILL CLINGING TO A LITTLE HOPE

UNFORTUNATELY THE BEARS TOOK THAT HOPE AWAY
WHEN A LINEBACKER SPRANG OUT FROM BEHIND A BACK
PICKED OFF A PASS—RAN IT IN FOR THE SCORE
PROVIDING THE POINTS THAT BEAT THE PACK

NOW THIS WEEK ON NEW YEAR'S DAY
A FACE FROM THE PAST WILL COME TO TOWN
AS MIKE HOLMGREN BRINGS THE SEAHAWKS IN
TO TAKE A TURN SHOVING THE PACKERS AROUND

THE 'HAWKS ARE HAVING A MARVELOUS YEAR
WITH SHAUN ALEXANDER RUNNING AMOK
AND WITH EX-PACKER HASSELBECK AT THE HELM
THE PASSING GAME NO LONGER DEPENDS ON LUCK

THE SEAHAWKS' DEFENSE MAY BE THEIR ACHILLES' HEEL
AS THEY HAVEN'T DOMINATED ANYONE THAT WAY YET
PERHAPS THIS WILL BE GREEN BAY'S WINDOW OF OPPORTUNITY
IF ONLY THAT OFFENSE COULD MUSTER A THREAT

~ ~ ~ ~ ~ ~ ~ ~ ~ ~ ~ ~ ~ ~ ~ ~

THE CHRISTMAS STOCKING WAS FILLED WITH COAL
FOR THE VIKES WHO NEEDED A MIRACLE IN GREEN BAY
TO PROVIDE A CHANCE TO WIN THE DIVISION TITLE
WHEN THEY PLAY THE BEARS ON NEW YEAR'S DAY

AN IMPRESSIVE COMEBACK STREAK FOR THE VIKES
WAS KEEPING THEM IN LINE FOR A PLAYOFF SPOT
BUT THE STEELERS' LOSS MEANT THEY'D NEED OTHERS TO HELP
AND THAT SURE WASN'T WHAT THEY GOT

STILL THEIR FATE WAS IN THEIR OWN HANDS
AS THEY TOOK THE FIELD AGAINST THE RAVENS' TEAM
ALL THEY HAD TO DO WAS WIN THE GAME
BUT THAT WASN'T QUITE AS EASY AS IT SEEMED

THEY MAY HAVE LOOKED PAST THE RAVENS A BIT
AS THEY WERE LOOKING FORWARD TO THE BEARS
BUT BALTIMORE MANAGED TO OUTPLAY THE VIKES
WHO WATCHED PLAYOFF HOPES VANISH INTO THIN AIR

SO NOW ON NEW YEAR'S IT'S STILL THE BEARS
ALTHOUGH THE GAME WILL BE MISSING SOME OF ITS DRAMA
WHILE THE VIKES TRY TO PLAY FOR A LITTLE PRIDE
BEFORE THEY GO CRYING HOME TO THEIR COLLECTIVE MAMAS

~ ~ ~ ~ ~ ~ ~ ~ ~ ~ ~ ~ ~ ~ ~ ~ ~

CAN THE VIKINGS PULL OFF A MIRACLE AND BEAT THE BEARS?
IF THEY CAN MIKE TICE PROBABLY WON'T GET FIRED
WHILE OVER IN GREEN BAY LET'S HOPE THIS GAME
WON'T PROVIDE THE REASON BRETT DECIDES TO RETIRE

HAPPY NEW YEAR!!

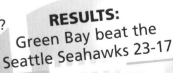

RESULTS:
Green Bay beat the
Seattle Seahawks 23-17

Minnesota beat the
Chicago Bears 34-10

PACKERS "VERSES" VIKINGS

~ Carl Nelson

Final Standings
GB: 4-12
MN: 9-7

THE PACKERS PUT FORTH A WINNING EFFORT
IN BEATING SOME OF THE SEAHAWKS ON NEW YEAR'S DAY
BUT ON THE WHIM OF MANAGER TED THOMPSON
MIKE SHERMAN WAS FIRED EARLY THE NEXT DAY

ONE CONTINGENT OF PACKERS FANS IS VERY HAPPY
AS MANY OF THEM USED SHERMAN FOR THEIR WHIPPING BOY
WHILE OTHERS THOUGHT HE WAS A PRETTY GOOD COACH
AND HAVEN'T FOUND THIS NEWS A SOURCE OF JOY

TED STILL HASN'T COME UP WITH A REASON
OTHER THAN "IT WAS TIME TO MAKE A CHANGE"
MANY FEEL THIS IS JUST A LITTLE WEAK
AND THAT THIS FIRING IS JUST A LITTLE STRANGE

BUT THAT'S WHY HE GETS PAID TO MAKE THESE CHOICES
AND ALL WE CAN DO NOW IS HOPE THAT HE IS WISE
AND SOMEHOW "MANAGES" TO FIND THE WINNER
AMONG ALL THOSE OTHER "WANNABE" KIND OF GUYS

~ ~ ~ ~ ~ ~ ~ ~ ~ ~ ~ ~ ~ ~ ~ ~ ~ ~

ALTHOUGH IT PERHAPS WASN'T QUITE SO SURPRISING
THE VIKINGS ALSO THOUGHT THEIR "MIKE" WAS DONE FOR
AND ONCE HIS TEAM HAD DISPATCHED THE BEARS
ZYGI QUICKLY SHOWED MIKE TICE THE DOOR

THE SEARCH FOR HIS SUCCESSOR HAS BEGUN
WITH ZYGI WILF LOOKING FAR AND WIDE
SPECULATION HAS BEEN THAT AN EX-COACH FROM THE GIANTS
MIGHT HAVE THE INSIDE TRACK TO BE "ZYGI'S GUY"

WITH DAUNTE'S RETURN FROM INJURY UNCERTAIN
AND GOOD RUNNING BACKS FEW AND FAR BETWEEN
WHETHER THAT "NEW GUY" CAN REASSEMBLE THE VIKINGS
IS SOMETHING THAT REMAINS TO BE SEEN

BUT NOTHING IS CERTAIN AT THIS STAGE OF THE GAME
OTHER THAN THERE WILL BE A NEW CAPTAIN OF THAT SHIP
HE IS GOING TO HAVE HIS HANDS FULL WITH THOSE VIKES
ESPECIALLY THE ONES WHO BOOKED THE "LOVE BOAT" TRIP

~ ~ ~ ~ ~ ~ ~ ~ ~ ~ ~ ~ ~ ~ ~ ~ ~ ~

WHILE NEITHER THE VIKES OR THE PACKERS WILL BE PLAYING
THIS YEAR'S PLAYOFF TOURNEY IS SET TO BEGIN
AS THESE TEAMS REALLY START TO MAKE THE MOVES
THAT MAY GET THEM TO SUPER BOWL AND WIN

TAMPA SHOULD GET PAST THE 'SKINS
WHILE THE PATS WILL CRUSH THE JAGS
THE STEELERS WILL GRIND UP THE BENGALS
WHILE A CAROLINA WIN IS IN THE BAG

WHILE THERE WILL ALWAYS BE SOME UPSETS
THE TRUE CREAM IS RISING TO THE TOP
AS THOSE TEAMS ARE GATHERING MOMENTUM
AND WILL NOT EASILY BE STOPPED

RESULTS:
The Washington Redskins beat the
Tampa Bay Buccaneers 17-10

The Carolina Panthers beat the
New York Giants 23-0

The Pittsburgh Steelers beat the
Cincinnati Bengals 31-17

The New England Patriots beat the
Jacksonville Jaguars 28-3

PACKERS "VERSES" VIKINGS

~ Carl Nelson

Seattle vs. Washington
New England vs. Denver

Pittsburgh vs. Indianapolis
Carolina vs Chicago

IN A MOVE THAT MAY SEEM A LITTLE CONFUSING
GREEN BAY MAY BE STARTING A DISTURBING TREND
AS TED THOMPSON (THE GM OF THE PACKERS)
TRIES TO REVIVE "MC CARTHYISM" ONCE AGAIN

FOR MIKE MC CARTHY IS THE MAN TAPPED BY THOMPSON
FOR THE HEAD COACH POSITION IN GREEN BAY
HE COMES TO THE PACKERS FROM SAN FRANCISCO
WHERE HE DEVISED THE OFFENSE EACH SUNDAY

THE QUESTIONS SURROUNDING HIM ARE MANY
LIKE "WHY DID THIS GUY GET THE JOB?"
HOPEFULLY THINGS WILL WORK OUT FOR MC CARTHY
OR "TEDDY T'"MIGHT HAVE TO OUTRUN A LYNCH MOB

REALISTICALLY THERE'S NOTHING FOR THE FANS TO DO
BUT CROSS OUR FINGERS AND HOPE FOR THE BEST
IF HE CAN GET THE PLAYERS TO BUY INTO HIS GAME PLAN
HE CAN STEP BACK AND LET THEM DO THE REST

~ ~ ~ ~ ~ ~ ~ ~ ~ ~ ~ ~ ~ ~ ~ ~ ~ ~ ~

MINNESOTA IS HOPING THAT BRAD CHILDRESS
CAN BRING THE VIKINGS TO A NEW BEGINNING
ONE BUILT ON RESPONSIBILITY AND DISCIPLINE
WHICH WILL HOPEFULLY LET THEIR TEAM START WINNING

BRINGING THE "WEST COAST" OFFENSE BACK
TO THE PLACE WHERE SOME SAY IT REALLY STARTED
WILL BE THE JOB ONCE HIS NEW STAFF IS COMPLETE
AND ALL OF TICE'S LEFTOVERS HAVE DEPARTED

BUT THERE'S SOMETHING INTERESTING ABOUT THOSE HIRES
AND WHILE IT'S SURE THAT BRAD REALLY KNOWS WHAT'S BEST
SO MANY OF THOSE COACHES HAVE SUCH STRONG BADGER TIES
WINTER PARK WILL BE KNOWN AS "MADISON-WEST"

~ ~ ~ ~ ~ ~ ~ ~ ~ ~ ~ ~ ~ ~ ~ ~ ~ ~ ~

FOR THOSE TEAMS WITH ESTABLISHED COACHING STAFFS
THE POSTSEASON CONTINUES THIS COMING WEEK
AS THE WINNERS OF THE "DIVISIONAL PLAYOFF" GAMES
MOVE CLOSER TO THE CHAMPIONSHIP THEY SEEK

IN SEATTLE THE SEAHAWKS WELCOME THE REDSKINS
BUT THAT'S ABOUT AS FRIENDLY AS THEY'LL GET
THE SEAHAWKS ARE GOING TO ROLL THE 'SKINS
AND SEND THEM PACKING OFF HOME ON THEIR JET

IN A GAME THAT WILL DRAW MUCH ATTENTION
THE PATRIOTS WILL INVADE THE BRONCOS' HOME
AND WHILE THE PATS HAVE HAD A MIRACLE SEASON
THROUGH THAT DEFENSE THE DENVER 'BACKS WILL ROAM

THE PANTHERS FACE OFF AGAINST CHICAGO'S BEARS
IN WHAT SHOULD BE A KNOCK-DOWN DRAG-OUT GAME
AND ALTHOUGH CAROLINA CAN PLAY TOUGH DEFENSE
THAT'S WHERE THE BEARS HAVE TRULY MADE THEIR NAME

THE COLTS HAVE ONLY LOST TWO GAMES
DURING THE COURSE OF THIS FOOTBALL SEASON
AFTER THE STEELERS HAVE TRIED TO TACKLE THEM THIS WEEK
PITTSBURGH WILL UNDERSTAND THE REASON THE REASON

RESULTS:
The Seattle Seahawks beat the Washington Redskins 20-10

The Carolina Panthers beat the Chicago Bears 29-21

The Denver Broncos beat the New England Patriots 27-13

The Pittsburgh Steelers beat the Indianapolis Colts 21-18

~ Carl Nelson

PACKERS "VERSES" VIKINGS

SUPER BOWL BERTHS WILL BE DETERMINED THIS WEEKEND
AS THE CONFERENCE CHAMPIONSHIP GAMES TAKE PLACE
THE WINNERS WILL HEAD OFF TO SPEND A WEEK IN DETROIT
WHICH DEFINITELY WILL BE A COLD AND WINTERY PLACE

THE OLD-TIMERS SAY "DEFENSES WIN CHAMPIONSHIPS"
WHILE "THE HOME TEAM HAS THE INSIDE TRACK"
OR IT'S "THE COACHES THAT MAKE THE DIFFERENCE"
AND "YOU NEED A VERY GOOD QUARTERBACK"

ALL OF THESE ADAGES WILL BE TESTED THIS WEEK
WITH ALL OF THEM COMING INTO PLAY
TWO OF THE TOP FIVE OFFENSES ARE THE HOME TEAMS
IN SEATTLE AND DENVER THIS SUNDAY

CAROLINA AND PITTSBURGH WILL COME ROLLING IN
WITH DEFENSES RATED IN THE LEAGUE'S FIVE BEST
BOTH MORE THAN WILLING TO PUT A LICK ON ANYONE
AND ARE LOOKING FORWARD TO THIS WEEK'S TEST

ALL THE COACHES HAVE ALREADY WON THE BIG ONE
AT VARIOUS TIMES IN SEASONS PAST
AND KNOW HOW TO PUT TOGETHER WINNING TEAMS
AND EXCELLENT SUPPORTING CASTS

ALL FOUR TEAMS HAVE SIMILAR STYLES
THAT DEPEND HEAVILY ON THE TALENT OF THEIR 'BACKS
AS WELL AS PLAYING TOUGH AND AGGRESSIVE DEFENSE
WHICH LEADS TO LOTS OF TACKLES AND SACKS

~ ~ ~ ~ ~ ~ ~ ~ ~ ~ ~ ~ ~ ~ ~ ~ ~ ~

SHAUN ALEXANDER IS THE NAME MOST MENTIONED
WHEN THE SEAHAWKS ARE BROUGHT UP IN DISCUSSION
BUT HASSELBECK AND THE DEFENSE BOTH STEPPED UP
LAST WEEK WHEN HE WENT DOWN WITH A CONCUSSION

BECAUSE OF DESHAUN FOSTER'S BROKEN ANKLE
THE PANTHERS WILL HAVE TO START NICK GOINGS
WHO'S TRUE ROLE WILL BE DISTRACTING THE HAWKS' "D"
WHEN TO STEVE SMITH JAKE DELHOMME STARTS THROWING

~ ~ ~ ~ ~ ~ ~ ~ ~ ~ ~ ~ ~ ~ ~ ~ ~ ~ ~

THE STEELERS AND BRONCOS ARE A LOT ALIKE
BOTH WILLING TO KEEP THE BALL ON THE GROUND
BEN ROETHLISBERGER MAY NEVER HAVE TO THROW THE BALL
IF "THE BUS" AND PARKER CAN SHOVE THE BRONCOS' "D" AROUND

THOSE BRONCOS ALSO HAVE TWO GOOD RUNNING BACKS
WITH MIKE ANDERSON BEING THE NUMBER-ONE GUY
BUT THEY'VE ALSO GOT JAKE "THE SNAKE" PLUMMER
IF THEY HAVE TO TAKE THEIR GAME TO THE SKY

~ ~ ~ ~ ~ ~ ~ ~ ~ ~ ~ ~ ~ ~ ~ ~ ~ ~ ~

THESE GAMES ARE OFTEN THOUGHT OF AS BETTER GAMES
THAN THE SUPER BOWL WILL TURN OUT TO BE
BUT WHEN THE SEAHAWKS FACE THE BRONCOS IN DETROIT
THAT WILL BE QUITE THE GAME TO SEE....

AFC
Broncos: 14-3
Steelers: 13-5
NFC
Seahawks: 14-3
Panthers: 13-5

RESULTS:
The Seattle Seahawks beat the Carolina Panthers 34-14

The Pittsburgh Steelers beat the Denver Broncos 34-17

Super Bowl Record
Pittsburgh: 4-1
Seattle: 0-0

PACKERS "VERSES" VIKINGS ~ Carl Nelson

FIVE LONG MONTHS AFTER THE SEASON STARTED
SUPER BOWL FORTY WILL BRING IT TO AN END
WITH THE SEAHAWKS AND THE STEELERS
BEING THE BEST TEAMS THE LEAGUE CAN SEND

THE SEAHAWKS HAD A TERRIFIC SEASON
COMING INTO THE PLAYOFFS RATED NUMBER ONE
AND WITH THE LEADERSHIP OF MIKE HOLMGREN
THEY'RE CONFIDENT THEY WILL "GIT 'ER DONE"

IN GETTING TO THIS YEAR'S EXTRAVAGANZA
THE STEELERS JOURNEYED THE ROAD LESS TRAVELLED
FIGHTING THEIR WAY THROUGH FROM THE WILDCARD SPOT
WITH COACH COWER NOT LETTING THEM UNRAVEL

THESE TEAMS ARE MORE ALIKE THAN DIFFERENT
EVEN IF THAT'S A LITTLE HARD TO SEE
BOTH OF THEM RELY HEAVILY ON THE RUNNING GAME
AND PLAYING OUTSTANDING "D"

BOTH TEAMS' QUARTERBACKS WILL FEEL THE PRESSURE
AS THE SACK-HAPPY SEAHAWKS BRING THE HEAT
BUT CONTAINING THE "BLITZBURGH" DEFENSE
WILL BE SEATTLE'S KEY TO AVOIDING DEFEAT

TROY POLAMALU LEADS THAT DEFENSIVE TEAM
CURRENTLY HE'S PLAYING LIKE A MAN POSSESSED
ALTHOUGH THE REST OF THE DEFENSE IS FIRST-RATE
THERE CAN BE NO ARGUMENT THAT AT SAFETY HE'S THE BEST

WHILE THE STEELERS HAVE QUITE A REPUTATION
THE SEATTLE DEFENSE HAS QUIETLY MADE ITS MARK
COMING UP WITH MORE SACKS THAN ANYONE ELSE
AND FLOWING TO THE BALL LIKE A SCHOOL OF SHARKS

SO HOW CAN MATT HASSELBECK SHOW HIS STUFF
AND BEN ROETHLISBERGER AIR IT OUT?
BOTH TEAMS WILL HAVE TO USE THE RUN
TO LET THE PASSING GAME COME ABOUT

SHAUN ALEXANDER LED THE NFL IN YARDS
AND ALSO LED THE LEAGUE IN SCORING
PITTSBURGH'S ATTEMPTS TO SLOW HIM DOWN
SHOULD BE ANYTHING BUT BORING

PITTSBURGH BRINGS JEROME "THE BUS" BETTIS
WHO'LL CLOSE OUT A LONG CAREER IN HIS HOME TOWN
AND ALTHOUGH THEY MAY BE A LITTLE OLD AND WORN
WE'LL SEE "THE WHEELS ON THE BUS GO 'ROUND"

WHILE IT WOULD BE NICE TO SEE MIKE HOLMGREN
ONCE AGAIN HOSTING THE LOMBARDI
THE STEELERS ARE ON TOO MUCH OF A ROLL
AND PITTSBURGH WILL HOST THE VICTORY PARTY

RESULTS:
The Pittsburgh Steelers beat the
Seattle Seahawks 21-10

AUTHOR BIO

Carl W. Nelson spent his early years on a small farm in Kingsdale, Minnesota. When Carl was seven, he and his six siblings moved with their parents to Dairyland, Wisconsin. He grew up wandering the north woods and rafting on the Spruce River, and from his lengthy periods alone came his very active imagination. In 1972, Carl graduated from Webster High School.

Following in his father's footsteps, Carl worked for the Soo Line Railroad and spent two years living in bunk cars. But a life on the (rail)road was not for Carl, and he decided he needed a "real" career once children became part of his life. Carl entered the St. Luke's School of Nursing in 1983 and graduated with honors in 1986. For the last nineteen years, he has worked in the operating rooms of St. Luke's Hospital in Duluth, Minnesota.

Hobbies include hunting, fishing, tinkering with old cars, and gardening. Carl loves being a parent and is now discovering the joys of grandchildren. Writing poetry began as an offshoot of writing parodies of songs. His first football poem, written in 1989, can be sung to *Oh, Susanna.*

Carl moved to Duluth two years ago and married Debbie Isabell. Fortunately, their home overlooks the St. Louis River and the land of his beloved Green Bay Packers.

Carl has always been an enthusiastic fan of the Green Bay Packers. His older brother taught him how to visualize the games broadcast on the radio—following the plays and key players. Carl first saw the hallowed ground of Lambeau Field in 2000 and has attended at least one game there every year since. Now, Carl hopes *Packers "Verses" Vikings* will justify even more trips to the land of Green-and-Gold.

CALIFORNIA
SCREAMIN'
GO PACK

STADIUM SPORTS
and Antiques

THEM,
NOT SO MUCH.
GO PACK

Cheeseheads Rule

SIDELINE SPORTS BAR & RESTAURANT

GOD BLESS CARL

DRAFT PARTY HERE

IMMEDIATE SEATING AVAILABLE

GREEN BAY FANS don't let FRIENDS be MINNESOTA FANS